er Universi'
rning Info

ND EDITION

Total Quality MANAGEMENT

Text, Cases and Readings

Joel E. Ross
Florida Atlantic University
Boca Raton, Florida

S^t_L

Library of Congress Cataloging-in-Publication Data

Ross, Joel E.
    Total quality management: text, cases and readings / by Joel E. Ross.—2nd ed.
      p. cm.
    Includes bibliographical references and index.
    ISBN 1-884015-08-5 (acid-free paper)
    1. Total quality management. 2. Total quality management—Case studies. I. Title.
    HD62.15.R67 1995
    658.5'62—dc20   94-9068
                                   CIP

Direct all inquiries to St. Lucie Press, Inc., 100 E. Linton Blvd., Suite 403B, Delray Beach, Florida 33483.

Phone: (407) 274-9906
Fax: (407) 274-9927

S^{t}L

Published by
St. Lucie Press
100 E. Linton Blvd., Suite 403B
Delray Beach, FL 33483

PREFACE

Since the publication of the first edition of this book, interest in and acceptance of TQM has accelerated around the world. It is now widely agreed that quality in products and services is a prerequisite for becoming a player in domestic and global markets.

The first edition of this book has been adopted by over 200 colleges and universities for courses in the topic. Many organizations and individual managers are using it as well. This reflects the growing recognition of the need to train and educate for quality management in all types of organizations.

This edition has been thoroughly revised, updated, and greatly expanded. The original seven chapters now number twelve and include additional textual material and examples. Extensive references are included at the end of each chapter. Five new chapters are presented:

- Organizing for Total Quality Management: Structure and Teams
- Benchmarking
- Productivity, Quality, and Reengineering
- The Cost of Quality
- ISO 9000: Universal Standards of Quality

New cases and readings have been added. The Varifilm case is an extensive comprehensive study that illustrates good and not so good practices. This is the 1993 case used by the Baldrige Award organization in preparing examiners to visit and evaluate companies that apply for that award. Each chapter contains an exercise which requires the reader to apply TQM principles to the practices contained in the comprehensive case.

Discussion questions, exercises, cases, and readings support the textual material. Together these tools provide reinforcement so that the reader is able to understand the principles and can apply them in practice.

The book is practical yet based on sound principles. It is not about the "hard" science of statistical quality control, although this topic is treated along with the other applied tools and techniques that are necessary for implementation of a quality program. It is an excellent text for college students as well as for organizational development programs directed to practitioners who are responsible for developing and implementing TQM programs in their own organizations, whether in manufacturing or service firms.

AUTHOR

Dr. Joel Ross is Senior Professor of Management at Florida Atlantic University in Boca Raton, Florida. He graduated from Yale University and received his doctorate in business administration from George Washington University. He has been Chairman of Management and Director of the MBA Program. Prior to his academic career, Dr. Ross was a Commander in the U.S. Navy.

Dr. Ross is widely known as a platform speaker, seminar leader, consultant, and author. He has developed and conducted management development programs for over one hundred companies and organizations in the areas of general management, strategy, productivity, and quality. He has been an invited lecturer on management topics in Israel, South Africa, Venezuela, Panama, India, Ecuador, the Philippines, and Japan.

His articles have appeared in such journals as *Journal of Systems Management, Business Horizons, Long Range Planning, Industrial Management, Personnel, Management Accounting,* and *Academy of Management Review.* He is the author of thirteen books, including the landmark *Management Information Systems, People, Profits, and Productivity,* and *Total Quality Management,* which has been adopted by over 250 colleges and universities.

Dr. Ross has the reputation of being able to integrate academic principle with real-world practice.

CONTENTS

INTRODUCTION TO TOTAL QUALITY MANAGEMENT

Total quality management (TQM) is the integration of all functions and processes within an organization in order to achieve continuous improvement of the quality of goods and services. The goal is customer satisfaction.

Of all the management issues faced in the last decade, none has had the impact of or caused as much concern as quality in American products and services. A report by the Conference Board indicates that senior executives in the United States agree that the banner of total quality is essential to ensure competitiveness in global markets. Quality expert J. M. Juran calls it a major phenomenon in this age.[1] This concern for quality is not misplaced.

The interest in quality is due, in part, to foreign competition and the trade deficit.[2] Analysts estimate that the vast majority of United States businesses will continue to face strong competition from the Pacific Rim and the European Economic Community for the remainder of the 1990s and beyond.[3] This comes in the face of a serious erosion of corporate America's ability to compete in global markets over the past 20 years.

The problem has not gone unnoticed by government officials, corporate executives, and the public at large. The concern of the President and Congress culminated in the enactment of the Malcolm Baldrige National Quality Improvement Act of 1987 (Public Law 100-107), which established an annual United States National Quality Award. The concern of business executives is reflected in their perceptions of quality. In a 1989 American Society for Quality Control

(ASQC) survey, 54 percent of executives rated quality of service as extremely critical and 51 percent rated quality of product as extremely critical.[4] Seventy-four percent gave American-made products less than eight on a ten-point scale for quality. Similarly, a panel of Fortune 500 executives agreed that American products deserved no better than a grade of C+.

Public opinion regarding American-made products is somewhat less than enthusiastic. In a 1988 ASQC survey of consumer perceptions, less than one-half gave American products high marks for quality.[5] Employees also have misgivings about quality in general and, more specifically, about quality in the companies in which they work. They believe that there is a significant gap between what their companies say and what they do. More importantly, employees believe that their talents, abilities, and energies are not being fully utilized for quality improvement.[6]

Despite the pessimism reflected by these groups, progress is being made. In a 1991 survey of American owners of Japanese-made cars, 32 percent indicated that their next purchase will be a domestic model, and the reason given most often was the improved quality of cars built in the United States.[7] Ford's "Quality Is Job One" campaign may have been a contributing factor. There is also evidence that quality has become a competitive marketing strategy in the small business community, as Americans are beginning to shun mass-produced, poorly made, disposable products.

Other promising developments include the increasing acceptance of TQM as a philosophy of management and a way of company life. It is essential that this trend continue if American companies are to remain competitive in global markets. Customers are becoming more demanding and international competition more fierce. Companies that deliver quality will prosper in the next century.

THE CONCEPT OF TQM

TQM is based on a number of ideas. It means thinking about quality in terms of all functions of the enterprise and is a start-to-finish process that integrates interrelated functions at all levels. It is a systems approach that considers every interaction between the various elements of the organization. Thus, the overall effectiveness of the system is higher than the sum of the individual outputs from the subsystems. The subsystems include all the *organizational functions* in the life cycle of a product, such as (1) design, (2) planning, (3) production, (4) distribution, and (5) field service. The *management* subsystems also require integration, including (1) strategy with a customer focus, (2) the tools of quality, and (3) employee involvement (the linking process that integrates the whole). A corollary is that any product, process, or service can be improved, and a successful organization is one that consciously seeks and exploits opportunities for improvement at all levels. The load-bearing structure is customer satisfaction. The watchword is *continuous improvement.*

Following an international conference in May 1990, the Conference Board summarized the key issues and terminology related to TQM:

- The **cost of quality** as the measure of non-quality (not meeting customer requirements) and a measure of how the quality process is progressing.

- A **cultural change** that appreciates the primary need to meet customer requirements, implements a management philosophy that acknowledges this emphasis, encourages employee involvement, and embraces the ethic of continuous improvement.

- **Enabling mechanisms of change,** including training and education, communication, recognition, management behavior, teamwork, and customer satisfaction programs.

- **Implementing TQM** by defining the mission, identifying the output, identifying the customers, negotiating customer requirements, developing a "supplier specification" that details customer objectives, and determining the activities required to fulfill those objectives.

- **Management behavior** that includes acting as role models, use of quality processes and tools, encouraging communication, sponsoring feedback activities, and fostering and providing a supporting environment.[8]

ANTECEDENTS OF MODERN QUALITY MANAGEMENT

Quality control as we know it probably had its beginnings in the factory system that developed following the Industrial Revolution. Production methods at that time were rudimentary at best. Products were made from non-standardized materials using non-standardized methods. The result was products of varying quality. The only real standards used were measures of dimensions, weight, and in some instances purity. The most common form of quality control was inspection by the purchaser, under the common law rule of *caveat emptor.*[9]

Much later, around the turn of this century, Frederick Taylor developed his system of scientific management, which emphasized productivity at the expense of quality. Centralized inspection departments were organized to check for quality at the end of the production line. An extreme example of this approach was the Hawthorne Works at Western Electric Company, which at its peak in 1928 employed 40,000 people in the manufacturing plant, 5,200 of whom were in the inspection department. The control of quality focused on final inspection of the manufactured product, and a number of techniques were developed to enhance the inspection process. Most involved visual inspection or testing of the product following manufacture. Methods of statistical quality control and quality assurance were added later. Detecting manufacturing problems was the overriding focus. Top management moved away from the idea of managing to achieve quality and, furthermore, the work force had no stake in it. The concern was limited largely to the shop floor.

Traditional quality control measures were (and still are) designed as defense mechanisms to prevent failure or eliminate defects.[10] Accountants were taught (and are still taught) that expenditures for defect prevention were justified only if they were less than the cost of failure. Of course, cost of failure was rarely computed. (Cost of quality is discussed further in Chapter 11.)[11]

Following World War II, the quality of products produced in the United States declined as manufacturers tried to keep up with the demand for non-military goods that had not been produced during the war. It was during this period that a number of pioneers began to advance a methodology of quality control in manufacturing and to develop theories and practical techniques for improved quality. The most visible of these pioneers were W. Edwards Deming, Joseph M. Juran, Armand V. Feigenbaum, and Philip Crosby.[12] It was a great loss to the quality movement when Deming died in December 1993 at the age of 93.

THE QUALITY GURUS

Deming, the best known of the "early" pioneers, is credited with popularizing quality control in Japan in the early 1950s. Today he is regarded as a national hero in that country and is the father of the world-famous Deming Prize for Quality. He is best known for developing a system of statistical quality control, although his contribution goes substantially beyond those techniques.[13] His philosophy begins with top management but maintains that a company must adopt the fourteen points of his system at all levels. He also believes that quality must be built into the product at all stages in order to achieve a high level of excellence. While it cannot be said that Deming is responsible for quality improvement in Japan or the United States, he has played a substantial role in increasing the visibility of the process and advancing an awareness of the need to improve.

Deming defines quality as a predictable degree of uniformity and dependability, at low costs and suited to the market. Deming teaches that 96 percent of variations have common causes and 4 percent have special causes. He views statistics as a management tool and relies on statistical process control as a means of managing variations in a process. Deming developed what is known as the Deming chain reaction; as quality improves, costs will decrease and productivity will increase, resulting in more jobs, greater market share, and long-term survival. Although it is the worker who will ultimately produce quality products, Deming stresses worker pride and satisfaction rather than the establishment of quantifiable goals. His overall approach focuses on improvement of the process, in that the system, rather than the worker, is the cause of process variation.

Deming's *universal fourteen points* for management are summarized as follows:

1. Create consistency of purpose with a plan.
2. Adopt the new philosophy of quality.
3. Cease dependence on mass inspection.
4. End the practice of choosing suppliers based solely on price.
5. Identify problems and work continuously to improve the system.
6. Adopt modern methods of training on the job.
7. Change the focus from production numbers (quantity) to quality.
8. Drive out fear.
9. Break down barriers between departments.
10. Stop requesting improved productivity without providing methods to achieve it.
11. Eliminate work standards that prescribe numerical quotas.
12. Remove barriers to pride of workmanship.
13. Institute vigorous education and retraining.
14. Create a structure in top management that will emphasize the preceding thirteen points every day.

Juran, like Deming, was invited to Japan in 1954 by the Union of Japanese Scientists and Engineers (JUSE). His lectures introduced the managerial dimensions of planning, organizing, and controlling and focused on the responsibility of management to achieve quality and the need for setting goals.[14] Juran defines quality as *fitness for use* in terms of design, conformance, availability, safety, and field use. Thus, his concept more closely incorporates the point of view of the customer. He is prepared to measure everything and relies on systems and problem-solving techniques. Unlike Deming, he focuses on top-down management and technical methods rather than worker pride and satisfaction.

Juran's ten steps to quality improvement are

1. Build awareness of opportunities to improve.
2. Set goals for improvement.
3. Organize to reach goals.
4. Provide training.

5. Carry out projects to solve problems.

6. Report progress.

7. Give recognition.

8. Communicate results.

9. Keep score.

10. Maintain momentum by making annual improvement part of the regular systems and processes of the company.

Juran is the founder of the Juran Institute in Wilton, Connecticut. He promotes a concept known as Managing Business Process Quality, which is a technique for executing cross-functional quality improvement. Juran's contribution may, over the longer term, may be greater than Deming's because Juran has the broader concept, while Deming's focus on statistical process control is more technically oriented.[15]

Armand Feigenbaum, like Deming and Juran, achieved visibility through his work with the Japanese. Unlike the latter two, he used a total quality control approach that may very well be the forerunner of today's TQM. He promoted a system for integrating efforts to develop, maintain, and improve quality by the various groups in an organization. To do otherwise, according to Feigenbaum, would be to inspect for and control quality after the fact rather than build it in at an earlier stage of the process.

Philip Crosby, author of the popular book *Quality is Free,*[16] may have achieved the greatest commercial success by promoting his views and founding the Quality College in Winter Park, Florida. He argues that poor quality in the average firm costs about 20 percent of revenues, most of which could be avoided by adopting good quality practices. His "absolutes" of quality are

- Quality is **defined** as conformance to requirements, not "goodness."
- The **system** for achieving quality is prevention, not appraisal.
- The performance **standard** is zero defects, not "that's close enough."
- The **measurement** of quality is the price of non-conformance, not indexes.[17]

Crosby stresses motivation and planning and does not dwell on statistical process control and the several problem-solving techniques of Deming and Juran. He states that quality is free because the small costs of prevention will always be lower than the costs of detection, correction, and failure. Like Deming, Crosby has his own *fourteen points:*

1. **Management commitment.** Top management must become convinced of the need for quality and must clearly communicate this to the entire

company by written policy, stating that each person is expected to perform according to the requirement or cause the requirement to be officially changed to what the company and the customers really need.

2. **Quality improvement team.** Form a team composed of department heads to oversee improvements in their departments and in the company as a whole.

3. **Quality measurement.** Establish measurements appropriate to every activity in order to identify areas in need of improvement.

4. **Cost of quality.** Estimate the costs of quality in order to identify areas where improvements would be profitable.

5. **Quality awareness.** Raise quality awareness among employees. They must understand the importance of product conformance and the costs of non-conformance.

6. **Corrective action.** Take corrective action as a result of steps 3 and 4.

7. **Zero defects planning.** Form a committee to plan a program appropriate to the company and its culture.

8. **Supervisor training.** All levels of management must be trained in how to implement their part of the quality improvement program.

9. **Zero defects day.** Schedule a day to signal to employees that the company has a new standard.

10. **Goal setting.** Individuals must establish improvement goals for themselves and their groups.

11. **Error cause removal.** Employees should be encouraged to inform management of any problems that prevent them from performing error-free work.

12. **Recognition.** Give public, non-financial appreciation to those who meet their quality goals or perform outstandingly.

13. **Quality councils.** Composed of quality professionals and team chairpersons, quality councils should meet regularly to share experiences, problems, and ideas.

14. **Do it all over again.** Repeat steps 1 to 13 in order to emphasize the never-ending process of quality improvement.

All of these pioneers believe that management and the system, rather than the workers, are the cause of poor quality. These and other trailblazers have largely absorbed and synthesized each other's ideas, but generally speaking they belong to two schools of thought: those who focus on technical processes and tools and those who focus on the managerial dimensions.[18] Deming provides manufacturers with methods to measure the variations in a production process in order to determine the causes of poor quality. Juran emphasizes setting specific annual goals and establishing teams to work on them. Crosby stresses a program of zero defects. Feigenbaum teaches total quality control aimed at managing by applying statistical and engineering methods throughout the company.

Despite the differences among these experts, a number of common themes arise:

1. Inspection is never the answer to quality improvement, nor is "policing."

2. Involvement of and leadership by top management are essential to the necessary culture of commitment to quality.

3. A program for quality requires organization-wide efforts and long-term commitment, accompanied by the necessary investment in training.

4. Quality is first and schedules are secondary.

Admiration for Deming's contribution is not confined to Japan. At the Yale University commencement in May 1991, Deming was awarded an honorary degree. The citation read:

> W. Edwards Deming, '28 PhD, *consultant in statistical studies*. For the past four decades, you have been the champion of quality management. You have developed a theory of management, based on scientific and statistical principles in which people remain the least predictable and most important part. Your scholarly insights and your wisdom have revolutionized industry. Yale is proud to confer upon you the degree of Doctor of Laws.[19]

ACCELERATING USE OF TQM

The increased acceptance and use of TQM is the result of three major trends: (1) reaction to increasing domestic and global competition, (2) the pervasive need to integrate the several organizational functions for improvement of total output of the organization as well as the quality of output within each function, and (3) the acceptance of TQM in a variety of service industries.

Aside from existing competitive pressures from Japan and the Pacific Rim countries, American firms are faced with the prospect of increasing competition from members of the European Economic Community. This concern is justified by the very nature of manufacturing strategy among European firms, where quality has replaced technology as the primary consideration.

Basic to the concept of TQM is the notion that quality is essential in all functions of the business, not just manufacturing. This is justified by reason of organization synergism: the need to provide quality output to internal as well as external customers and the facilitation of a quality culture and value system throughout the organization. Companies that commit to the concept of TQM apply quality improvement techniques in almost every area of product development, manufacturing, distribution, administration, and customer service.[20] Nowhere is the philosophy of "customer is king" more prevalent than in TQM. Customers are both external (including channels) and internal (including staff functions) to the business.

The paradigm of TQM applies to all enterprises, both manufacturing and service, and many companies in manufacturing, service, and information industries have reaped the benefits. Industries as diverse as telecommunications, public utilities, and health care have applied the principles of TQM.

Government agencies and departments have also joined the movement, although private sector efforts have been considerably more effective.[21] According to a 1992 General Accounting Office (GAO) special report, 68 percent of the federal organizations and installations surveyed had some kind of TQM effort underway. Productivity and quality improvement programs are expected to be initiated in almost 700 federal programs in 1993.[22] Defense contractors will be particularly affected as the government moves toward requiring suppliers to adopt the TQM concept.[23] Oregon State University is the first among academic institutions to make a commitment to adopt the principles of TQM throughout the organization.[24]

The widespread adoption of one or more approaches or principles of TQM does not mean that results have met expectations. According to the GAO survey mentioned earlier, only 13 percent of government agency employees actively participate in the TQM efforts.[25] Human resource professionals report a strong interest in TQM issues in 1993, ranking employee involvement, customer service, and TQM as the top three key issues, yet research shows that initiatives taken by organizations are not receiving as much praise as they did a few years ago.[26]

QUALITY AND BUSINESS PERFORMANCE

The relationship between quality, profitability, and market share has been studied in depth by the Strategic Planning Institute of Cambridge, Massachusetts. The conclusion, based on performance data of about 3000 strategic business units, is unequivocal:

> One factor above all others—quality—drives market share. And when superior quality and large market share are both present, profitability is virtually guaranteed.[27]

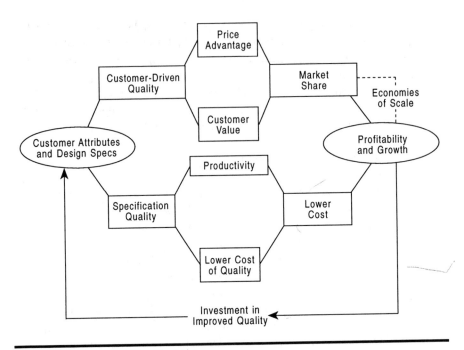

Figure 1-1   The Quality Circle

> There is no doubt that relative perceived quality and profitability are strongly related. Whether the profit measure is return on sales or return on investment, businesses with a superior product/service offering clearly outperform those with inferior quality.[28]

Even producers of commodity or near-commodity products seek and find ways to distinguish their products through cycle time, availability, or other quality attributes.[29] In addition to profitability and market share, quality drives growth. The linkages between these correlates of quality are shown in Figure 1-1.

Quality can also reduce costs. This reduction, in turn, provides an additional competitive edge. Note that Figure 1-1 includes two types of quality: customer-driven quality and conformance or internal specification quality. The latter relates to appropriate product specifications and service standards that lead to cost reduction. As will be discussed in Chapter 11, there is an inverse relationship between internal or conformance quality and costs, and thus the phrase coined by Crosby: "Quality Is Free."[30] As quality improves, so does cost, resulting in improved market share and hence profitability and growth. This, in turn, provides a means for further investment in such quality improvement areas as research and development. The cycle goes on. In summary, improving both internal (conformance) quality and external (customer perceived) quality not only lowers cost of poor quality or "non-quality" but also serves as a driver for growth, market share, and profitability.

The rewards of higher quality are positive, substantial, and pervasive.[31] Findings indicate that attaining quality superiority produces the following organizational benefits:

1. Greater customer loyalty
2. Market share improvements
3. Higher stock prices
4. Reduced service calls
5. Higher prices
6. Greater productivity

SERVICE QUALITY VS. PRODUCT QUALITY

It is paradoxical that there is more concern in the United States for product quality than there is for quality of services and service industries. Despite the fact that only 21 percent of total employment in the United States is in industries that produce goods (excluding agriculture with approximately 3 percent),[32] the emphasis has historically been on manufacturing industries. Consider also that up to half of employment in manufacturing is in such staff or white-collar jobs as marketing, finance, or the many other activities not directly involved in physically producing products. If it is accepted that quality improvement can only be achieved through the actions of people, the conclusion emerges that possibly 90 percent or more of the potential for improvement lies in service industries and service jobs in manufacturing firms. The concept of "white-collar quality" is becoming increasingly recognized as the service sector grows.[33]

Despite this rather obvious need for quality service, people directly employed in manufacturing functions tend to focus on production first and quality second. "Get out the production" and "meet the schedule" are common cries on many shop floors. A study conducted by David Garvin of Harvard Business School revealed that U.S. supervisors believed that a deep concern for quality was lacking among workers and that quality as an objective in manufacturing was secondary to the primary goal of meeting production schedules. This same conclusion is suggested in the experiences of over 100 companies. Supervisors almost invariably set targets related to productivity and cost reduction rather than quality improvement.[34]

This seeming manufacturing-service paradox is unusual in view of the several considerations which suggest that the emphasis on services should be substantially increased. The first of these considerations is the "bottom line" factor. Studies have shown that companies rated highly by their customers in terms of service can charge close to 10 percent more than those rated poorly.[35] People will go out of their way and pay more for good service, which indicates the importance placed on service by customers. Conference Board reports concluded that the strongest complaints of customers were registered not for products but rather for services. Recognizing this, executives rate quality of service as a more critical issue than quality of product.[36] Tom Peters, co-author of *Search for Excellence,* scolds U.S. manufacturers for allowing quality to deteriorate into a mindless effort to copy the Japanese and suggests that the best approach is to learn from America's leading service companies.[37]

> ■   Taking a cue from Domino's Pizza, their Michigan-based neighbor, Doctor's Hospital in Detroit is promising to see its emergency room patients in 20 minutes or the care will be free. During the first three weeks of the offer, no patients have been treated free of charge and the number of patients has been up 30 percent.[38]

As a strategic issue, customer service can be considered a major dimension of competitiveness. In the most exhaustive study in its history, the American Management Association surveyed over 3000 international respondents;[39] 78 percent identified improving quality and service to customers as *the* key to competitive success, and 92 percent indicated that providing superior service is one of their key responsibilities, regardless of position. To say that your competitive edge is price is to admit that your products and services are commodities.

After being viewed as a manufacturing problem for most of the past decade, quality has now become a service issue as well. TQM relates not only to the product, but to all the services that accompany it as well.

In many ways defining and controlling quality of service is more difficult than quality assurance of products. Unlike manufacturing, service industries share unique characteristics that make the process of quality control less manageable but no less important. Moreover, the level of quality expected is less predictable. Service company operations are affected by several characteristics, including the intangible nature of the output and the inability to store the output. Other distinguishing characteristics include:

1.   Behavior of the delivery person

2.   Image of the organization

3. The customer present during the production process and performing the final inspection

4. The measure of output is difficult to define

5. Variance and acceptance ranges may not apply

6. Adjusting the control system if the customer is present[40]

However, the most significant problem with the delivery of services is that it is typically measured at the customer interface—the one-on-one, face-to-face interaction between supplier and customer. If a problem exists, it is already too late to fix it.[41]

Wall Street Journal, March 4, 1993

Vice President Gore's sphere expanded yesterday with the announcement that he will lead the latest White House effort to answer the call for change in Washington: a task force that will supposedly examine each federal agency for ways to cut spending and improve services. The "total quality management" effort is an idea borrowed from industry.

THE BALDRIGE AWARD

An additional impetus was provided when Congress established the Baldrige Award in 1987 as a result of Public Law 100-107. Background information on the law mentions foreign competition as the major rationale. No other business prize or development in management theory can match its impact. As evidence of this impact, over twenty states are working to develop regional quality programs.[42]

The award has set a national standard for quality, and hundreds of major corporations use the criteria in the application form as a basic management guide for quality improvement programs. Although the award has its detractors,[43] it has effectively created a new set of standards—a benchmark for quality in U.S. industry.

Applicants must address seven specific categories. These categories of examination items and their respective point values are listed in Table 1-1. The Baldrige Award framework and the dynamic relationships among the criteria are shown in Figure 1-2.

Meeting the criteria is not an easy matter. A perfect score is 1000. The distribution of scores for the 203 applicants during the first three years (1988, 1989, 1990) is shown in Table 1-2. Of the 1203 applicants, only 9 were selected for the award.

An indication of the interest in the Baldrige is the number of application

Table 1-1   1994 Examination Items and Point Values[44]

Examination categories/items	Point values
1.0 Leadership	95
Senior executives' *personal* leadership and involvement in creating and sustaining a customer focus and clear and visible quality values. Also examined is how the quality values are integrated into the company's management system and reflected in the manner in which the company addresses its public responsibilities and corporate citizenship.	
1.1 Senior executive leadership	45
1.2 Management for quality	25
1.3 Public responsibility and corporate citizenship	25
2.0 Information and Analysis	75
The scope, validity, analysis, management, and use of data and information to drive quality excellence and to improve operational and competitive performance. Adequacy of company data, information, and analysis system to support improvement of the company's customer focus, products, services and internal operations.	
2.1 Scope and management of quality and performance data and information	15
2.2 Competitive comparisons and benchmarking	20
2.3 Analysis and uses of company-level data	40
3.0 Strategic Quality Planning	60
The planning process and how all key quality requirements are integrated into overall business planning. The company's short- and longer-term plans and how quality and operational performance are deployed to all work units.	
3.1 Strategic quality and company performance planning process	35
3.2 Quality and performance plans	25
4.0 Human Resource Development and Management	150
The key elements of how the work force is enabled to develop its full potential to pursue the company's quality and operational performance objectives. Also examined are the company's efforts to build and maintain an environment for quality excellence conducive to full participation and personal and organizational growth.	
4.1 Human resource planning and management	20
4.2 Employee involvement	40
4.3 Employee education and training	40
4.4 Employee performance and recognition	25
4.5 Employee well-being and satisfaction	25

Table 1-1 (continued)   1994 Examination Items and Point Values[44]

Examination categories/items	Point values
5.0 Management of Process Quality	**140**
Systematic processes the company uses to pursue ever-higher quality and company operational performance. The key elements of process management, including R&D, design, management of process quality for all work units and suppliers, systematic quality improvement, and quality assessment.	
5.1 Design and introduction of quality products and services	40
5.2 Process management: product and service production and delivery processes	35
5.3 Process management: business processes and support services	30
5.4 Supplier quality	20
5.5 Quality assessment	15
6.0 Quality and Operational Results	**180**
The company's quality levels and improvement trends in quality, company operational performance, and supplier quality. Current quality and operational performance levels relative to those of competitors.	
6.1 Product and service quality results	70
6.2 Company operational results	50
6.3 Business process and support service results	25
6.4 Supplier quality results	35
7.0 Customer Focus and Satisfaction	**300**
The company's relationships with customers and its knowledge of customer requirements and of the key quality factors that drive marketplace competitiveness. Also the company's methods to determine customer satisfaction, current trends and levels of customer satisfaction and retention, and these results relative to competitors.	
7.1 Customer expectations: current and future	35
7.2 Customer relationships management	65
7.3 Commitment to customers	15
7.4 Customer satisfaction determination	30
7.5 Customer satisfaction results	85
7.6 Customer satisfaction comparison	70
Total Points	**1000**

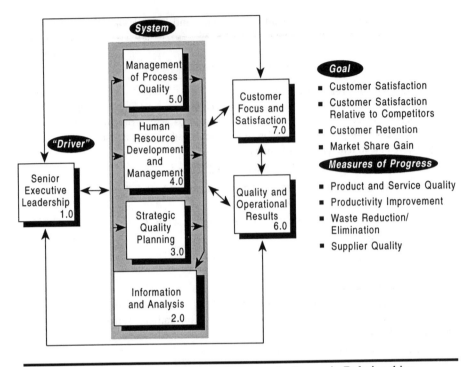

Figure 1-2   Baldrige Award Criteria Framework: Dynamic Relationships

Table 1-2   Distribution of Scores

Scoring range	Number of applications		
	1988	1989	1990
0–125	0	0	0
126–250	0	1	7
251–400	1	8	18
401–600	31	15	51
601–750	23	12	19
751–875	11	4	2
876–1000	0	0	0
Total	66	40	97

guidelines (167,000 in 1990) requested. In the first 3 years, 203 companies applied and 9 won: 6 manufacturers, 2 small companies, and 1 service company (Federal Express). Winners of the award are required to share their successful strategies with other companies. IBM's Rochester, Minnesota site, home of the Applications System/400 and a 1990 winner, attributes the success of the division to the way in which it appropriated the ideas of Motorola, Xerox, and Milliken, winners in prior years. This sharing of ideas is a central purpose of the National Institute of Standards and Technology, the administering agency.[45] The sharing policy by winners ensures a multiplier effect.

Another indication of the award's leverage is the stringent criteria related to quality assurance for products and services purchased by external providers (suppliers) of goods and services. It is clear that suppliers are a critical link in the chain of processes that constitute TQM. As a result, many companies require their suppliers to apply for the Baldrige. For example, Motorola and Westinghouse, two winners, will not do business with a supplier that has not applied for the award and does not use its criteria. Another winner, Globe Metallurgical, is certified as a supplier by Ford. Globe in turn requires certification by its suppliers. Thus, the number of firms using the Baldrige criteria may grow geometrically as first-tier suppliers certify second-tier suppliers and so on.

Hewlett-Packard, IBM, Motorola, Westinghouse, and 3M are among the many companies that use the application as a guide for managers and a checklist for internal quality standards:

■ But basically, the Baldrige criteria will be the way we judge our own operations from now on. The reason is simple: The Baldrige Award process is a basic blueprint on how to do the quality process.[46]

3M

■ Competing for the award motivated people to a level I didn't think possible.[47]

General Manager
GM Cadillac Division

■ The National Quality Award process enabled the company to look at itself through the eyes of the customer, and every aspect of the business came under scrutiny.[48]

Xerox

■ Managers of IBM's Santa Teresa, California lab are required to score their operations every 90 days using the criteria.

The winners for the six-year period since the beginning of the award in 1988 are shown in Table 1-3.[49]

Table 1-3   Award Winners: 1988 to 1993

1993 Award Winners

Manufacturing
Eastman Chemical Company
Kingsport, TN

Small Business
Ames Rubber Corp.
Hamburg, NJ

1992 Award Winners

Manufacturing
AT&T Network Systems Group
Transmission Systems Business Unit
Morristown, NJ

Texas Instruments, Inc.
Defense Systems & Electronics Group
Dallas, TX

Service
AT&T Universal Card Services
Jacksonville, FL

The Ritz-Carlton Hotel Company
Atlanta, GA

Small Business
Granite Rock Company
Watsonville, CA

1991 Award Winners

Manufacturing
Solectron Corp.
San Jose, CA

Zytec Corp.
Eden Prairie, MN

Small Business
Marlow Industries
Dallas, TX

1990 Award Winners

Manufacturing
Cadillac Motor Car Company
Detroit, MI

IBM Rochester
Rochester, MN

Service
Federal Express Corp.
Memphis, TN

Small Business
Wallace Co., Inc.
Houston, TX

1989 Award Winners

Manufacturing
Milliken & Company
Spartanburg, SC

Xerox Business Products and Systems
Stamford, CT

1988 Award Winners

Manufacturing
Motorola, Inc.
Schaumburg, IL

Westinghouse Commercial
Nuclear Fuel Division
Pittsburgh, PA

Small Business
Globe Metallurgical, Inc.
Cleveland, OH

QUESTIONS FOR DISCUSSION

1-1 Give one or more examples of products made in Japan or Western Europe that are superior in quality to American-made products. How do you explain this difference?

1-2 Illustrate how the TQM concept can integrate design, engineering, manufacturing, and service.

1-3 Explain why quality should be better by following the TQM concept than in a system that depends on final inspection.

1-4 What common elements or principles can you identify among (1) the Baldrige criteria and (2) Deming, Juran, and Crosby?

1-5 Describe how increased market share and profitability might result from improved quality.

1-6 Select one staff department (e.g., accounting, finance, marketing services, human resources) and describe how this department can deliver quality service to its *internal* customers.

1-7 Compare the Baldrige Award criteria to the principles promoted by Deming and Crosby. What are the similarities and/or differences?

ENDNOTES

1. J. M. Juran, "Strategies for World Class Quality," *Quality Progress,* March 1991, p. 81.
2. Armand V. Feigenbaum, "America on the Threshold of Quality," *Quality,* Jan. 1990, p. 16. Feigenbaum, a pioneer and current expert in quality, estimates that TQM could mean a 7 percent increase in the country's gross national product. See Armand V. Feigenbaum, "Quality: An International Imperative," *Journal for Quality and Participation,* March 1991, p. 16. Estimates from the United States Chamber of Commerce Department suggest that nearly 75 percent of all products manufactured in the United States are targets for strong competition from imports.
3. Ronald M. Fortuna, "The Quality Imperative," *Executive Excellence,* March 1990, p. 1. It is expected that competition from Europe may become more severe than that from Japan. Despite the surface congeniality at the G-7 meetings in London in mid-July 1991, it is apparent that the European Economic Community plans a united front against the United States. German Chancellor Helmut Kohl states, "Europe's return to its original unity means that the '90s will be the decade of Europe, not Japan. This is Europe's hour." (Peter Truell and Philip Revzin, "A New Era Is at Hand in Global Competition: U.S. vs. United Europe," *Wall Street Journal,* July 15, 1991, p. 1.)

4. American Society for Quality Control, *Quality: Executive Priority or Afterthought?* Milwaukee: ASQC, 1989.

5. American Society for Quality Control, *'88 Gallup Survey: Consumers' Perceptions Concerning the Quality of American Products and Services,* Milwaukee: ASQC, 1988, p. iv. This survey and the survey cited in Endnote 4 were conducted by the Gallup Organization.

6. American Society for Quality Control, *Quality: Everyone's Job, Many Vacancies,* Milwaukee: ASQC, 1990. This survey was conducted by the Gallup Organization. Other findings include: (1) where quality improvement programs exist the level of participation among employees is actually higher in small companies and service companies, (2) people who participate in quality improvement activities are more satisfied than non-participants with the rate of quality improvement their companies have been able to achieve.

7. A survey conducted by Integrated Automotive Resources, Wayne, Pennsylvania.

8. David Mercer, "Total Quality Management: Key Quality Issues," in *Global Perspectives on Total Quality,* New York: Conference Board, 1991, p. 11. See also Walter E. Breisch, "Employee Involvement," *Quality,* May 1990, pp. 49–51; John Hauser, "The House of Quality," *Harvard Business Review,* May/June 1988, pp. 63–73; W. F. Wheaton, "The Journey to Total Quality: A Fundamental Strategic Renewal," *Business Forum,* Spring 1989, pp. 4–7.

9. Claude S. George, Jr., *The History of Management Thought,* Englewood Cliffs, N.J.: Prentice-Hall, 1972, p. 53.

10. David A. Garvin, "Competing on the Eight Dimensions of Quality," *Harvard Business Review,* Nov./Dec. 1987, pp. 101–109. This same author has provided an excellent description of the background of quality developments in his book *Managing Quality* (New York: Free Press, 1988).

11. See Joel E. Ross and David E. Wegman, "Quality Management and the Role of the Accountant," *Industrial Management,* July/Aug. 1990, pp. 21–23.

12. Yunum Kathawala, "A Comparative Analysis of Selected Approaches to Quality," *International Journal of Quality and Reliability Management,* Vol. 6 Issue 5, 1989, pp. 7–17. Other writers and researchers with less visibility than those mentioned here have contributed to the literature. For a review of this rapidly expanding literature, see Jayant V. Saraph, P. George Benson, and Roger G. Schroeder, "An Instrument for Measuring the Critical Factors of Quality Management," *Decision Sciences,* Vol. 20, 1989. The research described in this article identified 120 prescriptions for effective quality management, which were subsequently grouped into 8 categories that are quite similar to the Baldrige Award criteria: (1) the role of management leadership and quality policy, (2) the role of the quality department, (3) training, (4) product/service design, (5) supplier quality management, (6) process management, (7) quality data and reporting, and (8) employee relations.

13. W. Edwards Deming, *Quality, Productivity, and Competitive Position,* Cambridge, Mass.: Center for Advanced Engineering Study, Massachusetts Institute of Technology, 1982. See also W. Edwards Deming, *Out of the Crisis,* Cambridge, Mass.: Center for Advanced Engineering Study, Massachusetts Institute of Technology, 1982.

14. Juran's early approach appears in J. M. Juran, *Quality Control Handbook,* New York: McGraw-Hill, 1951. For more recent contributions, see (all by Juran) "The Quality Trilogy," *Quality Progress,* Aug. 1986, pp. 19–24; "Universal Approach to Managing

Quality," *Executive Excellence,* May 1989, pp. 15–17; "Made in USA—A Quality Resurgence," *Journal for Quality and Participation,* March 1991, pp. 6–8; "Strategies for World Progress," *Quality Progress,* March 1991, pp. 81–85.

15. "Dueling Pioneers," *Business Week,* Oct. 25, 1991. This is a special report and bonus issue of *Business Week* entitled "The Quality Imperative."

16. Philip Crosby, *Quality Is Free,* New York: McGraw-Hill, 1979.

17. From *Quality,* a promotional brochure by Philip Crosby Associates, Inc.

18. Sara Jackson, "Calling in the Gurus," *Director (UK),* Oct. 1990, pp. 95–101. In this article, the author reports that in the U.K., it is not the quality gurus as much as government initiatives that have been responsible for raising quality awareness.

19. Marc Wortman, "Commencement," *Yale Alumni Magazine,* Summer 1991, p. 61. One of the authors happens to be a Yale graduate, although not of the class of '28.

20. Daniel M. Stowell, "Quality in the Marketing Process," *Quality Progress,* Oct. 1989, pp. 57–62. For the sales function, see Walt Williams, "Quality: An Old Objective but a New Strategy." For R & D, see Michael F. Wolff, "Quality in R & D—It Starts With You," *Marketing News,* Oct. 15, 1990, pp. 16–22.

21. Stanley Blacker, "Data Quality and the Environment," *Quality,* April 1990, pp. 38–42.

22. Carolyn Burstein and Kathleen Sediak, "The Federal Quality and Productivity Improvement Effort," *Quality Progress,* Oct. 1988, pp. 38–41.

23. General Dynamics and McDonnell Douglas are among the defense contractors that have achieved improvement through TQM. See Bruce Smith and William B. Scott, "Douglas Tightens Controls to Improve Performance," *Aviation Week & Space Technology,* Jan. 4, 1990, pp. 16–20. See also Glenn E. Hayes, "Three Views of TQM," *Quality,* April 1990, pp. 19–24.

24. Edwin L. Coate, "TQM at Oregon State University," *Journal for Quality and Participation,* Dec. 1990, pp. 90–101.

25. Jennifer Jordan, "Everything You Wanted to Know About TQM," *Public Manager,* Winter 1992–1993, pp. 45–48.

26. Karen Matthes, "A Look Ahead for '93," *HR Focus,* Jan. 1993, pp. 1, 4. See also Richard Y. Chang, "When TQM Goes Nowhere," *Training and Development,* Jan. 1993, pp. 22–29.

27. Robert D. Buzzell and Bradley T. Gale, *The PIMS Principles: Linking Strategy to Performance,* New York: The Free Press, 1987, p. 87. PIMS is the acronym for Profit Impact of Market Strategy. A PIMS study in Canada reached a similar conclusion. See William Band, "Quality Is King for Marketers," *Sales and Marketing Management in Canada,* March 1989.

28. Robert D. Buzzell and Bradley T. Gale, *The PIMS Principles: Linking Strategy to Performance,* New York: The Free Press, 1987, p. 107.

29. A good example is the "Perdue Chicken" produced by Perdue Farms. Owner Frank Perdue set out to differentiate his chicken by color, freshness, availability, and meat-to-bone ratio. These criteria of quality, as defined by the customer, led the company to growth and improved market share and profitability. See Diane Feldman, "Building a Better Bird," *Management Review,* May 1989, pp. 10–14.

30. Tom Peters reported in *Thriving on Chaos* (New York: Knopf, 1987) that experts agree that poor quality can cost about 25 percent of the people and assets in a manufacturing firm and up to 40 percent in a service firm.

31. See Joel E. Ross and David Georgoff, "A Survey of Productivity and Quality Issues in

Manufacturing: The State of the Industry," *Industrial Management,* Jan./Feb. 1991.

32. United States Bureau of Labor Statistics, *Monthly Labor Review,* Nov. 1989. Reported in *U.S. Statistical Abstract,* 1990, p. 395.

33. For example, Campbell USA has targeted the administrative and marketing side of the corporation in its latest quality program, "Quality Proud." See Herbert M. Baum, "White-Collar Quality Comes of Age," *Journal of Business Strategy,* March/April 1990, pp. 34–37.

34. David Garvin, "Quality Problems, Policies, and Attitudes in the United States and Japan: An Exploratory Study," *Academy of Management Journal,* Dec. 1986, pp. 653–673.

35. Frank K. Sonnenberg, "Service Quality: Forethought, Not Afterthought," *Journal of Business Strategy,* Sep./Oct. 1989, pp. 56–57.

36. American Society for Quality Control, *Quality: Executive Priority or Afterthought?"* Milwaukee: ASQC, 1989, p. 8. In this survey conducted by the Gallup Organization, 57 percent of service company executives rated service quality as extremely critical (10 on a scale of 1 to 10), while only 50 percent of industrial company executives gave service quality the same rating.

37. Tom Peters, "Total Quality Leadership. Let's Get It Right," *Journal for Quality and Participation,* March 1991, pp. 10–15.

38. "Hospital Delivers: Emergency Room Guarantees Care in 20 Minutes," Associated Press, July 15, 1991.

39. Reported in Eric R. Greenberg, "Customer Service: The Key to Competitiveness," *Management Review,* Dec. 1990, p. 29. Reported fully in AMA Research Report, *The New Competitive Edge,* New York: American Management Association, 1991.

40. See Terrence J. Smith, "Measuring a Customer Service Culture," *Retail Control,* Oct. 1989, pp. 15–18. See also Behshid Farsad and Ahmad K. Eishennawy, "Defining Service Quality Is Difficult for Service and Manufacturing Firms," *Industrial Engineering,* March 1989, pp. 17–19; Christian Gronroos, "Service Quality: The Six Criteria of Good Perceived Service Quality," *Review of Business,* Winter 1989, pp. 10–13; Carol King, "Service Quality Assurance Is Different," *Quality Progress,* June 1985, pp. 14–18.

41. Lawrence Holpp, "Ten Steps to Total Service Quality," *Journal for Quality and Participation,* March 1990, pp. 92–96. The major steps referred to in the title include: (1) creating an awareness and a philosophy of constant improvement, (2) making the vision of the organization a personal vision for every employee, (3) empowering employees to act, (4) surveying customers personally, (5) measuring meaningful information, and (6) adopting a performance management system that rewards teamwork, improvement, and new behaviors consistent with interdepartmental cooperation.

42. Curt W. Reimann, "America Unites Behind the Baldrige Quality Crusade," *Electronic Business,* October 15, 1990, p. 63. Reimann is Director of the Malcolm Baldrige National Quality Award and Associate Director for Quality Programs at the National Institute of Standards and Technology, the agency that administers the Baldrige Award program. A good summary of what it takes to compete for the Baldrige is contained in Curt Reimann, "Winning Strategies for Quality Improvement," *Business America,* March 25, 1991, pp. 8–11. See also "A Standard for All Seasons," *Executive Excellence,* March 1991, p. 9, and "The Baldrige Award: Leading the Way to Quality," *Quality Progress,* July 1989, pp. 35–39.

43. See Jeremy Main, "Is the Baldrige Overblown?" *Fortune,* July 1, 1991, pp. 62–65. Philip Crosby of *Quality Is Free* fame scorns the paperwork, thinks that customers rather than

the company applying should do the nominating, and deplores the lack of financial measures. Tom Peters, co-author of *Search for Excellence,* complains that the criteria are "strangely silent on the subject of bureaucracy." There was also a bit of sour grapes when Cadillac won the award in 1990.

44. A more detailed description is contained in The 1993 Award Criteria and The 1993 Application Forms and Instructions. These two documents can be obtained from Malcolm Baldrige National Quality Award, National Institute of Standards and Technology, Route 270 and Quince Orchard Road, Administration Building, Room A537, Gaithersburg, MD 20899 (Tel. 301-975 2036).

45. Michael Fitzgerald, "Quality: Take it to the Limit," *Computerworld,* Feb. 11, 1991, pp. 71–78.

46. Remarks of A. G. Jacobson in a presentation to the Conference Board Quality Conference, April 2, 1990.

47. Jeremy Main, "Is the Baldrige Overblown?" *Fortune,* July 1, 1991, p. 63.

48. Company brochure entitled "The Xerox Quest for Quality and the National Quality Award."

49. Texas Instruments is one of the several Baldrige winners that attribute their turnaround to the adoption of the principles of TQM. See *Fortune,* Nov. 30, 1992, p. 80–83. In October 1992 the Ritz-Carlton Hotel Company became the first hotel pcompany to win the Baldrige Award. Their approach to quality relies on traditional TQM principles. Edward Watkins, "How Ritz-Carlton Won the Baldrige Award," *Lodging Hospitality,* Nov. 1992, pp. 22–24. In 1990, AT&T chairman and CEO Robert Allen created the Chairman's Quality Award, the criteria and examination process for which were taken from the Malcolm Baldrige Award. See Rick Whiting, "AT&T Started a Quality Bonfire to Learn How to Put it Out," *Electronic Business,* Oct. 1992, pp. 95–103.

In the following article the author makes a good argument for adopting a total quality management approach and points out the substantial cultural and operational changes that are required. These changes may require a dismantling of top management's own bureaucratic creation. Several suggestions are made for the chief executive officer who is willing to make the necessary changes.

THE CATCH-22 OF TOTAL QUALITY MANAGEMENT

G. M. Harrington

In the quest for total quality, American business is going through a revolution. Or is it? There is certainly enough noise for a revolution. The eloquent and profound have learned all the catch phrases and make rousing speeches. Vice presidents and directors of total quality management are being added to CEO's staffs at a seemingly epidemic rate. The Malcolm Baldrige National Quality Award is becoming the standard of excellence in total quality management, and the winners of the past three years have indeed been very impressive in their quality achievements.

But how are we really doing? What is happening in the average American company? Vince Lombardi once said that the difference between a good team and a great team is not the performance of the superstars but, rather, the performance of the average players. If industrial America is going to be greatly improved by total quality management, it will not be as a result of improvement in the already excellent companies. Rather, it is the great mass of average companies that will have to do the job.

If you talk with the quality professionals in many companies, there is still much doubt that the revolution is spreading. In companies in which progress is

Reprinted with permission from *Across the Board,* September 1991.

slow, we hear the refrain, "This is a culture change, and culture changes take years." But this statement often hides the real fact that many companies are actually changing slowly, or not at all. Regrettably, these are the very companies where major change is not only attainable, but probably critical to survival.

To understand what is going on requires a knowledge of what the total quality culture change is really all about. The bedrock of total quality management is the combined behavior of the individuals in the company. The total quality culture change process is, therefore, a change in the behavior of these individuals. Yes, total quality management involves tools and techniques, such as statistical process control and problem solving. But as any teacher knows, it's the use of the tools, not the tools themselves, that matters.

The trick to total quality management is no secret: The leadership sets the vision that the customer is king, and provides the employees with support, tools, and rewards for doing their part. "Doing their part" means taking care of the customer and insuring that others dealing with the customer receive all the support they need. Any activities not contributing to this end are considered wasteful and must be eliminated.

When all this works, the customers will want you as their supplier, and will pay you a competitive price. At the competitive price, you will be so efficient that you will be able to make a nice profit. With this profit, you will have something with which to repay the shareholders for their investment.

If a company has not achieved total quality, it follows that most of the individuals in the company do not practice total quality behaviors. The combination of these behaviors is what forms the culture of the company. Over a period of time, the hiring and promotion practices of the company have reinforced and strengthened this culture.

Dominating the company's culture are the values and natural leadership style of the top people. If the company is "average," it's likely the result of the culture senior management has created. Thus, senior management has to dismantle and change its own creation to create a total quality environment. But first senior managers have to dismantle and change themselves. They cannot personally remain unchanged and hope that the rest of the people in the company will accomplish the change for them.

The Catch-22 is that the senior mangers who must personally change in order to instill a total quality environment may have the most to lose if the change succeeds. Senior managers have been promoted because they have succeeded in, and been role models for, the entrenched culture. The culture, in turn, has rewarded them with comfortable life styles and the perquisites of success.

One of the best examples of overcoming the Catch-22 of total quality management can be found in the Role Model Manager concept adopted by Xerox Corporation, a 1989 winner of the Baldrige Award. In employee surveys, the workers at Xerox made it clear to management that commitment to a quality improvement process, dubbed "Leadership Through Quality," was not evident from promotional practices. The feedback showed that there was a widely held perception among employees that promotions were based on reasons other than attaining quality. An analysis of past promotions confirmed this perception. So Xerox developed new criteria for promotions based on an individual's demonstrated practice of eight leadership characteristics critical to the success of the total quality process. Making these role-model behaviors a requirement for promotion was a key to the culture change that transformed Xerox into the world-class corporation recognized by the Baldrige Award examiners.

Obviously, such fundamental change in day-to-day conduct is difficult to achieve. For senior managers, who have done things the same way for 20 or 30 years, and who by all measures have been judged a success, it has been described as equivalent to asking someone who is right-handed to change permanently to being left-handed. In the case of senior managers, and especially for the CEO of an average company, changing to a total quality style of management is an uphill battle.

Does this mean that the total quality management transformation is impossible for the average-performing company? No, just difficult. In evaluating the successes of past Baldrige winners, I have found that there are three conditions that will yield success:

Impending financial collapse.   Nearly every winner of the Baldrige Award tells a story of believing it was on the verge of failure when it committed to total quality management. This was true of large companies such as Motorola Inc. and Xerox as well as small companies such as Globe Metallurgical Inc. They tried total quality management because everything else had failed, and no other option seemed available. While "impending collapse" has been demonstrated as a surefire way to foster a sincere commitment to total quality management, it is often too late—the patient may already be terminal.

Demanding customers.   Next best is customer demands that leave the company no alternative. Due to the heightened awareness of total quality among American companies, this is happening with increasing frequency. Demanding customers are being more specific about their expectations. In this situation, however, a company may still believe it is pretty good, and it may not totally embrace the total quality management concept. It will adopt the rhetoric but not the substance of true culture change. In other words, the Catch-22 may already be operating. The chance of success is greater than for the first group, however, because the company is healthier and has more time to make total quality management work.

"Born-again" CEO.   In the absence of customer pressures, about the only remaining hope is a "born-again" change of heart by the senior managers, particularly by the CEO. The evidence that total quality management works is growing, as is belief that success is attainable and that the risk of the effort is acceptable. But this "leap of faith" requires tremendous leadership—leadership not previously exhibited by the CEO, or the company would already be in the "excellent" category. This leadership must overcome the Catch-22 of total quality management. The good news is that if the CEO and senior management can truly, personally adopt the concepts of total quality management, their chance of succeeding is best of all.

What should you do if you are a CEO or senior manager of a company that is fortunate enough not to be subject to conditions one or two? There are several things you can do:

- **Study the leadership activities of the executives of excellent companies,** whether through personal discussions with these executives or by attending meetings and seminars given by Baldrige Award winners. Find out how they spend their time, what their priorities and values are and how they project them, what measurement system they used to gauge progress, and most importantly, how they reward, recognize, and promote employees.

- **Obtain and read the Baldrige Award criteria.** Even better, take a course in the use of the criteria for business assessment. The Baldrige standard is so comprehensive that is has to be studied thoroughly to grasp the scope of total quality.

- **Talk with quality experts and consultants.** The good ones will tell you the hard facts of what you, the executive, will have to do to clearly communicate to employees that you are truly committed to total quality management and that the company's criteria for individual success have changed.

- **Commission a customer survey.** This should only be done after spending several weeks or months doing the three steps outlined above. To insure objectivity, you should engage a professional to structure and conduct the survey. The aim should be to determine what is important to your customers, your company's level of performance, and how you compare to your competition. Most likely, you will learn that the system you have been using to measure business performance and to reward and promote managers has a different set of criteria than your customers use to evaluate your company. What is good for your managers may not be good for your customers. You should be prepared for feedback that is more negative than you expect. In the end, though, you will have the basis for establishing and communicating a new, quantifiable set of priorities. You will have the beginning of a new measurement system for rewarding performance.

- **Conduct an employee survey.** The survey should be designed to learn the extent to which total quality behaviors are part of your existing culture. Are employees rewarded for meeting customer expectations as much as they are for financial performance? Do the employees think that management really believes that employees are the company's most important asset? Do the employees have adequate training to be able to do their jobs? Is it safe to take risks? Do employees think their ideas are welcome, and likely to be acted upon?

By the time you complete these steps, you will be well on your way. You will understand your role as the leader. You will know what your customers really want and how they rate your performance. You will know what your employees think of their company, its priorities and values. And you will understand the Catch-22 of total quality management that has to be overcome to get your senior managers to do their part. Now comes the difficult work of total quality: changing.

To change requires methodically and systematically undertaking specific steps and actions that, in several years, will make your company world class. Much has been written about what these steps are—education, communications, reward and recognition, employee suggestion systems, involvement teams, benchmarking, statistical methods of management, and so on. You will already have learned a great deal about these from your journey thus far. As you go forward, you have to regularly repeat the customer and employee surveys to confirm that you are making acceptable progress. After all, only the judgment of your customers and the feedback of your employees will tell you if the Catch-22 of total quality has been defeated.

CASE

TQM IN A SERVICE ORGANIZATION

Macdonald, Levine, Jenkins & Company is a 20-person CPA firm located in Boston. For years, the firm offered the traditional CPA accounting services but differentiated these services by maintaining an early leadership in the computer field, a successful competitive edge that distinguished it from the competition in its market segment.

Following the widespread availability and use of computers, the directors came to realize that the differentiation of computer expertise had been diminished and the firm was becoming indistinguishable from other CPA firms, effectively reducing the company's services to commodity status. A commodity has but one differentiation: *price*! What had happened was that the firm had essentially lost its distinguishing differentiation and was concentrating on services as *it* defined them, not the way *the customer* defined them.

After the managing director had attended a TQM seminar, the firm's management decided to put more emphasis on continuous conformance to customer expectations and needs. Prior to this TQM "awakening," performance was measured by using the classical benchmarks such as number of new clients, total billings, etc. These measures, of course, are of little or no significance to the client. When submitting a sales proposal to a client, it had been customary to set high goals that promised service delivery without regard to the prospective client's desired level of service or what constituted satisfaction in the mind of the client. In other words, in order to increase the chances of obtaining a prospective client's business, the firm promised performance levels that were rarely kept in reality. The firm was in a double bind. On the one hand, the sales proposal was based on measures that the firm, *not the customer,* thought were appropriate, and the firm was setting itself up for failure by not delivering as promised. For example, one proposal offered to perform analytical reviews based on the client's internally generated financial information, but the product frequently was deliv-

Adapted from Constance Levine, "How TQM Worked for One Firm," *Journal of Accountancy,* September 1993, pp. 73–79.

ered late due to the difficulty of obtaining client information. The company was faced with the paradox of disappointing a client who never would have asked for the service if the CPA firm had not offered it in the first place. Following the company's conversion to TQM awareness, it was found that asking clients what they really wanted revealed that their needs were really very simple and unlike some of the performance measures or services that had been proposed.

Getting Started with TQM

Training was the initial and major step in implementing the TQM process. Everyone in the firm participated, including both owners and clerical staff. Each was asked to identify problems and possible solutions to selected topics such as communications. Brainstorming during group training sessions identified 52 possible quality improvement projects. It was decided to initially tackle the top five: (1) network office computers, (2) develop a strategic account process for managing client relationships, (3) improve the billing time and process, (4) improve the image of the firm, and (5) manage the overall TQM process. Teams were established to develop budgets and create timetables and action plans, so that each project could be accomplished during the following year.

Quality Indicators

Quality goals were established for clients, employees, and owners, and measures called "evidences of success" were developed. For example:

	Goal	Evidence of success
Clients	Satisfaction	(1) Bills paid on time
		(2) Score 93% on satisfaction survey
		(3) Reduce billing adjustments by 50%
		(4) Improve accounts receivable days outstanding by 30%
		(5) Increase referrals by 200%
		(6) Increase client retention rate by 50%
Employees	Satisfaction	(1) Decrease turnover rate
		(2) Lower absenteeism
		(3) Satisfaction survey
Owners	Growth	(1) Increase number of clients and revenue per client by 200% within 5 years
	Profit	(2) Increase per-shareholder profits by 200%
	Recognition	(3) Win Malcolm Baldrige Award

Annual planning includes both a quality as well as a business plan in which the "evidences of success" serve as a game plan for the entire firm. Each year, the plan is reviewed by the quality steering committee and changed as appropriate.

Client Input

The TQM needs of clients are determined through TQM awareness surveys. Questions are asked concerning activity-based costing, cost of quality, problem solving, product cost and/or process management, process costs, and product/service costs. From this client input, the firm is able to offer new and improved services. Examples include cost-of-quality analyses and activity-based costing.

Culture

A vision statement was developed during the training session:

■ We are an acknowledged leader in business and financial services, recognized for our dedication to providing valued services to our clients, our employees, and the business community by constantly meeting their needs and exceeding their expectations.

As a result of the firm's dedication to client satisfaction as reflected in the vision statement, it was recognized that several employees could not adapt to this cultural change that focused on communication and client service. These employees decided to leave the firm. Prospective employees are now screened to determine whether they can function in the changed environment.

Questions for Discussion

1   Compare the firm's actions in implementing TQM with the criteria of the Baldrige Award. What additional actions, if any, would you recommend?

2   Evaluate the firm's quality measures or "evidences of success." Do these indicators really measure quality as it is delivered to the customer? Why or why not?

3   Do the client TQM awareness surveys generate appropriate information to determine client needs? If so, do the "evidences of success" measure how well these needs are being met?

LEADERSHIP FOR TQM

Getting quality results is not a short-term, instant-pudding way to improve competitiveness; implementing total quality management requires hands-on, continuous leadership.

Armand V. Feigenbaum

The story is told of three executives traveling on the same flight to an international conference. One executive was British, one Japanese, and one American. They were hijacked by terrorists and immediately before execution were offered an opportunity to make a last request. The Englishman asked to sing a verse of "God Save the Queen." The Japanese executive wanted to give a lecture on Japanese management. Upon hearing this, the American said: "Let me be the first one to be shot. I simply can't take another lecture on Japanese management."

The point of this story is that many U.S. managers are growing weary of such comparisons in which Americans appear to be second best. One such comparison involved a visit to several Japanese companies by seven Leadership Forum executives. The experience left them with a profound belief that the reason why Japanese companies are beating U.S. companies has little to do with trade barriers, culture, cost of capital, sympathetic unions, or a supportive government. They found that the primary reason is simply that the United States is being out-led and out-managed. With some notable exceptions, U.S. firms are lagging behind because they lack clear, consistent, and persistent leadership from the top. Joseph Jaworski, chairman of the American Leadership Forum, is among the many CEOs who suggest that quality depends upon a vision of excellence and that a vision becomes reality through excellent, compelling leadership.[1]

Some principles and practices of total quality management (TQM) may differ among firms and industries, but there is unanimous agreement as to the importance of leadership by top management in implementing TQM. Such leadership is a prerequisite to all strategy and action plans. According to Juran, it cannot be delegated.[2] Those firms that have succeeded in making total quality work for them have been able to do so because of strong leadership.[3] A U.S. General Accounting Office study concluded, "Ultimately, strong visionary leaders are the most important element of a quality management approach."[4]

Dr. Curt Reimann, Director of the Malcolm Baldrige National Quality Award, has reviewed hundreds of applications, including those of the award winners. His review of key excellence indicators of quality management is insightful and helpful for an award applicant or anyone using the Baldrige criteria as a benchmark to evaluate the quality of management. He summarizes the characteristics of excellent leadership as follows:[5]

Visible, committed, and knowledgeable.   They promote the emphasis on quality and know the details and how well the company is doing. Personal involvement in education, training and recognition. Accessible to and routine contact with employees, customers and suppliers.

A missionary zeal.   The leaders are trying to effect as much change as possible through their suppliers, through the government and through any other vehicle that promotes quality in the United States. Active in promotion of quality outside the company.

Aggressive targets.   Going beyond incremental improvements and looking at the possibility of making large gains, getting the whole work force thinking about different processes—not just improving processes.

Strong drivers.   Cycle time, zero defects, six sigma or other targets to drive improvements. Clearly defined customer satisfaction and quality improvement objectives.

Communication of values.   Effecting cultural change related to quality. Written policy, mission, guidelines and other documented statements of quality values, or other bases for clear and consistent communications.

Organization.   Flat structures that allow more authority at lower levels. Empowering employees. Managers as coaches rather than bosses. Cross-functional management processes and focus on internal as well as external customers. Interdepartmental improvement teams.

Customer contact.   CEO and all senior managers are accessible to customers.

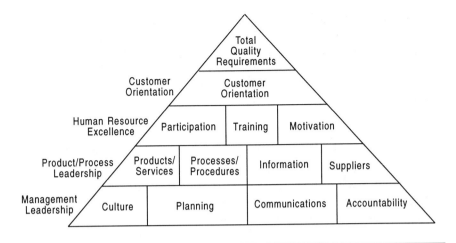

Figure 2-1   The Westinghouse Total Quality Model

Two of the many companies that have received a great deal of visibility for their TQM programs are Westinghouse and IBM, both with divisions that have won the Baldrige Award. Westinghouse committed significant capital resources to support the quality improvement efforts of all Westinghouse divisions, including the creation of the first corporate-sponsored Productivity and Quality Center in the United States. The company's Total Quality Model (Figure 2-1) was developed for use by all division managers. Note that it is built upon a foundation of management leadership. The framework of IBM's corporate-wide quality program, called "Market Driven Quality" is shown in Figure 2-2. Again, note that the input or "driver" of the system is leadership.

David Kearns, Chairman and CEO of Xerox, explains how the company's

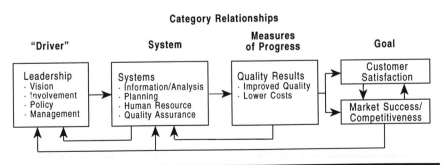

Figure 2-2   Framework of IBM's Market Driven Quality Program

"Leadership through Quality" process achieves commitment at every level: "training begins with our top-tier family work group—my direct reports and me. It then cascades through the organizations led by senior staff, gradually spreading worldwide to some 100,000 employees.[6] This "cascading" reflects the leverage effect of good leadership at all levels. As one executive remarked, "it goes up, down and across the organization chart."

ATTITUDE AND INVOLVEMENT OF TOP MANAGEMENT

It would not be unfair to say that there has been a tendency among U.S. managers to focus on technology and hard assets rather than soft assets such as human resources and organizational competence.[7] The tendency has been to emphasize the organizational chart and the key control points within it. Many managers place priority on the budget and the business plan (to many these are the same) and assume that rational people will get on board and perform according to standard. This popular perception does not fit with leadership and a philosophy of quality.

It is axiomatic that organizations do not achieve quality objectives; people do. If there is a big push for quality or a new program, each employee is justifiably skeptical (the BOHICA syndrome—bend over, here it comes again). According to A. Blanton Godfrey, chairman and CEO of the Juran Institute, top management should be prepared to answer the specific question that may be posed by each member of the organization: "What do you want me to do tomorrow that is different from what I am doing today?"[8] Thus, top managers need to be ambidextrous. They must balance the need for the *structural* dimension (e.g., hierarchy, budgets, plans, controls, procedures) on the one hand with the *behavioral* or personnel dimension on the other. The two dimensions need not be in conflict.

■ At 3M Company the leadership climate is proactive rather than reactive, externally focused rather than internally focused, and the quality perception views the totality of the business rather than just one aspect of it. In order to identify the gaps between its existing position and its vision of the future, 3M has developed "Quality Vision 2000" and implemented it through a process called Q90s which involves the total management system, making the process broader and deeper across the company worldwide.[9]

The commitment and involvement of management need to be demonstrated and visible. Speaking about his military experience, Dwight Eisenhower said: "They never listened to what I said, they always watch what I do."

Many managers send mixed signals. They endorse quality but reward bottom line or production. They insist on cost reduction even if it means canceling quality training. Still worse, some executives perceive the workers to be the cause of their quality problems.[10] This is hardly behavior that encourages individual involvement in decision making and personal "ownership" of the improvement process. Employee buy-in is unlikely in such a climate, where worker empowerment is talked about but not operationalized.

COMMUNICATION

Communication is inextricably linked in the quality process, yet some executives find it difficult to tell others about the plan in a way that will be understood. An additional difficulty is filtering. As top management's vision of quality gets filtered down through the ranks, the vision and the plan can lose both clarity and momentum. Thus, top management as well as managers and supervisors at all levels serve as translators and executors of top management's directive. The ability to communicate is a valuable skill at all levels, from front-line supervisor to CEO.

Quality-conscious companies are interested in the cost of poor communication in terms of both employee productivity and customer perception of product and service quality. More important than what is written or said is the recipient's perception of the message. Limited or inaccurate facts parceled out to employees may demoralize workers and lead to rumors.[11]

According to Peter Drucker, a true guru of management thought and practice, "The communications gap within institutions and between groups in society has been widening steadily—to a point where it threatens to become an unbridgeable gulf of total misunderstanding."[12] Having said that, he provides an easily understood and simple approach to help communicate the strategy, vision, and action plans related to TQM.

Communication is defined as the *exchange of information and understanding* between two or more persons or groups. Note the emphasis on exchange and understanding. Without understanding between sender and receiver concerning the message, there is no communication. The simple model is as follows:

Unless sender gets feedback that receiver understands the message, no communication takes place. Yet most of us send messages with no feedback to indicate that the recipient (or percipient) has understood the message.

Despite the sorry state of communication, Drucker concludes that we do know something about communication in organizations and calls it "managerial communications." Communication is an extremely complex process. Many universities provide a doctoral program in the topic. At the risk of oversimplifying both communication theory and Drucker's approach, the essence of his principles can be paraphrased:

- One can only communicate in terms of the recipient's language and perception, and therefore the message must be in terms of individual experience and perception. If the employee's perception of quality is "do a better job" or "keep the customer happy," it is unlikely that the message of TQM will be understood. Measures of quality are needed to ensure agreement on the meaning of the message.

- Only the recipient can communicate—the communicator cannot. Thus, management systems (including training) should be designed from the point of view of the recipient and with a built-in mechanism for feedback. Feedback and thus the exchange of information should be based on some measure, target, benchmark, or standard.

- All information is encoded, and prior agreement must be reached on the meaning of the code. Quality must be carefully defined and measures agreed upon.

- Communication downward cannot work because it focuses on what we want to say. Communication should be upward.

- Employees should be encouraged to set measurable goals.

Larry Appley, chairman emeritus of the American Management Association, has developed a company-wide productivity improvement program that has the model in Figure 2-3 as a centerpiece. Note that the direction of communication is *upward*. Recipient (subordinate) becomes sender, and sender (boss) becomes recipient. The message is specific and measurable, and the subordinate has ownership because he or she originated the message. Both parties can henceforth communicate about a message on which there is prior agreement. The Appley approach is therefore consistent with Drucker's ideas[13] and sound principles of communication. A modification tailored for a specific firm may be used as a vehicle for TQM implementation.

These concepts of effective communication can provide a practical approach for communicating about quality in the organization. It only remains to encode the message(s) in terms of recipient understanding. The vehicles for communicating about quality are selected components of the TQM system:

1. Training and development for both managers and employees. Managers must understand the processes they manage as well as the basic concept

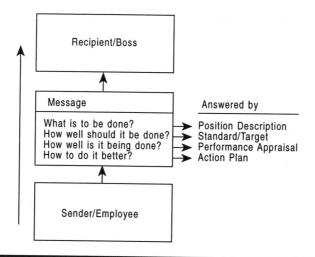

Figure 2-3   Effective Communication

of systems optimization. Employee training should focus on the integration and appropriate use of statistical tools and problem-solving methods.

2. Participation at all levels in establishing benchmarks and measures of process quality. Involvement is both vertical in the hierarchy as well as horizontal by cross-functional teams.

3. Empowerment of employees by delegating authority to make decisions regarding process improvement within individual areas of responsibility, so that the individual "owns" the particular process step.

4. Quality assurance in all organization processes, not only in manufacturing or operations but in business and supporting processes as well. The objective throughout is continuous improvement.

5. Human resource management systems that facilitate contributions at all levels (up and down and across) the organizational chart.

The Digital Switching and Customer Service Division of Northern Telecom Canada Ltd. has received awards and international recognition for its quality systems and procedures. Continually communicating the importance of quality to its 5000 employees is considered vital by division management. Three internal communications specialists generate daily newsletters, monthly newspapers, and videos.[14] One method used by Westinghouse Electric Corporation to spread the word about quality to its 118,000 employees is an annual symposium. For two days each October, more than 600 employees gather to hear colleagues' TQM success stories. The goals for the symposium are for the chairman and senior management to energize employees and to provide attendees an opportunity to talk to each other.[15]

CULTURE

Culture is the pattern of shared beliefs and values that provides the members of an organization rules of behavior or accepted norms for conducting operations. It is the philosophies, ideologies, values, assumptions, beliefs, expectations, attitudes, and norms that knit an organization together and are shared by employees.[16]

For example, IBM's basic beliefs are (1) respect for the individual, (2) best customer service, and (3) pursuit of excellence. In turn, these beliefs are operationalized in terms of strategy and customer values. In simpler terms, culture provides a framework to explain "the way things are done around here."

Other examples of basic beliefs include:

Company	Basic belief
Ford	Quality is job one
Delta	A family feeling
3M	Product innovation
Lincoln Electric	Wages proportionate to productivity
Caterpillar	Strong dealer support; 24-hour spare parts support around the world
McDonald's	Fast service, consistent quality

Institutionalizing strategy requires a culture that supports the strategy. For most organizations a strategy based on TQM requires a significant if not sweeping change in the way people think. Jack Welch, head of General Electric and one of the most controversial and respected executives in America, states that cultural change must be sweeping—not incremental change but "quantum." His cultural transformation at GE calls for a "boundary-less" company where internal divisions blur, everyone works as a team, and both suppliers and customers are partners. His cultural concept of change may differ from Juran, who says that, "When it comes to quality, there is no such thing as improvement in general. Any improvement is going to come about project by project and no other way."[17] The acknowledged experts agree on the need for a cultural or value system transformation:

■ Deming calls for a transformation of the American management style.[18]

■ Feigenbaum suggests a pervasive improvement throughout the organization.[19]

■ According to Crosby, "Quality is the result of a carefully constructed culture, it has to be the fabric of the organization."[20]

It is not surprising that many executives hold the same opinions. In a Gallup Organization survey of 615 business executives, 43 percent rated a change in corporate culture as an integral part of improving quality. The needed change may be given different names in different companies. Robert Crandall, CEO of American Airlines, calls it an innovative environment,[21] while at DuPont it is "The Way People Think"[22] and at Allied Signal "Workers attitudes had to change."[23] Xerox specified a 5-year cultural change strategy called Leadership through Quality.[24] Tom Peters even adds what he calls "the dazzle factor."[25]

Successful organizations have a central core culture around which the rest of the company revolves. It is important for the organization to have a sound basis of core values into which management and other employees will be drawn. Without this central core, the energy of members of the organization will dissipate as they develop plans, make decisions, communicate, and carry on operations without a fundamental criteria of relevance to guide them. This is particularly true in decisions related to quality. Research has shown that quality means different things to different people and levels in the organization. Employees tend to think like their peers and think differently from those at other levels. This suggests that organizations will have considerable difficulty in improving quality unless core values are embedded in the organization.[26]

Commitment to quality as a core value for planning, organizing, and control will be doubly difficult when a concern for the practice is lacking. Research has shown that many U.S. supervisors believe that a concern for quality is lacking among workers and managers.[27] Where this is the case, the perceptions of these supervisors may become a self-fulfilling prophecy.

Embedding a Culture of Quality

It is one thing for top management to state a commitment to quality but quite another for this commitment to be accepted or embedded in the company. The basic vehicle for embedding an organizational culture is a teaching process in which desired behaviors and activities are learned through experiences, symbols, and explicit behavior. Once again, the components of the total quality system provide the vehicles for change. These components as well as other mechanisms of cultural change are summarized in Table 2-1. Above all, demonstration of commitment by top management is essential. This commitment is demonstrated by behaviors and activities that are exhibited throughout the company. Categories of behaviors include:

Table 2-1   Cultural Change Mechanisms

Focus	From traditional	To quality
Plan	Short-range budgets	Future strategic issues
Organize	Hierarchy—chain of command	Participation/empowerment
Control	Variance reporting	Quality measures and information for self-control
Communication	Top down	Top down and bottom up
Decisions	Ad hoc/crisis management	Planned change
Functional management	Parochial, competitive	Cross-functions, integrative
Quality management	Fixing/one-shot manufacturing	Preventive/continuous, all functions and processes

- **Signaling.**   Making statements or taking actions that support the vision of quality, such as mission statements, creeds, or charters directed toward customer satisfaction. Publix supermarkets' "Where shopping is a pleasure" and JC Penney's "The customer is always right" are examples of such statements.

- **Focus.**   Every employee must know the mission, his or her part in it, and what has to be done to achieve it. What management pays attention to and how they react to crisis is indicative of this focus. When all functions and systems are aligned and when practice supports the culture, everyone is more likely to support the vision. Johnson and Johnson's cool reaction to the Tylenol scare is such an example.

- **Employee policies.**   These may be the clearest expression of culture, at least from the viewpoint of the employee. A culture of quality can be easily demonstrated in such policies as the reward and promotion system, status symbols, and other human resource actions.

Executives at all levels could learn a lesson from David T. Kearns, chairman and chief executive officer of Xerox Corporation. In an article for the academic journal *Academy of Management Executive,* he describes the change at Xerox: "At the time Leadership-Through-Quality was introduced, I told our employees that customer satisfaction would be our top priority and that it would change the culture of the company. We redefined quality as meeting the requirements of our customers. It may have been the most significant strategy Xerox ever embarked on."[28]

Among the changes brought about by the cultural change were the manage-

Total Quality Transition

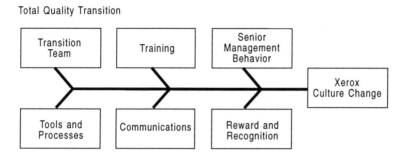

Figure 2-4   Transition to a Quality Culture at Xerox

ment style and the role of first-line management. Kearns continues: "We altered the role of first-line management from that of the traditional, dictatorial foreman to that of a supervisor functioning primarily as a coach and expediter."

Using a modification of the Ishikawa (fishbone) diagram, Xerox demonstrated (Figure 2-4) how the major component of the company's quality system was used for the transition to TQM.

MANAGEMENT SYSTEMS

No matter how comprehensive or lofty a quality strategy may be, it is not complete until it is put into action. It is only rhetoric until it has been implemented. Quality management systems are vehicles for change and should be designed to integrate all areas, not only the quality assurance department. They must be expanded throughout the company to include white-collar activities ranging from market research to shipping and customer service. They are directed toward achievement and commitment to purpose through four universal processes: (1) the specialization of task responsibilities through structure, (2) the provision of information systems that enable employees to know what they need to do in order to achieve goals, (3) the necessary achievement of results through action plans and projects, and (4) control through the establishment of benchmarks, standards, and feedback.

Each of these subsystems is the subject of a separate chapter in this book, but the implementation of each can only proceed from a base of clearly established goals. It is the specific task of top management to ensure that these goals are defined, disseminated, and implemented. Objectives in the areas of quality and productivity must be operationalized by establishing specific subobjectives for each function, department, or activity. Only then can courses of action be selected and plans implemented.

The problem, or conversely the opportunity, is to identify those *key* objectives and activities that are necessary in order to achieve a given strategy—in this case *quality*. The number of activities and processes in the typical organization is so large that a start-up quality management program cannot address all of them in the initial stages. Ultimately, every activity should be analyzed, its output evaluated in terms of value to both external and internal customers, and quality measures established.[29] Notwithstanding this longer term need, it is desirable to begin by setting goals only for those activities that are critical to achieving the mission statement and strategy.

What are these activities and processes that are critical to the mission of quality? The answer lies in identifying the key success factors that must be well managed if the mission or objective is to be achieved; that is, the limited number of areas in which results, if satisfactory, will ensure successful competitive performance for the organization.[30] Each activity or process can then be rated as to its importance. Advertising is a key success factor for Coca-Cola but not for McDonnell Douglas; design is critical to a hi-tech electronics firm but not to a bank.

This process can be used for any major objective, but it is also useful for providing a clear picture of things that must be done to implement a successful TQM program. Identification of key success factors emerges from three dimensions: (1) the drivers of quality such as cycle time reduction, zero defects, or six sigma; (2) operations that provide opportunities for reducing cost or improving productivity; and (3) the market side of quality, which relates to the salability of goods and services. These are converted to specific goals and targets which form the basis for subsequent programs and the universal processes identified earlier. Some U.S. managers have adopted ideas and language from Japanese companies, many of whom call the process *policy deployment.*[31]

QUESTIONS FOR DISCUSSION

2-1   List the characteristics of excellent leadership for TQM.

2-2   Describe how leadership by top management is the *driver* of quality.

2-3   How can top management communicate the need for quality throughout the organization?

2-4   Describe how setting targets for quality improvement helps to establish a culture and climate.

2-5 Give an example of a company culture as reflected in a statement of basic beliefs. Would such a statement help to institutionalize a quality culture? If so, how?

2-6 How would an organization's commitment to quality facilitate or improve the following:

- The planning process
- Organization
- Control

2-7 Choose a manufacturing company and a service company. Identify a key activity for improving quality in each.

ENDNOTES

1. See Richard C. Whiteley, "Creating a Customer Focus," *Executive Excellence,* Sep. 1990 pp. 9–10.
2. J. M. Juran, "Made in USA—A Quality Resurgence," *Journal for Quality and Participation,* March 1991 pp. 6–8.
3. Thomas C. Gibson, "Helping Leaders Accept Leadership of Total Quality Management," *Quality Progress,* Nov. 1990, pp. 45–47.
4. U.S. General Accounting Office, *Quality Management Scoping Study,* Washington, D.C.: U.S. General Accounting Office, Dec. 1990, p. 25.
5. Curt W. Reimann, "Winning Strategies for Quality Improvement," *Business America,* March 25, 1991, pp. 8–11.
6. David T. Kearns, "Leadership through Quality," *Academy of Management Executive,* Vol. 4 No. 2, 1990, p. 87.
7. Michael Moacoby, "How to Be a Quality Leader," *Research-Technology Management,* Sep./Oct. 1990, pp. 51–52. See also Brian L. Joiner and Peter R. Scholtes, "The Quality Manager's New Job," *Quality Progress,* Oct. 1986, pp. 52–56.
8. A. Blanton Godfrey, "Strategic Quality Management," *Quality,* March 1990, pp. 17–22.
9. Doug Anderson, "The Role of Senior Management in Total Quality," *Global Perspectives on Total Quality,* Conference Board Report Number 958, New York: Conference Board, 1991, p. 17. The author is Director, Corporate Quality Services, 3M Company.
10. Lance Arrington, "Training and Commitment: Two Keys to Quality," *Chief Executive,* Sep. 1990, pp. 72–73.
11. Dianna Booher, "Link between Corporate Communication & Quality," *Executive Excellence,* June 1990, pp. 17–18.
12. Peter Drucker, *Management: Tasks, Responsibilities, Practices,* New York: Harper & Row, 1973, p. 481.

13. The author had the pleasure and learning experience of working with Larry Appley on the development of this program, which had great success in a number of companies.

14. Bruce Van-Lane, "Good as Gold," *PEM: Plant Engineering & Maintenance (Canada),* April 1991, pp. 26–28.

15. Erika Penzer, "Spreading the Gospel about Total Quality at a Westinghouse Symposium," *Incentive,* Feb. 1991, pp. 46–49.

16. Ralph H. Kilmann, Mary J. Saxton, and Roy Serpa, "Issues in Understanding and Changing Culture," *California Management Review,* Winter 1986, p. 89.

17. See "Jack Welsch Reinvents General Electric—Again," *The Economist (UK),* March 30, 1991. See also Joseph M. Juran, *Juran on Leadership for Quality: An Executive Handbook,* New York: The Free Press, 1989.

18. Edwards W. Deming, "Transformation of Today's Management," *Executive Excellence,* Dec. 1987, p. 8.

19. Armand V. Feigenbaum, "Seven Keys to Constant Quality," *Journal for Quality and Participation,* March 1989, pp. 20–23.

20. Philip B. Crosby, *Eternally Successful Organization,* New York: McGraw-Hill, 1988.

21. Aaron Sugarman, "Success through People: A New Era in the Way America Does Business," *Incentive,* May 1988, pp. 40–43.

22. Thomas C. Gibson, "The Total Quality Management Resource," *Quality Progress,* Nov. 1987, pp. 62–66.

23. Syed Shah and George Woelki, "Aerospace Industry Finds TQM Essential for TQS," *Quality,* March 1991, pp. 14–19.

24. U.S. General Accounting Office, *Quality Management Scoping Study,* Washington, D.C.: U.S. General Accounting Office, Dec. 1990, p. 64.

25. Tom Peters, "Total Quality Leadership: Let's Get It Right," *Journal for Quality and Participation,* March 1991, pp. 10–15.

26. Frederick Derrick, Harsha Desai, and William O'Brien, "Survey Shows Employees at Different Organizational Levels Define Quality Differently," *Industrial Engineering,* April 1989, pp. 22–26.

27. David A. Garvin, "Quality Problems, Policies, and Attitudes in the United States and Japan: An Exploratory Study," *Academy of Management Journal,* Dec. 1986, pp. 653–673.

28. David T. Kearns, "Leadership through Quality," *Academy of Management Executive,* Vol. 4 No. 2, 1990, p. 87.

29. The need to set activity output and productivity measures (productivity being the ratio of output to input) has long been recognized, but little progress was made until recently, when a method known as *activity analysis* began to emerge. It is still in the early stages of implementation in industry. The accounting profession, recognizing the need to focus not only on cost but also on quality and productivity, is now promoting a related method known as *activity-based accounting.* See H. Thomas Johnson, "A Blueprint for World-Class Management Accounting," *Management Accounting,* June 1988, pp. 23–30. A very insightful and useful treatment of the shortcomings of traditional accounting systems is contained in H. Thomas Johnson and Robert S. Kaplan, *Relevance Lost,* Boston: Harvard Business School Press, 1991. Also included are excellent prescriptions for the improvement of accounting systems for managerial decision making.

30. Joel K. Leidecker and Albert V. Bruno, "Identifying and Using Critical Success Factors," *Long Range Planning,* Vol. 17 No. 1, 1984, pp. 23–32.

31. John E. Newcomb, "Management by Policy Deployment," *Quality,* Jan. 1989, pp. 28–30.

The following article reports on a number of comprehensive surveys and research studies which conclude, in general, that total quality management has been something less than a success in most companies. A number of reasons are proposed to explain these results and suggestions are offered for improvement. The article questions the extent to which leadership and commitment of top management are responsible for the "shoddy" results.

MANAGEMENT: QUALITY PROGRAMS SHOW SHODDY RESULTS

Gilbert Fuchsberg

The "total quality" movement, one of the biggest fads in corporate management, is floundering, a broad study suggests.

Despite plenty of talk and much action, many American companies are stumbling in their implementation of quality-improvement efforts, says the study, being released today. A key reason, the study concludes: Many quality-management plans are simply too amorphous to generate better products and services.

Rather than diffusing effort by addressing quality problems across the board, the report proposes that companies should focus on a small number of decisive changes.

"A lot of companies read lots of books, did lots of training, formed teams and tried to implement 9,000 new practices simultaneously," says Terrence R. Ozan, a partner with Ernst & Young, which ran the study with the American Quality Foundation. "But you don't get results that way. It's just too much."

The study represents one of the most comprehensive and critical reviews to date of quality-management programs. In recent years, thousands of organizations have embraced such efforts in a quest for improved performance. Based on a survey of 584 companies in the U.S., Canada, Germany and Japan, the study details failings across a range of quality-improvement activities in the auto, computer, banking and health-care industries. Among its U.S. findings:

- Computer companies involve only 12% of their employees in idea-suggestion programs. Auto makers, which rate highest in this area, involve just 28% of their workers.

- Customer complaints are of "major or primary" importance in identifying new products and services among only 19% of banks and 26% of hospitals.

- Quality-performance measures such as defect rates and customer-satisfaction levels play a key role in determining pay for senior managers among fewer than one in five companies across all four industries surveyed. Profitability still matters most.

The results seem even worse when compared with quality programs abroad. Some 73% of surveyed computer makers in Japan and 60% in Germany use customer complaints to help identify new products, compared with 26% in the U.S. Foreign employee-suggestion programs, meanwhile, include larger proportions of workers—34% among Canadian banks, for instance, and 78% among Japanese car makers.

To be sure, there are some bright spots in the U.S.: More than half of all workers in the surveyed companies participate in at least occasional meetings about quality. And the study reports marked increases in quality-related activities during the past three years. But among most U.S. companies, virtually no quality-boosting practices have reached what survey organizers consider lasting and meaningful levels.

"They've got to become habits," says Joshua Hammond, president of the American Quality Foundation, a New York think tank. "If quality is going to have a payoff, it's got to be a routine part of the way you do business."

The findings come at a critical point in the quality movement, which appears to be losing some of its allure after several years of steady growth. The Conference Board, a New York business research group, says attendance at seminars it runs on quality has fallen in the past year. Moreover, the number of companies competing for the Commerce Department's Malcolm Baldrige National Quality Award dropped to 90 this year from 106 last year.

Some experts trace the apparent slide in interest to the relative obscurity of last year's Baldrige winners, three small electronics suppliers. None of them have promoted their prizes in high-profile advertising, as did such earlier winners as Xerox Corp., International Business Machines Corp. and General Motors Corp.'s Cadillac division. "There just hasn't been as much excitement," says Kathryn Troy, a senior researcher with the Conference Board.

But others cite more profound reasons. Tom Vanderpool, a quality consultant with Gemini Consulting, Morristown, N.J., says many companies aren't seeing results—and may tire of trying—because they mistakenly isolate quality programs from day-to-day operations. "They tend to put it off as something special, as an objective with 10,000 activities unto itself," he says. "It is not. It is a way to meet business objectives."

Steven Walleck, director of consulting giant McKinsey & Co.'s operations practice, faults the sheer scale of many quality plans. "Most require so much groundwork before results can be expected that you're almost systematically doomed" to waste money on quality-related training and technology, he says. A recent McKinsey study of 30 quality programs found that two-thirds had stalled or fallen short of yielding real improvements, Mr. Walleck adds.

Mr. Hammond of the American Quality Foundation blames "the proliferation of consultants, each of whom preaches his own pet strategy." Indeed, the new study found that the surveyed companies used a total of 945 different quality-management tactics.

While concluding that companies should target their quality efforts more tightly—what some dub "partial quality management"—the $2 million study doesn't rank which practices work best. But Mr. Hammond suggests that the most successful programs typically include strong personal involvement by senior executives, company-wide awareness of strategic plans and goals, and an emphasis on simplifying processes.

One company that has already moved to focus its quality program is Johnson & Johnson. For most of the past decade, the giant health-products maker embraced a quality program based on "doing things right the first time," says Jeffrey M. Nugent, vice president, world-wide quality management. But after a review 18 months ago, the company refined its approach.

"It wasn't specific enough," Mr. Nugent says. So, the company established three more explicit quality goals: boosting customer satisfaction, reducing product introduction time and cutting costs. It then told each of its 166 operating units to "apply the principles of total quality management in a way that makes sense for them," Mr. Nugent says. Among other steps, he says, J&J has eliminated some of its broad quality-training programs in favor of more classes on narrow topics.

"We are doing fewer things better," Mr. Nugent says.

The study, despite its harsh findings, paints a rosy view of quality circa 1995. Most U.S. companies surveyed projected significant improvements in their quality practices three years from now. But by then, they will only reach levels that many surveyed companies in Japan, Germany and Canada have already attained.

"They're so far ahead of us that quality is no longer a competitive issue," Mr. Hammond says. "Now we've got to get into it to survive."

CASE

Representatives from three winners of the Malcolm Baldrige National Quality Award—Xerox, Federal Express, and IBM—tell how they overcame roadblocks to the total quality startup efforts and achieved success despite the reluctance to change from traditional mechanistic management practices. Major problems included institutionalizing a TQM vision and implementing the infrastructure required for success.

HOW TO IMPLEMENT A QUALITY MANAGEMENT INITIATIVE

Patricia L. Panchak

The term "quality management" has become so popular these days that we risk reducing it to a cliché, where the words become meaningless and serve no useful purpose. Only by translating those words into action can we use their message to help build better businesses.

Three Malcolm Baldrige National Quality Award-winning companies—Xerox Corp., Business Products and Systems (Stamford, CT), IBM Corp., Rochester Unit (Armonk, NY) and Federal Express Corp. (Memphis, TN)—successfully transformed quality management philosophies into quality management practices. The Malcolm Baldrige National Quality Award, created by Congress in 1987, is the highest form of recognition for quality management in the United States. Named after the late Secretary of Commerce, the award serves to promote quality awareness, recognize quality achievements and publicize successful quality strategies.

Here, representatives of each of these companies describe the steps they took to implement their award-winning quality initiatives.

Reprinted with permission from *Modern Office Technology,* Vol. 37 No. 2, February 1992, pp. 27–31. ©1992 by Penton Publishing, subsidiary of Pittway Corporation.

The Need for Change

"The first thing that has to happen is an understanding of a need for change," maintains Sam Malone, project manager, corporate communications for Xerox. At Xerox, he adds, "we faced a major crisis—in essence we were in a going-out-of-business strategy if we didn't change."

The awareness that change was needed at Xerox began in the mid-70s, when a series of events conspired to loosen Xerox' firm grip on the copier/duplicator market. Just as aggressive Japanese companies targeted the low end of the market with small, high-quality, low-priced copiers, and began to penetrate the mid-range market, Federal Trade Commission settlements required Xerox to open international access to key patents. Meanwhile Eastman Kodak (Rochester, NY) and IBM applied added pressure, entering the high end of the market.

By 1980, increased competition began to take its toll. Xerox' market share had dropped significantly. The resulting lower rates of return on assets threatened Xerox' ability to maintain long term business vitality. It was clear that drastic changes would be needed for Xerox to remain competitive.

In contrast, when FedEx embarked upon a quality management initiative, it began from a position of strength. Capitalizing on the management philosophy of "People, Service, and Profit" since its inception in 1973, the company had achieved high levels of customer satisfaction and experienced rapid sales growth. Within ten years, the company's annual revenues topped $1 billion; by 1990, revenues totaled nearly $7 billion. Domestic market share hit 43 percent in 1989, outdistancing the nearest competitor, which held 26 percent. But those achievements were history. Managements' understanding that past accomplishments do not ensure future success fueled the drive to improve, in order to retain their market dominance.

The management of IBM didn't have to look far to find a reason to initiate a company-wide quality management initiative. Their very own IBM Rochester, MN site (where intermediate computer systems and disk storage products are manufactured) had instituted quality management practices in 1981, and the results were compelling: a 30 percent improvement in productivity between 1986 and 1989; a 50+ percent reduction of product-development time for new mid-range computer systems; a 60 percent reduction in the manufacturing cycle since 1983; and impressive gains of IBM's world market share for intermediate computers achieved in 1988 and 1989, among other successes. In Rochester, corporate headquarters had found a way to translate a formidable technology leadership into market leadership in the face of an increasingly competitive computer industry. It was time to teach the rest of the computer giant how to capitalize on quality management.

A Vision Statement

Having made the difficult decision to embark on a quality management initiative, the companies entered the next stage of the process: formulating a clear vision of where the company will be once the quality initiative is in place. This entails, asserts Malone, "a coalescing of the senior management around the issue that we need to change the business, and some kind of an agreement as to what that change should result in."

To accomplish this, he adds, the company needs to develop "a desired-state document or vision statement that says, 'given we go through all this turmoil of change, how will we know if it's successful down the road: What would we look like? What are the key parameters? What are the specific elements that we want to focus on for change?'"

In most companies, if not all, the precepts of total quality management run counter to the very practices which brought success to the company and its managers in the past. Realizing this, the executives at Xerox, FedEx and IBM sought the advice of management experts to help identify those elements of change and to write a vision statement. Xerox selected an expert in organizational change and trained a group of senior executives to lead the initiative; FedEx opted for a quality consultant; and IBM found its experts among its executive ranks.

Xerox' decision was founded on the belief that senior executives educated in total quality management are "better able to understand the current environment and the current ills of the organization and will be better able to design an approach to fit," than an outside quality expert, says Malone. However, realizing they would need assistance, they felt the consultant would provide insights and expertise that were required to sustain a cultural change over a long period of time.

Even at the already successful FedEx, says John R. West, their manager of Corporate Quality Improvement, "the first step was to find some experts to lead the way." He too says management looked both inside the company and at outside consultants to find the experts. But time being a factor, he says, they opted to go primarily outside. After initially working with several consultants, they chose one who, among other things, provided them with a two-course quality curriculum, which launched the quality process companywide.

West cautions, however, that you should take care to find a consultant whose expertise matches your company's needs as a service or manufacturing company. "We ran into a few problems on the front end by concentrating too much on a manufacturing-type philosophy," confesses West. "We had too heavy an emphasis on statistical process control, and that turned some of our senior management off—to the extent that it took us about two years to get them interested again."

IBM found their quality experts and the makings of a vision statement at the award-winning Rochester site. Reviewing Rochester's management process, and using the Baldrige Award criteria as a guide, IBM executives identified the aspects of the process that made their latest intermediate computer, the AS/400, a success, and wrote those into the vision statement.

The Vision

While each of the companies' vision statements feature the quality principles that have come to be the buzzwords of quality management, they are tailored to suit the individual circumstances faced by each company. All of the initiatives focus on customer satisfaction, as determined by the customer, and as measured with verifiable facts. While it's impossible to discuss the intricacies of the companies' quality initiatives in this article, some main points provide insight into the more important aspects.

IBM's "Market Driven Quality" (MDQ) initiative, inspired in part by Rochester's success, focused on involving the customer more directly in the product planning and design decisions *before* beginning the development of a new product, say Paul Bergevin of IBM's corporate media relations. By involving the customer at the beginning, IBM believes they will "shorten cycle times and improve quality, which are fundamental to achieving higher levels of customer satisfaction from which everything else flows," he adds.

FedEx' new vision of a quality process, grafted onto the successful "People/ Service/Profit" philosophy, centers upon the replacement of the old quality measurement—percent of on-time deliveries—with a 12-component indicator that describes how its performance is experienced by its customers. Each item in the indicator, called a Service Quality Indicator (SQI), is weighted to reflect the "potential adverse impact" on customer satisfaction, explains West.

Xerox' "Leadership through Quality" process is "aimed at fundamentally changing the way Xerox people work and manage so they can continuously improve the way they meet the requirements of their customers," according to company literature. Six mechanisms for change, including management behavior and actions, transition teams, tools and processes, training, recognition and reward, and communications, provide the framework.

Benchmarking against other world-class companies and other measurement systems are key to visualizing the desired-state. Xerox began the quality initiative by benchmarking 14 performance elements; today they benchmark 350+ elements, taking care to analyze all this data not only "by the numbers," but also by processes.

In addition, all three companies rely on regular customer surveys to spawn new changes. Both the external customer, the purchaser of products, and the internal customer, any employee to whom another employee forwards material, are surveyed regularly to determine their constantly changing needs.

The Infrastructure

The integration of the vision into the business organization and strategy requires a strong infrastructure, which in business means strong leadership. At each of these three companies, senior executives are vested with the responsibility for quality, yet the responsibility for quality is not centralized. Though FedEx and Xerox both have formal quality management departments, they have kept the departments small to promote the premise that quality is everyone's job. To further emphasize that quality is everyone's job, each of the companies encourages employee involvement, by giving the employee authorization to make more day-to-day work decisions and by encouraging them to make suggestions.

To focus the organization around the topic of quality at Xerox, says Malone, "Xerox appointed vice presidents of quality very early in the process, and they participated in the design." The Corporate Management Team, in deciding to pursue a quality management initiative, had developed the quality policy and the broad outlines of a quality strategy and implementation plan. This group of VPs, called the Quality Implementation Team, fine-tuned the broad policy, designing Xerox' approach. The infrastructure is minimal: Workers throughout the company are vested with the authority over day-to-day work decisions.

FedEx' management infrastructure is a little more formal, in some cases. Senior managers head cross-functional teams, each of which focuses on one service component in SQI, and are responsible for assuring involvement of front-line employees, support personnel, and other managers on their team.

The senior managers are given the freedom to decide how to implement the quality initiative within their division. West explains; "Our effort has been to give the division the opportunity to 'invent it here.' We feel that's very important for long term viability of the process; that if the division, the managers and eventually the employees feel the ownership, they are much more likely to treat quality as a part of their daily activity."

For the same reason, the quality department is small. "On purpose, we have a very small staff," says West, "because we want the division to be out on their own and not to have anybody say 'quality isn't working, so it's the quality department's fault.'"

Two senior analysts, a quality coordinator and a secretary assist West, who reports to the VP of internal audit and quality assurance (IAQA), who in turn reports to the CEO. One other manager, currently on special assignment, answers to the VP of IAQA.

IBM's quality staff is also small. "The feeling is that you can't have quality implemented across a company like IBM by decree," says Bergevin. "What you really need to do is instill the notion of continuous improvement, the thirst for improvement, and the discipline of quality improvement across the entire enterprise—the people in the factories and branch offices are making quality happen, not some group of executives at headquarters."

The IBM quality department is headed by a Senior VP for MDQ. He answers to the Chairman, and his staff consists of about ten to eleven executives. In addition, he rotates another twelve "relatively senior" managers from all disciplines and geographic areas within the corporation into and out of his quality organization from the field for a ten- to twelve-month stint.

Other senior executives were named as owners, called "functional leaders," of the initiatives, adds Bergevin. Each functional leader is responsible for developing tailored sets of goals and strategies that apply to his department or function. The functional leaders, in turn, involve the employees.

With such an organization, work groups in each area of the business naturally form to identify sources of quality problems and ways to improve.

"So we have taken a look in a very systematic way at all the processes that make up the grand total of activity at IBM," Bergevin adds. "We sort of deconstruct these processes to look for ways that things can be streamlined and improved."

The Implementation

With the vision clear and the infrastructure in place, the companies began introducing quality management to the employees. Implementation of the quality initiatives is synonymous with employee training at all three companies. Training included courses in general quality principles, specific quality goals and, in some cases, measurement tools.

"The process we focused on at Xerox was to align the supporting mechanisms, and we used training in conjunction with communications as a vehicle to begin the deployment," explains Malone. Using the training program devised by the multi-national Quality Training Task Force, a group of senior executives, Xerox began the training/implementation. "We started at the senior-most level (CEO) and we cascaded that down the organization using the managers and 'family groups' as a focal point for training. The manager was trained by his or her immediate manager and then that manager, once trained, was responsible for training his or her immediate direct reports."

Likewise, at IBM, a multi-national training task force of training professionals designed the training, and the managers handled the training. All employees were first trained in overall quality and company goals, then attended follow-up sessions that pertained more specifically to the individual functions.

Similarly, at FedEx, the implementation strategy was to get key players—the executives responsible for a functional group—trained and then in turn have them train others. Says West, "We allowed the divisions—and still do today—to be pretty much on their own. We said, 'we're all going to use the same consultant and the same training package, but then it's up to you how you want to do this.'" Managers could have their employees trained by the consultant, or could have a selected employee trained as a trainer. The majority of the trainers selected were management.

Sustaining the Effort

Communication, in all its facets, is key to sustaining the quality initiative at each of these Baldrige Award-winning companies. Chief among the communication strategies, says Malone, "is getting management to 'walk like they talk.'" He explains: "It's very easy to get management to sign up and support quality verbally. It's much more difficult to get them to put it into practice and to use the tools day in and day out, and inspect for their use and apply the discipline required."

One of the ways Xerox insures managers implement quality practices is through promotions. Simply put, managers who support quality are promoted; those that don't, aren't. Malone explains: "What we are really doing is changing the role of the manager from a typical one-to-one supervisory style to one where the manager becomes the coach, the counselor, the facilitator." Most of the managers got to where they are by being autocratic, he points out.

"Not everybody is going to be successful in transforming himself from that old success model to the new success model. You better understand up front that there are some managers who will probably fall out of the equation. In our case we recognized that need and prepared to address it where and when that came up, by counseling, coaching and in some cases counseling out of the business."

Equally important, says Malone, is two-way communication. He advises, "No matter how much time you spend designing the process, you're probably going to have to make some adjustments so you want to have an early warning system that says there's something going awry that needs attention. Having two-way communication channels working will give you the insights and avenues to understand those things much earlier.

"And the one thing you don't want to do is shoot the messenger: if somebody brings bad news, you have to be open, willing to listen, to take the good with the bad. Also make sure you acknowledge their support and their contribution."

All three agree that simply passing on success stories contributes greatly to acceptance and use of the quality management practices.

To facilitate communication, FedEx has one person in the communications group dedicated to the quality process. She helps develop articles that are published in in-house publications, and produce video tapes and television segments to be shown on FedEx' closed circuit television network.

Constant feedback provided by the television network includes the closing New York Stock Exchange price of FedEx stocks, how the overall operations did the previous night and a quality success story.

He explains that approximately each quarter the twelve best quality success stories are chosen; the winning teams come to headquarters at the quality department's expense, to present before top management. The presentations are taped and edited for broadcast.

In addition to the recognition offered in the retelling of success stories, IBM also rewards employees who implement the quality process with luncheons, receptions, and monetary and non-monetary awards.

Also critical, says Bergevin, is translating the customer satisfaction goals to something everyone can instantly understand. "We've done some statistical work on the AS/400 category, for example, that shows that every point of customer satisfaction increase that we've been able to measure translates into a revenue effect of 250 million dollars over five years."

Starting Over

Self-assessment, along with communication, is key to sustaining the total quality management initiative beyond the achievement of your initial goals, say Malone, West and Bergevin. They add that a total quality management initiative, above all, is a never-ending process. It is a process of continuous improvement, of continuously questioning the way you do things, and of continuously reevaluating the market, customer needs, and work processes. It is a process which, done correctly, continuously renews itself.

Their companies, having won the Baldrige Award, continually return to the Baldrige criteria to reevaluate their processes. But whether you use the Baldrige Award assessment criteria is immaterial, maintains Malone. "The issue is evaluating 'how are we doing versus what we said we were going to do against the desired-state.'" This self-assessment, agree executives at Xerox, FedEx and IBM, makes even Baldrige Award-winning companies realize that quality is a continuous journey.

Questions for Discussion

1   What are the major steps in the TQM implementation program for these Baldrige winners?

2   Why would a successful company such as Federal Express embark on a TQM program? What risks, if any, are involved?

3   The article states that TQM runs counter to management practices that most companies follow. What management practices are these?

4   If, as these winners suggest, a culture represented by a vision is needed, how would you embed such a cultural change?

5   Why is it so important to involve customers at the beginning?

6   Describe the elements of the TQM infrastructure.

7   What is the role of communication in TQM implementation?

LEADERSHIP AT VERIFILM

Compare each of the following TQM criteria to Varifilm and indicate whether the practice in the company is a *strength (S)* or *needs improvement (I)*. Justify your answer.

1.0 Leadership	**(S)**	**(I)**
■ Senior executives are personally involved in Varifilm's quality vision and are actively driving the quality improvement initiative.	—	—
■ Personal leadership improvement plans are developed based on feedback mechanisms.	—	—
■ The approach to establishing specific expectations with other managers and supervisors is clearly defined.	—	—
■ I-Team members are committed to spending a minimum of one-third of their time on quality-related activities.	—	—
■ Varifilm's quality values are clearly summarized in the form of goals, policies, principles, and actions and serve as the foundation for strategic planning.	—	—
■ Senior executives are personally involved in the ongoing communication of customer focus and quality values.	—	—

Additional Areas for Improvement

_____

_____

_____

1.2 Management for Quality   (S)   (I)

- Key indicators are used to evaluate and improve awareness   —   —
  and integration of quality values.

- Unit managers are responsible for leading Varifilm's Con-   —   —
  tinuous Improvement Criteria (VCIC) and High Perfor-
  mance Work Systems (HPWS) process and reporting annually to the I-Team.

- Customer focus and quality values are aligned through a   —   —
  variety of approaches and the gain-sharing process is aligned
  with key performance indicators.

- There is a systematic process for deploying values and   —   —
  principles to all units and levels.

Additional Areas for Improvement

_____

_____

_____

3

INFORMATION ANALYSIS AND INFORMATION TECHNOLOGY

Since quality programs are dependent on good information systems, chief information officers have the opportunity to plan an integral and highly visible role in shaping the quality of the corporation.

Curt Reimann, Director
Malcolm Baldrige Award

Information is the critical enabler of total quality management (TQM). More and more successful companies agree that information technology and information systems serve as keys to their quality success. Conversely, this component of TQM is frequently the roadblock to improvement in many firms. In these firms better quality and productivity may not be the issue; rather, the real issue may be better quality of information. Dr. Curt W. Reimann, director of the Malcolm Baldrige National Quality Award, suggests that the critical constraint for many companies in applying for the award is the lack of a proper information system for tracking and improving areas in the remaining award categories.[1]

ORGANIZATIONAL IMPLICATIONS

John Sculley, former chairman of Apple Computer, concludes that information systems and technology can no longer be regarded as staff or service functions for management. Moreover, information systems will become the most important means for companies to create distinctive quality and unique service at the lowest possible cost.[2] At a 1988 symposium in Washington, D.C. for some 175 chief executive officers of major U.S. corporations, the main topic was quality improvement and the information systems to support that effort. Designing the product, the plant configuration, and even the organizational structure is less challenging than designing the information system, which is the central component of TQM that allows the process to function.[3] It may be that the rigor of the production process is not matched by that of the information system, and the cause may lie in the increased complexity and breadth of the latter. Information is critical to *all* functions, and *all* functions need to be integrated by information.

The natural progression of information systems (used interchangeably with management information systems) in the past has frequently resulted in "band-aids" or "islands of mechanization," as applications such as inventory control, production scheduling, and sales reporting were designed without much regard for integration among each other or among other functions and activities within the organization. In recent years, additional and more sophisticated applications have emerged, such as quality function deployment (QFD), Taguchi methods, statistical process control (SPC), and just-in-time (JIT). These are now considered basic to the TQM process.[4] The challenge remains the same: to integrate these techniques and principles into a structured approach that includes related decision-making requirements across the board.

Historically, companies have automated the easy applications: payroll, financial accounting, production control, etc. Today, the concept of *reengineering* is emerging. Rather than automating tasks and isolating them into discrete departments, companies are attempting to integrate the related activities of engineering, manufacturing, marketing, and support operations. Actions proceed in parallel, rather than sequential, order. Cycle time is reduced and products get to market faster with fewer defects. In short, the process is reengineered, and computer power is applied to the new process in the form of information systems. The focus is changing from buying information technology in order to automate paperwork to a focus designed to improve the process.

Information Technology

Systems design may be a constraint, but information technology (IT) is not. The geometric acceleration of developments is well known and can only be described as dramatic and spectacular.[5] If industry is capable of absorbing the technology, a further increase in the sophistication and importance of information will occur. Capital and direct labor will continue to be sources of value added, but the proportion contributed by intellectual and information activity will increase. Indeed, information can be considered to be a substitute for other assets because it can increase the productivity of existing capital and reduce the requirement for additional expenditures. It should be exploited.[6]

In 1990, Federal Express spent more than $243 million on IT. CEO Fred Smith stated that IT is absolutely the key to the organization's operations and that the entire quality process depends on statistical quantification which, in turn, depends on IT. Information is generated for both employees and customers.

Decision Making

The ability to make decisions quickly has always been critical to management at all levels, and information is essential to the process. It has emerged as a crucial competitive weapon.[7] Yet middle managers, who are the real change agents, spend most of their time exchanging information with subordinates, peers, or the boss, leaving little time for customers or for innovation and change. In the jargon of information systems, they need a decision support system.

Information Systems in Japan

In what continue to be customary comparisons between the United States and Japan, it is useful to examine how IT and information systems are perceived in Japan. Japanese executives believe that customer satisfaction drives the development of new services and products and that IT can be a vital means to facilitate strategies and operations to this end.[8] In true Japanese fashion, this view is apparently promoted by the national government as well. To build a foundation for future technicians and managers, the Ministry of Education has implemented national education policies for the full-scale use of computers in education.[9] There is also a national policy on software. The Ministry of International Trade and Industry (MITI) has launched the Sigma Project, which calls for computerizing the software process and industrializing and computerizing software production.[10]

The Deming Prize is awarded each year to Japanese companies that demonstrate outstanding improvement in quality control. Yokogawa Hewlett-Packard (YHP), a joint venture of Hewlett-Packard and Yokogawa Electric Works, was awarded the prize for an information systems approach that yielded dramatic increases in profit, productivity, and market share.

STRATEGIC INFORMATION SYSTEMS

The integration of management information systems (MIS) with strategic planning has been suggested as a necessary prerequisite to strategy formulation and implementation. If we assume, as we must, that the basic requirement of a strategy is environmental positioning in order to meet customer requirements and if we further assume that the ultimate purpose of each function and process within an organization is to contribute to strategy, the role of information becomes clear.

As will be discussed in Chapter 9, the value chain is a useful concept for determining the structure and processes needed by organization in order to achieve a competitive advantage, keeping in mind that competitiveness is decided neither by the industry nor by the company, but rather by the customer.

Beginning with the customer, integration of processes and information can proceed as follows:

■ Identify the market segment in which you want to compete.

■ Use data collection and analysis to define the customer requirements in the chosen segment.

■ Translate these requirements into major design parameters to develop, produce, deliver, and service the product that meets the customers' requirements. These are the primary functions and activities (processes) of the value chain.

■ Complement the primary processes with support activities such as planning, finance and accounting, MIS, personnel, etc.

■ Subdivide or "explode" the organization design parameters into the processes (functions, activities, etc.) that are necessary to achieve the quality differentiation.

■ Design the information requirements necessary to manage each process and to integrate all processes horizontally.

The support activities are sometimes taken for granted and their linking potential is often overlooked. Moreover, their potential contribution to differentiation may not be realized. Marketing services, for example, when combined with the customer's expertise, can generate differentiated product and service opportunities. The customer will place high value on a supplier who delivers the right information quickly. Engineering services, usually perceived as a commodity product, can also differentiate a firm. In both cases the information systems support is cost effective.

At Honeywell, Inc., translating long-term strategy into tactics that enhance short-term operations has resulted in new approaches that have shortened cycle time, improved quality, and reduced costs. The approach involves spreading information, standardizing, and measuring performance.

Environmental Analysis

Strategy formulation requires an analysis of the different environments: general, industry, and competitive (see Chapter 4 for further discussion). One study found that small business owners spend over one-fourth of the day in external information search activities.[11] Competitive information is particularly valuable but is difficult to obtain.[12] In general, the minimum information needed about competitors can be related to how they stand on the key success factors for a market segment. These may differ by industry and segment but usually include the following:[13]

Market share	Growth rate
Product line breadth	Distribution effectiveness
Proprietary advantages	Price competitiveness
Age and location of facility	Capacity and productivity
Experience curve effects	Value added
R&D advantage and position	Cash throw-off

Porter has identified the information needed for positioning in an industry and in a chosen market segment, and his system is widely used. His categories are (1) intensity of rivalry, (2) bargaining power of buyers, (3) bargaining power of suppliers, (4) threat of substitution, and (5) threat of new entrants.[13] Each category includes a number of elements or subtopics that should be determined and tracked with some type of information system.

Central to all information relating to strategy formulation and implementation is the need to *define and measure* the concept of quality of product and service— as determined by the customer. This step is fundamental to positioning and subsequent follow up.

SHORTCOMINGS OF ACCOUNTING SYSTEMS

Financial information is perhaps the most widespread indicator of performance, and for many firms is the only indicator. Critics of accounting systems claim that they do not really support the operations and strategy of the company, two dimensions in which quality plays a dominant role. Despite the widely held conclusion that we are in the information age, management accounting would probably be labeled inadequate by managers who seek to support company

Table 3-1   New Manufacturing Environment

Trend	Implication for quality
Focus on manufacturing strategy	Quality rapidly becoming the central competitive edge of strategy
Production of high-quality goods	Quality directly related to market share, growth, profits
Reduction of inventory levels by just-in-time (JIT) inventory	Reduction of costs associated with excess inventory
Tight schedules	Improves availability to customer, another competitive edge perceived as quality by the customer
Product mix and variety	Allows focus on strategy and market segmentation
Equipment automation	Provides justification for quality and productivity improvement
Shortened product life cycle	Provides opportunity to expedite market shifts and incorporate new technologies into the product, but imposes additional stress on the quality management program
Organizational changes	Responsibility for quality delegated to strategic business units and product managers
Information technology	Allows greater control of cost of quality, quality management, and cross-functional integration

operations and strategy through quality improvement. This is increasingly evident in the "new" manufacturing environment which is characterized by the trends and implications listed in Table 3-1.

Accountant bashing is becoming increasingly popular in the management literature. The trend is symbolized by Harvard Business School Professor Robert Kaplan in his popular book *Relevance Lost.*[14] He concludes that today's accounting information provides little help in reducing costs and improving quality and productivity. Indeed, he suggests that this information might even be harmful. Peter Drucker, another critic, describes some of the shortcomings that are generally recognized:[15]

1. Cost accounting is based on a 1920s reality, when direct labor was 80 percent of manufacturing costs other than raw material. Today it is 8 to 12 percent and in some industries (e.g., IT) it is about 3 percent.

2. Non-direct labor costs, which can run up to 90 percent, are allocated in proportion to labor costs, an arbitrary and misleading system. Benefits of a process change are allocated in the same way.

3. The cost system ignores the costs of *non-producing,* whether this be downtime, stockouts, defects, or other costs of non-quality.

4. The system cannot measure, predict, or justify change or innovation in product or process. In other words, accounting measures direct or real costs and not benefits.

5. Accounting-generated information does not recognize linkages between functions, activities, or processes.

6. Manufacturing decisions cannot be made as *business* decisions based on the information provided by accounting. The system confines itself to measurable and objective decisions and does not address the intangibles.

Efforts are underway to make accounting a true management and business system. For example, Computer-Aided Manufacturing-International (CAM-I) is a cooperative effort by automation producers, multinational manufacturers, and accountants to develop a new cost accounting system. Even internal auditors are examining their new role in TQM.[16]

ORGANIZATIONAL LINKAGES

The importance of data linkages is illustrated by data on service calls, a primary source of measuring product field performance. These are an important source of information for design, engineering, manufacturing, sales, and service. One research study[17] reported that in some cases among air conditioner manufacturers, the aggregative data on failure rates was of little use because of organization barriers.

■ The *service tracking report* at American Express monitors performance for all centers worldwide. For the credit card division, for example, performance is measured against 100 service measures, including how long it takes to process an application, authorize charges, bill card members, and answer customer billing inquiries. Each measure is based on customer expectations, the competition, the economy, and legislation. Application processing time has been reduced by 50 percent and the bottom line has been increased by $70 million.

This example illustrates the widespread need for organization linkages and cross-functional MIS and the need to track a process on a continuous basis. Figure 3-1 shows how each step in the life cycle of a product involves related processes as cross-functional lines.

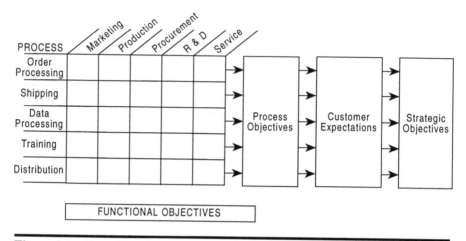

Figure 3-1   Cross-Functional Lines in the Life Cycle of a Product

Each step in the product life cycle involves a number of processes at these cross-functional lines in a continuous flow from design to preproduction planning to vendor management to incoming material to in-process control to finished goods to customer service. The steps along the flow should be accompanied by appropriate information.[18] Thus, the linkage concept may focus on internal customers (those who use products in a later step of the process) as well as external customers.

> ■ Federal Express, the first service sector company to earn the Baldrige Award, integrates a variety of internal measurement systems into the core of its business. The objective is "zero service defects." The system, SQI (service quality indicators) measures twelve critical points at which failure can occur in the service process and continually reinforces how employees are doing compared to their goals.

ADVANCED PROCESSES/SYSTEMS

SPC...QFD...CAD...CIM...MRP—one gets the impression of "alphabet management." These and other basic applications represent the major systems of TQM. None stand alone and there are overlaps among them. Some advocates promote one or more as the "total system." Most if not all of these processes depend upon IT and a sophisticated information system design. Because systems

Table 3-2   Objectives of Major Processes in Systems Design

Process/system	Objective
Statistical quality control (SQC)	Build in the control limits of a process that spots and identifies causes of variations
Statistical process control (SPC)	Provide information on how productivity and quality can be *continuously improved* through problem identification (it has been estimated that U.S. firms invest 20 to 25 percent of their operating budgets in finding and fixing mistakes[19])
Just-in-time (JIT)	Reduce inventory cost, production time, and space requirements
Computer-integrated manufacturing (CIM)	Lower cost, shorten lead time, and improve quality based on information sharing by linking management and financial information systems, departmental computing, process management systems, and factory systems for controlling machinery and manufacturing processes
Quality function deployment (QFD)	Integrate the three dimensions of (1) company-wide quality, (2) focus on customer requirements, and (3) translation of quality perceptions into product characteristics and then into the manufacturing process

design begins with the objective of the process, it is useful to list the objective of the major processes (Table 3-2).

At Motorola's Automotive and Industrial Electronics Group in Arcade, New York, over 1000 employees were trained in SPC. Operators then began doing their own inspections and plotting hourly control charts to control their own projects. Quality control inspectors were transferred out. Improvements included (1) achieving 10:1 goal of improvement, (2) significant increases in yields, and (3) reduction in scrap. The facility received the Q1 quality award as a supplier to Ford.

Donald Bell, general manager of Monsanto's Fibers Division, envisioned the "Plant of the 1990s." The scheme is a three-tiered approach encompassing human resources planning, total quality concepts, and computer-integrated manufacturing (CIM). Productivity gains of 40 to 50 percent have already been achieved. The program emphasizes the needs of internal customers—those who use products in a later step of the manufacturing process. Computer training has enabled greater acceptance of these concepts.[20]

INFORMATION AND THE CUSTOMER

According to examiners who visit companies that apply for the Baldrige Award, most companies lack the processes that ensure efficient flow of information on customer demands and related information throughout the organization.[21] In other words, most companies do not devote the same attention to the customer that they do to the internal processes of shipping, inventory, JIT, manufacturing, etc. This is unfortunate because the operating processes cannot be managed according to the principles of TQM unless the loop is closed with customer feedback. Information systems should be extended beyond the plant into the marketplace. Some companies tend to define quality in terms of customer satisfaction or some other non-specific term and then relax after shipment is made, overlooking the competitive success that accompanies after-the-sale service, spare parts, or distribution.[22]

Why do information systems directly related to customer satisfaction frequently take a back seat to what otherwise might be acceptable or excellent information systems in support of quality and process control? The answer may be that it is difficult to specify information needs for an elusive system to measure customer requirements and satisfaction, which in themselves are difficult to define. Or it may be that the pressures of crisis management and internal information exchange leave little time for the customer.[23] Whatever the cause, it is a good idea to design a system that measures the pulse of the market and the customer base. It is estimated that failure to do so will cost twice as much as poor internal quality.[24]

■   The First National Bank of Chicago found that quality can be the difference between acquiring and keeping customers. Because competitive pricing varies by only a few pennies, the customer must be enlightened as to the benefits of strong quality. The bank measures customer satisfaction by how often inaccurate information is given. In 1982, the error rate was 1 in 4,000 transactions; in 1990 it dropped to 1 in 810,000 transactions.

Information Needs

After the objective of an information system is established, the next step is to determine the information needs. This is the most difficult step in designing a MIS for customer satisfaction. Everything else is detail and technique. Manager/user involvement is essential here.

If there is one fundamental principle of TQM, it is that *quality is what the buyer defines it as,* and not what the company defines it to be. Ford learned this lesson in the late 1970s, when the company definition of DQR (durability, quality, and reliability) was found to be presented in terms (engineering design tolerances and specifications) understandable only within the company, rather than in terms that represented quality to the customer. Only after reassessing quality in terms understandable to the customer was Ford able to adopt a policy called "Ford Total Quality Excellence" and achieve organization-wide commitment to continuous improvement and customer focus.

The first step then is to define quality as perceived by the customer by viewing it *externally* from the customer's perspective. By profiling how customers make purchase decisions, it is possible to determine which product attributes are most important and to determine how customers rate each attribute. As will be discussed in Chapter 8, this process forms the basis of *benchmarking*.[25]

Market research methods ranging from focus groups to shopper surveys are means for profiling customers and defining quality as perceived by customers. The information system can then be designed to provide the input for decisions regarding the operating plan, organizational implications, and follow-up control.

SYSTEMS DESIGN

After reviewing hundreds of applications for the Baldrige Award, Curt Reimann, director of the award, concluded that the area of information and analysis represents a serious national problem.[26] Many firms have failed to design individual applications to fit an overall master plan. The result has been a "band-aid" solution with little integration between functions and activities.

A master plan should be centered around corporate goals and the critical success factors and cost-performance drivers related to these goals. In a manufacturing firm, data from engineering, production, and field service are used to improve product design and manufacturing techniques. If reducing cycle time in bringing a product to market is a critical success factor (as it is), a good deal of this information will flow sideways and across departmental lines, rather than upward and vertically as in the traditional model.

The individual manager/user has the job of designing his or her own system requirements and fitting these into the overall master plan. This is not easy. In discussions with dozens of system analysts, they almost always report that their number one difficulty in system design is the inability or unwillingness of the user to define information needs. This definition is not the job of the analyst—it is the job of the individual user. Before design can proceed, two critical steps must be taken: define *system objectives* and *information needs*.

Surprisingly, many users cannot define an objective. They will define it as "having the right part at the right place at the right time" or "preparing a field service report." Statements such as these are elusive, not quantifiable, and unsuitable for conversion to information needs. On the other hand, when objectives are stated in more specific terms (such as "reduce final inspection in the production process to the point of elimination" or "reduce throughput time to 6 days"), the designer has a benchmark from which to proceed.

The next step is to define *information needs,* another requirement that users have difficulty defining. The question is: "What information do I need to achieve the objective?" If performance measures are established, the determination of both objective and information needs will become more apparent. Successful companies benchmark their performance against world-class quality leaders. For example, Xerox measured its performance in about 240 key areas of product, service, and business performance. This process is discussed further in Chapter 8.

QUESTIONS FOR DISCUSSION

3-1   Describe how lack of information can be a roadblock to implementing one or more TQM actions.

3-2   How do traditional accounting systems provide inadequate information for control of processes in an industry with low labor content.

3-3   Choose two functions or activities (market research, R&D, design, production planning, procurement, human resources) and show how information can serve to integrate them across functional lines.

3-4   How does information technology affect organizational structure? Give an example of how information technology can facilitate TQM.

3-5   How would you go about designing an MIS for getting customer input for quality improvement?

3-6   How does market segmentation influence information needs?

ENDNOTES

1.   Telephone interview with Curt W. Reimann.
2.   John Sculley, "The Human Use of Information," *Journal for Quality and Participation,* Jan./Feb. 1990, pp. 10–13.

3. Elizabeth A. Haas, "Breakthrough Manufacturing," *Harvard Business Review,* March/April 1987, pp. 75–81. It is estimated here that companies adopting integrated strategies may succeed in increasing productivity by 10 or 15 percent annually. See also Julian W. Riehl, "Planning for Total Quality: The Information Technology Component," *Advanced Management Journal,* Autumn 1988, pp. 13–19.

4. Nael A. Aly, Venetta J. Maytubby, and Ahmad K. Elshennawy, "Total Quality Management: An Approach & A Case Study," *Computers and Industrial Engineering,* Issues 1–4, 1990, pp. 111–116.

5. For a description of what lies ahead, see Robb Wilmot, "Computer Integrated Management—The Next Competitive Breakthrough," *Long Range Planning,* Vol. 21 No. 6, 1988, pp. 65–70.

6. James Heskett, "Lessons in the Service Sector," *Harvard Business Review,* March/April 1987, pp. 118–126.

7. Kathleen M. Eisenhardt, "Speed and Strategic Choice: How Managers Accelerate Decision Making," *California Management Review,* Spring 1990, pp. 39–54.

8. Dennis Normile, "Japan Inc. Bows to the Customer," *CIO,* Aug. 1990, pp. 91–93. A major benefit of information systems is increasing the speed from product concept to marketing, an improvement that translates into customer satisfaction.

9. Takashi Yamagiwa, "Computer Use in the Japanese Educational System," *Business Japan,* March 1988, pp. 38–39.

10. Ryozo Hayashi, "National Policy on the Information Service Industry," *Business Japan,* March 1990, pp. 49–61.

11. J. Lynn Johnson and Ralph Kuehn, "The Small Business Owner/Manager's Search for External Information," *Journal of Small Business Management,* July 1987, pp. 53–60.

12. The pioneering book is Frank J. Aguilar, *Scanning the Business Environment,* New York: Macmillan, 1967.

13. For a comprehensive treatment of competitive information and its sources, see Michael E. Porter, *Competitive Advantage,* New York: The Free Press, 1985. Based on research data collected from more than 3000 strategic business units, The Strategic Planning Institute, through its PIMS program, has identified the following characteristics of the most profitable companies in an industry: (1) higher market share, (2) higher quality, (3) higher labor productivity, (4) higher capacity utilization, (5) newer plant and equipment, (6) lower investment intensity per sales dollar, and (7) lower direct cost per unit. See Robert D. Buzzell and Bradley T. Gale, *The PIMS Principles: Linking Strategy to Performance,* New York: The Free Press, 1987.

14. H. Thomas Johnson and Robert S. Kaplan, *Relevance Lost: The Rise and Fall of Management Accounting,* Boston: Harvard Business School Press, 1991.

15. Peter Drucker, "The Emerging Theory of Manufacturing," *Harvard Business Review,* May/June 1990, pp. 94–102. See also Robert S. Kaplan, "The Four Stage Model of Cost Systems Design," *Management Accounting,* Feb. 1990, pp. 22–26; James M. Reeve, "TQM and Cost Management: New Definitions for Cost Accounting," *Survey of Business,* Summer 1989, pp. 26–30.

16. Fred J. Newton, "A 1990s Agenda for Auditors," *Internal Auditor,* Dec. 1990, pp. 33–39.

17. David A. Garvin, *Managing Quality,* New York: The Free Press, 1988, pp. 167–169. In this study, the best plants maintained sophisticated systems to track data and report it back to interested departments and functions.

18. See Raymond G. Ernst, "Why Automating Isn't Enough," *Journal of Business Strategy,* May/June 1989, pp. 38–42. The author argues that companies too often attempt to improve manufacturing by making large investments in automation without improving their business processes. He estimates that the savings of 10 to 20 percent that can be derived from automating can be increased to 70 percent when improvements are made to existing business processes as well. The processes can be achieved through a product-information flow.

19. Otis Port, "The Push for Quality," *Business Week,* June 8, 1987, pp. 130–135.

20. For an excellent description of how QFD is implemented, see John R. Hauser and Don Clausing, "The House of Quality," *Harvard Business Review,* May/June 1988, pp. 63–73. See also Chia-Hao Chang, "Quality Function Deployment (QFD): Processes in an Integrated Quality Information System," *Computers and Industrial Engineering,* Vol. 17 Issues 1–4, 1989, pp. 311–316.

21. Peter Burrows, "Commitment to Quality: Five Lessons You Can Learn from Award Entrants," *Electronic Business,* Oct. 15, 1990, pp. 56–58.

22. Morris A. Cohen and Hau L. Lee, "Out of Touch With Customer Needs? Spare Parts and After Sales Service," *Sloan Management Review,* Winter 1990, pp. 55–66.

23. Robert W. Wilmot, "Computer Integrated Management—The Next Competitive Break-through," *Long Range Planning,* Dec. 1988, pp. 65–70. This author has found that typical middle managers spend less than 10 percent of their time with customers and a tiny fraction sponsoring innovation and orchestrating change.

24. John Goodman and Cynthia J. Grimm, "A Quantified Case for Improving Quality Now," *Journal for Quality and Participation,* March 1990, pp. 50–55.

25. Bradley T. Gale and Robert D. Buzzel, "Market Perceived Quality: Key Strategic Concept," *Planning Review,* March/April 1989, pp. 6–15.

26. Curt W. Reimann, "Winning Strategies for Quality Improvement," *Business America,* March 25, 1991, pp. 8–11.

*Peter Drucker is truly one of the great pioneers and global management schol-
ars. His writings are known and admired around the world. He has long been a
champion of management in a knowledge worker environment; that is to say, the
information environment. In the following article he encourages the reader to
ask the question: "What information do I need to do my job and in what form?"
He then demonstrates how the answer integrates with customer satisfaction, the
load-bearing component of total quality management.*

WHAT DOES IT ALL MEAN?

Peter F. Drucker

*Information we have plenty of, but what's really necessary to your
work, and what form should it take? Don't expect an "information
specialist" to tell you.*

Our relationship to information—and its tool, the computer—is changing. Most
of us continue to use computers primarily to crunch numbers, but attitudes and
applications are changing fast, and we are moving rapidly toward the information-based organization. Today, the big thing to learn is not how to use the
computer, or even how to organize information, but how to take information
responsibility.

Information responsibility means making information a tool of understanding, which in turn is the basis for common action. This idea is something that we
are just starting to nibble on. I know a few places where it's taken seriously, but
frankly, I don't know a single place where it's yet done. We are now only
beginning to ask the question: What does information mean, both for my work
and for other people's work?

Reprinted with permission from *Across the Board,* December 1991, pp. 12–14, The Conference Board, New York.

The first step in taking information responsibility is to ask the question: "What information do I need, and in what form?" Most of my friends, not just in industry but in all organizations, still believe that information specialists can tell them what information they need. This approach is like asking the traffic cop, "Where should I be going?" Executives and others will have to learn that information is their tool. They must think through the kind of information they need and make sure that the people on whom they depend to deliver it understand their needs.

The next question people have to learn to ask is: "How is this information important to people in other departments?" They have to consider the meaning of, for example, a piece of engineering information for the marketing people, or a piece of marketing information for the engineers. And to figure this out, they must learn not just to guess but to go and ask.

Today, we are simply providing data and leaving the interpretation to the users, who are notoriously poor interpreters. Instead, we need to look at the information from our own area of activity and ask, "What should this mean to people in other areas? What implications for action are there?" For example, if I receive information from market research about changes in distribution systems—which are changing faster today than anything else, much faster than technology—I need to think about what this means for the design of the product, the service of the product, and other efforts that are not within my area but that nonetheless have a direct effect on how well I can do my job. We have a long way to go in this area. Executives who understand their work in terms of a flow of information are still a very small minority.

Another challenge for managers in the information-based organization is to make sure that the information on hand does not become misleading. Most of the information capacity a company has is internal. In fact, fundamentally, the only data base it has is internal. External data are very poor, very abstract, and very late. Outside data will always remain unsatisfactory for the simple reason that the important things that happen outside the business happen at the margin. They are qualitative changes, so they are not expressed in figures until it's too late.

How do you tell whether a given qualitative change is meaningful or purely anecdotal? I've been struggling with this for 40 years, and I'm not the only one. The problem is that early qualitative changes have no solid geometry that can tell you whether they are significant or not. You cannot easily convert a qualitative change—say, an incipient change in a distribution system—into quantities. By the time you get outside quantitative information, it's obsolete, or at least it's so late that you are running behind the parade.

Basically, we have become internally focused, and that's very dangerous. Our new data-processing capacity, though not the cause of this imbalance, aggravates it by giving people the illusion that they have information, when, in fact, crucial pieces are missing. To balance the increasing accessibility of and increasing dependence on information from the inside, we will have to increase our experience and exposure to the outside.

Last year, for example, I worked on productivity and quality issues with the joint productivity committees of two large automobile manufacturers and the United Auto Workers. The committees consist of very able people working very hard—but their results are not terribly impressive. The reason for that is simple. They cannot see that what they mean by quality means nothing to the customer. They are manufacturing people, and they love to show you figures that demonstrate that the American-made car when it leaves the factory now has fewer defects than the Japanese-made car. (This is not true of all American models, but of quite a few.) Yet customers are deserting American car manufacturers in droves, switching to the likes of Honda, Nissan, Toyota, and Mazda.

What the engineers mean by quality and what the customer means are two different things. I live in southern California. Once a year, my wife and I drive the 1,300 miles to our summer home in Colorado. One year our car broke down in Delta, Colorado. What we mean by quality is not the shape the car was in when it came out of the factory, but the service we get in Delta, Colorado. No automotive manufacturer understands that because they're not out there listening to their customers.

In the 1930s, Alfred Sloan, who ran General Motors, would disappear from Detroit once every six weeks. The next morning he would walk into a dealership in Cincinnati or Kansas City and say, "I am Mr. Sloan from Detroit. Would you allow me to work for two days as your assistant service manager?" When he left, customers always asked, "Who was that incompetent clunk?" but that wasn't the point of the exercise.

Sloan would also pop into the dealership in Albany, New York. I know about this from the Albany dealer, who complained about it volubly. Sloan showed up one day and said, "Mr. Yeager, do you mind if I work for you as a salesman for three days? I don't want any commission." Afterward, Mr. Yeager said, "Alfred Sloan cost me more sales than I can possibly tell you." The point is that when Alfred Sloan went back to Detroit from these forays, he knew customers. Since World War II, nobody in Detroit has done that. But two weeks after I took my Japanese-made car in for its routine inspection, I got a telephone call from Nissan, asking, "Were you satisfied?" That has never happened with my Oldsmobile.

I have not been able to get the idea of knowing customers across to people, even people who have been my friends for 40 years. They don't get it because not one of them has gone to work as an assistant service manager for two days. Instead, they look at statistics. Their data show them that cars are complex. There are 38,000 parts, more or less, and something has got to go wrong. What matters to the customer is, "Do I get it fixed, and do they care?" That's customer service—not insuring that the car was in perfect shape when it left the factory. It's irrelevant to the customer what caused the problem—whether it was a pebble from the road that knocked the pipe galley west, or whether the bolt wasn't fastened.

We will have to learn to balance the increasing amount of hard information with meaningful market experience, especially as distribution channels continue to change quickly. Real market experience is the only way to get the critical information that is embodied in attitudes, expectations, and events.

The need for critical but unquantifiable information applies not only to markets but to technologies, which are changing just as fast and are becoming equally unstructured. It's no longer adequate for people in the paper industry, for example, to know all about paper chemistry and paper mechanics. Their industry will be affected by discoveries in solid-state physics that no paper-maker has ever heard of. Businesses need information on technologies that are being developed far beyond their narrow areas, and in most cases, they don't know how to get it.

Some companies are better at getting technology information than marketing information. Quite a few companies no longer subscribe to the belief that "only what goes on in our lab is technology; the rest is not relevant to us." But determining what is relevant to a company is not easy. So the next step is to define information. Information is not what the computer delivers but what executives need to take effective action.

One branch of the U.S. Armed Services, for example, recently faced a serious supply problem when the workers in a critical plant went on strike. The strike came as a shock to senior managers because they had been looking at personnel data over the whole system of plants, and they were very happy. Absenteeism was low, as was turnover. But the aggregated data failed to reveal that one of their smallest plants had absenteeism rates of 80 percent and extremely high turnover. This was a grotesquely mismanaged plant, and senior management had no inkling of that fact because the information that would have revealed years of neglect was masked by the wrong presentation of data.

So a key part of the job is to make sure that data are presented in the form in which they are capable of giving information. One has to ask not just, "Are the data reliable?" but, "Is this the right way of presenting them?"

In that light, you must also take into consideration the recipient of your information. The human race is split three ways: Some people can take in information by looking at figures, some by looking at graphs, and a third group only by touching it, feeling it, or writing it.

I learned a very valuable lesson about presenting information in 1942, when I was working for the Pentagon. I made my first appearance before a Congressional committee, which was headed by an obscure politician named Harry

Truman. He cut me into tiny little pieces and fed me to the fish. And then he became a kind old gentleman and invited me to his chambers. I am not a drinker, but he poured a bottle of bourbon into me without noticeable effect. And when I thought I would survive—though I didn't yet enjoy the prospect—he said, "Sonny, don't you ever do again what you did today." And I asked, "Sir, what did I do?" He said, "You quoted fractions to Senators. If we understood fractions, what would we be doing in the Senate?" And then he said, "Go back to that so-and-so general of yours and tell him never to do again what he did." I asked, "What did General Jones do, sir?" He said, "He did something that needs to be explained; there is nothing you can explain to a U.S. Senator." From that moment on I was the first Truman booster. He was absolutely right. This is wisdom.

So you need to know in what form your people can receive information. If you talk to me, for example, don't give me graphs covered with little colored men or I crawl up the wall. Give me solid black numbers, and don't carry them out to the seventh decimal place, because I'm better than you at forging and faking figures, and I know that the less reliable the information, the more decimals. Give me numbers and let me work through them, because I like doing that. Most executives are not yet thinking about the form in which they convey information because they have not yet addressed the problem of marketing their output, which always starts with the customer, not the product.

Information responsibility, then, begins with correctly identifying the information you need to effectively carry out your job, and extends to insuring that the information flows to people in other areas who stand to benefit from it, and in a form in which those people will readily understand it. Learning to exercise this responsibility will doubtless be a slow and difficult process, as forging new ground always is. Increasingly, however, the measure of the executive will not be his ability to interpret data, but his ability to define and exploit information.

CASE

INFORMATION SYSTEMS AT THREE COMPANIES

Company #1—Anderson Technology

Starting twenty years ago the top management of the company made a commitment to use computer technology to streamline operations. It was understood at that time that much of the effort would be assigned to manufacturing and related processes such as inventory, warehousing, and order processing. In 1987 the decision was made to adopt quality management as the basis for company operations and to incorporate computers as a tool for achieving this. Again, the focus was on manufacturing and related processes.

Anderson Technology produced sheet metal products for a variety of manufacturers. About half of total sales were comprised of metal housings for other manufacturers in the computer, electronic, small appliance, and automotive industries. Major processes consisted of cutting, bending, welding, painting and so forth. Sales were made on a special order basis as well as from finished goods inventory.

The company has six branch plants with a statistical process control (SPC) coordinator at each plant who evaluates the SPC data gathered at the branch by each SPC team comprised of production workers. The *critical factors* that are traced are those related to the manufacturing processes such as inventory, scheduling, on-time deliveries, and returned goods authorizations (RGAs). These factors are tracked on-line and the results posted at headquarters monthly.

The critical factors were developed by the teams with guidance from the coordinators. In addition to the critical factors there are 35 area measures that track such things as computer down-time, nonscheduled maintenance, or inventory accuracy. Because the Baldrige Award criteria placed so much emphasis on data gathering, it was desirable to get every plant employee (called associates) involved in the job of gathering data. Periodically the need and value of the different measures were reviewed and some were dropped. For example, it was decided that the tracking of inventory items in the proper location and lost-time accidents was a poor idea because there were so few transactions that were meaningful. Other measures were added as time progressed, such as the number of customers below a certain percentage of gross profit, so that these could be used as a target for improvement. Delivery performance of all accounts, not just the top five, was added for tracking.

Each customer special order is defined in terms of customer specifications and the process defined and tracked. Processes could be outside of manufacturing. For example, if the specification is on-time delivery, then pulling the item from inventory and transportation is part of the process. Continuous monitoring and study of a process reduced failures, rejects, or rework.

Employees were extensively trained in problem solving, SPC and topics related to TQM. On-the-job training (OJT) teams were organized to study a process within their work area, define the mission of the process, and produce an "Ideal Process Flow" that forms the basis for a standard operating procedure (SOP) and a specific job work instruction for each step in the process.

The company's computer system is the load-bearing structure of the entire system. All plants have computers hooked into the mainframe at headquarters where SPC measurements are tracked. Most of the company's orders come in via an Electronic Data Interchange (EDI) system.

The EDI system allows the company to build relationships with customers as well as suppliers. It also reduces errors, improves cycle time, and allows just-in-time principles to work.

Questions for Discussion

1   What additional information systems, other than the ones mentioned, would you recommend for this company?

2   Can SPC be used in processes outside of manufacturing? For example, order processing, accounting, billing?

3   Is it a good idea to "track" performance of plants at headquarters?

4   Choose two or three measures that you think would be desirable and describe (1) objective, (2) information needs, (3) and information sources.

Company #2—Wallace Co., Inc.*

The company is an industrial distributor of pipe, valves, fittings, and specialty products serving the refining, chemical, and petrochemical industries. Corporate offices are in Houston, Texas with nine branch offices in three states. Employees number 280 and sales were approximately $90 million in 1990. The company has long-term "partnering" relationships with such firms as Union Carbide, Monsanto, Hoechst Celanese, Dow Chemical, Bechtel, and Brown & Root Braun.

The following is quoted from the condensed version of the Baldrige Award application.

Information and Analysis

The Information and Analysis category examines the scope, validity, use, and management of data and information that underlie the company's total quality management system. Also examined is the adequacy of the data and information to support a responsive prevention approach to Quality based upon "management by fact."

We used the following criteria to determine the types of Quality-related data to be maintained in our information base:

- First, the data meet internal customers' needs (e.g., sales reports, branch financial statements and inventory records).
- Second, the data meet external customers' need (e.g., on-time delivery, supplier product quality).
- Third, the data help improve the company's Quality leadership practices (e.g., turnover, training, promotion data).

We maintain data in the following categories:

- Customer
- Internal Operations & Processes
- Associate
- Safety
- Health & Other Regulatory

- Competitive
- Benchmark Data
- Quality Results
- Vendor Quality

We have had a company-wide computerized information system since 1964. It has been consistently upgraded, most recently in 1988 and 1989. The system

---

*A condensed version of the Information and Analysis section of the company's application for the Malcolm Baldrige Award. Used by permission.

provides on-line data to all associates so that, for example, an inside sales person in Texas City can check the inventory available at any other district office. Validity of data within the system is audited by reviewing performance data with customers, by a perpetual inventory management system, and through an annual financial audit.

A recent innovation of the Wallace computer system also set a new standard for the distribution industry. Material Test Reports (MTRs) can now be scanned into our computer system for immediate customer access. For example, if a customer wants an MTR on carbon steel pipe sold six months ago, we can access the data, print a hard copy, and fax this hard copy to the customer.

We use our data base for SPC charting and analysis. Service performance trends, including on-time deliveries and invoicing errors, are monitored on control charts maintained by SPC Coordinators in each district office. These trends are used to project percentage improvements. Some processes where Quality data have been used for improvement include:

- On-the-Job Training Teams
- Sales Performance
- Electronic Data Interchange (EDI)
- Customer Base
- Inventory Trends
- Accounts Receivable

The QMSC reviews and analyzes all Quality data monthly to plan short- and long-range Quality Activities and to target specific processes for improvement.

Questions for Discussion

1 Wallace is a distributor, not a manufacturer. How would information needs for a distributor differ from those of a manufacturer?

2 What is the meaning of the statement "support a responsive prevention approach to Quality based upon 'Management by Fact?'"

3 The company maintains information systems for the purpose of meeting customers' needs. How are these needs determined for external customers? For internal customers?

4 Name two or three types of benchmark data that a distributor might collect.

5 Choose two of the processes mentioned (e.g., sales performance, customer base) and show how Quality data can be used for improvement.

Company #3—Bartlett Machine Tool Company

It was June 30, 1992 and the end of the company's fiscal year. Results had deteriorated to the point where dividends had to be eliminated and 25 percent of the work force let go. Reductions were made on an across-the-board basis rather than selectively because it could not be determined which jobs and activities were productive or non-productive.

Bartlett Machine Tool Company was an old line firm that had been well known in the industry for over 50 years. Manufacturer of cutting tools such as drills, reamers, chucks, cutters and gauges, the company's products were highly regarded for quality and durability as well as after-sale service. This reputation for quality and service had been achieved at a high cost. It was a matter of pride that no defective product left the plant and a policy of 100 percent final inspection insured that specifications were met. Frequent line stoppage and set up were necessary to meet the special orders that customers required. Rejects and rework amounted to approximately 5 percent of production. A service force of 65 highly skilled field technicians and engineers maintained contact with major customers. These individuals frequently doubled as salespersons.

Dave Hoover, President, blamed the poor financial results on the "double whammy" of the recession combined with increasing foreign competition whose wage rates were substantially below the rates at Bartlett. Privately, Hoover admitted that he really didn't know why the company's sales were declining while costs were rising. The management information system (MIS) did not provide adequate information to track results against plan.

Few problem causes could be identified or decisions made with the information available. The existing MIS was little more than a monthly report of actual costs compared to budgeted cost. Sales and cost data were aggregated and could not be broken down by customer, cost or process center, or major overhead category.

The situation regarding information systems had continued throughout 1991 and into 1992 despite the hiring of an MIS expert and a staff of four. The effort of this group had been spent on the conversion of a conventional accounting system to what the group hoped would be a financial planning system. This latter system was perceived as representing the business plan as well as the strategic plan although it was little more than a generalized projection of sales and expenses.

Dave Hoover knew that a more sophisticated approach to information was necessary in support of a strategic plan that was yet to be devised. The need for such a plan of action was reflected in the changing environment of the industry. Commodity products of the type manufactured by Bartlett were being replaced by laser cutting, bonding, and other more advanced technology. Hoover felt the need to keep abreast of these changes as well as customer needs. He was also concerned that personnel in design engineering and sales would become outdated if environmental trends continued.

Company headquarters were located on the fifth floor of the main manufacturing plant. Manufacturing was conducted in the main plant and three smaller buildings located nearby. Different processes were done in different areas; grinding in one, testing in another, milling in another, and finishing in the main plant. Some processes were not in the same building and goods had to be moved from one area to another for the next step in the manufacturing process. Each step could therefore become a bottleneck if scheduling was inaccurate, as it frequently was. Moreover, the constant moving from one process area to another resulted in an overhead rate that was much higher than the industry average. This system also required an unusual inventory of work-in-process and caused other delays and bottlenecks. For example, cycle time for a standard commodity drill was six months whereas other manufacturers could do it in less than an hour. "Firefighting" was common as the system had to adapt to production needs and customer demands.

The company had recently organized around three strategic business units (SBUs), each headed by a product manager who had bottom line responsibility for his product group. The reorganization had caused numerous problems. First, there was the matter of the product managers' profit and loss statements (P&L). Because existing information systems could not generate P&L data by product line, each product manager was at a loss to determine which of his products or customers were profitable. Cost and inventory figures for his stock keeping units (SKUs) and other information for adequate planning and control was not available.

There were frequent disagreements between the product manager, sales, manufacturing, and design. Besides the need to establish profitability figures, the product managers began to fall behind as their time was spent in negotiating production targets and pricing with other departments and responding to customer demands. An additional problem was the excess inventory that had been built up over time. Production targets had been set by sales forecasts made by field representatives but frequently these forecasts failed to materialize. Dave Hoover felt that up to 25 percent of inventory was obsolete or unsalable. He also felt that 80 percent of his sales were coming from about 20 percent of the items but he had no way to go about rationalizing inventory or production.

Questions for Discussion

Compare the quality information systems at Anderson Technology and Wallace Company with the needs at Bartlett Machine Tool Company. For Bartlett:

1 Identify the critical factors related to the manufacturing processes at Bartlett (see Anderson Technology).

2 Name five additional measures that should be tracked.

3 Would you organize one or more cross-functional teams? If so, what activities would be represented?

4 What are the top three priorities for internal customers' needs (e.g., sales reports, production schedule, etc.)?

5 In preparation for design of a management information system, name three categories of information that would be appropriate for beginning the design process (e.g., vendor, benchmarking, etc.).

6 Name three processes that lend themselves to improvement by the use of statistical process control (SPC).

7 How would you go about reducing the cycle time of a product from design to shipment?

8 What subsystems would you include if you were asked to devise an MIS master plan?

INFORMATION SYSTEMS
AND ANALYSIS AT VARIFILM

Compare each of the following TQM criteria to Varifilm and indicate whether the practice in the company is a *strength (S)* or *needs improvement (I)*. Justify your answer.

2.1 Scope and Management of Quality and   (S)   (I)
Performance Data and Information

■ The criteria for selecting types of data and information used   ___   ___
in quality and operational performance improvement are described. Selection factors include data related to customer satisfaction and data required for performance analysis, among others.

■ A wide range of customer-related, product and service per-   ___   ___
formance, internal operations and performance, supplier performance, and cost and financial data and information is used by Varifilm to improve quality and operational performance.

■ Key indicators used to evaluate and improve the alignment   ___   ___
of data and information with process improvement plans are clearly defined

■ Evidence is provided to determine how Varifilm ensures   ___   ___
data reliability.

■ A variety of methods are used to ensure rapid and accurate   ___   ___
data transfer throughout the company, including automated laboratory data entry at all manufacturing sites, electronic data interchange (EDI) with customers and suppliers, and electronic mail.

■ Principal roles for each type of data and information used   ___   ___
to improve quality and operational performance are provided.

	(S)	(I)

■ Improvements in the scope and management of data are   ___   ___
made through the assessment process, customer input, and
the process management system (PMS). In addition, the
use of EDI, electronic mail, and common databases has
helped to reduce cycle time.

Additional Areas for Improvement

_____

_____

_____

2.3 Analysis and Uses of Company-Level Data   (S)   (I)

■ Varifilm performs correlation analyses which compare   ___   ___
performance indicators to customer performance. This allows the company to improve its ability to predict how
products perform during end-use applications.

■ Performance in each of five customer satisfaction require-   ___   ___
ments is tracked against actual customer satisfaction and is
used as a determinant of customer actions.

■ Each functional organization performs its own data and   ___   ___
operational analysis for the business plan development process.

■ The analysis and priority-setting process considers "rev-   ___   ___
enue at risk" when prioritizing needs improvement.

■ A process exists for aggregating customer-related data with   ___   ___
other key data to set priorities.

■ The company aggregates performance data and results with   ___   ___
other key data to determine operations-related trends and
improvement requirements.

■ A method is in place to evaluate and improve data analysis   ___   ___
and capabilities.

Additional Areas for Improvement

_____

_____

_____

4

STRATEGIC QUALITY PLANNING

The basics of total quality management (TQM) can effectively govern executive-level strategic management and goal-setting

Executive
Academy of Management

Ford's slogan, "Quality Is Job 1," has caught on with increasing segments of the car-buying public. The company's North American Automobile Group is gaining market share among U.S. manufacturers and has a higher net income than General Motors with only two-thirds the amount of sales.[1] Things were not always this way. Between 1978 and 1982 market share slipped to 16.6 percent and sales fell by 49 percent, with a cumulative loss in excess of $3 billion. Ford was losing $1000 on every car it sold. The company sought advice from W. Edwards Deming. Reports John Betti, at that time a senior executive at Ford, "I distinctly remember some of Dr. Deming's first visits. We wanted to talk about quality, improvement tools, and which programs work. He wanted to talk to us about management, cultural change, and senior management's vision for the company. It took time for us to understand the profound cultural transformation he was proposing."[2] The company's subsequent turnaround is a classic example of the results that can be obtained from a strategic change based on quality. The major changes responsible for reversing the company's fortune were as follows:

- Emphasize quality and review new product planning and design.
- Keep investing in new products and processes.
- Make employee relations a source of competitive advantage.[3]

3M's approach to quality is so highly regarded that executives from leading U.S. companies travel to St. Paul to attend monthly briefings sponsored by 3M. In *Thriving on Chaos*,[4] Tom Peters described 3M as the only truly excellent company today. *Forbes* chose 3M as one of America's three most highly regarded companies. Their TQM implementation strategy includes:

- Defining 3M's quality vision
- Changing management perceptions through specialized training
- Empowering employees to focus on and satisfy customer expectations
- Sustaining the process through an ongoing culture change

One executive of the company explained it as follows: "How do you meet such a wide variety of expectations in a coherent way? I think you do it with a corporate philosophy on what constitutes a total quality process...a philosophy that you can apply across the company...to all your operations."[5]

These comments reflect the importance that successful companies place on the strategy issue. In the American Management Association's survey of over 3000 international managers, the key to competitive success was defined as the improvement of quality. There is little doubt that a strategy based on quality begins with strategic planning and is implemented through program and action planning.[6]

STRATEGY AND THE STRATEGIC PLANNING PROCESS

What is strategy and what is the strategic planning process? The answers to these questions are important because evidence suggests that those companies with strategies based on TQM have achieved stunning successes.[7]

Most of these successful companies will attribute their progress to a quality-based strategy that was developed through a formal structured approach to planning. The Commercial Nuclear Fuel Division of Westinghouse, another Baldrige winner, has discovered that the total quality concept must be viewed as a pervasive operating strategy for managing a business every day:

> Total Quality begins with a *strategic decision*—a decision that can only be made by top management—and that decision, simply put, is the decision to compete as a world-class company. Total Quality concentrates on quality performance—in every facet of the business—and the primary strategy to

achieve and maintain competitive advantage. It requires taking a systematic look at an organization—looking at how each part interrelates to the whole process. In addition, it demands continuous improvement as a "way of life."[8]

Major contributors to the development of the strategic concept and to the planning process include Professors Andrews, Christensen, and others in the Policy group at the Harvard Business School.[9] A recent definition by this group is contained in their highly regarded text on the subject:[10]

Corporate strategy is the pattern of decisions in a company that (1) determines, shapes, and reveals its objectives, purposes, or goals; (2) produces the principal policies and plans for achieving these goals; and (3) defines the business the company intends to be in, the kind of economic and human organization it intends to be, and the nature of the economic and non economic contribution it intends to make to its shareholders, employees, customers, and communities.

Michael Porter is perhaps the most highly regarded and certainly the most popular writer on the subject of strategy.[11] He describes the development of a competitive strategy as "a broad formula for how a business is going to compete, what its goals should be, and what policies will be needed to carry out those goals."

STRATEGIC QUALITY MANAGEMENT

This pattern of goals, policies, plans, and human organization is not something to be taken lightly. It is likely to be in place over a long period of time and therefore affects the organization in many different ways. The culture that guides members of the organization and other stakeholders, the position that it will occupy in an industry and market segments, and determining particular objectives and allocating resources to achieve them all follow from the decision processes determined by strategy. It is easy to see how pervasive a strategy based on quality can become. It provides the basis upon which plans are developed and communications achieved. A basic rule of strategic planning is that *structure follows strategy*. Although the process of formulation and implementation may require staff input, the ultimate decision is fundamental to the job of the chairman or CEO. It cannot be delegated.

The pervasive role that quality plays in strategic planning can best be understood by examining the components of a strategy:

- Mission
- Product/market scope

- Competitive edge (differentiation)
- Supporting policies
- Objectives
- Organizational culture

These components are developed through a process of strategy formulation, the outline of which is shown in Figure 4-1. Note that the process involves positioning yourself against forces in the environment in such a way that action plans can minimize your weaknesses and take advantage of your strengths relative to the competition. Quality is the means of differentiation for the satisfaction of customer needs. Research that includes over 300 U.S. companies indicates that firms

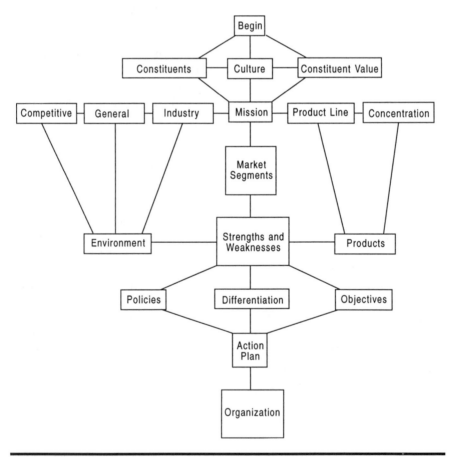

Figure 4-1 Strategic Planning

with superior quality address quality offensively, as a distinct competitive advantage, while firms with inferior quality treat it defensively (e.g., eliminate defects, lower cost of product failure).[12]

Mission

The mission is the primary overall purpose of an organization and its expressed reason for existence. The simplest statement of mission might be to "meet the needs/values of constituents."

■ The mission of NCR is stated simply: "Create Value for Our Stakeholders." Stakeholders are identified as employees, shareholders, suppliers, communities, and customers.[13] The mission can be operationalized by statements of how it will be implemented for each stakeholder.

■ At Goodyear, every employee carries a credit-card-sized mission statement: "Our mission is constant improvement in products and services to meet our customers' needs. This is the only means to business success for Goodyear and prosperity for its investors and employees."[14]

The mission statement includes the value that is being added and the direction the company intends to move. Because a mission can only be achieved by the people in an organization, it should have the commitment of the entire organization. Deming's first and what he considers his most important point of management obligation is to "create constancy of purpose for improvement of product and service with a plan to become competitive and stay in business."

This consistency must be achieved by a mission that can be operationalized and implemented. Consider the following examples:

■ All employees at Motorola consistently strive for a six sigma target.

■ 3M's mission focuses on innovation. To ensure consistency of purpose, the company established a requirement that 25 percent of each profit center's sales must come from products less than five years old.

■ Ford spent more than a year defining its mission. The real test of consistency and commitment came when the company withheld releasing a new Thunderbird, a "sure bet" for car of the year, because the car's quality was not yet suitable for a production model.

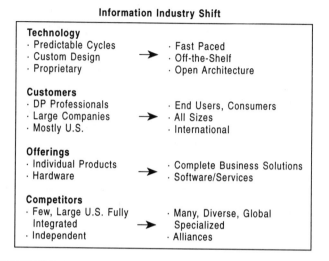

Figure 4-2   Defining the Environment

Environment

The major determinant of a mission is the environment in which the firm plans to operate: the general environment, the industry environment, and the competitive environment. Strategy is essentially the process of positioning oneself in that environment as trends and changes unfold. Thus, it is necessary to identify trends in the environment and how they affect the strategy of the firm. Figure 4-2 illustrates how a major U.S. manufacturer of computer equipment and software documented the major changes in that industry. The impact on strategy, as these issues relate to quality, is illustrated in Figure 4-3.

Product/Market Scope

This answers the questions: What am I selling and to whom am I selling it? The answers are more complex than they appear. What is Domino's Pizza selling: dough and tomato sauce or reliable delivery? What is a physician selling: surgery and diagnosis or patient involvement? Wal-Mart and Bloomingdale's are both in the retail business, but are their products simply what is on the shelves and racks in their stores? A company does not simply sell shoes or soap or banking services. It sells value to a particular segment of the market. The answers to these questions should be clear, as well as the role of quality in customer value.

What is value? It is, of course, what the customer—not the company—says it is. Timex sells watches, but does Rolex sell jewelry and prestige? Canada Dry

Re-Balancing for the '90s

Technology-Driven		Market-Driven
The Product	Focus	The Customer
Creating Demand	Approach	Providing Solutions
Price and Product Function	Marketing Strategy	Customer's Hearts and Minds
Product Volumes Revenue Profit	Measure of Performance	Customer Satisfaction Market Share Financial Returns

Figure 4-3   Impact of Changes in the Environment on Strategy

sells sparkling water, but does Perrier sell snob appeal? Thom-McCann sells loafers, but what does Gucci sell? This does not mean that Timex, Canada Dry, and Thom-McCann do not sell on the basis of quality. Indeed, they do. However, quality is defined differently for a different segment of the market. Each company must define its market segment and customer value in that segment. Ford's product mix includes the Lincoln Town Car and the Escort, but each is targeted at a different market segment, and quality (value) is different for each segment.

Every purchase decision is a function of price and quality. Price is generally known, but quality is in the mind of the individual customer. General Electric is aware of this and has broadened its perspective from "product quality" to "total customer satisfaction." The "product" is now defined by the customer.[15] It only remains to define customer satisfaction, perception, or expectation.

To repeat, in today's heightened competitive environment, a product or service is not simply sold to anyone who will buy it. To be effective, value must be sold to a particular market or customer segment. Strategic planning involves the determination of these strategy components, and quality plays a major role in this process.

Differentiation

Differentiation, frequently called the competitive edge, answers the question: Why should I buy from you? Michael Porter, in his landmark book *Competitive*

Strategy, identified two generic competitive strategies: (1) overall cost leadership and (2) differentiation.[16] Cost leadership in turn can be broad in market scope (e.g., Ivory Soap, Emerson Electric, Black & Decker) or market segment focused (e.g., La Quinta Motels, Porter Paint). The second strategy involves differentiating the product or service by creating something that is perceived by the buyer as unique. Differentiation can also be broad in scope (American Airlines in on-time service, Caterpillar for spare parts support) or focused (e.g., Godiva chocolates, Mercedes automobiles). Thus, there are four generic strategies, but each depends on something different—something unique or distinguishing. Even an effective cost leadership strategy must start with a good product.

Selecting a strategy and recognizing quality as the competitive dimension is important for strategic purposes. Product and service quality has become widely recognized as a major force in the competitive marketplace and in international trade.[17]

Research indicates that eight out of ten customers consider quality to be equal to or more important than price in their purchase decisions.[18] This is a doubling of buyer emphasis in ten years and the trend is expected to continue. The message here is that whether a cost leadership or differentiation strategy is chosen, quality must be a competitive consideration in either case.

Differentiation can command a premium price or allow increased sales at a given price. Moreover, differentiation is one of two types of competitive advantage, the other being price. Price, however, should not be the sole basis of differentiation unless the product is perceived to be a commodity. Even if the product is a commodity or near-commodity, it can still be differentiated by such service characteristics as availability or cycle time.

The several sources of differentiation are not well understood. Many managers perceive their uniqueness in terms of the physical product or in their marketing practices rather than in terms of value to the customer. They may waste money because their uniqueness does not provide real value to the buyer. Why spend money on extra tellers or checkout lines to reduce waiting time to one minute if the customers are willing to wait two minutes? On the other hand, buyers frequently have difficulty estimating value and how a particular firm can provide it. This incomplete knowledge can become an opportunity if the firm can adopt a new form of differentiation and educate the buyers to value it.

DEFINITION OF QUALITY

The concept and vocabulary of quality are elusive. Different people interpret quality differently. Few can define quality in measurable terms that can be operationalized. When asked what differentiates their product or service, the banker will answer "service," the health care worker will answer "quality health care," the hotel or restaurant employee will answer "customer satisfaction," and the manufacturer will simply answer "quality product." When pressed to provide a specific definition and measurement, few can do so.[19] There is an old maxim in management which says, "If you can't measure it, you can't manage it," and so it is with quality. If the strategic management system and the competitive advantage are to be based on quality, every member of the organization should be clear about its concept, definition, and measurement as it applies to his or her job. As will be discussed, it may be entirely appropriate for quality to be defined or perceived differently in the same company depending on the particular phase of the product life cycle.

Harvard professor David Garvin, in his book *Managing Quality,*[20] summarized five principal approaches to defining quality: transcendent, product based, user based, manufacturing based, and value based.

People from around the world travel to view the Mona Lisa or Michaelangelo's David, and most would agree that these works of art represent quality. But can they define it? Those who hold the *transcendental* view would say, "I can't define it, but I know it when I see it." Advertisers are fond of promoting products in these terms. "Where shopping is a pleasure" (supermarket), "We love to fly and it shows" (airline), "The great American beauty…It's elegant" (automobile), and "It means beautiful eyes" (cosmetics) are examples. Television and print media are awash with such undefinable claims and therein lies the problem: quality is difficult to define or to operationalize. It thus becomes elusive when using the approach as a basis for competitive advantage. Moreover, the functions of design, production, and service may find it difficult to use the definition as a basis for quality management.

Product-based definitions are different. Quality is viewed as a quantifiable or measurable characteristic or attribute. For example, durability or reliability can be measured (e.g., mean time between failure, fit and finish), and the engineer can design to that benchmark. Quality is determined objectively. Although this approach has many benefits, it has limitations as well. Where quality is based on individual taste or preference, the benchmark for measurement may be misleading.

User-based definitions are based on the idea that quality is an individual matter, and products that best satisfy their preferences (i.e., perceived quality) are those with the highest quality. This is a rational approach but leads to two problems. First, consumer preferences vary widely, and it is difficult to aggregate these preferences into products with wide appeal. This leads to the choice between a niche strategy (see later) or a market aggregation approach which tries to identify those product attributes that meet the needs of the largest number of consumers.

Another problem concerns the answer to the question: "Are quality and customer satisfaction the same?" The answer is probably not. One may admit that a Lincoln Continental has many quality attributes, but satisfaction may be better achieved with an Escort. One has only to recall the box office success of recent motion pictures that suffer from poor quality but are evidently preferred by the majority of moviegoers.

Manufacturing-based definitions are concerned primarily with engineering and manufacturing practices and use the universal definition of "conformance to requirements." Requirements, or specifications, are established by design, and any deviation implies a reduction in quality. The concept applies to services as well as products. Excellence in quality is not necessarily in the eye of the beholder but rather in the standards set by the organization. Thus, both Cadillac and Cavalier possess quality, as do Zayre and Bloomingdale's, as long as the product or service "conforms to requirements."

This approach has a serious weakness. The consumer's perception of quality is equated with conformance and hence is internally focused. Emphasis on reliability in design and manufacturing tends to address cost reduction as the objective, and cost reduction is perceived in a limited way—invest in design and manufacturing improvement until these incremental costs equal the costs of non-quality such as rework and scrap. This approach violates Crosby's concept of "quality is free" and is examined further in Chapter 11.

Value-based quality is defined in terms of costs and prices as well as a number of other attributes.[21] Thus, the consumer's purchase decision is based on quality (however it is defined) at an acceptable price. This approach is reflected in the popular *Consumer Reports* magazine which ranks products and services based on two criteria: quality and value. The highest quality product is not usually the best value. That designation is assigned to the "best-buy" product or service.

Which Approach(es)?

Which definition or concept of quality should be adopted? If each function or department in the company is allowed to pursue its own concept, potential conflicts may occur:

Function	Quality concerns
Marketing	Performance, features, service, focus on customer concerns
	User-based concerns that raise costs
Engineering	Specifications
	Product-based concerns
Manufacturing	Conformance to specifications
	Cost reduction

Adopting a single approach could lead to cost increases as well as customer dissatisfaction. Each function has a role to play, but it cannot be played in isolation. A blend is needed to coordinate meeting each of the concerns listed.

Market Segmentation (Niche) Quality

Quality means different things to different people. In terms of strategic quality management, this means that the firm must define that segment of the industry, that generic strategy, and that particular customer group which it intends to pursue. This can be called a segmented quality strategy. The big three automobile manufacturers have wide product lines, each of which is marketed to a different part of the market and each with differing quality attributes.

Recent efforts to codify the concepts of quality and provide baselines for measurement have yielded the characteristics listed in Table 4-1. None of these dimensions stands alone. Differentiation may depend on one or more or a combination, but the point is that when differentiating based on quality, quality must defined in terms that meet customer expectations, even if this is only what the customer perceives as quality.

A survey of purchasers of consumer products by the American Society for Quality Control summarized the factors influencing decisions to purchase (on a scale of 1 to 10) (Table 4-2).

Table 4-1   Measurement of Quality

Category	Example
Performance	On-time departure of aircraft Acceleration speed of automobile
Features	Remote control for stereo Double coupons at the supermarket
Reliability	Absence of repair during warranty 30-minute pizza delivery
Conformance	Supplier conforms to specifications Cost of performance failures
Durability	Maytag's 10-year transmission warranty Mean time between failures
Serviceability	Consumer "hot line" for repair information Time to answer the telephone for reservation or complaint
Aesthetics	Restaurant ambiance Perfume fragrance
Perceived quality	Japanese vs. American automobiles Doctor A is better than Doctor B

Table 4-2 Factors in
Decisions to Purchase

Factor	Mean
Performance	9.37
Lasts a long time	9.03
Easy to repair	8.80
Service	8.62
Warranty	8.13
Price	8.11
Ease of use	8.09
Appearance	7.54
Brand name	6.09

Objectives

Management statesman Peter Drucker has said, "a company has but one objective: to create a customer." Following this statement, he proceeded to popularize the concept of management by objectives (MBO) and identified eight key areas for which objectives must be set:[22] (1) marketing, (2) innovation, (3) human organization, (4) financial resources, (5) physical resources, (6) productivity, (7) social responsibility, and (8) profit requirements. These areas have been widely adopted by industry.

Within these eight broad areas, a company can set more specific objectives to identify the ends it hopes to achieve by implementing a strategy. Marketing becomes market share, innovation becomes new products, financial resources becomes capital structure, productivity becomes output per employee, profitability becomes return on investment or earnings per share, and so on.

Here, the question of quality becomes blurred. Is it a mission or an objective? It hardly matters if it is woven into the fabric of company strategy. If quality is chosen as central to a mission, other objectives begin to fall into place. For example, cycle time reduction, cost reduction, competitive standing, and return to shareholders can be related to the central mission.

■ Digital Equipment Corporation launched a TQM program in order to tie together various efforts scattered throughout the company. The goal is to have a consistent company vision and language. Included is a six sigma program motivated by a desire to improve competitive position.[23]

Many quality improvement programs were started in the 1980s and 1990s in reaction to the increasing importance of quality and the need to compete for market share. Many companies failed, often because they had no action plan for implementing a strategy that was based on objectives, a prerequisite for follow-on operational planning.[24]

Supporting Policies

Policies are guidelines for action and decision making that facilitate the attainment of objectives. Taken together, a company's policies delineate its strategy fairly well. Tell me your policies and I can tell you your strategy.

The role of policies as a critical element of strategy is displayed in Figure 4-4, which can be called the *policy wheel*. In the center are the mission (the purpose of the organization), the differentiation (how to compete in the market), and the key objectives of the business. The spokes of the wheel represent the functions of the business. Each function requires supporting policies (functional strategies) to achieve the *hub*. If the firm's strategy calls for competing on quality, then this becomes the impetus for policy determination. Each functional policy supports this central strategy and the objectives that are determined during the planning process.

A firm's policy choices are essential as drivers of differentiation. They determine what activities to perform and how to perform them. Grey Poupon's advertising policy for its premium mustard sets the product apart. Bic Pen's manufacturing policy of low-cost automation supports its low price. Avon's door-to-door distribution policy sets it apart. McDonald's policy of strict franchisee training and control allows it to retain its quality image. An airline's policy

Figure 4-4 Policy Wheel

Table 4-3   Consistency of Supporting Policies

Function	Illustration of policy
Target market	Map the industry and seek out those segments where we have the advantage
Product line	Product line breadth is confined to those products where our value chain is appropriate for focus segment
Marketing	Market research to be directed toward defining customer expectations
Sales	Sales force hired and trained to promote our competitive edge
Distribution	Select distributors that complement our quality edge
Manufacturing	Invest in automation for improvement of quality and productivity
Supplier	Select suppliers that have applied for Baldrige Award Make life contracts
Human resources	Require skill and experience level for new hires Partnership relations with union
Research and development	Percentage of budget devoted to quality improvement Products designed for ease of repair
Finance	Service procedures in billing activity Financial arrangements with suppliers

of "answering the phone on the third ring" reinforces a competitive edge of service.

Testing for Consistency of Policies

Assuming that the company has decided to make quality the central focus of its strategy, objectives are then set for profitability, growth, market share, innovation, productivity, etc. The test for consistency of supporting policies for a hypothetical firm is provided in Table 4-3. Of course, each policy is related to the hub and radiates from it. Like a wheel, the spokes must be connected.

CONTROL

The propensity of the American manager to focus on short-term financial goals is well known. In its simplest and most prevalent form, the control system consists of setting financial standards (the budget), getting historical feedback on performance (the variance report), and trying to meet targets after deviations have occurred.

Much has been written about the shortcomings of this approach. The major problem is the lack of focus on productivity (absolute, not financial measures), quality, and other strategic issues.

A system to control quality objectives, as distinct from quality on the shop floor, requires measures and standards designed for that purpose. Indeed, Juran suggests that the traditional control process may be put on hold while increasing the emphasis on quality planning and improvement.[25] Thus, planning and control of quality come together in an integrated system. The focus is on quality improvement set out in the planning process. The difference between traditional dollar accounting budgeting and the control of quality objectives is the participation of those who set standards and targets. Each function, department, or individual sets targets and provides real-time feedback as operations unfold.

SERVICE QUALITY

The differences between service and product quality were discussed in Chapter 1. This topic will be examined further in Chapter 7 (Customer Focus and Satisfaction). It is both more difficult and yet simpler to plan and control service quality than it is to plan and control product quality. It is more difficult because measurement is elusive and production is frequently one-on-one. Like product quality, service quality should live up to expectation, but this can be a pitfall if too much service is promised.

Service quality may be more easily planned, provided objectives are defined and people committed. In any case, the payoff can be years away, and no service can overcome other weaknesses in a business.[26] The system for quality service also requires new approaches, such as restructuring incentives. In any case, a good beginning approach can be based on the Baldrige Award criteria, which are the same for both product and service. Process control in service industries is discussed further in Chapter 6.

SUMMARY

Quality has taken center stage as the main issue in both national and corporate competitive strategies. Those organizations that adopt quality as a differentiation and a way of organizational life will, over the longer term, pull ahead of competition. Achieving this goal is not easy. It is more than just issuing pronouncements and engaging in company promotion.

When an organization chooses to make quality a major competitive edge, it becomes the central issue in strategic planning—from mission to supporting policies. An essential idea is that the product is customer value rather than a physical product or service. Another concept that is basic to the process is the need to develop an organizational culture based on quality. Finally, no strategy or plan can be effective unless it is carefully implemented.

QUESTIONS FOR DISCUSSION

4-1   Assume that an airline, a hotel, and a hospital have chosen quality for differentiation. Identify two or more measures of quality for a firm in each of these industries.

4-2   Illustrate a definition of
- *Transcendental* quality
- Product-based quality
- User-based quality
- Value-based quality

4-3   Choose an industry and a product or service within that industry and show how quality may differ for different segments or customer groups within that industry.

4-4   Is the objective of cost reduction in conflict with quality improvement? If so, illustrate how.

4-5   How can quality be reflected in the following:
- Distribution policy
- Human resources
- Sales
- Suppliers

4-6   Illustrate how trends in an industry can change a company's strategy.

ENDNOTES

1. United States General Accounting Office, *Quality Management: Scoping Study,* Washington, D.C.: U.S. General Accounting Office, Dec. 1990, p. 67.

2. United States General Accounting Office, *Quality Management: Scoping Study,* Washington, D.C.: U.S. General Accounting Office, Dec. 1990, p. 15.

3. The details of Ford's transformation are contained in HBS Case 390-083, available from HBR Publications, Harvard Business School, Boston, MA 02163. See also Richard T. Pascale, *Managing on the Edge,* New York: Simon & Schuster, 1990.

4. Tom Peters, *Thriving on Chaos: Handbook for a Management Revolution,* New York: Knopf, 1987.

5. Remarks of A. F. Jacobson at the Conference Board Quality Conference in Dallas, April 2, 1990.

6. Eric Rolf Greenberg, "Customer Service: The Key to Competitiveness," *Management Review,* Dec. 1990, pp. 29–31.

7. J. M. Juran, "Made in USA—A Quality Resurgence," *Journal for Quality and Participation,* March 1991, pp. 6–8.

8. "Performance Leadership through Total Quality," a presentation made to the Conference Board Quality Conference, April 2, 1990. Two other Westinghouse divisions were runners-up for the Baldrige Award in 1989 and 1990.

9. Kenneth R. Andrews, *The Concept of Corporate Strategy,* New York: Dow Jones-Irwin, 1971.

10. Joseph L. Bower, Christopher A. Bartlett, C. Roland Christensen, Andrall E. Pearson, and Kenneth R. Andrews, *Business Policy: Text and Cases,* 7th ed., Homewood, Ill.: Irwin, 1991, p. 9.

11. Michael Porter, *Competitive Strategy: Techniques for Analyzing Industries and Competitors,* New York: The Free Press, 1980. See also his *Competitive Advantage: Creating and Sustaining Superior Performance,* New York: The Free Press, 1985, and *The Competitive Advantage of Nations,* New York: The Free Press, 1990.

12. Joel Ross and David Georgoff, "A Survey of Quality Issues in Manufacturing: The State of the Industry," *Industrial Management,* Jan./Feb. 1991.

13. Company brochure entitled "NCR Mission."

14. U.S. General Accounting Office, *Quality Management: Scoping Study,* Washington, D.C.: U.S. General Accounting Office, Dec. 1990, p. 23. T. Boone Pickens, the quintessential LBO raider, was not very charitable to Goodyear. In a speech to the Strategic Planning Institute in Boston on October 23, 1989, he used Chairman Robert Mercer as an example of corporate America in the early 1980s: "bloated, uncompetitive, bureaucratic and barely accountable to anyone...what I call the BUBBA syndrome."

15. Elyse Allan, "Measuring Quality Costs: A Shifting Perspective," a presentation made to the Conference Board Quality Conference, April 2, 1990. *Global Perspectives on Total Quality,* Report Number 958, New York: The Conference Board, 1990, p. 35.

16. Michael Porter, *Competitive Strategy: Techniques for Analyzing Industries and Competitors,* New York: The Free Press, 1980, pp. 35–37.

17. J. M. Juran, "Strategies for World-Class Quality," *Quality Progress,* March 1991, pp. 81–85.

18. Armand V. Feigenbaum, "How to Implement Total Quality," *Executive Excellence,* Nov. 1989, pp. 15–16.

19. Y. K. Shetty and Joel Ross, "Quality and Its Management in Service Businesses," *Industrial Management,* Nov./Dec. 1985, pp. 7–12; Joel Ross and Y. K. Shetty, "Making Quality a Fundamental Part of Strategy," *Long Range Planning (UK),* Feb. 1985, pp. 53–58.

20. David A. Garvin, *Managing Quality,* New York: The Free Press, 1988, pp. 40–46.

21. In a survey of consumers' purchasing decisions conducted by the Gallup Organization, consumers were asked to rank (on a scale of 1 to 10) the importance of selected factors in the decision to purchase; 42 percent ranked price as 10. Other factors ranked as 10 were performance (72 percent), lasts a long time (58 percent), easily repaired (52 percent), service (50 percent), warranty (48 percent), ease of use (37 percent), appearance (28 percent), and brand name (15 percent). See *'88 Gallup Survey of Consumers' Perceptions Concerning the Quality of American Products and Services,* Milwaukee: American Society for Quality Control, 1988, p. 9.

22. Peter F. Drucker, *Management: Tasks, Responsibilities, Practices,* New York: Harper & Row, 1973, p. 100.

23. Rick Whiting, "Digital Strives for a Consistent Vision of Quality," *Electronic Business,* Nov. 26, 1990, pp. 55–56.

24. A. Blanton Godfrey, "Strategic Quality Management," *Quality,* March 1990, pp. 17–22.

25. J. M. Juran, "Universal Approach to Managing for Quality," *Executive Excellence,* May 1989, pp. 15–17. See also Bradley Gale and Donald J. Swmre, "Business Strategies that Create Wealth," *Planning Review,* March/April 1988, pp. 6–13. Traditional strategic planning based on financial measures is being called into question because they do not look beyond more important measures such as quality.

26. David Eva, "The Myth of Customer Service," *Canadian Business,* March 1991, pp. 34–39.

A total quality management approach to strategy is needed, based on the benefits derived from a focus on quality and in line with emergent beliefs about employee-driven, customer-centered business practices. The author argues that the basics of TQM can effectively govern much of what is required in modern strategic planning.

IS STRATEGY STRATEGIC? IMPACT OF TOTAL QUALITY MANAGEMENT ON STRATEGY

Richard J. Schonberger

If the TQM agenda is as substantive, stable, and competitively potent as it is made out to be, then it is time to consider its strategic impact. Is TQM becoming a dominant component of strategic planning? If so, it might be good news, in view of the often turbulent economic effects of conventional business strategies—which have tended toward outwitting the tax system, playing follow-the-leader, pick-a-number target setting, trying to outguess the competition, shuffling resources, and so on.

In the remaining discussion, we examine the influence of TQM and note, further, the weaknesses of conventional strategic thought, which seems out of phase with emergent beliefs about employee-driven, customer-centered business practices. The intent is not to pose a complete, revised, ironclad "theory of business strategy." Rather it is to show that:

1. The basics of total quality management, which may be reduced to a few principles, can effectively govern much of what conventionally required executive-level strategic planning and goal-setting.

Abridged with permission from *Academy of Management Executive,* Vol. 6 No. 3, August 1992, pp. 80–87.

2. Remaining competitive issues (those not clearly covered by generally accepted TQM principles) are best resolved by organization-wide planning, with executive oversight.

From Basics to Principles

I'll restate what I believe to be basic pursuits, as reflected by total quality management practices and policies of our newly enlightened companies and managers. They are:

■ Ever better, more appealing, less variable quality of the product or service itself.

■ Ever quicker, less variable response—from design and development through supplier and sales channels, offices, and plants all the way to the final user.

■ Ever greater flexibility—in adjusting to customers' shifting volume and "mix" requirements.

■ Ever lower cost—through quality improvement, rework reduction, and non-value-adding (NVA) waste elimination.

These four objects of continuous improvement are general categories. For application, they must be translated into—or supported by—specific operational guidelines. Table 1 is a 19-point list of such guidelines, each of which furthers one, more than one, or all of the four basic objects of improvement.

This tentative (not definitive) list, which is based on observations of improvement practices in TQM-oriented firms, has been modified a few times, as firms in more and more lines of business catch continuous improvement fever. Manufacturing firms, under the withering heat of Asian competition, caught the fever first, and earlier published versions of the lists contained manufacturing language. The list in Table 1 is neutral as to type of business.

The nineteen items, in eight categories, are labeled "principles of total quality management." To be a *principle*, an item must apply nearly all the time. The idea is simply to (a) do what is consistent with the principles and (b) avoid doing anything that would violate any of them.

Though the nineteen TQM principles reach across most business functions, it is not hard to think of strategic questions that are not directly answered by them. When should capacity be added? Where should the new facility be built? What emphasis (i.e., money) should be given to in-house R&D? Is this the time to cut prices and put the heat on the competition in the northeastern market?

Each such critical question begs consideration of a prodigious number of variables, and rarely do executives make the decision with much confidence. While the TQM principles won't make the decision, they can improve the odds

Table 1   Principles of Total Quality Management

General

1. Get to know the next and final customer
2. Get to know the direct competition, and the world-class leaders (whether competitors or not)
3. Dedicate to continual, rapid improvement in quality, response time, flexibility, and cost
4. Achieve unified purpose via extensive sharing of information and involvement in planning and implementation of change

Design and Organization

5. Cut the number of components or operations and number of suppliers to a few good ones
6. Organize resources into chains of customers, each chain mostly self-contained and focused on a product or customer "family"

Operations

7. Cut flow time, distance, inventory, and space along the chain of customers
8. Cut setup, changeover, get-ready, and startup time
9. Operate at the customer's rate of use (or a smoothed representation of it)

Human Resource Development

10. Continually invest in human resources through cross-training (for mastery), education, job switching, and multi-year cross-career re-assignments; and improved health, safety, and security
11. Develop operator-owners of products, processes, and outcomes via broadened owner-like reward and recognition

Quality and Process Improvement

12. Make it easier to produce or provide the product without mishap or process variation
13. Record and own quality, process, and mishap data at the workplace
14. Ensure that front-line associates get first chance at process improvement—before staff experts

Accounting and Control

15. Cut transactions and reporting; control causes and measure performance at the source, not via periodic cost reports

Capacity

16. Maintain/improve present resources and human work before thinking about new equipment and automation
17. Automate incrementally when process variability cannot otherwise be reduced
18. Seek to have multiple work stations, machines, flow lines, cells for each product or customer family

Marketing and Sales

19. Market and sell your firm's increasing customer-oriented capabilities and competencies

that a good decision will be made. This is especially true of principle number 4, achieve unified purpose via extensive sharing of information and involvement in planning and implementation of change.

Principles 5 through 18, collectively, are aimed at driving out costly overhead, speeding up the design and production process, improving flexibility of human and physical resources, and eliminating uncertainties caused by rework and shaky suppliers.

Goals and Policies

If TQM principles can, in fact, ease the burden of knotty strategic decisions facing senior management, how does the executive art change? We have been told, in the business press, that our newly made executives should be managing the pace of continuous improvement via "stretch" goal-setting, building teamwork and trust among the key department and business unit managers, developing a corporate culture, and—newly arrived from Japan—policy deployment.

Today, a minority opinion is that high-level managers should *not* engage in numerical goal-setting. Perhaps this opinion is related, in part, to points 10 and 11 of Dr. W. Edwards Deming's well-known 14 points; the tenth and eleventh call for elimination of numerical *productivity* and *work standard* goals.

What about numerical cost, profit, sales, market share, capacity utilization, and return-on-investment goals? Preoccupation with such goals sometimes is cited as a reason why our executives find it hard to look beyond the next quarterly report. The numbers in that report are, in the main, the ones referrred to by those who ridicule "by-the-numbers management." Pressures to meet them tend to push managers into making ill-advised decisions: keeping prices high (eroding sales volume) to meet a tough profit target, cutting prices below costs to prop up current sales, foregoing machine maintenance to meet a productivity (or cost or utilization) goal, and so on.

On the other hand, numerical targets for sales, profit, and so forth are necessary for budgeting and financial management—the need for which no one seriously questions. The TQM line of thought on goals vs. budgets might be as follows:

- Budgetary accuracy is an appropriate object of continuous improvement, and TQM data analysis methods offer an excellent way to improve the accuracy of budgeting (or accuracy of nearly any process, for that matter).

- Deviation from the budget is like deviation from tolerances on a component part; it is suitable for monitoring on statistical process control charts, so that a point out of the control limits may be easily spotted and dealt with. Zytec Corporation, the previously cited 1991 Baldrige prize winner, pioneered in the use of control charts for this purpose.

■ Meeting the budget is, inherently, neither good nor bad. More sales, more profits, and lower costs than budgeted usually are happy events (unless at the expense of future results). Thus, budget items *should not be goals*! Quick reaction to take advantage of a good situation or a bad one, reflected by a sharp deviation from the budget, is what's important.

In today's admired companies, of course, executive goal-setting is not limited to items on the P&L statement and balance sheet. It extends to goals that are close to the essence of total quality management—for example, cycle time, quality, skill-upgrading, and machine up-time goals.

Self-imposed or team-imposed numerical goals are a different story—quite acceptable as long as they do not stray out of TQM boundaries. In fact, when a team sets its own goals, numerical or just indefinitely rapid, it *owns* goal setting, which is consistent with the ownership principle, number 11.

A tenet of TQM is that "you only improve what you measure." But aggregate numbers planned and measured high in the organization ("management by the numbers") have little relevance to the work of most people in the organization. Total quality management requires everyone to be working on measurable improvement meaningful in their own jobs.

CASE

Peter Drucker is perhaps the most highly regarded management philosopher in the Western world. In the following article he describes how Japan is restructuring around "brain power" rather than "manufacturing power." This means moving from total quality management toward zero defects management. This dual movement means increased emphasis on cycle time in bringing products to market, along with implementing organizational devices such as cross-functional teams and empowerment.

DRUCKER ON MANAGEMENT: JAPAN: NEW STRATEGIES FOR A NEW REALITY

Peter F. Drucker

Quietly, and with a minimum of discussion, the leading Japanese companies are moving to new business strategies. They are embracing two radically new theories: To do blue-collar manufacturing work in Japan is a gross misallocation of resources that weakens both the company and the national economy. And leadership throughout the developed world no longer rests on financial control or traditional cost advantages. It rests on control of brain power.

These companies are also fast restructuring their organizations on the assumption that the winner in a competitive world economy is going to be the firm that best organizes the systematic abandonment of its own products. And they are moving from Total Quality Management toward Zero Defects Management based on drastically different principles and methods.

The Japanese now hold about 30% of the U.S. automobile market and expect to increase this share substantially in the next few years. Yet they also expect to stop exporting Japanese-made cars to the American market within the next three to five years; by 1995 or so, most Japanese marques sold in the U.S. should be manufactured in North American plants.

Similarly, the Japanese expect to have something like one-third of the automobile market of the European Economic Community by the year 2000 (whatever their present promises to the EC to the contrary), but again without exporting many cars from Japan. And Japanese multinationals—Toyota, Honda, Sony, Matsushita, Fujitsu, the ceramics leader Kyocera, and the Mitsubishi companies—are pouring staggering amounts of money into manufacturing plants in developing countries. They are in Tijuana on the U.S.–Mexican border, throughout South America, in Southern Europe, and in Southeast Asia.

The standard explanations for moving manufacturing out of Japan are "foreign protectionism" and "Japan's growing labor shortage." Both explanations are legitimate, but they are also smoke screens. The real reason is the growing conviction among Japan's business leaders and influential bureaucrats that manufacturing work does not belong in a developed country such as Japan.

Before youngsters can go to work on the assembly line, my Japanese friends say again and again, Japan pours $100,000 in school expenses into them. And then they have to get a middle-class income, lifetime security, a pension and health care. In Bangkok or in Tijuana, youngsters require very little capital investment in their educations; and they are "middle class" if paid a 10th the wages of the U.S. or Japan. Yet their productivity after two or three years of training is as high in Tijuana or in Bangkok as it is in Nagoya or Detroit. When you figure the enormous social capital invested in them, my friends say, the return that blue-collar workers make to society in developed countries is at most 1% or 2%; in Latin America or Indonesia, it's 20 times that.

Whenever I then argue that a country is highly vulnerable without a strong manufacturing base, they respond that the supply of young people in the developing world will be so large in the next 30 years that it's absurd to worry about the "manufacturing base," the way Americans do. Indeed it's my friends' social responsibility to Japan, they say, to make sure that as few as possible of its high-investment, high-cost young people are being misused for low-yield manufacturing work.

Instead, the new Japanese strategies call for total control of what now matters. To be competitive, the argument goes, Japan requires leadership in technology, marketing and management, and firm control of what my Japanese friends are beginning to call "brain capital."

The Japanese are willing to pay large sums to gain access to knowledge—through a minority participation in a Silicon Valley computer specialist; through similar investments in U.S. and European pharmaceutical or genetics entrepreneurships; above all, through financing research in Western (mainly

U.S.) universities. The direct financial return is usually zero. But the Japanese are paying not for dividends but access to the knowledge their partners will produce, and control over it—or at least priority in using it.

Increasingly Japanese companies employ foreigners in their international operations, both as professionals and as executives. The large Japanese auto makers now all have design studios in Southern California and Westerners running their international marketing. But the use of the knowledge these foreigners produce is "proprietary" and tightly held within the Japanese management team. And while in the past some Japanese companies granted licenses on their knowledge to Western companies—e.g., on some Japanese-developed cardiac drugs—they are now revoking or not renewing them.

Every major Japanese industrial group now has its own research institute, whose main function is to bring to the group awareness of any important new knowledge—in technology, in management and organization, in marketing, in finance, in training—developed world-wide. On my last trip to Japan, a few months ago, I spoke at the 20th anniversary of one of these think tanks, that of the Mitsubishi Group. At lunch after my talk, one of the most respected elders of the Mitsubishi clan said to me: "In another 20 years the entire Mitsubishi Group will be organized around this research institute."

Everybody now knows that the Japanese can bring out a new product in half the time it takes their American competitors and in one-third the time it takes the Europeans. And everybody also knows that major U.S. companies are reorganizing their research and development work on the Japanese model, along cross-functional lines. But the Japanese are already moving to the next stage.

They are reorganizing R&D so that it simultaneously produces three new products with the effort traditionally needed to produce one. And they do this by starting out with a deadline for abandoning today's new product on the very day it is first sold. "The faster we can abandon today's new product, the stronger and the more profitable we'll be" is the new motto.

To most Western businessmen, this is madness. They believe that a product becomes more profitable the longer its product life—for then the money spent on developing it has been written off. But "writing off" to the Japanese is useful to cut taxes but otherwise self-delusion.

Money spent on developing a product or a process is not "investment" to the Japanese; it is "sunk cost." But the main reason the leading Japanese businesses are now shifting the life cycle of their products is their conviction that the only alternative is for a competitor to do so—and then the competitor will have not only the profits but the market.

My Japanese friends acknowledge that some Western companies—3M, for example—have long operated on the policy that 70% of their sales five years hence will have to come from products that do not exist today. But these companies rely on a spontaneous upswelling of entrepreneurship from within.

By deciding in advance that they will abandon a new product within a given period of time, the Japanese force themselves to go to work immediately on replacing it, and to do so on three tracks:

One track ("kaizen") is organized work on improvement of the product with specific goals and deadlines—e.g., a 10% reduction in cost within 15 months and/or a 10% improvement in reliability within the same time, and/or a 15% increase in performance characteristics—and enough in any event to result in a truly different product. The second track is "leaping"—developing a new product out of the old. The best example is still the earliest one: Sony's development of the Walkman out of the newly developed portable tape recorder. And finally there is genuine innovation.

Increasingly, the leading Japanese companies organize themselves so that all three tracks are pursued simultaneously and under the direction of the same cross-functional team. The idea is to produce three new products to replace each present product, with the same investment of time and money—with one of the three then becoming the new market leader and producing the "innovator's profit."

Finally, the leading Japanese companies are moving from Total Quality Management to Zero Defects Management. "We can't use TQM," one of the top manufacturing people at Toyota recently said. "At its very best—and no one has reached that yet—it cuts defects to 10%. But we turn out four million cars, and a 10% defect rate means that 400,000 Toyota buyers get a 100% defective car. But Zero Defects Management is now possible and actually not too difficult."

What the Japanese now practice is very much a return to Frederick Taylor's Scientific Management. Only the operators themselves, rather than the industrial engineer, take the initiative in studying the task, the work and the tools. And instead of stopwatch and camera, they use computer simulation.

What triggered this shift was an American import: the huge and hugely successful Disneyland that opened outside of Tokyo. "We all knew that it would take Disney three years to work the bugs out of this huge undertaking," a leading Japanese industrialist told me. "Instead, it ran with zero defects the day it opened. Every single operation had been engineered all the way through and simulated on the computer and trained for—and it suddenly dawned on us that we could do this too."

Since the mid-1980s, he said, American firms have been rushing to install TQM. "That'll take 10 years before it really works—at least that's what it took here. This means it will work in America around 1995. By that time we'll have Zero Defects Management and will again be 15 years ahead of you."

These new Japanese strategies may not work. Or they may work only for the Japanese. But even if they are the wrong responses, they are at least responses to reality: the emergence of the highly competitive and world-wide knowledge economy.

Questions for Discussion

1   Compare the Japanese approach to cycle time and new product development with the approach used in the United States.

2   What is the difference, according to Drucker, between TQM and zero defects?

3   Drucker suggests that the Japanese practice is very much a return to Frederick Taylor's Scientific Management. To what extent does TQM and/or zero defects reflect the principles of Taylor? What are the differences?

4   How does zero defects management relate to the accelerating growth of information workers and the predicted emergence of a worldwide knowledge economy?

5   From the reading "Is Strategy Strategic?" in this chapter, illustrate how the 19 principles of total quality management listed in Table 1 can be applied in a service firm.

STRATEGIC PLANNING AT VARIFILM

Compare each of the following TQM criteria to Varifilm and indicate whether the practice in the company is a *strength (S)* or *needs improvement (I)*. Justify your answer.

3.1 Strategic Quality and Company Performance   (S)   (I)
      Planning Process

■ An integrated strategic quality planning process (SQPP)   —   —
   exists, which incorporates a wide variety of internal and
   external information sources, including customer, competitive, environmental, supplier, co-worker, and society data.

■ The process to determine resource commitments to meet   —   —
   the plan requirements is made clear.

■ Productivity improvement is considered when developing   —   —
   operational performance improvement plans.

■ A partnership process has been developed to facilitate pro-   —   —
   cess analysis and redesign within work units.

■ Each work unit develops implementation action plans based   —   —
   on critical operating tasks presented by business leaders.

■ Each business develops a portfolio that includes an assess-   —   —
   ment of financial performance and strategies, key indicators, and the total VCIC assessment score and goal. This
   information is reviewed by the I-Team to verify alignment
   with company vision and mission, as well as to authorize
   resource plans.

■ Human resource development requirements are considered   —   —
   during the planning process.

Additional Areas for Improvement

_____

_____

_____

3.2 Quality and Performance Plans   (S)   (I)

■ Key quality factors and requirements to achieve leadership   —   —
   include product quality, on-time delivery, partnership, responsiveness to and understanding of customer requirements, commitment to the customer's industry, and new
   product development.

■ Specific short-term and longer term quality and perfor-   —   —
   mance goals, including a goal to achieve substantial improvement in key indicators, have been set.

■ Longer term plans are committed for such expenditures as   —   —
   plant modernization, research, and training.

■ Key quality factors and requirements to achieve leadership   —   —
   have been deployed to all work units.

■ Longer term goals have been set and requirements on how   —   —
   to achieve them have been addressed.

■ Projected quality and operational performance of key com-   —   —
   petitors has been addressed.

Additional Areas for Improvement

_____

_____

_____

5

HUMAN RESOURCE DEVELOPMENT AND MANAGEMENT

At the heart of Total Quality Management (TQM) is the concept of intrinsic motivation. Empowerment—involvement in decision making—is commonly viewed as essential for assuring sustained results.

Healthcare Forum

Kaizen is a Japanese concept that means *continuous improvement.* Despite the perception of many U.S. managers that kaizen is not appropriate for American firms, there is abundant evidence that the concept is entirely in keeping with American values and norms. The approach offers a substantial potential for improvement if accompanied by an appropriate human resources effort. Indeed, it is becoming a maxim of good management that *human factors* are the most important dimension in quality and productivity improvement. People really do make quality happen.

Chief executive officers of some of America's most quality-conscious companies are quick to point out that the best way to achieve organization success is by involving and empowering employees at all levels. Some even say that employee empowerment is a revolution that will turn top-down companies into democratic workplaces.

The whole employee involvement process springs from asking all your workers the simple question, "What do you think?"

Donald Peterson
Former Chairman of Ford

To get every worker to have a new idea every day is the route to winning in the '90s.

John Welch, Chairman
General Electric

The teams at Goodyear are now telling the boss how to run things. And I must say, I'm not doing a half-bad job because of it.

Stanley Gault
Chairman

Recall W. Edwards Deming's fourteen points discussed in Chapter 1. The basis of his philosophy is contained in the following principles: (1) institute training on the job, (2) break down barriers between departments to build teamwork, (3) drive fear out in the workplace, (4) eliminate quotas on the shop floor, (5) create conditions that allow employees to have pride in their workmanship and abolish annual reviews and merit ratings, and (6) institute a program of education and self-improvement.

Total quality management (TQM) has far-reaching implications for the management of human resources. It emphasizes self-control, autonomy, and creativity among employees and calls for greater active cooperation rather than just compliance.

INVOLVEMENT: A CENTRAL IDEA OF HUMAN RESOURCE UTILIZATION

■ Back in 1987 the Ames Rubber Corporation decided to adopt a TQM strategy as a major change for implementing their determination to become more competitive. The executive committee identified its best and brightest managers and asked them to reorganize around functional processes. By 1992, every employee was assigned to an *involvement* group or team.

The human resource professional magazine *HR Focus* asked over 1000 readers to rate the key issues they faced in 1993. Employee involvement was rated as one of the top three concerns by 46 percent of the respondents. Customer service followed with 39 percent and TQM with 34 percent.[1]

At the heart of TQM is the concept of intrinsic motivation-involvement in decision making. Employee involvement is a process for *empowering* members of an organization to make decisions and to solve problems appropriate to their levels in the organization. The logic is that the people closest to a problem or opportunity are in the best position to make decisions for improvement if they have ownership of the improvement process. Empowerment is equally effective in service industries, where most frequently the customer's perception of quality stands or falls based on the action of the employee in a one-on-one relationship with the customer.

At Federal Express the driver represents the company. He or she *is* the company and must deal directly with customer problems. Quality in an airline is represented not by CEOs and pilots, but by counter personnel and flight attendants.

■ One of the more successful efforts to *empower* employees was the Astronautics Groups at Martin Marietta's Denver, Colorado operation (MMAG). The group instituted a TQM process. To build employee support, the group dropped its pyramid hierarchy of management in favor of a flatter structure and a more participative management approach. High-performance work teams were organized to *empower* people closest to the work to make decisions about how the work is performed. Aside from the substantial production area savings, less tangible benefits included improved morale.

Quality improvement can result from a reduction in cost or cycle time, an increase in throughput, or a decrease in variation within the process. In the past, the focus in achieving such improvement was frequently the *system*—traditional techniques and methods of quality control. Such a focus may overlook the fact that operation of the system depends on people, and no system will work with disinterested or poorly trained employees. The solution is simple: coordinate the system and the people.

Contrast two production management styles in manufacturing industries. The "buffered" approach is characterized by large stocks of inventory and narrowly specialized workers. "Lean" systems, utilizing just-in-time (JIT) techniques, operate with small inventory stocks, multi-skilled workers, and a team approach to work organization. Lean plants are more productive because they do not have valuable resources tied up in idle inventory. Plants are smaller and more efficient, with increased communication among departments, and workers tend to have a view of the organization as a whole.

Two examples of the lean approach involving worker participation are General Motors' New United Motor Manufacturing (NUMMI) plant (a joint venture with Toyota) and Dynatech's automotive test division. In both companies, *inter-*

nalization of the JIT philosophy and worker participation have increased worker pride and involvement on the shop floor. At GM, productivity levels are 40 percent higher than typical GM plants, and the plant has the highest quality levels GM has ever known. At Dynatech, cycle time was reduced by as much as 90 percent and setup by 67 to 100 percent.

TRAINING AND DEVELOPMENT

Increased involvement means more responsibility, which in turn requires a greater level of skill. This must be achieved through training. Baldrige Award winners place a great deal of emphasis on training and support it with appropriate provision of resources. Motorola allocates about 2.5 percent of payroll costs or $120 million annually to training, 40 percent of which goes to quality training. The company calculates the training return at about $29 for each $1 invested. Additional benefits include (1) improved communications, (2) change in corporate culture, and (3) demonstration of management's commitment to quality. (Xerox has extended quality training to 30,000 supplier personnel.)

■ Since the early 1980s, Hughes Aircraft has made quality one of its chief operating philosophies. The cornerstone of the company's TQM thrust is continuous measurable improvement (CMI). Recently, the firm has championed a unique "trickle-down" training system to sustain its quality and productivity improvements. Under CMI (Cascaded Training Program), the managers responsible for achieving improvement teach the philosophy and principles of CMI leadership throughout the organization.[2]

Although the type of training depends on the needs of the particular company and may or may not extend to technical areas, the one area that should be common to all organization training programs is *problem solving*. Problem solving should be institutionalized and internalized in many, if not most, companies. This would be a prerequisite to widespread empowerment.

Training usually falls into one of three categories: (1) reinforcement of the quality message[3] and basic skill remediation, (2) job skill requirements, and (3) knowledge about principles of TQM. The latter typically covers problem-solving techniques, problem analysis, statistical process control, and quality measurement—areas that go beyond typical job skills. If groups or teams are utilized, training in the group process and group decision making is included. According to a survey conducted by the Conference Board, top companies commonly address the following topics in quality training curricula:

- Quality awareness
- Quality measurement (performance measures/quality cost benchmarking, data analysis)
- Process management and defect prevention
- Team building and quality circle training
- Focus on customers and markets
- Statistics and statistical methods
- Taguchi methods

> - Research Testing Laboratories, Inc., a TQM company providing clinical research services, encourages employees to make changes in processes in order to minimize and eliminate errors early in the work process. The goal is 100 percent customer satisfaction. To achieve this goal, employees are provided with a 25-hour training program in which they learn (1) effective interactive skills, (2) the problem-solving process, and (3) the quality improvement process.

Managerial training may take the form of item 3 above (TQM principles). In addition, programs often are directed toward sensitizing individuals to the strategic importance of quality, the cost of poor quality, and their role in influencing the quality of products and services.

The International Quality Study (IQS) was conducted among 584 companies representing four industries. The use of quality tools in the American auto industry is expected to increase 1.5- to 6-fold over the next three years. Quality training was found to have the greatest impact when coupled with other practices, such as measurement and reward systems.[4]

SELECTION

Selection is choosing from a group of potential employees (or placement from existing employees) the specific person to perform a given job. In theory, the process is simple: decide what the job involves and what abilities are necessary, and then use established selection techniques (ability tests, personality tests, interviews, assessment centers) as indicators of how the candidate will perform.

The process is not so simple, however, when TQM enters the picture. The job requirements for a typist, a machinist, or even a manager can be determined by job analysis, and the qualifications of a candidate can be compared to these requirements. When a company commits to TQM, an entirely new dimension is introduced. The skills and abilities required for a specific job can usually easily be identified and then matched with an individual. People well suited for operating in a quality climate may require additional characteristics, such as attitude, values, personality type, analytical ability.

Persons working in a quality environment need sharp problem-solving ability in order to perform the quantitative work demanded by statistical process control, Pareto analysis, etc. Because of the emphasis on teams and group process, personnel must function well in group settings. Motorola shows applicants video tapes of problem-solving groups in action and asks them how they would respond to a particular quality issue. Presumably this technique encourages *self-selection*.

What is perhaps different in the selection process in a TQM environment is the emphasis on a *quality-oriented organization culture* as the desired outcome of the selection process.[5]

PERFORMANCE APPRAISAL

The purpose of performance appraisal is to serve as a diagnostic tool and review process for development of the individual, team, and organization. Appraisals are used to determine reward levels, validate tests, aid career development, improve communication, and facilitate understanding of job duties.[6]

Deming cites *traditional* employee evaluation systems as one of seven deadly diseases confronting U.S. industry. He states that *individual* performance evaluations encourage short-term goals rather than long-term planning. They undermine teamwork and encourage competition among people for the same rewards. Moreover, the overwhelming cause of non-quality is not the employee but the system; by focusing on individuals, attention is diverted from the root cause of poor quality: the system.

Many TQM proponents, like Deming, argue that traditional performance appraisal methods are attempts by management to pin the blame for poor organization performance on lower level employees, rather than focusing attention on the system, for which upper management is primarily responsible.

Should individual performance appraisal be eliminated, as Deming suggests?[7] This is unlikely in view of the historical and widespread use of this human resource management tool. What, then, can be done to relate individual and group performance to a total quality strategy?

Performance appraisals are most effective when they focus on the objectives of the company and therefore of the individual or group. Because the eventual outcome of all work is quality and customer satisfaction, it follows that appraisal should somehow relate to this outcome—to the objectives of the company, the group, and the individual. In other words, a performance appraisal system should be aligned with the principle of shared responsibility for quality. This can be accomplished by focusing on development of the skills and abilities necessary to perform well and, as such, directly support collective responsibility.

■ In a model used by the Hay Group (a consulting organization), individuals are evaluated for base pay on such variables as ability to communicate, customer focus, and ability to work as a team. Managers are rated on employee development, group productivity, and leadership. Variable pay for both is based on what is accomplished. Because customer focus is a critical part of any TQM effort, a three-category rating system that involves (1) not meeting customer expectations, (2) meeting them, and (3) far exceeding them is easy to implement.[8]

Answering Deming and the other critics is not easy. The integration of total quality and performance appraisal is necessary. One should reinforce the other. One approach might be to modify existing systems in accordance with the following principles:

■ Customer expectations, not the job description, generate the individual's job expectation.

■ Results expectations meet different criteria than management-by-objectives statements.

■ Performance expectations include behavioral skills that make the real difference in achieving quality performance and total customer satisfaction.

■ The rating scale reflects actual performance, not a "grading curve."

■ Employees are active participants in the process, not merely "drawn in."

Regardless of which specific system is adopted, there seems to be little question that performance management practices need to be in line with and supportive of TQM.

COMPENSATION SYSTEMS

This may be one of the most elusive and controversial of all systems that support TQM. Historically, compensation systems have been based on (1) pay for performance or (2) pay for responsibility (a job description). Each of these is based on individual performance, which creates a competitive atmosphere among employees. In contrast, the TQM philosophy emphasizes flexibility, lateral communication, group effectiveness, and responsibility for an entire process that has the ultimate outcome of customer satisfaction. No wonder research and writing have offered little in the way of new approaches that are more in tune with the needs of TQM.

■ Shawnee Mission (Kansas) Medical Center attempted to set up an infrastructure to push TQM ideals throughout the organization. In 1992 the center operationalized its new evaluation system based on personal development, education, and teamwork. Everyone receives the same raise.

Both training and performance appraisal are desirable components of a TQM implementation strategy, but compensation is an equally necessary dimension. Employees may perceive the system as a reflection of the company's commitment to quality.

Individual or Team Compensation?

A company's infrastructure, specifically its reward and compensation systems, provides an accurate picture of its strategic goals. If compensation criteria are focused exclusively on individual performance, a company will find that initiatives promoting teamwork may fail. A TQM vision and the principles supporting it are unlikely to take hold unless the values on which they are based are built into the underlying structure.

■ Target Stores is among the growing number of companies in the retail industry that are going beyond logistics-specific performance measures and are tying pay into the effectiveness of TQM programs. Throughout the logistics field, pay for performance and pay for quality appear to becoming more entrenched.

There is no lack of compensation plans in U.S. industry. Gain sharing, profit sharing, and stock ownership are among the systems designed to create a financial incentive for employees to be involved in performance improvements. Gain sharing is one of the most rapidly growing compensation and involvement systems in U.S. industry. It is a system of management in which an organization seeks higher levels of performance through the involvement and participation of its people. Employees share financially in the gain when performance improves. The approach is a team effort in which employees are eligible for bonuses at regular intervals on an operational basis. Gain sharing reinforces TQM, partially because it contains common components, such as involvement and commitment.[9]

The jury is still out on the effectiveness of these plans, but evidence suggests that effectiveness is a function of strong communication programs and widespread employee involvement.

Summary

Many reasons have been offered as the cause of poor performance in organizations: (1) system failure; (2) misunderstanding of job expectations; (3) lack of awareness about performance; (4) lack of time, tools, or resources to succeed; (5) lack of necessary knowledge or skills; (6) lack of appropriate consequences for performance; and (7) bad fit for the job. Although a compensation system supportive of TQM is not the only remedy, combined with other human resource management systems it will go a long way toward improvement of performance and development among individuals, groups, and the organization.

TOTAL QUALITY ORIENTED
HUMAN RESOURCE MANAGEMENT

Human resource executives are faced with both a challenge and an opportunity. They are not generally perceived with the same regard as line managers. Philip Crosby describes the human resource department as behind the times and the human resource executive as his or her own worst enemy. On the other hand, the department can play a critical role in the implementation of a holistic quality environment in support of a strategic initiative. To accomplish this role, the function should not only be designed to support TQM throughout the organization, but should make sure that good quality management practices are followed within the processes of the function itself. This means continuous improvement as a way of department life. Bowen and Lawler suggest putting the following principles of TQM to work *within* the human resource department:[10]

1. Quality work the first time
2. Focus on the customer
3. Strategic holistic approach to improvement
4. Continuous improvement as a way of life
5. Mutual respect and teamwork

It is evident that some modification of traditional human resource management practices is required if the function is to support the TQM program throughout the company. Planning is the first step. The 1993 Baldrige Award criteria describe human resource planning:[11]

Human resource plans might include the following: mechanisms for promoting cooperation such as internal customer/supplier techniques or other internal partnerships; initiatives to promote labor–management cooperation, such as partnerships with unions; creation and/or modification of recognition systems; mechanisms for increasing or broadening employee responsibilities; creating opportunities for employees to learn and use skills that go beyond current job assignments through redesign of processes; creation of high performance work teams; and education and training initiatives. Plans might also include forming partnerships with educational institutions to develop employees or to help ensure the future supply of well-prepared employees.

QUESTIONS FOR DISCUSSION

5-1   Would a quality improvement program based on process control be more appropriate for employee involvement than a system based on traditional production methods? If so, explain why.

5-2   What effect does employee involvement have on motivation? Explain the effect in terms of motivational theory.

5-3   Contrast the benefits of the different types of small groups or teams. Which would be more appropriate for achieving integration across organizational functions or departments?

5-4   A Deming principle advises to "create conditions that allow employees to have pride in their workmanship." What are these conditions and how can they be implemented?

5-5   Assume that a company has just committed to change from a traditional style of management to one based on TQM. What topics would you include for

- Shop floor employees
- Front-line supervisors
- Middle-level managers

5-6   Describe how training in problem solving would improve

- Process control
- Employee motivation

ENDNOTES

1. *HR Focus,* Jan. 1993, pp. 1, 4.
2. Judy Rice, "Cascaded Training at Hughes Aircraft Helps Ensure Continuous Measurable Improvement," *National Productivity Review,* Winter 1992/1993, pp. 111–116.
3. Bernie Knill, "The Nitty-Gritty of Quality Manufacturing," *Materials Handling Engineering,* July 1992, pp. 40–42. In a Conference Board survey, training is first used to reinforce the quality message and then to build skills. Another finding of the survey is that leaders link TQM to performance review and compensation.
4. Trace E. Benson, "When Less Is More," *Industry Week,* Sep. 7, 1992, pp. 68–77.
5. David E. Bowen and Edward E. Lawler III, "Total Quality-Oriented Human Resource Management," *Organization Dynamics,* Spring 1992, pp. 29–41.
6. David E. Bowen and Edward E. Lawler III, "Total Quality-Oriented Human Resource Management," *Organization Dynamics,* Spring 1992, p. 36.
7. Some recent articles that treat performance appraisal in a TQM context include Kathleen A. Guinn, "Successfully Integrating Total Quality Management and Performance Appraisal," *Human Resource Professional,* Spring 1992, pp. 19–25; Mike Deblieux, "Performance Reviews Support the Quest for Quality," *HR Focus,* Nov. 1991, pp. 3–4; Jean B. Ferketish and John W. Hayden, "HRD & Quality: The Chicken or the Egg?" Jan. 1992, pp. 38–42.
8. Linda Thornburg, "Pay for Performance: What You Should Know (Part 1)," *HR Magazine,* June 1992, pp. 58–61.
9. Robert L. Masternak, "Gainsharing at B. F. Goodrich: Succeeding Together Achieves Rewards," *Tapping the Network Journal,* Fall/Winter 1991, pp. 13–16.
10. David Bowen and Edward Lawler, "Total Quality-Oriented Human Resources Management," *Organizational Dynamics,* Spring 1992, p. 29.
11. *Malcolm Baldrige National Quality Award. 1993 Award Criteria,* Gaithersburg, Md.: U.S. Department of Commerce, National Institute of Standards and Technology, 1993, p. 21.

READING

The author describes the bridge between the commitment to TQM and the reasons why the bridge can fail to be completed and the return on investment achieved. Using TQM/SPC as an example, failure patterns are examined and a model for successful training is developed.

THE TRAINING CHALLENGE

For over a decade, companies in the U.S. have undertaken the challenge of implementing a total quality management/statistical process control (TQM/SPC) initiative. And a recent study of over 325 companies by the Quality Alert Institute has shown what historically has been assumed: The quality training given to the work force is a critical variable in the success or failure of TQM/SPC programs. The report also revealed that many companies make a major investment in quality training, with only between a quarter to a third of them able to significantly reduce the cost of nonconformance.

What appears to be happening in many companies is that an initial commitment is made to quality and TQM/SPC training, but the bridge between the classroom and the functional area is never completed and return on investment never happens. As a result, anticipated excitement, enthusiasm and payoff turn into failure, disillusionment and resentment.

Failure Patterns

Unfortunately, what the quality training investment has produced in some instances is:

■ *The fizzle effect.* Quality enthusiasm is generated and training is provided, but the workers are not given the opportunity to use the tools and techniques

---

Reprinted by permission of *Quality*, August 1990.

acquired in training. Workers perceive TQM/SPC as a management program that is visible until it's replaced by another that is more in vogue. As many workers have said, "There's the training…and then we go back to work." The result: TQM/SPC dies a slow, predictable death.

■ The TQM/SPC *charade.* Training in the tools and techniques of TQM/SPC is provided for the workers, but management does not expose itself to the same training for understanding. Or TQM/SPC training is given to workers by a trained TQM/SPC instructor who provides no insight, understanding or enthusiasm for those who have the most to gain from its implementation.

The end product of both these scenarios is the appearance of TQM/SPC. There are control charts in place, but most of the workers fail to internalize the value of TQM/SPC, ignoring the process insights provided by control charts and, in some cases, taking a pro forma approach to data collection, giving management the numbers it wants. Because the quality training effort does not produce worker understanding of the TQM/SPC philosophy and tools, the following occurs:

■ Team membership is created through conscription vs. volunteers.

■ Teams meet regularly, but, in some cases, the project charter is ill-defined or too broad for team success.

■ Only one or two team members dominate most of the work.

■ Workers see team participation as a *pro forma* responsibility rather than an opportunity for improvement.

Although quality training serves as the foundation for all quality improvement, if training strategies, methods and materials are not congruent with the target audience, certain negative outcomes are inevitable:

■ Loss of training dollars.

■ Work force resentment.

■ Lost quality improvement opportunities and competitive advantage.

■ Investment in SPC data collection with no discernible return on investment.

■ Disinterested and disillusioned workers.

Who Should Be Trained

Regardless of whose teachings you look to—Deming, Juran, Crosby or others—there is a common agreement: For a company to derive the benefits of the tools of TQM and SPC, everyone must be trained. Figure 1 offers a

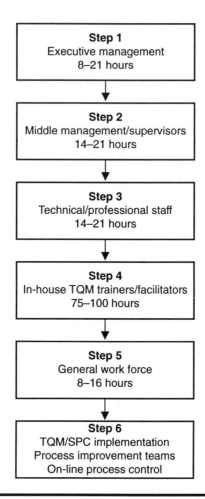

Figure 1   Total Quality Management/Statistical Process Control Training

TQM/SPC training plan that has proved successful for both small and large companies and has delivered significant dollar return on investment.

In Step 1, executive management is given an orientation to the TQM philosophy, including in-depth exploration of what TQM is, the benefits of TQM implementation, barriers to success, and use of TQM/SPC tools. Critical components of this training are executive management's role and responsibilities, required long-term investment, strategic and operational planning, and the difference between management's commitment to or endorsement of TQM.

In Step 2, middle level manager/supervisors are given training experience similar to that of step 1, but there is less emphasis on strategic planning and the macromanagement of the TQM process. More time is spent on the tools and techniques of TQM/SPC, with specific attention given to environmental issues and behavioral actions that will facilitate TQM/SPC.

In Step 3, technical/professional staffs are given training on problem-solving skills along with the quantitative tools and techniques—Pareto charts, frequency distributions, histograms, sampling plans, and control chart construction and interpretation. This is supported by a comprehensive overview of the TQM philosophy.

In Step 4, training is given to those individuals who will serve as the in-house TQM/SPC facilitators and trainers. This group will then:

- Provide TQM/SPC training to workers before implementation.
- Serve as facilitators of process improvement teams to ensure the teams function effectively and use the TQM/SPC tools and techniques properly.
- Serve as a continuing resource for departments and individuals who are using TQM/SPC.
- Provide refresher TQM/SPC training to individuals and teams.
- Train new employees.

Training for trainers includes a solid grounding in the TQM philosophy, the use of all SPC tools, problem solving, group leadership and communication skills.

Where to Train

There are distinct advantages and disadvantages to both on-site and off-site training. But the factors of both must be carefully weighed when making the decision to train on- or off-site. On-site training provides:

- Reduced training costs.
- Elimination of lost travel time.
- Flexible training schedules.
- Less disruption to daily operations.

Off-site training provides:

- A message to workers that quality is important.
- Fewer distractions.
- Fewer interruptions.
- An educational setting matched to the size and composition of the class.

How Much, How Fast?

There are two schools of thought about the amount of training and how fast it should be presented. Those concerned with overloading trainees prefer to spread training out. The most frequently used model is two to four hours of training a week until the sequence is completed. Production requirements and logistics also sometimes create the need to take this approach.

Although a strong trainer and well-thought-out training materials can make this approach work, consolidation of the training experience has proved more desirable. By providing training on consecutive or alternate days, students get an opportunity to let enthusiasm build gradually and continuously as the training proceeds; spend more time learning new material rather than review previously covered material; experience teaching continuity and timely sequencing of workshops and demonstrations; and have the opportunity to internalize the "big picture" regarding quality improvement, now viewing TQM/SPC as a set of separate, independent tools.

To address material overload and operation issues, training in daily three to four hour sessions has proved fruitful.

Materials and Content

Complex issues affect quality training and the selection and development of training materials. But ultimately, the choices depend mostly on course content, instructional design and training aids. Figure 2 presents a systems approach to the TQM/SPC course development challenge. Ensuring TQM/SPC training success depends on specific strategies:

- **Develop training objectives first.** Only by first coming to grips with what the trainees need to come away with can a successful training experience be provided. The objectives should be clear, performance-oriented and quantitatively measurable. Good objectives are not limited to mastery of the technical content but should be more action-oriented and geared to the work place. The true goal of a good quality training program is not to learn control chart formulas but to equip employees with tools that they will comfortably use to ferret out and attack process improvement opportunities.

- **Provide a training manual to match course objectives.** When it comes to quality training manuals, bigger isn't necessarily better. Large manuals, particularly those with highly technical concepts and terms, can certainly send a message that the quality improvement is important. But when used in the classroom, they can be intimidating and overwhelming. Many trainers have learned that the larger the manual and the more sophisticated the

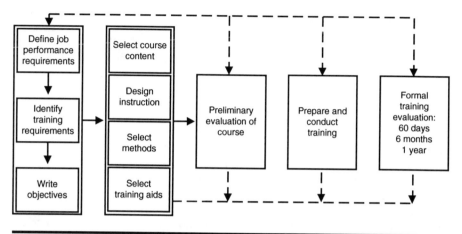

Figure 2   A Systems Approach to TQM/SPC Training

language, the less often it is used after training. Good TQM/SPC training manuals minimize the use of technical jargon and sophisticated language and offer a wealth of customized examples that enable the trainee to directly link the TQM/SPC tools with his/her own job responsibilities.

■ **Quality training content should include technical and behavioral components.** This is especially true for the training given managers and supervisors. The traditional technical component of quality training and implementation includes the well-accepted menu of TQM concepts, principles and techniques.

Equally important is the behavioral component of TQM implementation, dealing with the skills and techniques needed by managers and supervisors to get the work force to buy in to the TQM concept and participate in continuous quality improvement. What many experienced quality coordinators acknowledge is that many quality training programs either provide only a superficial treatment of this issue or avoid it all together.

Training/Evaluation

Paper-and-pencil evaluation forms are not enough. These measure more the charisma of the instructor than the skills, principles and applications acquired by trainees. The barometer of success for the training effort is whether the employees are using the TQM tools and techniques in their process improvement teams and as they execute their job responsibilities. Formal follow-up evaluation should be developed and executed at about 60 days, six months and a year after training.

CASE

EMPLOYEE INVOLVEMENT AT
BAY CITY MACHINE TOOL COMPANY

Bay City Machine Tool Company is a manufacturer of machine tools and chuck jaws for the manufacturing industry. Although 80 percent of production goes to customers in the aerospace and automobile industry, the company is trying to expand its product line and customer base to a variety of other applications.

The company was founded in 1964 in Bay City, Michigan. Bob Parsons, founder and CEO, moved the home office to Fort Lauderdale, Florida in 1979 in order to "achieve a lifestyle of sun and surf." Parsons was also a boating enthusiast. The main plant was still located in Bay City, with additional plants in Fort Lauderdale and San Juan, Puerto Rico. Only the main plant was unionized.

Parsons was concerned about the recent changes in the machine tool industry. His product line had historically been comprised of high-speed steel drills which were now approaching commodity status. New materials, technologies, and methods were reducing the demand for the company's bread-and-butter products. Titanium nitride coatings and carbide-tipped tools had a longer wear life and were priced higher. Lasers were increasingly being used as a cutting medium, and a shift from fastening to bonding of metal parts eliminated the need for drills. Thus, the company was faced with the dual problems of updating a product line and modernizing the manufacturing equipment and methods to meet the increased demand for high-quality specialty tools.

During the late 1980s and early 1990s, the machine tool industry was hit particularly hard by a combination of foreign competition, the worldwide recession, and the strength of the dollar. Because demand had fallen off considerably, Bay City was required to lay off (downsize) about 25 percent of its work force. It was during this time that the company attempted a changeover to a new production line that demanded tighter specifications and machine tolerance and higher quality product. New equipment was installed and a few new salespersons were hired.

Not long after the production changeover in the Bay City plant, many of the old-line customers, who themselves had to make the change, began to complain about quality, price, missed delivery dates and similar related problems not previously encountered. Returns were increasing and accounts receivable began to grow at a rate twice the rate of sales growth. No problems were encountered at the San Juan plant because that operation was still producing the commodity drills as they had been doing since the plant opened in 1981.

The situation began to get out of hand in late 1993, when a large order at the Michigan plant was canceled. Bob Parsons decided to go to Bay City to see what could be done to correct this incident and to figure out how to improve quality and production levels. He left the Fort Lauderdale operation in the hands of his son, Bob Jr.

Parsons had previously attended a three-day TQM seminar and came away with a conviction that the company's problems could only be solved by getting production employees more involved in problem solving at the shop floor level. He did not know exactly how to implement such an approach, but he knew that something had to be done quickly and effectively. He was aware that a failure to achieve some success and acceptance would doom this and subsequent efforts. On the other hand, he did not trust the shop floor supervisors to cooperate because of their perception that their authority might be circumvented. For this reason, he decided to put the manager of human resources in charge of the employee involvement effort.

Because a long-standing adversarial relationship existed between the union and the Human Resources Department, it was decided that the union should not be involved during the effort. Parsons did not want the union to stop it before it began.

Shortly after his arrival at Bay City, Parsons became convinced that part of the problem could be traced to the new machines that were necessary for the revised production process. His conviction was based on what he had been told by several shop floor supervisors. The machine manufacturer in turn suggested that the workers had not been adequately trained and offered to conduct training for supervisors, who would then train their workers. No concessions or reductions in production schedules were made however.

Based on what he learned during his visit and what he already knew, Parsons summarized the situation:

- According to an attitude survey conducted by the Human Resources Department, worker satisfaction had been declining and had reached an all-time low.
- The supervisors were generally of the opinion that many of the problems were the fault of the workers who did not care about quality. All supervisors had previously been shop floor workers.

■ The focus had historically been on getting out the production, and this remained the focus under the new production system. Compensation was tied to production levels. It was assumed that any quality problems would be solved by the Quality Control Department.

■ Outside industrial engineers had developed specific and detailed work procedures and job standards for each job on the shop floor. Work was organized around a traditional assembly line.

■ The chain of command went from the vice president of manufacturing (in Fort Lauderdale), to the plant manager, to the superintendent of production, to department managers, to shift supervisors, and finally to workers.

Questions for Discussion

1   What advice would you give to Bob Parsons? What concerns do you have? For example,

   ■   Is he moving too fast?

   ■   Is the shop floor the place to start?

   ■   Should the union be excluded?

   ■   Should a line manager lead the effort rather than Human Resources?

   ■   What is the culture of the organization? Does it need to be changed? Would work teams be appropriate? If so, what kind?

   ■   How can the supervisors' perception of workers be changed? Is training needed? If so, what kind and at what stage?

2   What plan of action do you recommend?

HUMAN RESOURCES AT VARIFILM

Compare each of the following TQM criteria to Varifilm and indicate whether the practice in the company is a *strength (S)* or *needs improvement (I)*. Justify your answer.

EMPLOYEE INVOLVEMENT

4.1 Human Resource Development and Management (S)   (I)

■ Plans have been established that address education and training, empowerment, recognition, and recruitment. —   —

■ Employee satisfaction factors are used to reduce adverse human resource indicators. —   —

■ Key performance indicators are used for human resource processes and practices. —   —

■ Key diversity goals have been established for achieving a workplace diversity balance. —   —

■ Reductions in cycle time have been achieved in bonus delivery, flexible benefits, travel expense reimbursement, and benefits. —   —

■ Third-party co-worker climate surveys that monitor key indicators have been administered and appropriate improvement actions identified. —   —

■ Short-term plans have been distinguished from longer term plans. —   —

4.2 Employee Involvement

■ A wide variety of teams are used to promote ongoing co-worker contributions. —   —

■ Involvement goals are established for all employees, based on the most important requirements. —   —

	(S)	(I)

- Evidence is maintained to show how involvement is linked to key quality and operational performance improvement results. — —

- All categories of employees are linked to empowerment through the business objectives. — —

- Co-worker entrepreneurship is encouraged by cash grants or other means. — —

- Co-worker involvement is evaluated by such means as self-managed team participation, co-worker climate survey, and participation in a suggestion system. — —

Additional Areas for Improvement

_____

_____

_____

HUMAN RESOURCES DEVELOPMENT AND MANAGEMENT

4.3 Employee Education and Training

- Adequate training for both new plant workers and non-plant workers should include orientation about policy, principles and values, self-managed team training, and safety. Quality training comprises a significant portion of the overall training. — —

- Training and course effectiveness are evaluated and improved through the use of skill testing and participant feedback. — —

- Trend data regarding the effectiveness of training and key indicators of effectiveness are maintained. — —

- Training is regularly delivered and reinforced. — —

- Acceptable methods of determining the "soft skill" training needs for management are used. — —

	(S)	(I)
4.4 Employee Performance and Recognition		

- Key indicators are used to evaluate and improve recognition approaches.   —   —
- The objectivity of any quality award process is ensured.   —   —
- A wide and appropriate variety of reward and recognition methods are used for both teams and individuals.   —   —
- A worker climate survey or other means is used to obtain feedback on how workers rate the recognition program.   —   —
- Recognition processes ensure that quality is reinforced relative to short-term financial considerations.   —   —

4.5 Employee Well-Being and Satisfaction

- Periodic audits are conducted to determine employee well-being and satisfaction. Other methods are used as well.   —   —
- Improvement goals are set for important factors.   —   —
- Key indicators are used and tracked.   —   —

Additional Areas for Improvement

_____

_____

_____

6

MANAGEMENT OF PROCESS QUALITY

A Deming-style "total quality management" approach to improving service quality is rooted in the unglamorous and never fashionable discipline of statistics. Using Mr. Deming's statistical approach to total quality management, we have reduced service expenses 35% over the past 12 months while improving service quality.

President
Savin Copiers

The need for top management to display leadership in setting the climate and culture for total quality management was outlined in Chapter 2. Climate and culture, however, are not enough. It is unlikely that exhortations and slogans will be effective unless accompanied by action planning and implementation. A statement such as "We Are the Quality Company" convinces no one—not the employees and not the customers. The company should be organized for quality assurance in the context of modern quality management.

Assume that the criteria of the Baldrige Award fairly represent what is generally accepted as the national standard for management of process quality:

■ The *Management of Process Quality* category examines systematic processes the company uses to pursue ever-higher quality and company operational performance. The key elements of process management are examined, including research and development, design, management of process quality for all work units and suppliers, systematic quality improvement, and quality assessment.

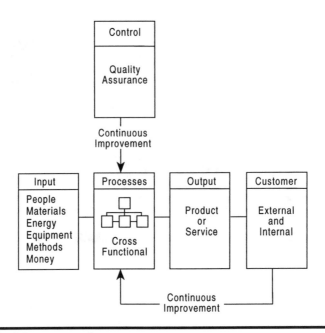

Figure 6-1   Management System

It is apparent that this definition is directly related to how well the *processes* are managed—*all* of the processes in the organization that contribute directly or indirectly to quality as the customer defines it. The concept is illustrated in Figure 6-1. Note that the control component (quality assurance) has moved from measuring output (the traditional control system) to controlling the *continuous improvement of the process.*

The traditional approach to quality control was inspection of the final product, and this approach is still practiced by many firms. This chapter will introduce methods and techniques that are significantly more advanced and more effective than the practice of "final inspection," which has been used for so long. Although the concepts in this chapter are not the last word in modern total quality management (TQM), they represent substantial potential for improving quality, cost, and productivity in almost any company.

A BRIEF HISTORY OF QUALITY CONTROL

Concern for product quality and process control is nothing new. Historians have traced the concept as far back as 3000 B.C. in Babylonia. Among the references to quality from the Code of Hammurabi, ruler of Babylonia, is the following excerpt: "The mason who builds a house which falls down and kills the inmate shall be put to death." This law reflects a concern for quality in antiquity.[1] Process control is a concept that may have begun with the pyramids of Egypt, when a system of standards for quarrying and dressing of stone was designed. One has only to examine the pyramids at Cheops to appreciate this remarkable achievement. Later, Greek architecture would surpass Egyptian architecture in the area of military applications. Centuries later, the shipbuilding operations in Venice introduced rudimentary production control and standardization.

Following the Industrial Revolution and the resulting factory system, quality and process control began to take on some of the characteristics that we know today. Specialization of labor in the factory demanded it. Interchangeability of parts was introduced by Eli Whitney when he manufactured 15,000 muskets for the federal government. This event was representative of the emerging era of mass production, when inspection by a skilled craftsman at a workbench was replaced by the specialized function of inspection conducted by individuals not directly involved in the production process.

Specialization of labor and quality assurance took a giant step forward in 1911 with the publication of Frederick W. Taylor's book *Principles of Scientific Management*.[2] This pioneering work had a profound effect on management thought and practice. Taylor's philosophy was one of extreme functional specialization and he suggested eight functional bosses for the shop floor, one of whom was assigned the task of inspection:

> The inspector is responsible for the quality of the work, and both the workmen and the speed bosses [who see that the proper cutting tools are used, that the work is properly driven, and that cuts are started in the right part of the piece] must see that the work is finished to suit him. This man can, of course, do his work best if he is a master of the art of finishing work both well and quickly.[3]

Taylor later conceded that extreme functional specialization has its disadvantages, but his notion of process analysis and quality control by inspection of the final product still lives on in many firms today. Statistical quality control (SQC), the forerunner of today's TQM or total quality control, had its beginnings in the mid-1920s at the Western Electric plant of the Bell System. Walter Shewhart, a Bell Laboratories physicist, designed the original version of SQC for the zero defects mass production of complex telephone exchanges and telephone sets. In 1931 Shewhart published his landmark book *Economic Control of Quality of Manufactured Product*.[4] This book provided a precise and measurable definition of quality control and developed statistical techniques for evaluating production and improving quality. During World War II, W. Edwards Deming and Joseph Juran, both former members of Shewhart's group, separately developed the versions used today.

It is generally accepted today that the Japanese owe their product leadership partly to adopting the precepts of Deming and Juran. According to Peter Drucker, U.S. industry ignored their contributions for 40 years and is only now converting to SQC.[5]

■   The Willimatic Division of Rogers Corporation, an IBM supplier, uses just-in-time techniques along with X-bar and R charts for key product attributes to achieve statistical process control. Rework is reduced by 40 percent, scrap by 50 percent, and productivity is increased by 14 percent.[6]

PRODUCT INSPECTION VS. PROCESS CONTROL

Structure follows strategy.

Nothing happens until a sale is made.

If you can't measure it, you can't manage it.

These statements are typical of the popular catchphrases adopted by particular functions (e.g., planning, sales, accounting) within the business. The popularity of the expression usually means that there is a measure of truth behind it. Truisms in the field of quality management include "don't inspect the product, inspect the process" and "you can't inspect it in, you've got to build it in."

There is sound thinking behind these two statements. In the previous discussion of the control process, the point was made that controlling the output of the system *after the fact* was historical action and nothing could be done to correct the variation after it had already occurred. This is feedback control. The same is true of inspecting the product. The variation or the defect has already occurred. What is needed is a feedforward system that will prevent defects and variations. Better yet is a system that will improve the process. This is the idea behind process control (Figure 6-1).

What is the process? Does it begin with material inspection at the receiving dock and end with final inspection, or does it begin with design and end with delivery to the customer? Does it begin with market research and end with after-sale service? If we take the broader view, the process might begin with the concept of the product idea and extend through the life cycle of the product to ultimate maturity and phase out. This definition matches the concept of TQM.

It is clear that in the philosophy of TQM, most (if not all) business functions and activities (i.e., processes) are interrelated and none stand alone—not purchasing, engineering, shipping, order processing, or manufacturing. Key business objectives and organization success are dependent on cross-functional processes. Moreover, these processes must change as environments change. The conclusion emerges that true process optimization requires the application of tools and methods in all activities, not just manufacturing.

Historically, there have been two major barriers to effective process control. The first has been the tendency to focus on volume of output rather than quality of output. Volume of production has been the major objective in the mistaken notion that more units of output means lower unit cost. Another barrier is the quality control system that measures products or service against a set of internal conformance specifications that may or may not relate to customer expectations. The result in many cases has been inferior quality products that are reworked or scrapped or, worse, products that customers *did not buy*. As will be discussed in Chapter 11, the cost of poor quality can amount to 25 to 30 percent of sales revenues. The profit potential in quality improvement is greater than simply improved production of inferior quality.

■ Bytex Corporation manufactures electronic matrix switches for Citicorp, MasterCard, American Express, and others. The company has focused on understanding the process, concentrating on eliminating non-value-added transactions. Cycle time is down by 60 percent, inventory down by 43 percent, final assembly time down by 52 percent, and floor space down by 30 percent. The resulting product is superb.[7]

MOVING FROM INSPECTION TO PROCESS CONTROL

Process control may still require measurement that is determined by inspection, but the activity of inspection is now transformed into a diagnostic role. The objective is not merely to discover defects, but rather to identify and remove the cause(s) of defects or variations. Process control now becomes problem solving for *continuous improvement*. Moving from inspection to process control takes place in steps or phases:

Step	Action
1	Process characterization Definition of process requirements and identification of key variables
2	Develop standards and measures of output Involve work force
3	Monitor compliance to standards and review for better control Identify any additional variables that affect quality
4	Identify and remove cause(s) of defects or variations (this requires a step-by-step documentation of the process and process control charting)
5	Achievement of process control with improved stability and reduced variation

STATISTICAL QUALITY CONTROL

This is the oldest and most widely known of the several process control methods. It involves the use of statistical techniques, such as control charts, to analyze a work process or its outputs. The data can be used to identify variations and to take appropriate actions in order to achieve and maintain a state of statistical control (predetermined upper and lower limits) and to improve the capability of the process. It is the best-known innovation among Deming's ideas.

Rigorously applied, SQC can virtually eliminate the production of defective parts.[8] By identifying the quality that can be expected from a given production process, control can be built into the process itself. Moreover, the method can spot the causes of variations—incoming materials, machine calibration, temperature of soldering iron, or whatever.

Despite the maturity of the method and its proven benefit, many firms do not take full advantage of it. One survey found that 49 percent of responding electronic manufacturers reported using SQC techniques, but 75 percent of them also continued to use traditional 100 percent inspection. This is in an industry where quality in the manufacturing process is essential.

■ At Motorola, SQC has been integrated into the corporate culture and is being applied in all areas of the plant. Steps to place a process under statistical control include (1) characterizing the process, (2) controlling it, and (3) adjusting the process when non-random deviations are observed. Six sigma is the goal.

The term *statistical process control* can be misleading because it is so frequently confined to manufacturing processes, whereas the methods can be useful for improving results in other non-manufacturing areas such as sales and staff activities. Moreover, the methods can be used in many of the activities and functions of service industries. It is also worth noting that the only universal technique for SQC is logical reasoning applied to the improvement of a process. Thus it is a systematic way of problem solving.

A *process* is a set of causes and conditions and a set of steps comprising an activity that transforms inputs into outputs. Consider the number of processes involved in the airline industry: the process of taking and confirming a reservation, of baggage handling, of loading passengers, of meal service, etc. The process is any set of people, equipment, procedures, and conditions that work together to produce a result—an output.

The process is expected to add value to the inputs in order to produce an output. The ratio of output to input is called productivity and the objectives are to (1) increase the ratio of output to input and (2) reduce the variation in the output of the process. If the variation is too small or insignificant to have any effect on the usefulness of the product or service, the output is said to be within tolerance. Should the output fall outside the desired tolerance, the process can be improved and returned to tolerance by defining the cause of the change (the problem) and taking action to make sure that the cause does not recur.

BASIC APPROACH TO
STATISTICAL QUALITY CONTROL[9]

SQC and its companion *statistical process control* (SPC) were developed in the United States in the 1930s and 1940s by W. A. Shewhart, W. E. Deming, J. M. Juran, and others. These techniques (some call them philosophies) have been used for decades by some American firms and many Japanese companies. Despite the proven effectiveness of the techniques, many U.S. firms are reluctant to use them.[10]

The approach is designed to identify underlying cause of problems which cause process variations that are outside predetermined tolerances and to implement controls to fix the problem. The basic approach contains the following steps:

1. Awareness that a problem exists.
2. Determine the specific problem to be solved.
3. Diagnose the causes of the problem.
4. Determine and implement remedies to solve the problem.
5. Implement controls to hold the gains achieved by solving the problem.

TOOLS FOR STATISTICAL QUALITY CONTROL

Process improvement depends to a large extent on the gathering and analysis of data which are abundant in any organization that is involved in process problems. The basic techniques are (1) data collection, (2) data display, and (3) problem analysis.

■ To illustrate the use of these SQC tools, consider the case of the National Machine Tool Company, a manufacturer of chuck jaws for the metals working industry. The company is experiencing rejects and reworked jobs due to unknown causes. A chuck jaw is made from metal bar stock (grinding, drilling, cutting, etc.) and is a holding device used on a machine for metal turning and indexing.

Weeks

Department	No. 1	No. 2	No. 3	No. 4	No. 5	No. 6	No. 7	No. 8	TOTAL
11		I		II		I			4
66	I		I		II		II	I	7
55	III	I	II	II	I	ЖI	II	IIII	20
22	I	II		III	II		I	I	10
Other			I		I		II		4

Figure 6-2   Check Sheet of Reworked Jobs

Data Collection

A **check sheet** is an aid used in assembling and compiling data concerning a problem. It is used to collect data on a process in order to determine whether any unusual or unwanted elements are present. The functions of a check sheet are

■ Production process distribution checks
■ Defective item checks
■ Defect location checks
■ Defect cause checks
■ Checkup confirmation checks

■ At the National Machine Tool Company (discussed earlier), a team (quality circle) identified the problem as "loss of time due to reworked jobs" and agreed that in order to determine the cause(s) of the problems it would be necessary to find out which department(s) were experiencing excessive rework. As a result, data were collected and recorded on the check sheet shown in Figure 6-2. It was evident from this check sheet that department number 55 has excessive rework.

Data Display

After data are collected, they can be converted into a variety of forms for *display* and *analysis*. The most common forms are shown in Figure 6-3.

A **control chart** reflects the ongoing control of a process and signals an alarm when the process exceeds the control limits. When the line moves beyond the control limit (dotted line in Figure 6-3a), it can signal a problem. Once

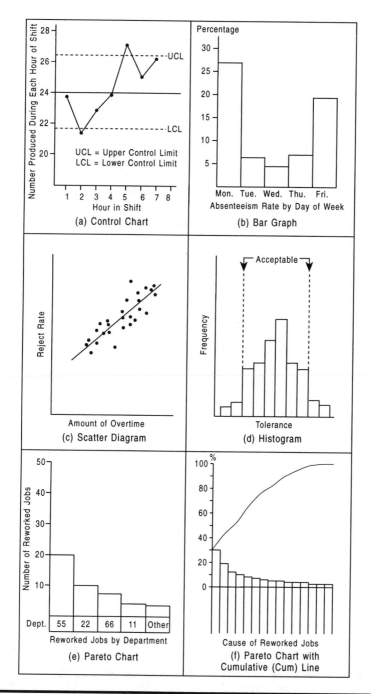

Figure 6-3   Methods of Displaying Data

set up, it is an effective tool for day-to-day monitoring and management of a process.

A **bar graph** (Figure 6-3b), or column graph, summarizes and presents data in an easily understood manner.

A **scatter diagram** (Figure 6-3c) depicts the relationship between two kinds of data, and the relationship forms a pattern.

A **histogram** (Figure 6-3d) is a vertical bar graph showing the distribution of data in terms of the frequency of occurrence for specific values of data.

A **Pareto diagram** (Figure 6-3e) is the most widely used statistical tool in problem analysis. Indeed, it is almost universal in process control problem solving. It is a graphic way of summarizing data in order to focus attention on the main reason(s) why some result is occurring and to produce a cause-and-effect relationship. The *cumulative distribution line,* or "cum" line (Figure 6-3f), is an additional dimension of the Pareto diagram. The "cum" line displays the cumulative distribution of events by percentage. The total of all events is 100 percent.

PROBLEM ANALYSIS

The **cause-and-effect diagram,** sometimes known as the "fishbone" or Ishikawa diagram, was developed and named by Professor Kaoru Ishikawa of the University of Tokyo in 1950. It is an excellent tool for organizing and document-ing potential causes of problems in all areas and at all levels in the organization. As a *brainstorming* device, it is a good way to stimulate ideas during problem-solving meetings.[11]

■   Returning to the case of the National Machine Tool Company, the fishbone diagram was used to brainstorm about possible causes of excess reworked jobs. The result of the brainstorming session is shown in Figure 6-4, which also illustrates the construction and use of the cause-and-effect (fishbone) diagram.

This technique, as demonstrated in the National Machine Tool case, consists of defining an *effect* (reworked jobs) and then determining its contributing factors (*causes*).

Cause-and-effect diagrams are drawn to clearly illustrate the various factors that affect product quality and productivity by sorting out and relating the causes of problems. In a brainstorming session, the causes identified by group members or the team can be listed on a blackboard or flip chart and later transferred to a cause-and-effect diagram. A more experienced group might prepare the diagram directly as the causes are given. Reasons for using the cause-and-effect diagram include:

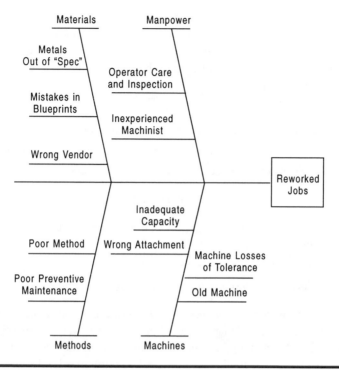

Figure 6-4   Cause-and-Effect Diagram

1. The diagram is a guide for discussion and focuses on the subject at hand. It serves as a measure of progress and indicates how far the discussion has progressed.

2. By encouraging group members to participate, it becomes an educational tool. Knowledge is also shared.

3. It encourages data gathering. Examination of the causes of problems leads to the gathering of additional data in order to support and validate the causes.

PARETO ANALYSIS

Dr. J. M. Juran popularized the term "the Pareto principle" while teaching quality control methods to the Japanese following World War II. This process is derived from *Pareto's law,* named for the Italian economist Alfredo Pareto (1848–1923). The concept of this law is that any cause that results from a multiplicity of effects is primarily the result of the impact of a minor percentage of all the causes. Conversely, a majority of the causative factors play a minor role in the observed effect. In his study of the distribution of wealth and income, he observed that wealth was concentrated in the hands of the few, while the great majority of the population was poor.

This technique is similar to the "80-20" rule:

1. 80 percent of inventory value is in 20 percent of the inventory items
2. 80 percent of sales volume comes from 20 percent of the customers
3. 80 percent of overdue accounts are owed by 20 percent of the customers

Some examples where Pareto analysis is a universal tool include:

1. A problem in inventory reduction where there are large numbers of separate items
2. An analysis of sales volume by product
3. A breakdown of accounts receivable by dollar amount and customer

Dr. Juran, in his book *Managerial Breakthrough,* stated it succinctly: "The vital few are everywhere, but masquerading under a variety of aliases. In their more benevolent forms they are known by such names as key accounts or star salesmen. In their weak moments they are known as the bottlenecks, chronic clinkers, deadbeats, most wanted criminals, critical components." Thus, this separation of the *vital few* from the *trivial many* has universal application in identifying the important problems and establishing priorities.

■   In the case of the National Machine Tool Company, the data from the check sheet (Figure 6-2) were transcribed and converted to the Pareto chart shown in Figure 6-5. It becomes evident that the major problem can be traced to department 55.

The Case of the Printing Company

The more sophisticated problem of sorting a conglomerate mixture into the vital few and the trivial many is illustrated by a cause-and-effect diagram (Figure 6-6) and a subsequent Pareto analysis (Figure 6-7) for a specific case involving a company using plastics for printing and packaging materials. The company was concerned about the number of defects coming off the machine production line, such as misprints, print out of register, warpage, etc.

Team members selected this as a project and through brainstorming prepared a cause-and-effect diagram, as shown in Figure 6-6. After a throrough study of the causes and the effect, the team agreed that a monitor would be appointed to

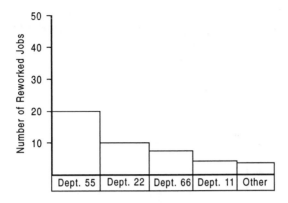

Figure 6-5   Pareto Chart of Reworked Jobs

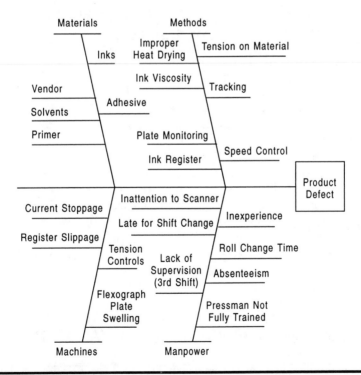

Figure 6-6   Cause-and-Effect Diagram

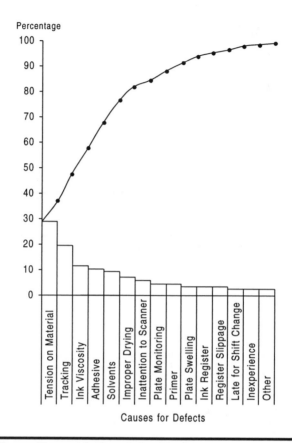

Figure 6-7   Pareto Chart with Cumulative Total

check the causes of all defects over a four-week period. From the information collected during this period, with the use of a check sheet, a Pareto chart was developed for the circle meeting (Figure 6-7).

As can be seen from the Pareto chart in Figure 6-7, the vital few (e.g., "tension material" and "tracking") made up 46 percent of the causes for defects. This graphically illustrates the major areas that need attention.

MANUFACTURING TO SPECIFICATION VS. MANUFACTURING TO REDUCE VARIATIONS

Among production managers who manufacture to specifications or those who depend upon final inspection, the common problem can be traced to the control loop. Defect statistics are generated by inspection, but appropriate action is not taken to define problems, determine cause(s), and correct variations. Companies continue to live with a reject rate that is considered to be "normal," as typified by statements such as "We can live with X percent defectives" or "that's fairly common in the industry."

The benefit of manufacturing to reduce variations (process control) is generally recognized.[12] It is the purpose of SQC to *identify* and *reduce* variations from standard and *continuously improve* the process until a theoretical condition of "zero defects" is achieved.[13] The causes of variations are many and vary from industry to industry. Common sources include (1) material balance disturbances, (2) energy balance changes, (3) process instabilities, (4) equipment failure and wear, and (5) poor control loop performance.[14] SQC is used to develop control limits for each step within the process. Measuring sample parts and graphing trends leads to identification of the cause(s) of any erratic (non-random) behavior in the process.

The objective of process control is not only production of quality output, but reduction of costs as well. Quality is defined as the total acceptable variation divided by the total actual variation or Cp index. When used alone, this measure may be misleading because it assumes acceptable quality product design.[15] This, of course, is not always the case and suggests the need for the cross-functional process control mentioned earlier.

Data acquisition and monitoring is an essential step if the process is to remain in control. This tracking is generally accomplished by the operator concerned. In more sophisticated plants, particularly in unattended manufacturing, the goal is to have in-process measurement and correction in real time through the use of sensors or other measuring devices.[16] Devices such as bar code readers, vision systems, and counters are some of the tools available for collection of data. Of course, data alone is not enough. Data must be organized in such a way that process decisions can be made.

PROCESS CONTROL IN SERVICE INDUSTRIES

Examination of the U.S. Government Standards Industrial Classification of Industries suggests many industries in which the use of SPC would be appropriate. Use of the techniques is spreading to such industries as transportation,[17] health care, and banking.[18]

To some extent the service process is more difficult to control than manufacturing because quality is typically measured at the customer interface, when it is already too late to fix the problem. Hence, "final inspection" will always be a part of the process; the customer serves as the inspector.

Service failures are analogous to bad parts in manufacturing, and measures of service may be compared to manufacturing tolerances or standards. SPC can be used to measure consistency of service and determine causes of deterioration from prescribed standards and the cause(s) of variations. In transportation the cause may be missed appointments, refusals, or weekend closures.[19] At the First National Bank of Chicago, a number of processes are checked weekly against over 500 customer-sensitive measures.[20]

■   L. L. Bean, a mail order company in Freeport, Maine, is known worldwide for its outstanding distribution system. It is the ideal company to benchmark for that function. The company analyzed all key activities and processes, including benchmarking competitors. It is ranked number 1 in virtually every product category in which it is evaluated by outside sources.[21]

Customer Defections: The Measure of Service Process Quality

Measures of output, as the customer defines them, are not too difficult to identify in service firms. An airline can measure on-time departures and the time it takes to make a reservation. A bank can measure the ratio of ATM downtime to total number of ATM minutes available and so on. Measures such as these are necessary, but the most important measure is *customer defections* or customers lost to the competition.

What is the cost of a customer defection? Conversely, what is the value of a customer retention? Defections have a substantial effect on profits and cost, more so than market share, economies of scale, or unit costs. Simply put, losing a customer costs money and retaining one makes money.

The initial cost of acquiring a new customer involves a number of one-time costs for prospecting, advertising, records, and such. Banks, attorneys, mutual funds, and credit card companies are examples of firms that spend to recruit a customer and establish an account. However, once a relationship is established, the marginal cost of each additional dollar of sales *diminishes*—provided the customer does not defect.

Improving the processes and reducing the process variations that reduce customer defections can be perceived not as a cost but as an investment. Consider the following examples:

■   Taco Bell calculates that the lifetime value of a retained customer is $11,000.

■   An auto dealer believes that the lifetime value of retaining a customer is $300,000 in sales.

■ MBNA America, a credit card company, has found that a 5 percent improvement in defection rates increases its average customer value by 125 percent.

PROCESS CONTROL FOR INTERNAL SERVICES

■ Until it moved to Raleigh, North Carolina, IBM's personal computer assembly operation was located at its plant in Boca Raton, Florida. The general manager was committed to internal as well as external quality. In support of this commitment, the following policy was adopted, widely disseminated, and implemented through "Excellent Plus" groups:

Excellence Plus Commitment

IBM Boca Raton will deliver defect-free, competitive products and services, on time, to all customers. Quality will be the primary consideration in all decisions related to cost and delivery. *Likewise, each department will provide defect-free work to the next user of its output or service* (italics added).

An inventory of the many functions and activities in an organization will reveal that each activity is responsible for the operations of one or more processes where the customer is an *internal* user of its output or service. Many, if not most, of these processes lend themselves to process control methods.

AT&T's support services organization in Chicago is responsible for word processing and reprographics. Through SPC, a fivefold improvement in typing accuracy and a halving of turnaround time in reprographics was achieved. Most of the gain was attributed to better communications with customers.[22]

QUALITY FUNCTION DEPLOYMENT

For centuries, and even today, navies have built ships in the same process sequence:

Design → Build hull and launch → Outfit →

Trial run → Return to shipyard → Rework →

Operational check → Return → Fix → Operational

This sequence in modern construction of ships and other weapon systems almost always results in time and cost overruns and subsequent operational deficiencies.

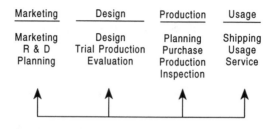

Figure 6-8   Quality Function Deployment Chart

This is evidence of inadequate process control, which may change as a result of the Defense Department's shift from testing the product to testing the process. This shift is a part of the Pentagon's recent TQM strategy.[23]

It is generally agreed that maybe nine out of ten new product developments end up as a design, manufacturing, or marketing failure. These failures may be more the fault of the organization than the market. Many firms lack a system to integrate the market demands with the organization processes. Most applicants for the Baldrige Award, according to examiners, lack management processes that ensure the efficient flow of customer demands throughout the organization.[24]

If quality definition (customer expectation) is not introduced early in the concept or design stage, there is the risk (indeed the probability) that design errors and product defects will only be discovered at later stages of production or final inspection. The worst scenario is discovery by the customer in the marketplace. Motorola estimates that whereas design accounts for only 5 percent of product cost, it accounts for 70 percent of the influence on manufacturing cost.

The major functions of the organization and the matching activities/processes are shown in Figure 6-8. Each is necessary throughout the life cycle of the product, but if the beginning of each process or activity must wait for the end of the preceding one, the time to market is lengthened and the product may be obsolete or overtaken by competition midway through the processes. A method is needed to integrate all processes and relate them to the customer.

Every chief executive officer would welcome a TQM system that would:

■ Implement strategic quality management, including market segment differentiation based on customer expectations

■ Communicate a culture of quality throughout the organization

■ Translate technical requirements into process requirements and then to production planning

■ Organize the potential for world-class competition

■ *Integrate*
1. The special interest functions of the company
2. The stream of processes and provide a basis for process design and control
3. Suppliers and customers
4. Everyone in the process while promoting a team culture with interfunctional teams

This is a lot to ask of any method, but proponents of quality function deployment (QFD) suggest that this method has the potential to achieve many of these requirements. It has proven so effective as a competitive advantage in some companies (e.g., Ford, Digital Equipment, Black & Decker, Budd, Kelsey Hayes) that they are unwilling to talk about it.[25] In Japan, where the method was first used, companies have achieved dramatic improvement in the design-development process, including reductions of 30 to 50 percent in engineering changes and design-cycle time and 20 to 60 percent in start-up costs.[26]

QFD is a group of techniques for planning and communicating that coordinates the activities within an organization. It is a dynamic, iterative method performed by interfunctional teams from marketing, design, engineering, manufacturing engineering, manufacturing, quality, purchasing, and accounting and in some cases suppliers and customers as well. Thus, a common quality focus is achieved across all functions: quality function deployment. The basic premise is that products should be designed to reflect the desires and tastes of customers. An additional benefit is improvement of the company's management processes.[27]

The primary technique is a visual planning matrix called the "House of Quality" which links customer requirements, design requirements, target values, and competitive performance in one easy-to-read chart. The concept, but not the details, is illustrated in Figure 6-9.[28]

QFD unfolds in the following steps or phases. Note that step numbers for product planning and design processes are entered in the sections of the House of Quality in Figure 6-9.

Step 1   **Product planning.** This begins with customer requirements, defined by specific and detailed phrases that the customers in their own words use to describe desired product characteristics.

■ Eaton Corporation, a supplier to the automobile industry, selected a control device for a QFD pilot process. A matrix chart was prepared that related desired product features to part quality characteristics. Each quality characteristic was ranked. Through QFD, selling price and engineering expenses were reduced by 50 percent.[29]

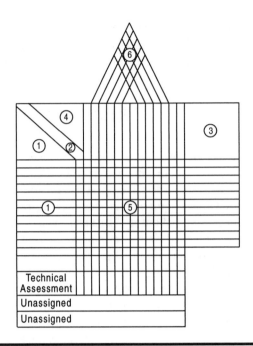

Figure 6-9   House of Quality Concept

Step 2   **Prioritize** and **weight** the relative importance that customers have assigned to each characteristic. This can be done on a scale (e.g., 1 to 5) or in terms of percentages that sum to 100 percent.[30]

Step 3   **Competitive evaluation.**   For those who want to be world-class or meet or beat the competition, it is essential to know how their products compare. Specifically, will the characteristics identified in steps 1 and 2 provide a strategic competitive advantage? (See Chapter 8 for further information on benchmarking.)

Step 4   **The design process.**   This is where the customer's product characteristics meet the *measurable* engineering characteristics that directly affect customer perceptions.

Step 5   **Design** (continued).   The central relationship matrix indicates the degree to which each engineering characteristic affects the customer's characteristics. Strengths of relationships are entered.

Step 6   **Design** (continued).   The roof of the "house" matrix encourages creativity by allowing changes between steps 4 and 5 in order to judge potential trade-offs between engineering and customer characteristics.

Step 7   **Process planning.** Output from the design process goes to process planning, where the key processes (e.g., cutting, stamping, welding, painting, assembly, etc.) are determined. This step may have its own matrix.

Step 8   **Process control.** Output from step 7 goes to process control, where the necessary process flows and controls are designed.

The entire QFD process is "deployed" as illustrated in Figure 6-10. The "hows" of one step become the "what's" of the next. Many of the statistical techniques mentioned previously can be used. Market research has particular methods for that function.

In all cases the interfunctional teams are involved. This is necessary to avoid rework and redesign as well as overruns in cost and time. Questions need to be answered along the way: "What does the customer really want?" "Can we design it?" "Can we make it?" "Is it competitive?" "Can we sell it at a profit?" "Do the processes support it?" Hewlett-Packard estimates that quality programs have saved the company $400 million in warranty costs. Prior to implementing QFD and quality programs, the company estimated that non-quality costs added up to 25 to 30 percent of sales dollars.[31]

The essential prerequisite for QFD is the determination of customer requirements that are defined by specific and detailed phrases that customers in their own words use to describe desired product characteristics. To achieve this degree of specificity, it may be necessary to communicate with customers one-on-one or in focus groups. A less desirable method is to use surveys or other means.

JUST-IN-TIME (JIT)

■   By the third year of JIT implementation, Isuzu (a Japanese company) had reduced the number of employees from 15,000 to 9,900, reduced work-in-process from 35 billion yen to 11 billion yen, and decreased the defect rate by two-thirds.[32]

■   Hewlett-Packard has spread JIT to all areas, including cost accounting, procurement, and engineering. At one plant where 290 pieces of equipment are hand assembled, product reliability has improved sixfold and productivity is up considerably.[33]

■   As part of its conversion to JIT, Westinghouse Electric's Asheville, North Carolina plant was run as a number of mini plants. Cycle time has been reduced two to four times, on-time performance is up over 90 percent, and shop productivity is up by 70 percent. Employees are

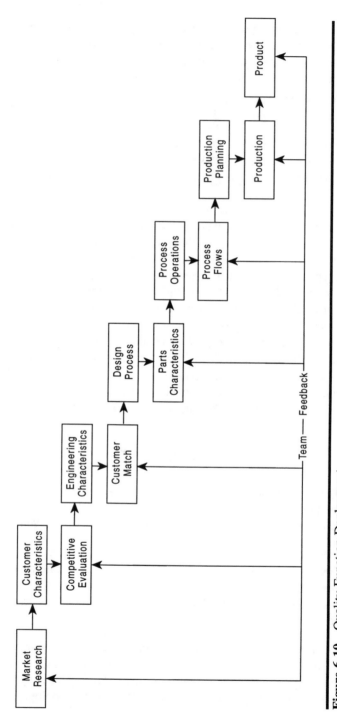

Figure 6-10   Quality Function Deployment

trained to perform multiple functions, and each will end up knowing how to build the complete product.

U.S. manufacturing has been characterized by mass production, high-volume output, and machine capacities that are pushed to the limit. This is changing as American managers begin to discover a production method called just-in-time (JIT). Proponents say that it is more than a manufacturing system; they call it a philosophy and a way of approaching business goals that incorporates (1) producing what is needed when it is needed, (2) minimizing problems, and (3) eliminating production processes that make safety stocks necessary.[34]

Prior to the 1960s, the goal of production planning was cost optimization. In the early 1970s it became requirements planning, and the technique of materials requirements planning (MRP) computed material needs to meet a sales forecast and production plan. MRP was, and is, an effort to balance the sometimes conflicting demands of safety stocks, inventory carrying costs, economic order quantity, and risk factors related to possible stockouts. Today, the modern corporation is turning to manufacturing as a crucial strategic resource and is adopting JIT as a basic component of manufacturing strategy. The view is that the expense and risk of maintaining inventory can be reduced so that lower costs becomes a way of improving both productivity and quality. Of course, inventory is not the only consideration of JIT. It involves all functions and all processes.

JUST-IN-TIME OR JUST-IN-CASE

JIT infers that "less is best," while just-in-case (JIC) involves the use of buffer or safety stocks. Conventional reasons given to explain the need for buffer stock include avoiding risks of stockouts or failure of suppliers, getting a better price for volume purchasing, or avoiding an anticipated price increase. The presence of such "excess" inventory increased the risk of obsolescence and deterioration, increased the need for warehouse and shop floor space, and by "pushing" parts through the assembly process encouraged a number of wasteful practices. Operators were unconcerned with workstations other than their own. The attitude became "there's plenty more where that came from." If a defective part was discovered, the tendency was to blame it on a previous operation or assume that it would be corrected later in the process or at the rework area.

Shigeo Shingo, who is credited with designing Toyota's JIT production system, believes that the "push" process used in the United States generates process-yield imbalances and interprocess delays.[35] *Kanban,* as JIT is called in Japan, means "visible record." It is a means of pulling parts through the assembly process; production is initiated only when a worker receives a visible cue that assembly is needed for the next step in the process. The worker orders the product from the previous operation so that it arrives just when needed. If one of the key processes fails to produce a quality part, the production line stops. Individual operators are their own inspectors and are cross-trained for a number of tasks. The system is continuously being fine tuned.

Benefits of JIT[36]

JIT is not just an inventory control method. It is a system of factory production that interrelates with all functions and activities. The benefits include:

- Reduction of direct and indirect labor by eliminating extraneous activities
- Reduction of floor space and warehouse space per unit of output
- Reduction of setup time and schedule delays as the factory becomes a continuous production process
- Reduction of waste, rejects, and rework by detecting errors at the source
- Reduction of lead time due to small lot sizes, so that downstream work centers provide feedback on quality problems
- Better utilization of machines and facilities
- Better relations with suppliers
- Better plant layout
- Better integration of and communication between functions such as marketing, purchasing, design, and production
- Quality control built into the process

THE HUMAN SIDE OF PROCESS CONTROL

One study found that a very small percentage of employees could define quality or could relate what their companies were doing to improve it.[37]

The problems of managing streams of processes are both methodological and organizational. Peter Drucker concludes that SQC has its greatest impact on the factory's social organization.[38] The essence of his argument relates to the way that the use of statistical tools in the production process places information and hence accountability in the hands of the machine operator rather than nonoperators such as inspectors, expediters, repair crews, and supervisors. Each operator becomes his or her own inspector. Operators "own" the machines, which allows them to spot malfunctions and correct problems. The concept is known as "workstation ownership" at IBM, where each employee is responsible for an entire operation in the production line.[39]

If Drucker is right, as he probably is, the potential exists for significant improvement in quality, cost, and productivity. However, there is a down side. Strict adherence to rigid methods and procedures means that workers and teams may lose the autonomy they previously enjoyed, only to have it replaced by the regimentation necessitated by process control. By their very nature SPC and JIT require a focus on the process as a whole, an environment that may be strange to an operator accustomed to the segmented approach previously in effect.[40]

It is probably almost universally accepted that control of any process rests upon measuring against some standard, measure, benchmark, or target. Yet in many organizations, workers and managers operate with two different sets of goals and in two different cultures. It becomes an "us versus them" split culture. As we move from inspection to process control, it is essential that control measures become the property of the workers. SPC and JIT achieve this. Workers are involved in measures over which they have some control in monitoring continuous improvements. Control of measures alone, however, may not be enough. Understanding of and involvement in the system would enhance job satisfaction, which is a necessary dimension. Moreover, like any process or system, the people with hands-on involvement are a valuable resource for refinement and improvement.

Attention to the human resource dimension provides a basis for significant improvements in job development, job satisfaction, training, and morale. Suggested actions to improve the changes include:

- Like all major change, top management support is essential.

- Change the focus from production volume to quality, from speed to flow, from execution to task design, from performing to learning.

- Invest in training, a necessary prerequisite.

QUESTIONS FOR DISCUSSION

6-1 Explain the difference between feedforward and feedback (final inspection) control. Why is feedforward more appropriate for TQM?

6-2 What are the steps in moving from a system of final inspection to process control?

6-3 Choose a non-manufacturing (service) process and show how statistical quality control would be appropriate.

6-4 How would a *sequential* approach to product design and introduction result in overruns in time, cost, and quality? How would quality function deployment improve the system?

6-5 Is customer defections a measure of service quality? If so, how can the measure be used to reduce customer defections?

6-6 Explain the benefits of just-in-time (JIT).

ENDNOTES

1. Claude S. George, Jr., *The History of Management Thought,* Englewood Cliffs, N.J.: Prentice-Hall, 1972, p. 10. For an excellent summary of sources that have traced the history of the quality movement, see David A. Garvin, *Managing Quality,* New York: The Free Press, 1988, p. 251.
2. Frederick W. Taylor, *Principles of Scientific Management,* New York: Harper & Row, 1911.
3. Frederick W. Taylor, *Shop Management,* New York: Harper & Row, 1919, p. 101.
4. W. A. Shewhart, *Economic Control of Quality of Manufactured Product,* New York: E. Van Nostrand Company, 1931.
5. Peter Drucker, "The Emerging Theory of Manufacturing," *Harvard Business Review,* May/June 1990, p. 95.
6. Harry W. Kenworthy and Angela George, "Quality and Cost Efficiency Go Hand in Hand," *Quality Progress,* Oct. 1989, pp. 40–41.
7. Barbara Dutton, "Switching to Quality Excellence," *Manufacturing Systems,* March 1990, pp. 51–53.
8. Bob Johnstone, "Prophet with Honor," *Far Eastern Economic Review (Hong Kong),* Dec. 27, 1990, p. 50. A survey of Japanese automobile parts suppliers showed that 93 percent used SPC in their operations.
9. For a detailed treatment of SQC and SPC, see Kaoru Ishikawa, *Guide to Quality Control,* rev. ed., 1982 (available in the United States from UNIPUB [Tel. 800-274-4888]). See also J. M. Juran, *Quality Control Handbook,* 3rd ed., New York: McGraw-Hill, 1974. For application of process control charts, see such standard texts as J. M. Juran and Frank Gryna, Jr., *Quality Planning and Analysis,* New York: McGraw-Hill, 1980 and E. L. Grant and R. S. Leavenworth, *Statistical Quality Control,* 5th ed., New York: McGraw-Hill, 1980.
10. One research study of over 300 U.S. firms found that less than half believed that they had a state-of-the-art quality control program that includes SQC and SPC and utilizes a computer support system. Joel E. Ross and David Georgoff, "A Survey of Productivity and Quality Issues in Manufacturing: The State of the Industry," *Industrial Management,* Jan./Feb. 1991.
11. For a summary discussion of the various techniques used in brainstorming, see Ron Zemke, "In Search of...Good Ideas," *Training,* Jan. 1993, pp. 46–52.

12. Ken Jones, "High Performance Manufacturing: A Break with Tradition," *Industrial Management (Canada),* June 1988, pp. 30–32.
13. Genichi Taguchi and Don Clausing, "Robust Quality," *Harvard Business Review,* Jan./ Feb. 1990, pp. 65–75. This article provides a summary of the collection now known as Taguchi methods, a popular approach that is opposed to the zero defects concept, based on the conclusion that the concept promotes quality in terms of acceptable deviation from targets rather than a consistent effort to hit them. Zero defects, according to Taguchi, fixes design before the effects of the quality program are felt.
14. Kenneth E. Kirby and Charles F. Moore, "Process Control and Quality in the Continuous Process Industries," *Survey of Business,* Summer 1989, pp. 62–66.
15. Larry H. Anderson, "Controlling Process Variation Is Key to Manufacturing Success," *Quality Progress,* Aug. 1990, pp. 91–93.
16. Chester Placek, "CMMs in Automation," *Quality,* March 1990, pp. 28–38.
17. Ray A. Mundy, Russel Passarella, and Jay Morse, "Applying SPC in Service Industries," *Survey of Business,* Spring 1986, pp. 24–29.
18. Aleta Holub, "The Added Value of the Customer–Provider Partnership," in *Making Total Quality Happen,* Research Report No. 937, New York: The Conference Board, 1990, pp. 60–63.
19. John E. Tyworth, Pat Lemons, and Bruce Ferrin, "Improving LTL Delivery Service Quality with Statistical Process Control," *Transportation Journal,* Spring 1989, pp. 4–12.
20. Aleta Holub, Endnote 18.
21. Thomas C. Day, "Value-Driven Business = Long-Term Success," in *Total Quality Performance,* Research Report No. 909, New York: The Conference Board, 1988, pp. 27–29.
22. Laurence C. Seifert, "AT&T's Full-Stream Quality Architecture," in *Total Quality Performance,* Research Report No. 909, New York: The Conference Board, 1988, pp. 47–49.
23. Pam Nazaruk, "Commitment to Quality: Test Process Not Product, Orders Pentagon," *Electronic Business,* Oct. 15, 1990, pp. 163–164.
24. Peter Burrows, "Commitment to Quality: Five Lessons You Can Learn from Award Entrants," *Electronic Business,* Oct. 15, 1990, pp. 56–58.
25. Gary S. Vasilash, "Hearing the Voice of the Customer," *Production,* Feb. 1989, pp. 66–68.
26. Ronald Fortuna, "Beyond Quality: Taking SPC Upstream," *Quality Progress,* June 1988, pp. 23–28. The author is manager of the Chicago office of Ernst & Young and observes that the control charts of SPC are considered one of the "Seven Old Tools" in Japan, along with Pareto analysis, cause-and-effect diagrams, data stratification, histograms, and scatter diagrams.
27. William Band and Richard Huot, "Quality & Functionality Equal Satisfaction," *Sales and Marketing Management in Canada (Canada),* March 1990, pp. 4–5.
28. For a more detailed and practical description of how to formulate and implement the method, see John R. Hauser and Don Clausing, "The House of Quality," *Harvard Business Review,* May–June 1988, pp. 63–73. Clausing, one of the authors, introduced QFD to Ford and its supplier companies in 1984 and the process was used in the successful design and introduction of the Taurus.
29. Dennis De Vera et al., "An Automotive Case Study," *Quality Progress,* June 1988, pp. 35–38.

30. At a Conference Board Quality Conference on April 2, 1990, A. F. Jacobson of 3M described how the Commercial Office Supply division brings customer expectations into the design process: "Let's say, they're going to develop an improved tape of some kind. They don't wait until the product is finished...or nearly finished...to take it to their customers. They take the idea to customers right at the beginning of the process. They ask customers what they want from a particular tape. Very often, they'll hear things like: 'Don't make it too sticky.' 'I want to be able to pull it off the roll easily.' and, 'It's no good unless I can write on it.' Now, collecting opinions is the easy part of the process. The tough part is converting these soft expectations into technical requirements. This is done on a matrix *before* the development process gets very far. These soft expectations are converted into technical specifications for, say, adhesion, roughness and reflectance."

31. Robert Haavind, "Hewlett-Packard Unravels the Mysteries of Quality," *Electronic Business,* Oct. 16, 1989, pp. 101–105.

32. Ronald M. Fortuna, "The Quality Imperative," *Executive Excellence,* March 1990, p. 1.

33. Steve Kaufman, "Quest for Quality," *Business Month,* May 1989, pp. 60–65.

34. Jack Byrd, Jr. and Mark D. Carter, "A Just-in-Time Implementation Strategy at Work," *Industrial Management,* March/April 1988, pp. 8–10. See also Ira P. Krespchin, "What Do You Mean by Just-in-Time?" *Modern Materials Handling,* Aug. 1986, pp. 93–95.

35. John H. Sheridan, "World-Class Manufacturing: Lessons from the Gurus," *Industry Week,* Aug. 6, 1990, pp. 35–41. Shingo also believes that JIT extends to plant maintenance, and with a participative environment operators will protect their own equipment.

36. There are a number of references that point out the benefits as well as the pitfalls of JIT. These sources also contain suggestions for implementation. See the following: Bruce D. Henderson, "The Logic of Kanban," *Journal of Business Strategy,* Winter 1986, pp. 6–12. The author describes how the technique can provide a competitive advantage. The need to rethink traditional practices is discussed in Lynne Perry, "Simplified Manufacturing Is Best," *Industrial Management,* July/Aug. 1986, pp. 29–30. The way that small manufacturers can adapt the technique is described in Byron Finch, "Japanese Management Techniques in Small Manufacturing Companies," *Production & Inventory Management,* Vol. 27 Issue 3, 3rd Quarter 1986, pp. 30–38. The need for continued quality control and other requirements is outlined in Mark R. Jamrog, "Just-in-Time Manufacturing: Just in Time for U.S. Manufacturers," *Price Waterhouse Review,* Vol. 32 Issue 1, 1988, pp. 17–29. The interface with other functions of the company is provided by R. Natarajan and Donald Weinrauch, "JIT and the Marketing Interface," *Production & Inventory Management Journal,* Vol. 31 Issue 3, 3rd Quarter 1990, pp. 42–46.

37. Joel E. Ross and Lawrence A. Klatt, "Quality: The Competitive Edge," *Management Decision (UK),* Vol. 24 Issue 5, 1986, pp. 12–16.

38. Peter Drucker, "The Emerging Theory of Manufacturing," *Harvard Business Review,* May/June 1990, p. 95.

39. James J. Webster, "Pulling—Not Pushing—For Higher Productivity," *Mechanical Engineering,* April 1988, pp. 42–44.

40. Gervase R. Bushe, "Cultural Contradictions of Statistical Process Control in American Manufacturing Corporations," *Journal of Management,* March 1988, pp. 19–31.

The Taguchi Method for design of experiments is a tool used to reduce the inherent variability in a product or process. The concept of process variation is introduced and expanded, and the use of Taguchi Method in statistical process control (SPC) is explained. A good introduction to and explanation of the basics of SPC are provided.

REDUCING VARIABILITY— KEY TO CONTINUOUS QUALITY IMPROVEMENT

Gregg D. Stocker

In recent years, quality has undoubtedly become a strategic focus of companies expecting to do business in the 1990s and beyond. In the summer of 1988, the Department of Defense released the Total Quality Management (TQM) Master Plan to achieve continuous improvement of products and services offered and used by the department. A major component of this philosophy is the concept of variability reduction. As a result of DoD's move, many organizations are beginning to understand that reducing the variability of a process results in improved quality and reduced costs.

The concept of variability reduction has its origins in the 1920s with Dr. Walter Shewhart of Bell Laboratories. It has been expanded through the works of W. Edwards Deming, J. A. Juran, Armand Feigenbaum and Genichi Taguchi. Although variability reduction is only one of many components in a continuous improvement process, it is one whose importance calls for further examination.

The Concept of Variation

Understanding variability reduction requires an understanding of basic statistics. This fundamental requirement has apparently frightened a number of people

Reprinted by permission of *Manufacturing Systems*, March 1990.

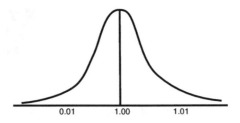

Figure 1   Distribution of a Drilling Operation

away from employing many proven quality improvement techniques. Fortunately, the level of statistical knowledge required to understand the underlying philosophies for quality improvement is not great.

Statistically every process experiences variation in one form or another. It is this variation that leads to quality problems. Methods employed to reduce the amount of variation will, therefore, improve quality and reduce cost.

The philosophy of variability reduction is based on the fact that there is a "best" value for a product's function, fit and appearance. This value is the target that must be achieved to ensure the highest level of quality. To address the existence of variation in a process, traditionally engineering and manufacturing have relied on tolerance or specification limits. This approach must be changed because although parts produced within the specification limits may be functional, their quality decreases and cost increases as the process varies from the target. And this variability can lose business. The company that best meets the needs of the customers within a specific market will gain the greatest share of the market.

Variability is illustrated by the normal distribution, also known as the bell-shaped curve. Figure 1 presents the output of a process that drills holes to a target value of one inch. The normal distribution states that, as long as the process is operating in a statistical state of control, most of the holes will be drilled at exactly one inch. The curve also shows that an equal portion of parts will vary above and below the one inch target, called the "spread."

Figure 2 presents a comparison of distribution of three different processes. Process A produced a greater amount of variation than process B or C, as shown by the wider and flatter curve. In terms of variability, therefore, process C is the best of the three processes for this particular part, i.e., it is the most centered around the target value.

Process A will produce parts that will be scrapped or require rework. Although process B produces virtually every piece within the tolerance limits, the increased variability over process C could result in increased assembly time or possible tolerance stackup problems.

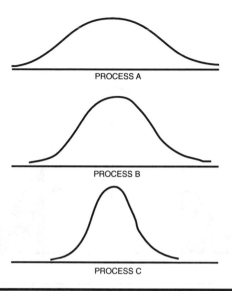

Figure 2   Comparison of Three Processes

The principles relating to variability of quality and cost are represented by the Quality Loss Function (QLF) which was developed by Taguchi and is discussed later in this article under "Taguchi Methods."

Statistical Process Control (SPC)

SPC is a tool used to measure the variability of a process and determine its capability to produce a particular part. The method was developed by Shewhart in 1924 and was used extensively by government contractors during World War II.

A process consistently and predictably producing parts within three standard deviations of the average is considered in a state of statistical control. This means all the special causes of variation within the process have been removed.

A process in a state of statistical control refers *only* to the ability to predict the amount of inherent variation. It does not make any reference to the capability of the process to produce high quality parts on a consistent basis.

Figure 3 presents a process in a state of control, but only able to produce acceptable parts 60 percent of the time. This is because the spread of variation inherent in the process carries outside-the-product specification limits. The measure used to determine if the process can produce acceptable parts on a consistent basis is the process capability (C_p) index.

The C_p index is a measure of the variation of a process with respect to the

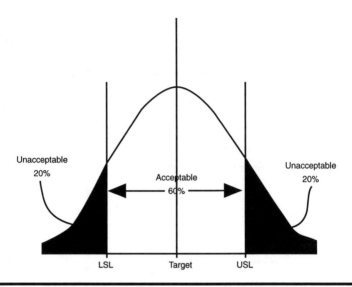

Figure 3 Distribution 60% Acceptable

acceptable tolerance limits for an item. The formula for C_p is: [Tolerance/Process Spread]. The higher the C_p index, the smaller the variation within the process in relation to the tolerance specifications. As a general rule, any C_p greater than 1.33 is considered acceptable—although statistically the process will continue to produce 66 defects per million.

The problem with the C_p index is that it does not take into account the process average. The process variability may be shifted to one side or the other of the specification limits which will result in a greater number of rejected items than the measure indicates. This situation has led to the development of the C_{pk} index, which is a measure of the process in relation to the item's target value and specification limits. C_{pk} is calculated as the lower of:

$$\frac{(\text{Upper Spec Limit}) - (\text{Process Average})}{\text{Process Spread}}$$

$$\frac{- (\text{Lower Spec Limit}) - (\text{Process Average})}{\text{Process Spread}}$$

The process spread is calculated as 3 sigma. As with the C_p index, the general rule is to consider any process capable that has a value of 1.33 or greater. The higher the C_{pk} value, the less variation inherent in the process, or the larger the specification limits.

As mentioned earlier, any item produced that exhibits a value outside the 3 sigma limit for that process identifies a *special* cause of variation. Statistically, this refers to a problem not attributable to the natural variation causes that can be identified and eliminated on the shop floor by the production worker.

The problems associated with the natural variation within the process are referred to as *common* causes. The common causes, resulting in a flatter and wider curve for the process, can only be eliminated by management action through improvements in the overall system. The philosophy of TQM is based on the premise that the variation must be reduced to improve quality and that a reduction in this variation will automatically result in lower costs for the company.

Companies that use quality levels denoted by sigma are referring to the capabilities of their processes. Motorola, one of the winners of the 1988 Malcolm Baldrige National Quality Award, has targeted its quality level at 6 sigma by 1991. In terms of the normal distribution, this means they are improving their processes to produce less than 3.4 defects per million parts produced.

It is important to note that SPC is only a tool to monitor the process and identify the special causes. Although it is a very important tool for quality improvement, it is not useful in reducing the natural variation inherent within the process.

Figure 4 presents a simple example of the control chart developed by Shewhart. The chart is basically the same as the normal curve except it is presented

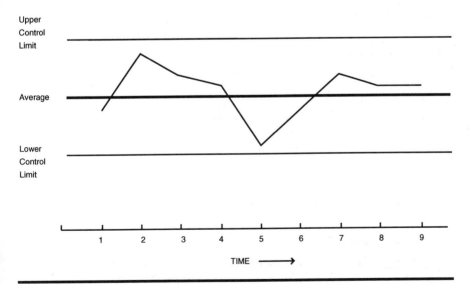

Figure 4   Shewhart Control Chart

horizontally and includes a time element. The sample measurements are plotted on the chart, and the process average and control limits (average ± 3 standard deviations) are calculated and drawn as straight lines. This chart does not refer to the specification limits in any way. It is hoped that the specifications of the items to be manufactured within that process are well outside the control limits. If not, the process is not considered capable of producing the item(s) in question.

Any point outside the control limits identifies a special cause of variation that can be corrected by the operator. If the part specifications are well outside the control limits the special causes can be identified and corrected before unacceptable parts are produced.

Other signals to special causes of variation include:

- Seven consecutive points on the same side of the centerline;
- Seven consecutive points that increase or decrease;
- Two out of three consecutive points on the same side of the centerline outside the ±2 sigma zone;
- Other *non-random* patterns—trends, cycles, etc.

Any efforts to bring the control limits closer to the mean need to address the (common) causes of natural variation. One method proven very successful in the reduction of the natural process variation was developed by Taguchi.

Taguchi Methods

The Taguchi Method for design of experiments is a tool used to reduce the inherent variability in a product or process. It combines engineering and statistics to directly address the process variability problem. The tool is employed primarily in product and process engineering to identify and optimize conflicting inputs (factors) to enable improved quality and reduced cost. Developed by Taguchi, it has enabled him to win the coveted Deming Prize in Japan four times.

The factors in product and process design are defined by Taguchi as controllable and uncontrollable. The interaction of these factors has a direct impact on the performance variation inherent in the product. By concentrating solely on the controllable factors, and their resultant effect on variation, the engineer can design a product or process that minimizes variation, thereby increasing quality and reducing cost.

Definition of Quality

The Taguchi philosophy is based on the premise that cost can be reduced by improving quality and that quality will automatically improve by reducing varia-

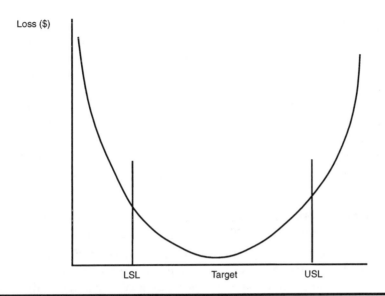

Figure 5   Taguchi Loss Function

tion. This philosophy strongly disagrees with Philip Crosby's statements that quality is solely *conformance to specifications.*

Taguchi believes that tolerance limits are defined to cover up problems in design of the product or process. Minimal variation around the target value is the only true way to achieve high levels of quality. Taguchi states that the difference between an item that is barely within specification and one that is barely out of specification is very little; yet one is considered good and the other is considered bad. Following this philosophy, Taguchi defines quality as *"the loss a product causes to society after being shipped, other than any losses caused by its intrinsic functions."* Any product characteristic that varies from its intended value causes a loss to society, hence poor quality.

To quantify his definition of quality, Taguchi has developed the Quality Loss Function (QLF). The QLF is a graphic representation of the loss to society caused by product/process variation. The graph is a parabola in which the lowest point represents the minimal loss (expressed in monetary terms) to the customer and company. As the target value is missed in either direction, the cost to society increases. Deviations from the target can also represent an over-designed product—heavier, larger, less efficient, etc. The QLF is a tool to be used during the early stages of design, thereby enabling changes to be made as quickly and efficiently as possible (see Figure 5).

By emphasizing a long-term focus on the customer's and society's needs and continuous improvement, Taguchi's philosophy closely follows the teachings of Deming and Juran. In particular, Taguchi's practice of designing a product or process that is insensitive to noise will enable the final product to be of consistent quality, thereby reducing the dependence on inspection as a means to achieve quality.

Within his method, Taguchi differentiates between the controllable and uncontrollable (noise) factors. These factors consist of any design characteristic that can cause variation in the product's performance. Examples of design factors include tubing wall thickness, screw thread length, wire diameter, cooling method and coating material. Definitions of the two types of design characteristics are as follows:

- **Control Factors:** Factors affecting product/process performance that can be easily controlled during the production of a product.

- **Noise Factors:** Factors affecting product/process performance that are impossible or too expensive to control, i.e., environmental conditions. There are three types of noise factors: external (environmental), internal (wear, shrinkage, etc.), and product-to-product (resulting from part-to-part variation).

The objective of the Taguchi Method is to reduce the effect of noise factors on variation by concentrating on their interaction with the control factors. Therefore, the control factors are the only factors that can be changed.

Design Process

In accordance with the TQM concept, Taguchi has made improvements in product/process design by concentrating on the process itself. He has formalized the design process by defining three distinct stages for all products and processes:

- **System Design:** Determine the product's intended function and build a prototype to accomplish objectives. Tentative parameters are defined to construct a prototype.

- **Parameter Design:** Determine the factors affecting product performance and distinguish between controllable and uncontrollable. The objective is to determine the combination of factors least sensitive to changes in the noise factors through design of experiments.

- **Tolerance Design:** If the reduced variation determined through parameter design is not acceptable, design changes are made to attempt to achieve objectives. This usually involves increasing manufacturing and purchase costs, i.e., improved grades of material, tighter tolerances, etc.

Signal-to-Noise Ratio

The effect of a specific noise factor on the quality of the design is described by its signal-to-noise (S/N) ratio. The S/N ratio refers to statistical measurement of the stability of a quality characteristic's performance. The S/N ratio objective is usually determined by the QLF, and is the target for the parameter design stage. The larger the S/N ratio, the more *robust* the design, i.e., the less sensitive performance will be to noise. If the actual S/N ratio is less than the target value, tolerance design will need to be performed.

Taguchi uses orthogonal arrays to simulate the results of different factor combinations to greatly reduce the number of experiments needed to complete the design. Statistical analysis, utilizing the arrays, quickly aids the engineer in eliminating the factors that will not affect the quality of the design.

Results

Taguchi Methods are slowly gaining popularity in the United States. In a book published by the American Supplier Institute—the U.S. Center for Taguchi Methods—it was estimated that approximately 5,000 Taguchi Methods case studies are completed annually in the U.S. Although this number sounds impressive, estimates of the method's use in Japan exceed 100,000. Akashi Fukuhara, one person credited with the implementation of TQC at Toyota, stated that the use of Taguchi Methods is the single most important quality improvement tool used by the company.

Continuous process improvement includes (1) defining the problem and possible solutions, (2) selecting and implementing the most cost-effective solution, and (3) re-evaluating, standardizing, and then repeating the process. This article identifies the seven basic tools of problem solving and process improvement and explains how these can be introduced by training and employee involvement.

BEYOND STATISTICAL PROCESS CONTROL

Robert E. Stein

The benefits derived by the effective implementation of total quality control and continuous process improvement have been considered the equivalent of an industrial revolution, as well they should. Until recently, most traditional productivity/quality improvement programs have been characterized by a product/inspection orientation and have ignored employee contributions; productivity improvement was assumed to involve high capitalization expenditures.

Statistical process control, the application of statistical principles to reduce defects, is one of seven elementary tools used by first-line supervisors and their employees. Emphasis is on continuous process monitoring; the assumption is that a process under control will yield acceptable product. The operator establishes the average value and range of deviations from the mean in a process and plots those values in the form of X-bar and R charts (Figure 1). Precontrol limits are set and sample measurements are taken from the products being produced. The operator then monitors the outcome of each plot or group of plots to determine if a trend is developing or if the process is out of control. If it is out of control, the process is stopped, the cause determined, and a solution is implemented.

Reprinted with permission from The American Production and Inventory Control Society, Falls Church, VA, *Production and Inventory Management Journal,* First Quarter, 1991.

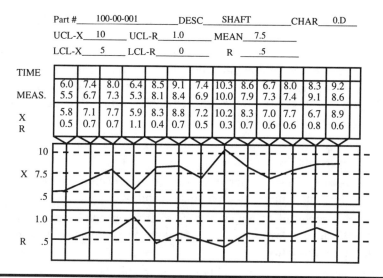

Part #_____100-00-001_____DESC____SHAFT_____CHAR___O.D___

UCL-X__10____ UCL-R___1.0____ MEAN___7.5____

LCL-X___5____ LCL-R____0____ R ___.5____

Figure 1   X-bar and R Chart

Precontrol, a simplified version of SPC, focuses more on process control/ capability verification and less on charting (Figure 2). Precontrol process lines (PC lines) are set in the middle half of the product specification width. Process capabilities are established at the beginning of production by measuring five consecutive occurrences, each of which must appear in the green zone. Periodic sampling indicates whether the process is under control. (The frequency of sampling is determined by dividing the time interval between failures by six.)

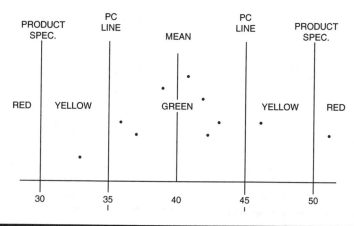

Figure 2   Precontrol

Two units are measured during each sample, and the process is stopped if two measurements are in the yellow zone or one is in the red.

Statistical process control is not a prerequisite to total quality control, and SPC alone will not yield a high-quality product. Total quality control is much more than the application of statistics in quality problem resolution. A successful quality program involves a three-pronged approach including people, product and process, the key issues being:

- The consignment of a workable methodology to the shop floor which maximizes individual worker input

- The concept of manufacturability of design, reducing product/production variability, and emphasizing process capability

- The philosophy of continuous process improvement, de-emphasizing acceptable quality levels and concentrating on continually measuring and improving the status quo

- The changing role of the quality control organization.

Methodology

Shop-floor methodology consignment places proven technology into the hands of the individual contributor within the production environment. It allows for the development of a statistical base for problem analysis and resolution, provides a forum for group involvement, and capitalizes on the effectiveness of peer pressure in human interaction. Specific areas of interest include employee involvement teams, the seven elementary tools (see next page), source inspection, manufacturability of design, and continuous process improvement.

Individual workers are trained to:

- Identify the seven wastes (overproduction, time on hand, transportation, unnecessary processing, excess inventory, unnecessary motion, and poor quality) as they apply to their environment.

- Understand and utilize the elementary tools of analytical problem resolution (Pareto charts, cause-and-effect diagrams, check sheets, histograms, scatter diagrams, control charts, and graphs).

- Participate in relevant employee involvement teams (work improvement groups, swat teams, and quality circles).

- Understand and apply the concepts of continuous process improvement.

The first step in the development of an employee-involved quality program is to establish a focus on quality issues. The next step is to re-inforce the first by changing the employee's environment, the method by which feedback is received, and the way individual work goals are established:

- Increase the individual's level of visibility.

- Clear and simplify his environment; have a place for everything and keep the work area cleared of any tool or product that is not currently being used.

- Standardize tool locations between similar operations.

- Insure that workers can immediately determine their next priority.

- Keep inventories at a low enough level that any problems involving quality or delivery become readily noticeable.

- Establish a pull system of shop-floor control where work priorities are determined by downstream requirements which will allow the proper synchronization of work flow.

- Convert to U lines and group technology cells wherever possible.

- Use scoreboards, signal lights, and alarms to emphasize key issues such as production goals, work stoppages, and quality levels.

Employee Involvement Teams

A forum must be provided for the address of problems which will begin to surface after shop restructuring. Work improvement groups and quality circles include three to fifteen shop, technical, and supervisory people meeting on a regular basis: the former trained in problem-solving techniques and the latter in quality improvement. Swat teams consist of three to five people who meet during crisis situations to solve problems and focus on the immediate resumption of production.

The Seven Elementary Tools

1. **Pareto charts** rank problems/defects according to the level of occurrence.

2. **Cause-and-effect diagrams** establish probable relationships between defects and their causes.

3. **Check sheets** are a physical mechanism for collecting data.

4. **Histograms,** designed to show the distribution of occurrences, establish mean values and their associated variances.

5. **Scatter diagrams** are a basic method for determining the extent of correlation between two or more measured defects or actions (for instance, machine temperature variances may cause problems associated with diameter measurements in lathe operations).

6. **Control charts** (X-bar and R/precontrol) monitor the output of a specific process to determine its viability.

7. **Graphs** monitor/track performance measurements over time.

Source Inspection

Source Inspection is at the heart of TQC. Conceptually, the emphasis is on inspecting and correcting problems as close to the object process as possible. Operator feedback is immediate, inspection levels reach 100% without additional costs, and social pressures require performance. Poka-yoke devices (categorized by purpose and method) prevent defects from occurring: control devices prevent defects, and warning devices give notice of pending defects. A machine modified to allow a part to be installed only one way is a control device; a buzzer which sounds when a defect is about to occur is a warning device. Poka-yoke devices include pressure-sensitive switches, thermometers, electrical current sensors, light-activated switches, and counters.

Process inspection uses the next person in the process to inspect the work of the previous process. Discovered defects result in work being returned immediately to the causing departments or operations.

Manufacturability of Design

Perhaps the largest contributor to product quality is the concept of the manufacturability of design. As products become easier to make, track, and store, quality increases and the gap between cost and time of production for high- and low-end products narrows. Factors which have a direct effect on manufacturability include:

- Number of parts (minimize)
- Variability of components (minimize)
- Process requirements (simplify)
- Degree of design detail (simplify)
- Technology employed (should be proven)
- Availability of materials (high)
- Degree of production involvement (high)
- Design for yield (within process capabilities).

Process capability levels are determined by dividing the product specification width by the process width. As the level increases, the probability of product rejection decreases. A level of 1.66 or higher guarantees a 100% yield. The two methods for increasing process capability levels are reducing variables which tend to widen process width and increasing the specification width through product design.

Continuous Process Improvement

Traditional measurements have been against standards (standard versus actual labor expenditures). Primary concerns have been bottom-line comparisons to return on assets employed. In a highly competitive environment the utilization of standards can be a disadvantage; the key to success is in staying ahead of the opponent, not the standard. While return on assets employed will remain a large part of corporate life, current tendencies have been toward measuring operational successes against continual improvement. Comparisons are not against standards or acceptable levels, but against measurements previously taken, such as:

- Process capability
- Product design lead time
- Production cycle time
- Inventory levels
- Product cost
- Setup time
- Number and duration of line stoppages
- Equipment down time
- Defect rates
- Number of suggestions per person
- Number of parts per assembly
- Number of processes per assembly
- Travel distances.

The operation of continuous process improvement includes:

- Defining the problem and possible solutions
- Selecting and implementing the most cost-effective solution
- Re-evaluating, standardizing, then repeating the process.

Problem definition sets the stage for what is to follow. Formalized definition procedures allow groups to collectively agree or disagree on key issues and to collect pertinent information. The use of cause-and-effect diagrams is excellent for subdividing more complex issues and for further defining probable solutions. Maximum benefits are realized by standardizing the process across numerous work cells or operations. The key issue is "never accept the status quo."

CASE

The author, a Deming disciple, now a top manager at the Savin Corporation, relates how Deming's techniques and principles are transferable to the service functions.

PUTTING DEMING'S PRINCIPLES TO WORK

Robert Williams

Before I joined Savin Corp., I spent 10 years working with W. Edwards Deming while he was consulting with my previous employer. Mr. Deming's statistical analysis approach to quality helped get Japanese industry back on its feet after World War II and, to borrow a phrase, the rest is history. In the 1990s, this total quality approach will make history again. Not in Japan, and not in manufacturing, but in the service industry.

The service sector in the U.S. in 1991 bears an eerie resemblance to American manufacturing 10 or 15 years ago. Costs are high. Profit margins are narrowing. Quality standards are inconsistent at best, and competitive pressures are mounting each year.

A Deming-style "total quality management" approach to improving service quality is rooted in the unglamorous and never fashionable discipline of statistics. I speak from Savin's experience in the copier industry, where a company's fortunes ride on the quality of its services. Using Mr. Deming's statistical approach to total quality management, we have reduced service expenses 35% over the past 12 months while improving service quality. Here are some examples of how it was done:

Reprinted with permission from *Wall Street Journal,* November 4, 1991, Section A, p. 18.

■ "Callbacks" are anathema to every business that sends technicians on service calls. A customer callback means the job wasn't completed right the first time, and the service provider has to eat the cost of a second visit. Early last year, a careful study by Savin found that the callbacks were related to deficiencies in our training process. One of our branch managers suggested stripping our dealer training centers of their instructors so we could run marathon training programs for all of our branch technicians.

While this approach could have corrected our callback problem, the time and expense involved had the potential to outrun the cost of making the callbacks, in addition to disrupting dealer support. To find an affordable solution that would reduce callbacks sharply at an affordable cost, we turned to the tools of statistical analysis.

I asked our branch service managers to prepare a Pareto diagram of callbacks for each field engineer. The Pareto principle states that cause and effect are not linearly related. There usually will be a few causes—20% or fewer by volume—that will account for 80% or more of the effect.

Using the Pareto principle against our callback problem in one branch showed that if we retrained only five field engineers—those with the record number of callbacks—we could drop the branch average for callbacks by 19%. Retraining five engineers was a lot less daunting than retraining 45, many of whom didn't really need to be retrained. Of course, this was a process that could be repeated whenever the callback situation got out of control again. This was a case where using a statistical tool focused our corrective action to where it was needed, and helped us reduce waste at an affordable cost.

■ In a technical service business, small details gone awry can collectively kill productivity and drain the profitability from a service call. We found, for instance, that significant time was being wasted on service calls when our engineers had to go back to their vehicles for spare parts. It is physically unrealistic and impractical to expect a field engineer to carry every conceivable part that might be needed. Considering, however, the salaries paid to skilled technicians, the time they spent shuttling back and forth for parts represented some of the most expensive travel in corporate America.

By using statistical analysis, we were able to determine those parts that the engineers were most likely to use on a call. We were able to assemble a call kit containing those parts with the highest probability for use, and this is what our field engineers began carrying onto customers' premises. The result was a significant decrease in the time spent retrieving extra parts. Service calls are now finished much faster, which pleases customers. And we are able to make more service calls, which delights Savin.

■ Even a problem as small as tiny screws being occasionally dropped into machines during service calls can be helped by statistical analysis. When we studied the variation found in the service call process, we were able to quantify the time being wasted retrieving those little screws. As a result, we equipped each technician with a magnetic screwdriver and the problem of wayward screws was virtually eliminated.

One should not conclude that total quality management and statistical analysis are the exclusive territory of a handful of specialists. Total quality management is an approach to doing business that should permeate every job in the service industry. For that reason, I have fought against designating TQM as a "program" at Savin. Programs tend to be finite efforts that get the full attention only of those people whose careers are directly tied to the program. If the U.S. service industry is to survive and prosper, TQM should be the approach followed by everyone in the industry.

That's not to say that a company's TQM resources shouldn't include an in-house statistician. I know from personal experience that they are hard to recruit. If your company is fortunate enough to have one, that statistician should be an in-house consultant who provides the mathematical expertise managers need to implement their own TQM efforts.

Ideally, the corporate statistician will work almost exclusively at the invitation of operating managers. And as those managers come to appreciate the value of total quality management as a tool, the statistician should be one of the busiest people in the company.

Questions for Discussion

1   How did statistical analysis improve productivity at Savin? Give examples.

2   Based on your own experience, give one or two examples of situations where Pareto analysis might help improve quality or productivity.

CASE

The following case takes us through the chip-making process from design to supplier selection and to manufacturing and demonstrates how cycle time and quality were improved through improved process management.

CONTINUOUS PROCESS IMPROVEMENT AT BROOKTREE

Diane D. Pattison, James M. Caltrider, and Robert Lutze

In today's highly competitive marketplace continuous improvement is very difficult to achieve because oftentimes no one knows where to begin. Brooktree Corporation's experience provides insights into how continuous improvement can be achieved.

Brooktree Corporation designs, develops, and markets a broad family of proprietary mixed-signal VLSI integrated circuits (computer chips) that solve complex technical problems in computer graphics, imaging, and automatic test equipment (ATE) systems. Brooktree is a leading supplier of RAMDACs (random access memory digital to analog converters) that enable vendors of computer workstations, personal computers and laptop computers to offer cost-effective color and grey-scale graphics. These mixed-signal circuits are used by leading computer system manufacturers including IBM, Hewlett-Packard, Sun Microsystems, DEC, Compaq, and many others.

Brooktree was founded in 1981 by Myron Eichon and Henry Katzenstein, began operations in 1983, shipped its first product in 1985, achieved profitability in 1988, and went public in 1991. Current year's sales were over $80 million. Brooktree currently employs approximately 540 people worldwide.

Reprinted with permission from *Management Accounting,* Vol. 74 No. 8, February 1993, pp. 49–52. Copyright 1993 by Institute of Management Accountants, Montvale, N.J.

Computer Chip Production

Computer chips are designed at the San Diego development center after one of Brooktree's Strategic Business Units identifies an opportunity to fill a need in one of the corporation's target markets. The design process generally takes from eight to 18 months.

When the design phase is complete, production occurs in a four-step process. The first step is the production of the wafers, which contain the die that will become the heart or the "mind" of a computer chip. Brooktree contracts with several "foundries" located in the United States and Japan to produce the die used in its products. Specifications for the wafer are communicated to one or more of these "foundries" that fabricate Brooktree wafers. Finished wafers are shipped to San Diego where they are tested in the second step of the production process.

In the second step, wafer probe, all the die in a wafer are tested. Bad die are marked so that they will not be built into finished chips at assembly. This phase requires about seven days from the time the wafers arrive at Brooktree until they are tested and ready to ship out for assembly.

The third phase of the production process also is outsourced. The wafers are sent to assembly houses that cut the die out of the wafers and package the good ones in the ceramic or plastic packages that form most of the bulk of a computer chip.

Packaged parts are then sent back to San Diego for final testing. This final testing is considered to be the fourth phase of the production process. The finished goods inventory is maintained in San Diego. The entire production process—fabrication, probe, assembly, and final test—takes about 14 weeks. A flowchart of this process is shown in Figure 1.

Total Quality Management Background

In mid-1989 Brooktree management committed the company to Total Quality Management and continuous process improvement. Managers began a sustained effort to promote the understanding and improvement of the capabilities of the Brooktree processes. Many of the initial efforts focused on classic "factory problems" including inventory and cycle time reductions, improvement in outgoing quality, and on-time delivery performance. These efforts have been rewarded with improvements—in some cases dramatic improvements—in these measures.

About the same time, Brooktree management began to focus on forging a closer working relationship with its many suppliers. This supplier-management effort was driven by the knowledge that Brooktree's ability to meet the quality, cost, and performance needs of its customers would be determined by its suppliers. In order for Brooktree to perform better, it had to improve the performance of its suppliers.

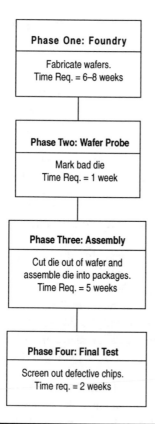

Figure 1 Production Process

Brooktree originally had established the Brooktree Foundry Coordination Committee (BFCC) to provide a single foundry interface or point of contact with all foundries. Late in 1991 BFCC began to hold quarterly strategy meetings with representatives from various foundries to explore ways in which all foundry groups could work together to improve Brooktree's relationship with them.

When the meetings began, foundries would often take as long as three weeks to commit to a delivery time to Brooktree. Of course, long and inconsistent commitment times make it harder to plan and control operations and respond quickly to customer requirements. Bob Lutze, Brooktree's manager of device engineering, noted, "Wafer ordering is a black hole."

One of the Foundry Coordination Committee's goals was to reduce the time required for foundries to commit to the dates that wafer orders would be delivered to Brooktree. The Brooktree contingent—including Quality Assurance Director Ted Holtaway, Manager of Device Engineering Bob Lutze, and Purchasing Manager Claudia Johnson—knew that the first step to solving the long-lead-time problem was to understand the way the current process worked. All the steps involved and the linkages or "products" that passed from group to group along the way would have to be understood. If the goal was to reduce the time requirement, then it also would be necessary to determine which steps in the process took the longest and which, if any, added no real value to the process.

It soon became apparent that none of the Brooktree personnel or the foundry representatives in question understood the whole process. Although the group had the collective knowledge to understand and describe the entire process, they never had "talked to each other" regarding the way the process worked. Each individual was expert in one or more of the steps required to get a wafer order committed, but nobody at the table had a good feel for the "big picture" and how all the pieces fit together.

Before a meaningful improvement effort could get under way, it was necessary to educate everyone in the room regarding the way the whole process worked at the time. A process flowchart was used to try to gather and display the collective knowledge present in the room. The entire flowchart development took about an hour. The group created the process flowchart capturing the current process and the time requirements for each step in that process. A "clean" version of that chart, including standard times, is presented in Figure 2.

Often participants in this type of exercise have trouble believing that the process under examination actually works the way the flowchart suggests it does. It's not uncommon to hear comments such as: "That can't be right!" or "We don't really do that, do we?" At this BFCC meeting such comments were made. And such comments are apt to be heard anytime a process consists of a series of functions performed by different companies, different divisions, or even different departments within one company. This lack of understanding occurs anytime management focuses on function (production control, customer service, marketing, accounting) rather than the process of meeting customer needs. This clearly was the case in this instance. Order commitments generally cross functional boundaries. And as long as an organization's vision is aligned with functional axes, managers and their accounting reports will operate in "functional chimneys." These chimneys make it easy for redundancies and inefficiencies in the process to grow and make it difficult if not impossible for these same redundancies and inefficiencies to be detected and ultimately corrected.

Process flowcharts are a simple way to begin to understand and communicate how a process actually works. Once one can "see the process" managers may be able to break down the walls of the functional chimneys and manage the process rather than the pieces.

Once the current wafer-commit process was visible, the group began devising

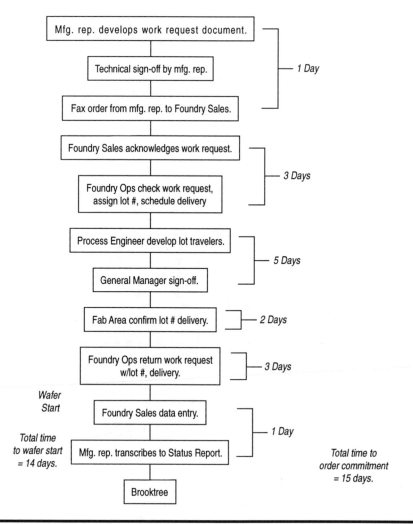

Figure 2   Original Process Flowchart

a plan to reduce the time required to commit wafer orders. The first flowchart shows that orders were not committed until the wafers had been started. After brief discussion, it became clear to everyone in the group that the time required to commit an order could be reduced by decoupling the commit process from the rest of the process of starting wafers. In other words, the two processes could run in parallel instead of serially as they are shown in Figure 2. Other changes included reducing the number of approvals required to move from step to step in the process.

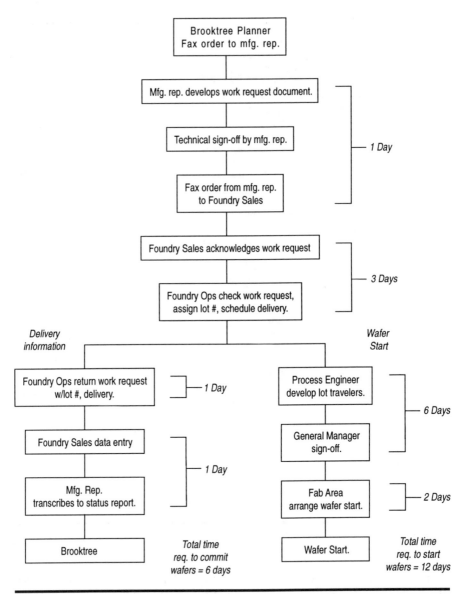

Figure 3 Improved Process Flowchart

The flowchart shown in Figure 3 maps the "improved process." It was expected that the process changes made as a result of this analysis would reduce the time required to obtain foundry commitments for wafers from 15 to six working days. Thus, what used to require three weeks now requires one week. This 67% reduction in process time is significant.

According to Brooktree participants, there were two characteristics of this improvement effort that made it successful. The first was that all parties recognized that everyone involved—Brooktree, distributors, and foundries—would benefit from streamlining the process. The second was that all the right people—people who knew the current process and who could make decisions regarding changes—were committed to the improvement and participated in the discussions at the meeting.

Committee members also were surprised at how quickly the supplier companies were able to agree to the changes that were necessary to streamline this process. They attributed this quickness, at least in part, to the clear picture that the flowchart provided.

Benefits of Flowcharting the Process

As a result of this exercise, wafer commit times have been reduced by about 67%. That reduction greatly simplifies the process of planning and managing Brooktree's purchasing and material control activities. It allows better and faster service to the ultimate customers. Because these gains were made by streamlining the process so that it works smarter and is more efficient (as opposed to acceleration by pushing harder), these process changes also should save suppliers time and money. A final result of this process evaluation and change is a tighter working relationship between Brooktree and its suppliers. That should continue to pay dividends, in terms of competitiveness, for a long time into the future.

Flowcharting and Analysis

One of the key requirements to the successful use of flowcharts as a process improvement tool is capturing the process as it actually works. This information is usually harder to obtain than expected. It is easy to fall into the trap of drawing the process as it should be or as it is assumed to be. But it should make sense that if the goal of the exercise is to improve the process, then neither of those approaches will be as effective as charting the actual process as it currently functions.

People involved in the flowcharting must have a good working knowledge of the process and how it actually works.

Once the chart is drawn, ideas for changing the process often begin to flow spontaneously. But there are some general guidelines or approaches, summarized below, that have proven useful in evaluating flowcharts.

General Guidelines

Be sure the flowchart reflects the way that the process actually works. The best way to do that is to have the people who are actually involved in the process develop the chart. Once that real chart is drawn, look for the following:

- **Steps that require lots of time or cost.** Are they necessary? Are there better alternatives available?

- **Bottlenecks or poorly designed steps in the process.** Would changes here improve the ability of the process to get its job done?

- **Critical relationships or interfaces among different groups.** How well managed are the interfaces? How well does the "product" that is provided by the supplier, or sender, in that relationship meet the needs of the customer, or receiver? Don't guess. Get some data! Ask the customer.

- **Loops in the flow.** These indicate that something is being redone (or reworked as it would be called in manufacturing) because it wasn't done correctly the first time. Find out why that happens, and work to remove the cause of the problem.

Questions for Discussion

1   The case describes a four-phase production process that is flowcharted in Figure 1. What actions would you take to reduce the cycle time of the production process?

2   How would a cross-functional team improve the process improvement?

3   Why does a flowchart such as Figure 2 help in reengineering the process?

4   Review the revised process and show how cycle time was reduced.

CASE

Chicago's Rush-Presbyterian-St. Luke's Medical Center is comprised of a 983-bed flagship facility, two suburban hospitals, a health science university, Rush Health Plans, a home health nursing service, and a subsidiary that markets health care products to corporations and other health care users. The following article identifies the many opportunities for process improvement and how these were attempted at the center.

CASE STUDY: QUALITY IMPROVEMENT IN A DIVERSIFIED HEALTH CENTER

Mary T. Koska

Applying industry models of quality improvement to the health care setting made perfect sense to Marie Sinioris, corporate vice-president of Rush-Presbyterian-St. Luke's Medical Center, Chicago.

When Sinioris began investigating the idea, she had already seen several concepts borrowed from industry—such as strategic planning and product-line management—successfully applied in the health care setting. And she believed that the Rush health system, with its diverse mix of for-profit and not-for-profit services, shared many similarities with the industries that had integrated quality management principles.

Sinioris was particularly impressed with the quality management philosophies in place at the Minnesota Mining and Manufacturing (3M) Co., St. Paul.

3M defines quality as a "consistent conformance with customer expectations." Its total quality management (TQM) process requires the commitment of top management and draws on employee insights to discover ways to better meet customer needs.

Reprinted with permission from *Hospitals*, Vol. 64 No. 23, December 5, 1990, pp. 38–39.

When Sinioris approached 3M for advice in implementing a TQM program, the company had already marketed its TQM process to other corporations. Sinioris offered 3M a new challenge: the chance to study how well TQM principles applied to the health care setting. In 1987, Rush became 3M's alpha site for testing TQM in health care.

TQM in a complex system.   At Rush, 3M had the opportunity to test the TQM process in a variety of health care settings. In addition to Rush's urban, 983-bed flagship facility, the system includes two suburban hospitals; a health sciences university; Rush Health Plans (which includes an HMO with 16 sites, a preferred provider organization, and an independent practice association); a home health nursing service; ArcVentures, a for-profit subsidiary that markets health care products to corporations and other health care settings; and six occupational health clinics.

The challenge of attaining a uniform standard of quality across Rush's diverse assemblage of organizations has never daunted Sinioris. And after three years, the TQM program at Rush is steadily moving toward its goal of achieving "uniform quality across the whole system," she says. The entire Rush system is scheduled to be using the TQM process in some form by July 1995.

Everyone counts.   3M's TQM process is built on the belief that every hospital staff member can have an impact on improving patient care. Therefore, Rush employees must be trained in the TQM philosophy. Currently, all senior managers and 5,000 of Rush's 8,000 employees have completed TQM training. All Rush employees are scheduled to have completed training when its fiscal year ends June 31, 1991.

Eighty departments have already completed initial training, and 32 departments have completed quality improvement plans. TQM philosophies have been linked to job descriptions and job appraisals throughout the system.

Sinioris is the first to say that not everyone in the institution is committed to applying TQM. There are still employees and managers who have a "wait and see" attitude or regard TQM as the newest management fad. But for the most part, the response has been overwhelmingly positive. "It was a surprise to me to see how dedicated employees have been to making improvements in their work," she notes.

Return on investment.   Rush commits $100,000 a year in direct operating expenses for the TQM program. That covers the salaries of two full-time TQM staff members and expenses for training materials, promotional posters and mugs, and other motivational and educational tools. Another $60,000 to $100,000 was initially spent on customer research to determine areas in need of improvement. That research will be repeated periodically to measure improvements.

Rush is already seeing a return on its investment. The TQM process has been credited with such departmental improvements as:

■ Decreasing the x-ray repeat rate in diagnostic radiology and reducing the department's absentee rate by 22.7 percent from 1987 to 1988

■ Reducing laboratory result turnaround time by an average of 25 percent, resulting in a $10,000 savings

■ Reducing the number of checks manually typed by the accounts payable department by 25 percent

■ Improving patient transport by adding eight additional FTEs

Beyond hospital care.   Rush and 3M are working on applying the TQM process to Rush subsidiaries such as the Home Pharmacy service, the university, and the managed care plans.

Home Pharmacy, Rush's for-profit mail-order pharmacy service that operates under ArcVentures, Inc., began using TQM concepts in pilot projects three years ago. The process is a good fit for the pharmacy service, says Ed Fischer, ArcVentures' vice-president.

That may be because the Home Pharmacy division has many of the same qualities of other small industries: It sells a service—home delivery of maintenance medication combined with claims processing—to employee benefits purchasers. Home Pharmacy's 160 clients include self-insured companies, third-party administrators, insurance companies, and managed care organizations.

The 40 Home Pharmacy employees applied 3M's concepts to the day-to-day problems that occur when filling 35,000 prescriptions per month.

For example, the employees suggested streamlining the nine separate forms used for customer service, order delays, and prescription returns into just three forms. The resulting reduction in paperwork saved one penny per each prescription filled.

Another project pinpointed the most common reasons that prescription orders were returned unfilled to the patient. Using a customer survey, Home Pharmacy determined that prescriptions were returned most often because patients were either ordering refills too early or ordering refills on prescriptions that had expired.

Before the survey, Home Pharmacy didn't know that many patients were unaware of the one-year limit on prescriptions. It then decided to include an editorial on prescription limits in most issues of the Home Pharmacy's semiannual newsletter.

TQM concepts apply readily to measuring improvements in error rates or response time in the mail-order pharmacy setting, says Fischer. Most of all, the program has helped Home Pharmacy employees know where to concentrate their energy when making improvements. In some cases, that has meant redesigning standard forms; in other cases, it has meant increasing patient education.

"Ultimately, the feedback in the TQM process can take virtually any operation ahead in its quest for customer satisfaction," says Fischer.

TQM in the university. Rush is one of the first universities to begin applying the TQM process, says John Trufant, Ed.D., vice-president of academic resources and dean of Rush's College of Health Sciences and graduate schools. He believes that many of the basic principles of TQM are already present in good university management. "The tenets underlying TQM—empowerment of the staff, pushing decisionmaking down to the lowest possible levels, and participatory management—are things that university settings are good at anyway," he says.

Rush has not yet applied TQM to any academic program, although a few health sciences departments are gearing up for it. However, Rush has successfully applied TQM to academic support services, particularly the university library and biomedical communications department. Both of these divisions have applied classic TQM principles to determine how they could better meet their customers' expectations.

The university library is currently developing a system to ensure that its resources are available to those who make specific requests for them. In particular, the library noticed that many books put on hold were not available when borrowers came to pick them up. The library designed a flow chart of the entire "hold" process and pinpointed exactly where the current system broke down.

For example, some books requested to be held were not designated as "holds" in the library computer system, and others requested to be held were accidentally reshelved and then checked out again before an existing hold request was fulfilled. Library personnel are now in the process of developing a system to ensure that hold requests are honored.

Another result of TQM has been increased use of the university's biomedical communications department. As part of TQM, the department launched a self-promotion campaign. The campaign was so effective in increasing use of department services that the department had to add two new full-time employees.

TQM has been applied for a year in the academic support service areas. During this time, Trufant admits he has seen a few false starts. For example, a survey of library customers turned up little new or interesting information to use for quality improvement projects. In fact, the majority of respondents said the library was already doing a good job meeting their needs.

Although library staff were glad to discover that they had satisfied customers, "It didn't mean we couldn't do things better or that there weren't ways of increasing our efficiency," Trufant points out. "That's really what we're working on."

The managed care frontier. The introduction of TQM principles to Rush Health Plans, Inc. (RHPI) is just now getting under way. The plans hope to use the TQM process to help achieve their long-term goal of becoming the most well-known and respected managed health care plans in the Chicago area.

But the plans don't expect to be able to supply the TQM process overnight, says Barb Wener, RHPI's quality improvement process coordinator. The Rush Health Plans umbrella includes three distinct product lines: a staff model HMO, an independent practice association (IPA), and a preferred provider organization (PPO).

The diversity of each entity will make coordinating the TQM process an ongoing challenge. Each plan has a different customer group to please and thus different problems to address, Wener says.

For example, improving patients' access to care will be the goal at the 16 HMO sites. For the PPO and IPA plans, the focus will be on improving contractual arrangements with vendors and providers.

The success of the quality improvement efforts at RHPI will rest on identifying customer needs. To do this, Wener will rely heavily on the plans' 800 employees to devise solutions to identified problems.

That's the heart of the 3M/Rush TQM process. "We realize that we must focus on the customer's expectations when we plan our improvements," notes Wener. "We're going to do that with employee participation, because they know best."

Questions for Discussion

1   Can the principles of TQM that are appropriate for manufacturing be applied in a service industry such as health care? Explain.

2   What kind of training would you recommend for the 8,000 employees at Rush?

3   Choose two or more of the tools/techniques/methods discussed in Chapter 6 and show how they could be used to improve cycle time and quality at Rush.

4   Choose another service company and show how it could be improved by using the same or similar methods.

PROCESS QUALITY AT VARIFILM

Compare each of the following criteria to Varifilm and indicate whether the situation in the company is a *strength (S)* or *needs improvement (I)*. Justify your answer.

PROCESS MANAGEMENT

5.2 Process Management: Product and Service Processes   (S)   (I)

- Key indicators are used to evaluate quality and operational performance.   —   —

- The process management system provides for a controlled process for each product through documentation and standard systems.   —   —

- A controlled operating system incorporates equipment specifications, production orders, controlled operations, controlled processing procedures, and measurement test methods.   —   —

- Documentation is available on how to handle out-of-control occurrences for automated processes.   —   —

- Customer input is reviewed to determine how quality, cycle time, and overall performance can be improved.   —   —

5.3 Process Management: Business Processes and Support Services

- Internal and external customer requirements are determined through customer discussions, benchmark studies, and internal and external audits.   —   —

- Support service functions need key indicators with formal charts and regular reviews.   —   —

- A systematic approach is required for gathering and considering information from customers of the business processes and support services.   —   —

	(S)	(I)

■ Information concerning business and support services leads to corrective actions and documentation.

■ Support services are prioritized according to importance (e.g., finance and accounting, MIS, human resources, facilities, etc.).

■ Business processes are improved through the application of statistical analysis of process data and statistically designed experiments. In addition, benchmarking, process mapping, and process simplification are used.

SUPPLIER QUALITY AND QUALITY ASSESSMENT

5.4 Supplier Quality

■ Supplier quality requirements are defined, including product quality, value added, service, and capability and technology. Key indicators for each requirement are also defined.

■ A system of supplier certification is in place, as well as a supplier recognition process.

■ Supplier input is sought for improvement in supplier specifications, which in turn improves company specifications.

■ Specific methods are used for gathering data from suppliers so that procurement activities can be improved.

■ Supplier benchmarks are used to improve supplier quality.

5.5 Quality Assessment

■ Internal audits, TQM fitness reviews, customer surveys, and supplier audits are among the methods for assessing systems and processes.

■ Assessment findings lead to specific improvement actions.

■ Who assesses the systems and processes, what is assessed, and how often the assessment takes place are clearly defined.

Additional Areas for Improvement

_____

_____

_____

7

CUSTOMER FOCUS AND SATISFACTION

Quality begins and ends with the customer.

Joel Ross

Of all the Baldrige Award criteria, none is more important that customer focus and satisfaction. This category accounts for 300 of the 1000-point value of the award.

> This category examines the company's relationships with customers and its knowledge of customer requirements and of the key quality factors that drive marketplace competition. Also examined are the company's methods to determine customer satisfaction, current trends and levels of customer satisfaction and retention, and these results relative to the competition.[1]

The principles discussed in this chapter and in the entire book apply equally to both service and manufacturing firms. Judging from what is known about U.S. manufacturing and service firms, not many companies would not receive a grade of "A" for customer focus. A comprehensive study by the consulting firm Ernst & Young of 584 companies found that customer complaints were of "major or primary" importance in identifying new products and services among only 19 percent of banks and 26 percent of hospitals.

The widespread tendency to ignore complaints or track them and identify the cause(s) can have very serious consequences. This is particularly true in services, where it is estimated that for every complaint a business receives, there are 26 other customers who feel the same way but do not air their feelings to the company.[2]

Failure to identify the root cause of complaints means that reduction of variation in the causative process is more difficult. A customer unable to get through to a sales representative is evidence of a malfunction in the telephone procedure (process) or the sales and marketing function. Thus, it becomes necessary to tie the customer to the process.

Evidence indicates that part of the cause of this failure to close the customer-process loop is inadequate support from top management for the total quality management (TQM) infrastructure and a continued focus on the techniques of TQM, particularly statistical process control (SPC).

The Ernst & Young study mentioned previously found that quality-performance measures such as defect rates and customer satisfaction levels play a key role in determining pay for senior managers in only fewer than one in five companies. *Profitability* is still king. There is, of course, nothing wrong with a focus on cash flow and short-term profits, but long-term profit and market share require a base of satisfied customers that are retained by a focus on satisfaction. Some top executives may not like to believe the level or severity of customer complaints or may be offended by them. When Amtrak was criticized in the *Wall Street Journal* by a transportation analyst (Lind), the president of Amtrak responded (in the same paper):

■ My own conclusion is that this [comment] is based on hopelessly incorrect assumptions about Amtrak and the railroad industry, and that Mr. Lind would be well advised to limit his comments and suggestions to the streetcar and transit business with which he is familiar and to avoid getting over his depth.[3]

While it may be true that the president of Amtrak is correct in this case, such an attitude expressed publicly could very well pervade the work force, who might perceive the message as justification for continuing the existing level of service.

Another reason for the lack of customer focus is the tendency of many firms to emphasize the techniques of TQM such as SPC and other outcome-oriented methods such as productivity and cost reduction. Again, these are desirable and necessary, but a singular emphasis on these areas is to put the cart before the horse.

The customer is not really interested in the sophistication of a company's process control, its training program, or its culture. The bottom line for the customer is whether he or she obtains the desired product. This truism is recognized by Deming, Juran, and Crosby.

PROCESS VS. CUSTOMER

Customer complaints are analogous to process variation. Both are undesirable and must be addressed. In both cases, the optimum output must be compared against an objective, a standard, or a benchmark. Both are integral parts of the quality improvement process. The integration of the customer and the process is shown conceptually in Figure 7-1.

From the company's point of view, customer satisfaction is the result of a three-part system: (1) company processes (operations), (2) company employees who deliver the product, and service that is consistent with (3) customer expectations. Thus, the effectiveness of the three-part system is a function of how well these three factors are integrated.

This concept is shown in Figure 7-2. The overlap (shaded area) represents the extent to which customer satisfaction is achieved. The objective is to make this area as large as possible and ultimately to make all three circles converge into an integrated system. The extent to which this condition is achieved depends on the effectiveness of (1) the process, (2) employees, and (3) determination of what constitutes "satisfaction." Like any system, control is necessary. Thus, standards are set, performance is measured, and variation, if any, is corrected.

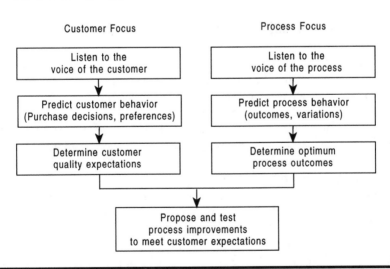

Figure 7-1   Integration of Customer and Process (Adapted from Dean E. Headley and Bob Choi, "Achieving Service Quality through Gap Analysis and a Basic Statistical Approach," *Journal of Services Marketing,* Winter 1992, p. 7.)

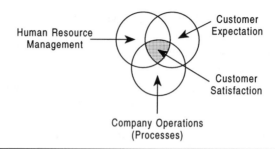

Figure 7-2 Customer Satisfaction: Three-Part System

■ Ritz-Carlton Hotel Company won the Baldrige Award in 1992. Many people thought that no hotel could do this because service in this industry is so difficult to measure and to deliver. The company meticulously gathers data on every aspect of the guest's stay to determine if the hotels are meeting customer expectations. Key to the research are the daily quality production reports that identify all problems and defects reported in each of 720 work areas. The data compiled range from the time it takes for housekeepers to clean a room to the number of guests who must wait in line to check in.[4]

INTERNAL CUSTOMER CONFLICT

Internal customers are also important in a TQM program. These are the people, the activities, and the functions within the company that are the customers of other people, activities, or functions. Hence, manufacturing is the customer of design, and several departments may be customers of data processing.

Conflict frequently arises between the needs of internal and external customers. In many cases, processes are designed to meet the needs of internal customers. Any "customer" who has been admitted to a hospital or outpatient service understands this. The registration process is designed to meet the needs of the admitting department, business office, or medical records. The result is a long wait to give information that will be provided again and again to personnel who represent admitting, the laboratory, finance, social work, and medicine. Who is the customer? Who is the beneficiary? Who is the recipient of the output? The patient gets the impression that he or she is a piece of raw material being moved along an amorphous assembly line known as health care.

It is not too difficult to identify other examples in both the private and public sectors. How about a university? It has been said that if you want to find out what kind of organization you are about to do business with, call on the phone!

A balance needs to be struck between the needs of these two customer groups. The solution is to determine the real needs of each and design the process to meet both.

DEFINING QUALITY

Supreme Court Justice Potter Steward once said that while he could not define "obscenity," he knew it when he saw it. Wrestling with a definition of quality is almost as difficult but necessary nevertheless. You cannot manage what you cannot measure.

The several dimensions of quality (performance, features, reliability, etc.) were discussed in a previous section.[5] However, the shortfall regarding product quality is that the services connected with it are so frequently overlooked. Good packaging, timely and accurate shipping, and the ability to meet deadlines matter as much as the quality of the product itself. Customers define quality in terms of their total experience with the company. Many companies approach customer satisfaction in a narrow way by confining quality considerations to the product alone.[6]

A QUALITY FOCUS

It is impossible to avoid the constant bombardment of "quality" and "satisfaction" messages in advertising on television and radio and in print media. Much of this advertising, and the actions to deliver the product or service, is little more than vague rhetoric. Even the popular phrases "satisfaction guaranteed" or "low price guaranteed" do not state what the customer is supposed to get for his or her purchase.

Some companies have attempted to improve this rhetoric by supplementing the message with additional definitions of satisfaction. McDonald's guarantees customer satisfaction with the pledge: "If you are not satisfied, we'll make it right or the next meal is on us." What does the phrase *make it right* mean? The question is whether this guarantee relates to product quality and customer satisfaction or is merely a promotion. Perhaps the slogan should be changed to "enjoyment guaranteed."

Many firms back up a satisfaction guarantee with promises of a reward if they fail to meet their own standards or those of the customer. Hampton Inns refunds your money. At Pizza Hut you get it free if not served in five minutes. Some firms give you a $5 bill. Delta Dental Plans of Massachusetts sends you a check for $50 if you get transferred from phone to phone while seeking an answer to an insurance question. Automobile dealers and manufacturers are fond of promoting "quality service" without defining just what this is. Some back it up with such specifics as towing service, free rides to work, or loaner cars when the customer's car is kept overnight.

There are two advantages to backing up a guarantee with some penalty for failure to deliver. It can cure employee apathy and bring quality to the attention of employees on a personal basis. It also may leave the buyer with a perception of dedication and thereby serve to retain what otherwise may have been a lost customer. These customers may say to themselves and others: "Well, my pizza was ten minutes late but they gave me a free one, so that proves they are serious about quality." Retaining this customer, who now has a better perception and higher expectation, may be worth the cost of the pizza and the foregone sale.

It should be remembered that any effort to tie the message of satisfaction to a failure-to-deliver penalty is ineffective if the variation or failure is not traced back to process improvement and the cause of the variation. Why was the pizza delivered late? Why was the customer shifted from phone to phone? Why did the dealer keep the car overnight? The variation-cause connection is identified by problem solving and the process improvement through process control.

Break Points

The need to improve customer satisfaction in *measurable* amounts is well known. But what is the measure and how much improvement is needed? If a customer is willing to stand in line for two minutes but finds five minutes unacceptable, anything between is merely satisfactory. Zero to one minute is outstanding. On-time delivery below 90 percent may be judged by customers as unacceptable, while over 98 percent is considered outstanding. Improvement programs should be geared toward reaching either a two-minute or five-minute range for standing in line and either 90 or 98 percent for delivery times. These are the market *break points,* where improving performance will change customer behavior, resulting in higher prices or sales volume. Forget the improvement program that targets one minute waiting in line or the delivery program that targets between 90 and 98 percent.

A Central Theme

Although individuals and teams may have targets that are directed at process improvement in their specific activities, a common theme or focus may integrate the many individual or group efforts that may have their own priority. At Motorola the theme is *six sigma;* at Hewlett Packard it is a *tenfold reduction in warranty expense.* At General Electric no part will be produced that cannot meet a *one-part-in-a-million* defect rate. At MBNA of America (a credit card company), the target is *customer retention.* In other companies it can be a reduction in defects or cycle time. Such a theme tends to be pervasive because so many individuals can relate their activities to it. It can serve to mobilize employees around an overall quality culture.

THE DRIVER OF CUSTOMER SATISFACTION

The benefits of having customers who are satisfied is well known and was outlined in Chapter 1. The issues in building customer satisfaction are to acquire satisfied customers, know when you have them, and keep them.[7]

The obvious way to determine what makes customers satisfied is simply to ask them. Before or concurrently with a customer survey, an audit of the company's TQM infrastructure needs to be made. IBM is one company that has identified the key excellence indicators for customer satisfaction. These key indicators are listed in Table 7-1.[8]

Despite the obvious need for customer input in determining new product/ service offerings and improving existing ones, the widespread tendency is to determine perceived quality and perceived customer satisfaction based almost

Table 7-1   Key Excellence Indicators for Customer Satisfaction

- Service standards derived from customer requirements
- Understanding customer requirements
  - Thoroughness/objectivity
  - Customer types
  - Product/service features
- Front-line empowerment (resolution)
- Strategic infrastructure support for front-line employees
- Attention to hiring, training, attitude, morale for front-line employees
- High levels of satisfaction—customer awards
- Proactive customer service systems
- Proactive management of relationships with customer
- Use of all listening posts
  - Surveys
  - Product/service follow-ups
  - Complaints
  - Turnover of customers
  - Employees
- Quality requirements of market segments
- ■ Surveys go beyond current customers
  - Commitment to customer (trust/confidence/making good on word)

solely on in-house surveys.[9] Even when the company does attempt to get input, the survey may suffer from methodology shortcomings. Mailed questionnaires lose control over who responds, and respondents are less likely to reply if they are dissatisfied or if the name of the company or product is indicated. Just what is satisfaction? If the customer's expectation is low, satisfaction may be acceptable but perception will not improve. If perception is low but satisfaction is acceptable, how is this determined and what can be done? Suppose that 95 percent of respondents indicate satisfaction but do not perceive the product as one of the best. Survey results can be misconstrued and lead to complacency.[10]

■   The hotel chain Ritz-Carlton, a Baldrige winner, relies on technology to keep comprehensive computerized guest history profiles on the likes and dislikes of more than 240,000 repeat guests. Researchers survey more than 25,000 guests each year to find ways in which the chain can improve delivery of its service.[11]

GETTING EMPLOYEE INPUT

Employee input can be solicited concurrent with customer research. It could help identify barriers and solutions to service and product problems, as well as serving as a customer-company interface.[12] Such surveys can help identify changes that may be necessary for quality improvement. In addition to customer-related considerations, employee surveys can measure (1) TQM effectiveness, (2) skills and behaviors that need improvement, (3) the effectiveness of the team problem-solving process, (4) the outcomes of training programs, and (5) needs of internal customers.[13]

■   Corning Inc., a leader in the glassware industry, asked line and staff groups worldwide to assess themselves using the Baldrige criteria. Each group was to develop a few quality strategies that would address the most critical elements identified in the assessment. Measures, referred to a Key Result Indicators, that focused on evidence of customer deliverables and process outcomes were required.[14]

MEASUREMENT OF CUSTOMER SATISFACTION

The accelerating interest in the measurement of customer satisfaction is reflected in the over 170 consulting firms that specialize in this activity.[15] Some firms use the "squeaky wheel" or "if it ain't broke, don't fix it" approach and measure customer satisfaction based on the level of complaints. This has a number of disadvantages. First, it focuses on the negative aspects by measuring dissatisfaction rather than satisfaction. Second, the measure is based on the complaints of a vocal few and may cause costly or unneeded changes in a process. As indicated at the beginning of this chapter, for every complaint, there are 26 others who feel the same way but do not air their feelings.

There are two basic steps in a measurement system: (1) develop key indicators that drive customer satisfaction and (2) collect data regarding the perceptions of quality received by customers.[16]

Key indicators of customer satisfaction are what the company has chosen to represent quality in its products and services and the way in which these are delivered. The building blocks that the system is designed to track are (1) expectations of the customer and (2) company perceptions of customer expectations.

In Chapter 1 a number of indicators for the physical product (e.g., reliability, aesthetics, adaptability, etc.) were identified. For service businesses or for services that accompany a product, the range of indicators depends on the nature of the service. One authority[17] has suggested that some important areas to consider are outcome, timeliness of the service, satisfaction, dependability, reputation of the provider, friendliness/courteousness of employees, safety/risk of the service, billing/invoicing procedures, responsiveness to requests, competence, appearance of the physical facilities, approachability of the service provider, location and access, respect for customer feelings/rights, willingness to listen to the customer, honesty, and an ability to communicate in clear language. These indicators, if appropriate and addressable, are converted to action items that reflect specific delivery systems where the product or service meets the customer. For example, in a bank customer needs and systems would combine to deliver short teller lines, friendly and courteous staff, ATMs that work, and low fees on accounts.

Data collection is required in order to identify the needs of customers and the related problems of process delivery. The data gathering process surveys both customers and employees. By including employees, customer needs and barriers to service can be identified, as well as recommendations for process improvement. Different orientations are emphasized for customers and employees; the former are asked for *their* expectations and the latter are asked what they think *customers* expect.

THE ROLE OF MARKETING AND SALES

Marketing and sales are the functions charged with gathering customer input, but in many firms the people in these functions are unfamiliar with quality improvement.[18] Shortcomings in marketing as identified by critics include:[19]

- Partnering arrangements with dealers and distribution channels
- Focusing on the physical characteristics of products and overlooking the related services
- Losing a sense of customer price sensitivity
- Not measuring or certifying suppliers such as advertisers
- Failing to perform cost/benefit analyses on promotion costs
- Losing markets to generics and house brands

> - According to one source, Motorola is a world-class producer of products but is less than world class in marketing. Historically, the company has been oriented toward engineering and technology. Its six sigma quality is well known. The publisher of *Technologic Computer Letter* says, "With many product lines Motorola has an extremely compelling story to tell but it is used to hiding its light under a bushel and does not make its advantages heard."[20]

Quality and customer satisfaction have not played an important role in the sales function (*process*). Consider the stereotype of a salesperson. He or she is detail (rather than process) oriented and trained in technical product knowledge (rather than customer knowledge). Salespeople are feature oriented: "We've got six models, four colors, and it comes with a money-back guarantee." They are trained and rewarded for getting new customers, as opposed to retaining existing ones.

THE SALES PROCESS

According to Hiroshi Osada of the Union of Japanese Scientists and Engineers (JUSE), TQM needs to begin with the salespeople.[21] Yet TQM has migrated to the sales force in only a few companies.[22] Even fewer perceive sales as a *process* that lends itself to analysis and improvement for customer satisfaction. To repeat a previous caveat, "If you can't measure it, you can't manage it." Another can be added: "You can't measure it if its not a process." Both of these cliches are as true for sales and marketing as for any other process. The objective is quality outcomes. In order for TQM to become a part of sales and marketing, managers and employees must move toward a deeper understanding of its processes—selling, advertising, promoting, innovating, distribution, pricing, and packaging—*as they relate to customer satisfaction.*

Marketing applications need not be confined to the marketing department. Other functions can borrow these techniques to improve the satisfaction of external and internal customers. A brokerage firm should care not only about sending accurate statements on time, but should also be concerned with whether the statement format fits the customer's needs. In an issue of *Marketing News,* Research Professor Eugene H. Fram of the Rochester Institute of Technology suggests the following types of non-traditional marketing extensions:[23]

- **Adapted** marketing refers to a non-marketing function that adapts traditional techniques. Relationship selling is an example. If a human resource department sends the same recruiter each year to a campus, this person can use principles of relationship selling to further company goals. This type of selling can also be used within the organization and between departments. The classic conflict between production (cost) and sales (delivery) can be reduced.

- **Morale** marketing can improve morale. Consider what the terms "Team Taurus" or "Team Xerox" did for morale in those companies.

- **Sensitivity** marketing borrows from the basic marketing principle which says that one must understand the customer's needs in order to fulfill them and to build long-term relationships. In a marketing sense, individuals, groups, and departments are better able to achieve quality and productivity if they are sensitive to the needs, concerns, and priorities of both internal and external customers.

SERVICE QUALITY AND CUSTOMER RETENTION

Customer defection is a problem and customer retention an opportunity in both manufacturing and service firms. Manufacturers have generally been good about measuring satisfaction with products, but now they are moving into service areas. The publicity surrounding the Baldrige Award accounts for much of this. Other reasons relate to the size and growth of service industries and the growing importance of service as a means of strategically competing in the marketplace.

Service industries are playing an increasingly important role in a nation's economy. Over 75 percent of the working population in the United States is employed in the service sector and the percentage is growing. When this employment is combined with service jobs in the manufacturing sector, it becomes evident that the importance of services is increasing. Many executives feel that the management of services is one of the most important problems they face today. Yet most of us know from personal experience that the quality of services is declining, despite the efforts of some companies to improve it.

Because so many services are intangible, the interaction between employees and customers is critical. Chase Manhattan Bank realizes that an employee's ability to meet or exceed customer expectations when conducting a routine transaction influences the customer's satisfaction with the organization. In fact, this interaction influences satisfaction more than the actual product or service obtained. The one-on-one or face-to-face contact between the customer and the deliverer of the service (nurse, flight attendant, retail clerk, restaurant server) is extremely important.

Manufacturers are careful to measure material yield, waste scrap, rework, returns, and other costs of poor quality processes. Service companies also have these costs, which are reflected in the cost of customers who will not come back because of poor service. These are customer defections and they have a substantial impact on cost and profits. Indeed, it is estimated that customer defections can have a greater impact than economies of scale, market share, or unit cost.[24] Despite this, many companies fail to *measure* defections, determine the *cause* of defections, and improve the *process* to reduce defections.

CUSTOMER RETENTION AND PROFITABILITY

What is the ultimate desired outcome of customer focus and satisfaction? Is it achieving profit in the private sector or productivity in the public or non-profit sectors? The answer must be yes. Oddly enough, however, an accurate cause-and-effect relationship has yet to be established between profit and customer satisfaction. This is due, in part, to the difficulty of measuring satisfaction and relating it to profit. However, there is a proven relationship between *customer retention and profit.*

One way to put a value on customer retention is to assign or estimate a "lifetime retention value," the additional sales that would result if the customer were retained. Taco Bell calculates the lifetime value of a retained customer as $11,000. An automobile dealer believes that the lifetime value of retaining a customer is $300,000 in sales.[25] Conversely, MBNA America (a credit card company) has found that a 5 percent improvement in customer *defections* increases its average customer value by 125 percent.

The system for improving *customer retention* and profit is illustrated in Figure 7-3. The drivers are *employee satisfaction* and employee retention. The system components are

- **Internal service quality,** which establishes and reinforces a climate and organization culture directed toward quality.

- **Employee retention,** which is achieved through good human resource management practices and organization development methods such as teams, job development, and empowerment. Employee retention depends on employee satisfaction, which in turn can be related to external service and customer satisfaction.

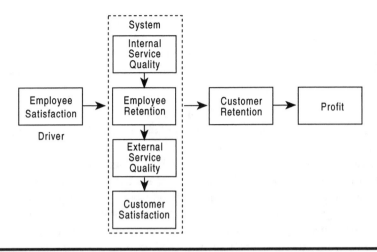

Figure 7-3   Profitability and Customer Retention

- **External service quality,** which is delivered through the organization's quality infrastructure.
- **Customer satisfaction** and follow up, in order to reduce customer defections and improve retention.

To reiterate, there is a proven relationship between customer retention and profit.

BUYER–SUPPLIER RELATIONSHIPS

Almost every company purchases products, supplies, or services in an amount that frequently equals around 50 percent of its sales. Traditionally many of these companies have followed the "lowest bidder" practice where price is the critical criterion. The focus on price, even for commodity products, is changing as companies realize that careful concentration of purchases, together with long-term supplier–buyer relationships, will reduce costs and improve profits.[26] Deming realized this and suggested that a long-term relationship between purchaser and supplier is necessary for best economy.[27] If a buyer has to rework, repair, inspect, or otherwise expend time and cost on a supplier's product, the buyer is involved in a "value/quality-added" operation, which is not the purpose of having a reliable supplier. In that never-neverland of the perfect buyer–supplier relationship, no rework or inspection is necessary.

A partnership arrangement is emerging between a growing number of manufacturers and suppliers. At Eastman Kodak, the Quality Leadership Process

(QLP) has improved the company's production processes, reduced overall manufacturing costs, and improved quality by transforming traditional manufacturer–supplier roles. Because one-half of all components used in manufacturing are supplied by outside vendors, realignment of the supplier base has become a central strategy of QLP.[28]

> ■ Motorola has advanced the supplier–customer relationship further than most companies. The system is based on a basic economic principle: whenever someone buys from someone else, there is a mutually beneficial transaction and pleasing both sides is important. With this in mind, Motorola has begun to market itself as a customer. The company's director of materials and purchasing says, "If the sauce is good for the goose, it should be good for the gander, and we are genuinely trying to cooperate, collaborate and do some strategic things with our suppliers. Our goal is to become a world-class customer and that means that it is important for use to learn what the buyer needs to do in order for suppliers to see us as a world-class customer."[29]

Several guidelines will help both the supplier and customer benefit from a long-term partnering relationship:

■ **Implementation of TQM by both supplier and customer.** Many customers (e.g., Motorola, Ford, Xerox) are requiring suppliers to operationalize the basic principles of TQM. Some have even required the supplier to apply for the Baldrige Award. This joint effort provides a common language and builds confidence between both parties.

■ **Long-term commitment to TQM and to the partnering relationship between the parties.** This may mean a "life cycle" relationship that carries partnering through the life cycle of the product, from market research and design through production and service.

■ **Reduction in the supplier base.** One or more automobile companies have reduced the number of suppliers from thousands to hundreds. Why have ten suppliers for a part when the top two will do a better job and avoid problems?

■ **Get suppliers involved in the early stages of research, development, and design.** Such involvement generates additional ideas for cost and quality improvement and prevents problems at a later stage of the product life cycle.

■ **Benchmarking.** Both customer and supplier can seek out and agree on the best-in-class products and processes.

How does one become a quality supplier? This of course depends on the criteria of the buyer, but it is reasonably safe to assume that if the following criteria are met, a company can reasonably expect to be classified in the quality category. The following criteria are required to be certified as *quality* in the automobile industry:

1. *Management philosophy* of the CEO should support TQM
2. Techniques of *quality control* should be in place (SPC, etc.)
3. Desire for a long-term *life cycle relationship*
4. Best-in-class *inventory and purchasing systems*
5. *Facilities* should be up to TQM standards
6. *Automation* level should meet quality standards
7. *R & D and design* should support customer expectations
8. Willing to *share costs*

QUESTIONS FOR DISCUSSION

7-1 Describe how a program directed toward customer focus and satisfaction interacts with

- The information and analysis component of the TQM approach
- Strategic quality planning
- Human resource development and management
- Management of process quality

7-2 Select a function or activity (e.g., design, order processing, accounting, data processing, engineering, market research) and identify a measure of quality that you would expect if you were an *internal* customer of that function or activity.

7-3 Choose a specific product or service in a particular industry and devise an action plan for obtaining customer input and feedback. How would the information generated by such a plan be used for process improvement?

7-4 Illustrate how a firm might focus on *internal* product or service specifications rather than customer expectations and desires.

7-5 Choose a product or service and list four or five characteristics that you as a customer would want and expect. Based on your experience, do you think that the firm will deliver?

7-6 How would you establish a system to measure customer satisfaction?

ENDNOTES

1. *Malcolm Baldrige National Quality Award Criteria—1993,* Washington, D.C.: U.S. Department of Commerce, National Institute of Standards and Technology, 1993, p. 29.
2. "Satisfaction-Action," *Marketing News,* Feb. 4, 1991, p. 4.
3. "Management: Quality Programs Show Shoddy Results," *Wall Street Journal,* May 14, 1992, Section B, p. 1.
4. Edward Watkins, "How Ritz-Carlton Won the Baldrige Award," *Lodging Hospitality,* Nov. 1992, p. 23.
5. See David A. Garvin, *Managing Quality,* New York: The Free Press, 1988, pp. 49–59. Garvin has defined the eight dimensions of quality as performance, features, reliability, conformance, durability, serviceability, aesthetics, and perceived quality. Computer-maker NCR goes to great expense to define quality as appropriateness, reliability, aesthetics, and usability. Industrial designers have given the company a silver medal for design. For a comprehensive report on how product design enhances profits and market share, see a special report, "Hot Products: How Good Design Pays Off" (cover story), *Business Week,* June 7, 1993, pp. 54–78.
6. Oren Harari, "Quality Is a Good Bit-Box," *Management Review,* Dec. 1992, p. 8.
7. Gerald O. Cavallo and Joel Perelmuth, "Building Customer Satisfaction, Strategically," *Bottomline,* Jan. 1989, p. 29.
8. These indicators are taken from class material in an IBM in-house workshop, "MDQ (Market Driven Quality) Workshop." The company was kind enough to share this class material with the author and several other professors from the College of Business, Florida Atlantic University. For this, I thank them.
9. It was found, for example, that in the hospital industry fewer than 5 percent of referring physicians play a prominent role in identifying new service opportunities. Nearly 40 percent of U.S. hospitals indicate that senior management "always or almost always" takes the dominant role in identifying new services." U.S. hospitals seek minimal input from patients. *The international Quality Study, Healthcare Industry Report,* American Quality Foundation and Ernst & Young, 1992.
10. For some ideas on getting customer input, see Joel E. Ross and David Georgoff, "A Survey of Productivity and Quality Issues in Manufacturing: The State of the Industry," *Industrial Management,* Jan./Feb. 1991.
11. Edward Watkins, "How Ritz-Carlton Won the Baldrige Award," *Lodging Hospitality,* Nov. 1992, p. 24.
12. Luane Kohnke, "Designing a Customer Satisfaction Measurement Program," *Bank Marketing,* July 1990, p. 29.
13. Kate Ludeman, "Using Employee Surveys to Revitalize TQM," *Training,* Dec. 1992, pp. 51–57.
14. David Luther, "Advanced TQM: Measurements, Missteps, and Progress through Key Result Indicators at Corning," *National Productivity Review,* Winter 1992/1993, pp. 23–36.
15. Lynn G. Coleman, "Learning What Customers Like," *Marketing News,* March 2, 1992, pp. CSM-1–CSM-11. This article contains a directory of 170 customer satisfaction measurement firms.
16. For a more detailed description of how to establish a measurement system, see J. Joseph

Cronin, Jr. and Steven A. Taylor, "Measuring Service Quality: A Reexamination and Extension," *Journal of Marketing,* July 1992, pp. 55–68. See also Luane Kohnke, "Designing a Customer Measurement Program," *Bank Marketing,* July 1990, pp. 28–30; Gerald O. Cavallo and Joel Perelmuth, "Building Customer Satisfaction, Strategically," *Bottomline,* Jan. 1989, pp. 29–33.

17. Dean E. Headley and Bob Choi, "Achieving Service Quality through Gap Analysis and a Basic Statistical Approach," *Journal of Services Marketing,* Winter 1992, pp. 5–14. This is a good primer on gap analysis and the use of basic statistical techniques.

18. Joe M. Inguanzo, "Taking a Serious Look at Patient Expectations," *Hospitals,* Sep. 5, 1992, p. 68. This article points out that there is very little employee involvement in measuring satisfaction and practically none from patients.

19. Allan J. Magrath, "Marching to a Different Drummer," *Across the Board,* June 1992, pp. 53–54.

20. B. G. Yovovich, "Becoming a World-Class Customer," *Business Marketing,* Sep. 1991, p. 16.

21. Dick Schaaf, "Selling Quality," *Training,* June 1992, pp. 53–59.

22. John Franco, president of Learning International in Stamford, Connecticut, has conducted a series of round table discussions with sales executives. He reported: "When we ask participants how many of them are from companies that have a quality movement underway, we find about half do. But when we ask them whether that effort has migrated to the sales force, fewer than 10 percent say it has." Dick Schaaf, "Selling Quality," *Training,* June 1992, pp. 53–59.

23. Eugene H. Fram and Martin L. Presberg, "TQM Is a Catalyst for New Marketing Applications," *Marketing News,* Nov. 9, 1992.

24. Frederick F. Reicheld and W. Earl Sasser, Jr., "Zero Defections: Quality Comes to Services," *Harvard Business Review,* Sep./Oct. 1990, pp. 105–111. Reprint No. 90508.

25. Harvard Business School video series, "Achieving Breakthrough Service," Boston: Harvard Business School, 1992.

26. Robert D. Buzzell and Bradley Gale, *The PIMS Principles,* New York: The Free Press, 1987, p. 62. The data from over 3000 strategic business units show that concentrating purchases *improves* profitability, at least up to a point. "The positive net effect of a moderate degree of purchase concentration suggests that the efficiency gains that can be achieved via this approach to procurement are usually big enough to offset the disadvantages that might be expected as a results of an inferior bargaining position."

27. W. Edwards Deming, *Out of the Crisis,* Cambridge, Mass.: Massachusetts Institute of Technology, Center for Advanced Engineering Study, 1986, p. 35.

28. Joseph P. Aleo, Jr., "Redefining the Manufacturer–Supplier Relationship," *Journal of Business Strategy,* Sep./Oct. 1992, pp. 10–14.

29. B. G. Yovovich, "Becoming a World-Class Customer," *Business Marketing,* Sep. 1991, p. 29.

READING

McKinsey and Company, a major U.S. management consulting firm, found that as many as two of three TQM programs have "stalled" in terms of customer satisfaction, service quality, and operations performance. The firm suggests that it is necessary to make quantum changes rather than just taking an incremental approach. Emphasis should be on results, not process. McKinsey gives a number of illustrations and makes suggestions for achieving results.

WHEN QUALITY CONTROL
GETS IN THE WAY OF QUALITY

Graham Sharman

U.S. industry has plowed several million dollars into quality programs over the past decade. So much so, that many U.S. managers are convinced they make quality products. Unfortunately, customers don't always think so. IBM's CEO John Akers probably put it best, when he was quoted in this newspaper as saying, "I am sick and tired of visiting plants to hear nothing but great things about quality and cycle time—and then to visit customers who tell me of problems."

Mr. Akers isn't alone. Our experience suggests that as many as two out of every three quality management programs in place for more than a couple of years are stalled; they no longer meet the CEO's expectations for tangible improvement in product or service quality, customer satisfaction, and operating performance.

What is to be done with these "stalled" programs? We at McKinsey have found the following to be useful:

■ **Shut down programs in businesses where dramatic change in economic performance is needed.**   Quality management programs yield incremental, not dramatic, improvements. Sagging profits and depressed sales call for tougher measures, such as radical downsizing, restructuring, or purging of superfluous management layers. If you have a gradual improvement program in place to sap losses, bite the bullet and shut it down.

After taking over as CEO of Alcoa, one of Paul O'Neill's first initiatives was to shut down Alcoa's decade-long quality effort because, he told *Business Week* last October, "the business needed restructuring and dramatic change, not gradual improvement over several years." To close the gap in competitiveness and productivity between Alcoa and some of the leading aluminum companies, such as Kobe Steel, he opted for a "quantum improvement" program like benchmarking.

■ **Link programs to strategic planning processes.** If incremental improvement is what you need, make sure you evaluate programs as part of your strategic planning processes; set specific goals for your senior managers and make these goals part of their performance reviews. Some companies like Allen-Bradley and Corning are already doing this. They incorporate quality improvement objectives in the bonus plans of senior executives.

But while you set priorities and objectives for your managers, do not let them, in turn, set goals for lower-level employees. It is demotivating and ineffective. Over and over we find that, given some guiding principles or areas for improvement, they set much higher goals for themselves. Reward them for reaching their goals. John Cleghorn, president of Royal Bank of Canada, was recently quoted in the *Toronto Globe & Mail* as saying that "quality companies put faith in their people....When employees see their opinions are valued, they see themselves making a difference to the success of the company. And they do."

■ **Focus programs outward on market "break points."** It is one thing to stress the importance of customer satisfaction; it is quite another to actually achieve measurable improvements. For a computer company, achieving on-time delivery rates below 90% may be judged by customers as unacceptable, while above 98% is judged clearly outstanding; anything in between is just satisfactory. On-time delivery improvement programs should be geared toward reaching either 90% or 98%—the market "break points" where improved performance will change customer behavior, resulting in higher prices or sales volume. Forget the improvement program that targets between 90% and 98%. You are wasting money.

MBNA Corp., the fourth-largest credit card issuer in the U.S., keeps its customers twice as long as the industry average because it religiously focuses on 14 items that it believes are break-point issues to its customers, including answering every phone within two rings and processing every credit-line increase request within an hour. Emphasizing the notion of break points pushes improvement efforts to understand customer behavior, focuses on what is deemed by customers as most important, and measures impact.

■ **Choose a single theme.** Nothing is more counterproductive than tens or sometimes hundreds of teams chasing wildly different "quality" priorities. Team A slashes cycle time in a components warehouse, while Team B reduces defects in circuit-board assembly, and so on. At year end, despite these small wins, neither cycle time nor defects, measured at the business or company level, demonstrates any tangible improvement.

Contrast this with Hewlett Packard, where CEO John Young focused the entire company by, in 1979, setting a goal of a tenfold reduction in warranty expenses and following it up, as Hewlett Packard neared that, with a goal of a 90% reduction in software defects. However, focusing on a single goal carries a risk: It may be inappropriate for the company at that time or may be viewed as an end in itself, rather than as the means to achieve a much higher and broader goal.

■ **Emphasize results, not process.** It is remarkable how often the focus with process diverts attention from results and creates excess staff and bureaucracy. (Before it was rolled back, the TQM effort at Florida Power & Light included a staff and a group of "quality consultants" that had swelled to 75.)

The Baldrige Award criteria are useful for an assessment of the completeness of a TQM effort, but making the prize the goal puts too much emphasis on process, and arguably yields mainly PR, not sustainable competitive wins. Motorola won the Baldrige Award in its inaugural year (1988). But its chairman, George Fisher, remarked then: "Yes we won the Baldrige Award. But all that means is that we are on our way with an effective process aimed at achieving total customer satisfaction. We still have a long way to go."

A result that Motorola wants out of its investments is a reduction of defects to within "six sigma" (no more than 3.4 defects per million—or 99.9997% perfect). Mr. Fisher is even trying to set exacting standards in such areas as basic research and meetings, where standards are not easily set. Alcoa's use of benchmarks was also driven by a need to set exacting standards, because, as Mr. O'Neill says, "world standards are measurable, and they are practiced somewhere."

A combination of these suggestions can help restart a stalled program by tying it to measurable achievements that make a real difference.

CASE

You may have come up with what you think customers want from your company's product or service. But how do you compare your processes with customer needs to ensure a quality fit? This company has an approach that works.

HEWLETT-PACKARD COMPANY

Have you ever sat down with other people at your company to look for a better way to meet customers' quality needs, only to have been disappointed with the results? The reason for your disappointment may be that one important element was missing from the equation: your customers themselves. Listening to them is what provides real insight into meeting their quality requirements.

While Hewlett-Packard Company's Northwest Integrated Circuit Division (Corvallis, OR) is in business to sell chips to other divisions inside Hewlett-Packard (HP), it also serves customers outside of HP. The problem that it faced about five years ago, however, was that many employees either didn't know who their customers were or actually believed that the customers were interfering with them as they performed their work.

Fortunately, management saw the obvious need to address these problems. "We wanted our people to become very familiar with our customers and realize that they were here to serve those customers," says Casey Collett, Ph.D., Total Quality Control manager. "Our goal was to become so responsive to our customers that we would be the only supplier with which they would want to do business."

A Four-Step Process

To meet that goal, the Division launched its Total Quality Control effort in 1983. Collett says it involves four steps:

Step #1 On your own, identify what you feel your major business processes are.

Step #2 On your own, determine how you are being measured by your customers.

Step #3 Go out and verify these two perceptions with your major customers.

Step #4 Develop a program to improve these processes.

To execute these four steps, division management created a small group of TQC experts, who currently report directly to the division manager and work closely with a steering committee of top managers. TQC members have expertise in manufacturing, teaching, statistics, and group facilitation. Together, the division quality and TQC departments attack customer satisfaction and internal process improvement issues, respectively.

The Division has also created a three-point TQC model, which has expanded to a seven-point model over the years. (See Figure 1.)

HP'S 10-Step Planning Process

The key to achieving TQC from the customer's point of view at HP is a 10-step business planning process pioneered by planning expert Scott Feamster. This process requires the division to understand and analyze each of the following:

1. Purpose
2. Objectives
3. Customers and distribution channels
4. Competition
5. Necessary products and services
6. Plans for necessary products and services (research, manufacturing, financial, and marketing plans)
7. Financial analysis
8. Potential problem analysis
9. Recommendations
10. Next year's tactical plan

The 10-step business planning process, then, is a systematic way of:

- Understanding the business you're proposing to be in;
- Understanding your customers' needs;

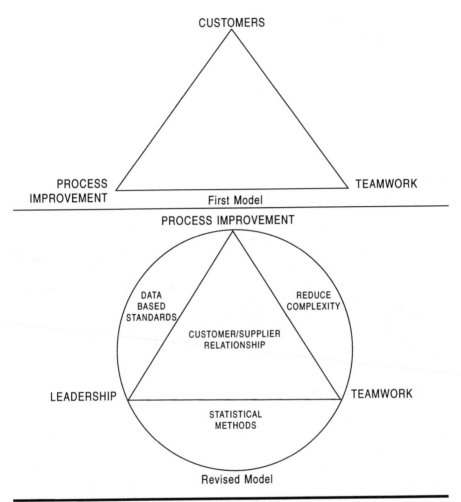

CUSTOMERS

PROCESS
IMPROVEMENT

TEAMWORK

First Model

PROCESS IMPROVEMENT

DATA
BASED
STANDARDS

REDUCE
COMPLEXITY

CUSTOMER/SUPPLIER
RELATIONSHIP

LEADERSHIP

TEAMWORK

STATISTICAL
METHODS

Revised Model

Figure 1   The *customer/supplier relationship* is central to the model. *Process improvements* occur through quality *leadership* and *teamwork*. *Reducing complexity,* setting *data-based (meaningful) standards,* and using appropriate *statistical methods* are the tools used to achieve the process improvements.

- Understanding the market and competitive environment you're entering, and as a result of these understandings
- Making solid, well-thought-out plans to meet your objectives.

"When you have developed your strategy, you should have an objective, methodical business plan that looks at what customers need and what you are going to do about those needs," says Collett. "Then you can take this document back to the customer and verify its accuracy."

A crucial element of making the 10-step business planning process work is what John Doyle, HP executive vice president for Systems Technology, calls "imaginative understanding of users' needs" (IUUN). "IUUN is becoming an integral part of how HP does business," Collett reports, adding that the philosophy of IUUN is to hear what customers say their needs are, and apply the creativity and knowledge you have to create solutions for customers.

Quality Function Deployment

While IUUN is critical to the success of the business planning process, Quality Function Deployment (QFD) is critical to the success of IUUN. QFD is the philosophy of designing your processes in response to customer needs.

"Before QFD, we didn't always realize the importance of understanding customer needs," says Collett. "As a result, we often invented products that we thought people such as ourselves would want, instead of asking our customers what they wanted."

Currently, the Division uses QFD in its R&D and marketing areas. "It helps us find out what our customers need so that we can build these needs into the next generation of our products."

QFD's Planning Matrix

One of the most important tools in QFD is the Planning Matrix. Once you know what your customers' requirements are, the next step is to translate these data into product development plans. The Planning Matrix plots customer requirements on one axis and business processes and their measures or product features on the other axis. The idea is to be able to determine the fit between customer needs and product features. "The Planning Matrix puts a lot more objectivity into the product development process," notes Collett.

Here's How It Works

Down the left side of the matrix are rows of user needs. Across the top of the matrix are columns of product features. With the matrix, you can see where a row intersects with a column and, in that cell, ask yourself if there is a strong relationship, a weak relationship, or no relationship between what the customer requires and what your company is doing.

If you find no relationship on a highly rated need as ranked by the customer, then you need to look at your product design plan and address the problem, since the customer considers it important. Conversely, if you are building in steps in the design process that have no bearing on customer needs, you may be able to eliminate them. For example, you may be doing test procedures on something that the customer doesn't care about.

R&D then creates another matrix of customer needs by process control characteristics (or internal manufacturing control characteristics) that will have to be met in order to give customers the features that they want. In short, the system translates raw customer data into focused activities for helping Marketing, R&D, Manufacturing, and Quality to make the desired product a reality.

Two More Tools for Success

HP uses two other tools to ensure that it is responding to the quality requirements of customers:

- **Customer Quality Engineers** are electrical engineers who work with Marketing to gather customer data, and with R&D and Manufacturing to make sure customer issues are addressed. The task is not always easy. "Clients ask questions in their own terms," says Collett. Customer quality engineers thus need to translate these terms so that answers to their real, often unarticulated problems can be found. Then they need to translate the solutions developed by the Division back into language that the customers will be able to understand and utilize.

- **Process Improvement Teams** attack customer issues throughout the Division's team concept. "A few of these teams interface so closely with customer divisions that they ask the customers to be on one of our teams," says Collett. "This certainly gives teams direct feedback from customers."

The teams solve customer problems and then return to customer locations to show them what they have accomplished. "The concept works well, because customers essentially drive the improvement process," she adds.

Focus on the Future

Things have been improving. "Our quality is better, our planning processes are improving, and teams are busy with improvement projects," says Collett. "Sales are up, but we never take customer satisfaction for granted. On an annual basis, we verify with our customers that our processes and the way we are measuring ourselves reflect customer satisfaction. We refine the measures more and more over time to make sure that they accurately reflect what the customer wants."

Questions for Discussion

1 Why is it important to understand a company's basic business processes in order to deliver customer satisfaction? Illustrate your answer.

2 How do you determine customers' perceptions of your product or service?

3 What are the basic differences between the first model and the revised model in Figure 1?

4 Explain the necessity for steps 3 and 4 of Hewlett-Packard's 10-step planning process.

5 How would you verify that customers are satisfied? What key result indicators (KRI) might be used?

CUSTOMER FOCUS AT VARIFILM

Compare each of the following TQM criteria to Varifilm and indicate whether the practice in the company is a *strength (S)* or *needs improvement (I)*. Justify your answer.

7.1 Customer Expectations: Current and Future	(S)	(I)
■ Surveys, partner feedback, complaints, gains and losses of customers, and trade literature are among the approaches to understanding customer requirements and expectations.	—	—
■ Third-party telephone surveys are conducted and reviewed periodically.	—	—
■ Selected methods can be used to project the relative importance of key future product and service features.	—	—
■ Cross-functional teams conduct post-mortem and root-cause analysis to determine why projects are not on target.	—	—
■ Different product requirements are considered for different market segments.	—	—
■ A systematic improvement approach to evaluating and improving the process for determining customer requirements is in place.	—	—

7.2 Customer Relationship Management

■ Specific service standards are deployed to all customer contact personnel and evaluated for service quality.	—	—
■ A customer satisfaction survey is used to evaluate the effectiveness of relationship management and customer contact performance.	—	—
■ Complaint data are systematically used to set priorities for improvement projects.	—	—

	(S)	(I)

■ Customer contact personnel maintain partnerships with strategic customers through meetings and TQM fitness reviews. — —

■ Response time standards are maintained for customer inquiries and followed up on. — —

■ A variety of customer contact approaches are used to provide easy access for customers. — —

Additional Areas for Improvement

_____

_____

_____

7.3 Commitment to Customers

■ Warranties and commitments to customers are compared to those made by key competitors. — —

■ Commitments extend beyond direct customers to the consumer. Methods include warranties and a toll-free number. — —

■ Determination of whether the customers understand and value commitments is made by customer contact personnel. — —

■ Whether or not company commitments address the principal concerns of customers is the subject of surveys and analysis. — —

■ Commitments such as warranties and guarantees are incorporated into every order and customer invoice along with the toll-free number. — —

7.4 Customer Satisfaction Determination

■ Key customer satisfaction requirements include product quality, on-time delivery, ease of access, price, and worker knowledge. Actual satisfaction is determined through personal contact, third-party surveys, and fitness reviews. — —

	(S)	(I)

■ Future market behavior is determined by interviewing key customer decision makers in functions such as R&D or purchasing.   —— ——

■ Competitive position relative to competitors on some appropriate index is conducted by a third-party survey.   —— ——

■ Customer satisfaction data are used to improve those processes where key indicators suggest improvement.   —— ——

Additional Areas for Improvement

_____

_____

_____

7.5 Customer Satisfaction Results

■ The five key measures of customer satisfaction show overall improvement trends. The company appears to be performing at or better than the best competitor.   —— ——

■ The three key measures of customer dissatisfaction show overall improvement trends.   —— ——

■ The number of awards received from customers has increased.   —— ——

■ Trend data by business segment are not presented.   —— ——

■ Little evidence is provided to determine whether or not the key indicator measures for customer dissatisfaction address the principal concern of customers.   —— ——

7.6 Customer Satisfaction Comparison

■ When compared to key competitors on an overall customer satisfaction rating, customers rated Varifilm higher than the average of all competitors.   —— ——

■ The Customer Assessment Index shows that Varifilm became the industry leader.   —— ——

■ Gains in market share relative to competitors have shown improvement during the past 2 years.   —— ——

	(S)	(I)
■ It is not clear how many customers were included in the overall customer satisfaction comparison rating.	—	—
■ Trend data in gaining and losing customers or customer accounts to competitors are not provided.	—	—

Additional Areas for Improvement

_____

_____

_____

8

BENCHMARKING

Benchmarking is a way to go backstage and watch another company's performance from the wings, where all the stage tricks and hurried realignments are visible.

Wall Street Journal

In Joseph Juran's 1964 book *Managerial Breakthrough,* he asked the question: "What is it that organizations do that gets results so much better than ours?" The answer to this question opens the door to *benchmarking,* an approach that is accelerating among U.S. firms that have adopted the total quality management (TQM) philosophy.

The essence of benchmarking is the continuous process of comparing a company's strategy, products, and processes with those of world leaders and best-in-class organizations in order to learn how they achieved excellence, and then setting out to match and even surpass it. For may companies, benchmarking has become a key component of their TQM programs. The justification lies partly in the question: "Why re-invent the wheel if I can learn from someone who has already done it?" C. Jackson Grayson, Jr., chairman of the Houston-based American Productivity and Quality Center, which offers training in benchmarking and consulting services, reports an incredible amount of interest in benchmarking. Some of that interest may be explained by the criteria for the Malcolm Baldrige Award, which includes "competitive comparisons and benchmarks."[1]

THE EVOLUTION OF BENCHMARKING

The method may have evolved in the 1950s, when W. Edwards Deming taught the Japanese the idea of quality control. Other American management innovations followed. However, the method was rarely used in the United States until the early 1980s, when IBM, Motorola, and Xerox became the pioneers. The latter company became the best-known example of the use of benchmarking.

Xerox

The company invented the photocopier in 1959 and maintained a virtual monopoly for many year thereafter. Like "Coke" or "Kleenex," "Xerox" became a generic name for all photocopiers. By 1981, however, the company's market share shrank to 35 percent as IBM and Kodak developed high-end machines and Canon, Ricoh, and Savin dominated the low-end segment of the market. The Xerox vice president of copier manufacturing remarked: "We were horrified to find that the Japanese were selling their machines at what it cost us to make ours...we had been benchmarking against ourselves. We weren't looking outside." The company was suffering from the "not invented here" syndrome, as Xerox managers did not want to admit that they were not the best.

The company instituted the benchmarking process, but it met with resistance at first. People did not believe that someone else could do it better. When faced with the facts, reaction went from denial to dismay to frustration and finally to action. Once the process began, the company benchmarked virtually every function and task for productivity, cost, and quality. Comparisons were made for companies both in and outside the industry. For example, the distribution function was compared to L. L. Bean, the Freeport, Maine catalog seller of outdoor equipment and clothing and everyone's model of distribution effectiveness.

By the company's own admission, it would probably not be in the copier business today if it were not for benchmarking. Results were dramatic:

- Suppliers were reduced from 5000 to 300.
- "Concurrent engineering" was practiced. Each product development group has input from design, manufacturing, and service from the initial stages of the project.
- Commonality of parts increased from about 20 percent to 60 to 70 percent.
- Hierarchical organization structure was reduced, and the use of cross-functional "Teams Xerox" was established.
- Results included:
  - Quality problems cut by two-thirds
  - Manufacturing costs cut in half

- Development time cut by two-thirds
- Direct labor cut by 50 percent and corporate staff cut by 35 percent while increasing volume

It should be noted that all of these improvements were not the direct result of benchmarking. What happened at Xerox (and what happens at most companies) is that in adopting the process, the climate for change and continuous improvement followed as a natural result. In other words, benchmarking can be a very good intervention technique for positive change.

Ford

The entire automobile industry may have undergone substantial change as a result of Ford's Taurus and Sable model cars. Operating performance and reliability were significantly improved, and the gains were recognized by U.S. car buyers as well as others in the industry. "Team Taurus," a cross-functional group of employees, was empowered to bring the car to market and was given considerable authority to act outside of the normal company bureaucracy.

The team defined 400 different areas that were considered important to the success of a mid-size car. A best-in-class competition was chosen for each area. Fifty different mid-sized car models were chosen. Few were Ford models. Based on the 400 benchmarks, specific teams were assigned responsibility to meet or beat the best-in-class for each area of performance, and 300 features were "copied" and incorporated into the car design. Target dates were set for beating the remaining features. "Quality Is Job One" became the fight song for Ford employees.

The Taurus was, and is, a resounding success. Some auto analysts credit the Taurus experience with the partial resurgence of quality in the U.S. automobile industry. The benchmarking process provided additional benefits. During the examination of competitors' features, valuable insights into the design process were gained. Cycle time was reduced. Buyer–supplier relationship was improved as supplier input was solicited for the design. All manufacturing processes were improved as a by-product of the benchmarking process.

Motorola

In the early 1980s, the company set a goal of improving a set of basic quality attributes *tenfold* in five years. Based on *internal* benchmarking, the goal was reached in three years. The company then began to look outside, sending teams to visit competitor plants in Japan. To their chagrin, the teams found that Motorola would have to improve its tenfold improvement level another two to three times just to match the competition.

Borrowing process benchmarks from companies as diverse as Wal-Mart, Benetton, and Domino's Pizza, the company now routinely fields benchmarking requests from those same Japanese companies it toured the first time around.[2]

THE ESSENCE OF BENCHMARKING

The process is more than a means of gathering data on how well a company performs against others both in and outside the industry. It is a method of identifying new ideas and new ways of improving processes and hence meeting customer expectations. Cycle time reduction and cost cutting are but two process improvements that can result. The traditional approach of measuring defect rates is not enough. The ultimate objective is *process improvement* that meets the attributes of customer expectation. This improvement, of course, should meet both strategic and operational needs.

A properly designed and implemented benchmarking program will take a total system approach by examining the company's role in the supply chain, looking upstream at the suppliers and downstream at distribution channels. How competitive are suppliers in the world market and how well are they integrated into the company's own core business processes—product design, demand forecasting, product planning, and order fulfillment.[3]

BENCHMARKING AND THE BOTTOM LINE

There are two basic points of view regarding how to get started in benchmarking. One minority view maintains that an *initial* action plan that tries to match the techniques used by world-class performance may actually make things worse by doing too much too soon. A three-year study of 580 global companies conducted by the management consulting firm Ernst & Young concluded that it may be best to start measuring existing financial performance measures. Two key measures are return on assets (which is simply after tax income divided by total assets) and value added per employee. Value added is sales minus the costs of materials, supplies, and work done by outside contractors. Labor and administrative costs are not subtracted from sales to arrive at value added.[4]

The focus on financial results is not recommended by the majority of executives familiar with the benefits of benchmarking. Some believe that it is easy to be fooled by financial indicators that lull the company into thinking that it is doing well when what in reality occurs is a transitory financial phenomenon that may not hold up over the longer term. A more important payoff is quality processes that lead to a quality product.

Robert C. Camp headed up the now-famous study at Xerox in which the buzzword "benchmarking" was coined in 1980. When asked whether the best work practices necessarily improve the bottom line, he replied: "The full definition of benchmarking is finding and implementing best practices in our business, practices that meet customer requirements. So the flywheel on finding the very best is, 'Does this meet customer requirements?' There is a cost of quality that exceeds customer requirements. The basic objective is satisfying the customer, so that is the limiter."[5]

THE BENEFITS OF BENCHMARKING

Given the considerable effort and expense required for effective benchmarking, why would an organization embark on such an effort? The answer is justified by three sets of benefits.

Cultural Change

Benchmarking allows organizations to set realistic, rigorous new performance targets, and this process helps convince people of the credibility of these targets. This tends to overcome the "not invented here" syndrome and the "we're different" justification for the status quo. The emphasis on looking to other companies for ideas and solutions is antithetical to the traditional U.S. business culture of individualism. Robert Camp, the former Xerox guru quoted earlier, indicates that the most difficult part for a company that is starting the process is getting people to understand that there may be people out there who do things better than they do. According to Camp, overcoming that myopia is extremely important.

Performance Improvement

Benchmarking allows the organization to define specific gaps in performance and to select the processes to improve. It provides a vehicle whereby products and services are redesigned to achieve outcomes that meet or exceed customer expectations. The gaps in performance that are discovered can provide objectives and action plans for improvement at all levels of the organization and promote improved performance for individual and group participants.

Human Resources

Benchmarking provides a basis for training. Employees begin to see the gap between what they are doing and what best-in-class are doing. Closing the gap points out the need for personnel to be involved in techniques of problem solving and process improvement. Moreover, the synergy between organization activities is improved through cross-functional cooperation.

STRATEGIC BENCHMARKING

It is paradoxical that two AT&T divisions (AT&T Network Systems Group, Transmission Systems Business Unit, and AT&T Universal Card Services) were 1992 winners of the Baldrige Award. Like several other winners, the company has turned this win into an advantage and organized a separate operation to market this expertise. Training is the product offered by the AT&T Benchmarking Group of Warren, New Jersey.[6] The process is illustrated in Figure 8-1.

The paradox is that ten years earlier, in 1983, AT&T was convinced that it could be a major player in the computer industry. The company owned Bell Laboratories, the largest R&D facility in the world, and had extensive experience in the manufacture of telecommunications equipment, a related product.

Five years after entering the industry and after losing billions of dollars, the company was still trying to be a significant player in the market. The near disaster could be traced directly to the company's failure to (a) realize that the key success factors in the industry included sales, distribution, and service (functions that AT&T had very little experience in) and (b) conduct *strategic benchmarking* against such best-in-class competitors as IBM and Compaq. Moreover, the company apparently failed to define its market segment, the criteria used for customer purchasing decisions, and how the company's product could be differ-

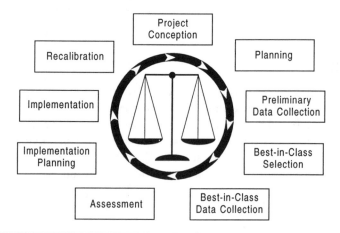

Figure 8-1 AT&T Benchmarking Process

Competitive Analysis
Computer Industry
_____ **Segment**

Key Success Factors	Weight	Performance Rating		
		Our Company	Competitor #1	Competitor #2
Sales Force				
Distribution				
Suppliers				
R&D				
Service				
Cost Structure				
etc.				
etc.				

Figure 8-2   Key Success Factor Matrix

entiated in the chosen segment. If, for example, IBM, Compaq, or AT&T wanted to benchmark NCR, they would find that NCR has gone to great expense to define the criteria of product quality as "usability, aesthetics, reliability, functionality, innovation and appropriateness."[7]

One way to determine how well you are prepared to compete in a segment and to help define a best-in-class competitor is to construct a key success factor (KSF) matrix similar to the one shown in Figure 8-2. Following this determination, a matrix such as the hypothetical one shown in Figure 8-3 can be constructed to measure market differentiation criteria against competitors. Note that the criteria

Computer Industry
_____ **Segment**
Customer's Purchase Decision

Criteria	Weight	Performance Rating			
		Our Company	Competitor #1	Competitor #2	etc.
Reliability					
Performance					
Features					
Durability					
Service					
Software					
etc.					
etc.					

Figure 8-3   Measuring Market Differentiation Criteria against Competitors

for comparison are based on the customer's purchase decision. This type of strategic analysis can be followed by one involving specific processes—operational benchmarking. Strategy drives performance and hence quality. Indeed, quality can and should become the central theme of strategy. Note that Figures 8-2 and 8-3 can be used to benchmark best-in-class *outside* the industry.[8]

OPERATIONAL BENCHMARKING

This category focuses on a particular activity within a company's functional operations and then identifies ways to emulate or improve on the practices of best-in-class. Whereas strategic benchmarking is largely concerned with the macro analysis of the environment, the industry, and the competitors, operational benchmarking is more detailed in terms of data gathering and the rigor of the analysis. Most of the focus is on cost and differentiation. Because the customer's purchasing decision (PD) is a function of price and differentiation, it is necessary to differentiate through *quality* $[PD = f(P \times Q)]$ and improve price through *cost* reduction. Both lead to an analysis of the cost and activity chains of interconnected processes.

The scope of benchmarking extends to both strategic and operational processes. The scope of these two categories of benchmarking at Westinghouse (a Baldrige winner) is displayed in Table 8-1.

THE BENCHMARKING PROCESS

There is no standard or commonly accepted approach to the benchmarking process. Each consulting group[9] and each company[10] uses its own method. Whatever method is used, the major steps involve (1) measuring the performance of best-in-class relative to critical performance variables, (2) determining how the levels of performance are achieved, and (3) using the information to develop and implement a plan for improvement. These steps are discussed in further detail in the following sections.

Determine the Functions/Processes to Benchmark

Those functions or processes that will benefit the most should be targeted for benchmarking. It is wise to choose those that absorb the highest percent of cost and contribute the greatest role in differentiation, always thinking in terms of process improvements that will have a positive impact on the customer's purchasing decision. Because no company can excel at everything, it is necessary

Table 8-1   How Westinghouse Uses Competitive Benchmarking Data

Process benchmarks	Product benchmarks
Categories	**Categories**
Assessment	Development
Performance	Features
Technology	Functionality
Financial	Architecture
Organizational	Availability
Development	**Marketing**
Goals	Target markets
Analysis	Market positioning
Countermeasures	Price strategies
Implementation	
Improvement	**Sales**
Gap analysis	Product positioning
Targets	Bid responses
Countermeasures	Customer talks
Comparisons and competitive analysis	**Comparisons and competitive analysis**
Scope	Features
Complexity	Functionality
Technology	Architecture
Performance	Availability
Cost	Market position
Strength/weakness	Price
Documentation	Strength/weakness
	Documentation

to delineate targets. Benchmarking "manufacturing," for example, is much too broad and the subject is too ill-defined. If the elements to be benchmarked cannot be framed, data gathering is not focused and subsequent actions may be destructive.

Many companies focus their efforts on product comparisons. In manufacturing industries this may mean product tear-downs (e.g., Ford, Xerox) and re-engineering of design standards and assembly processes. This approach should take second place to improving time to market, first-time quality of design, and design for purchasing effectiveness, which are the primary drivers of both quality and cost. Of course, these actions should be undertaken after customer satisfaction has been defined with customer input.

■ The health care industry provides an example of the potential for cost and quality improvement. For one procedure alone, coronary artery bypass grafts (CABGs, DRGs 106-7), Americans paid for more than 130,000 in 1991. Of the patients treated, 6,033 died. Ancillary charges alone reached $2.67 billion. Baxter Healthcare Corporation of Deerfield, Illinois, which benchmarked CABGs in ten hospitals, calculated that $1.57 billion in ancillary charges alone could be saved if all hospitals benchmarked the processes of the benchmarked ten.[11]

Select Key Performance Variables

Functions, activities, and processes can be measured in terms of specific output measures of operations and performance. In general, these measures fall into four broad categories.

Cost and productivity, such as overhead costs and labor efficiency. Total dollars per unit or per ton is a starting point in manufacturing. Other variables might include production yield of raw material, direct labor per unit produced, etc. Unless the project team begins with total costs before it breaks them down by process or activity, some very important overhead charges may be neglected when benchmarked against firms with different accounting systems. See Chapter 10 (Productivity and Quality) for additional measures.

Comparing one company's financial statements and cost breakdowns against those of another would be a good method for a "me-too" strategy *if* access were available to the detailed statements of a competitor or the best-in-class and *if* they were based on similar accounting methodology. These are two big "if's." A better way is to identify the underlying cost *drivers* of the many functions and activities that, when combined, make up total costs. For example, raw material costs may be driven by sales, purchase volume, source, or freight; direct labor by wage and benefit rates, skilled vs. unskilled, or union vs. non-union; indirect labor by the ratio of direct to indirect, salary levels, and so on.

■ A team at Mercy Hospital in San Diego decided to benchmark medical records because the activity represented the largest portion of clinical support. The team left a benchmarking visit to a sister hospital empty-handed because they found that the two hospitals were quite different in this activity. A team member commented: "They weren't equivalent to us at all. It didn't do the functions we did, it wasn't open 24 hours a day like us, and it was more decentralized—a lot of what we do, they do in various other departments and clinics"

Timeliness. Often overlooked, timeliness is a major factor in internal processes as well as customer satisfaction. The measure is frequently expressed in cycle time or turnaround time such as time to fill an order or time to answer the phone. Some manufacturing executives have been known to visit automobile races to measure pit stops as benchmarks for set-up time or line changeover time.

Differentiation and quality. Measures of differentiation and quality are needed for both processes and product. Quality measures should capture the errors, defects, and waste attributable to an entire process and express them relative to the total output achieved. Defects tend to cascade down a chain of processes, becoming increasingly expensive to correct.

Differentiation and quality of product are essentially the same, because quality is what differentiates a product. The variables should include any factors that affects a customer's purchasing decision (see, for example, Figure 8-3).

Business processes. These are the processes not directly related to product design, production, sales, and service. They include the many staff and internal service activities that are costed under general and administrative (G&A) expense. One has only to look at the organizational chart to identify areas for cost reduction and for improvement of productivity and quality. Human resources, data processing, accounts receivable, marketing services, maintenance, security, data center, warehousing, public relations...the list goes on. Many companies have had severe cash flow and profit problems due to a failure to control the cost and output of these business or support processes. Whereas direct labor and material costs may make up the largest segment of total costs in a manufacturing firm and can be benchmarked more easily, G&A costs are more elusive and more difficult to measure; however, they represent fertile ground for improvement. Another area is internal quality and internal customers. A good place to start may be to use the techniques of activity analysis and activity-based costing.

IDENTIFY THE BEST-IN-CLASS

This is a major step in the benchmark analysis. The objective is to identify companies whose operations are superior, the so-called best-in-class, so that the company's own operations can be targeted.

The quickest way to identify excellent performers is simply to visit some companies that have won the Baldrige Award. A lot could be learned in a hurry, but these companies may not have the time or may not have similar processes. Other sources include (1) available databases, (2), sharing agreements between companies, and (3) out-of-industry companies.

Databases are an expanding source of comparison information. The most current and most comprehensive of these is maintained by the Houston-based American Productivity & Quality Center (AP&QC). Some of the chief difficulties that organizations encounter are identifying top-performing companies in specific functions and finding companies that have already conducted studies in specific areas. Helping others overcome these difficulties is the role of the AP&QC. It serves as a central networking source and has the support of top benchmarkers.

The cost of membership in the AP&QC ranges from $6,000 to $12,500, depending on the number of employees. Dissemination of benchmarking information is through face-to-face networking meetings, electronic bulletin boards, and on-line access to abstracts of company benchmark studies.[12]

As the popularity of benchmarking accelerates, so does the number of consortium efforts among industry peer groups. For example, a number of hospitals have formed the MECON-PEER database to provide information and analysis software for examining individual operations and compare them with similar operations nationwide. Some of the participants have discovered an additional use for the database: putting muscle into a budget squeeze and justifying additional resources based on benchmarking activities of peers.

Even universities are emerging as benchmarkers. Oregon State University pioneered the process in the academic world, and their success led to the creation of NACUBO, a database of the National Association of College and University Business Officers.

A number of companies are also developing *in-house* databases. This is particularly effective in large multi-division companies, where economies of scale in data sharing can be achieved. One such company is AT&T. The extent of the competitive benchmarking data maintained by the Network Systems Group for use by all company divisions is shown in Table 8-1 (see earlier).[13]

Cooperative sharing agreements between companies is another source of best-in-class identification. Members of the agreement may or may not be competitors and may or may not be in the same industry. DEC, Xerox, Motorola, and Boeing joined forces to standardize benchmarking procedures in training.

Out-of-industry companies may be the best source of information for many firms in the early or intermediate stages of project implementation. A benchmark planner at Johnson & Johnson suggests that 90 percent of all opportunities for breakthrough improvement lie in studying practices outside the industry. Perishable food companies often teach other manufacturers about supply-demand balancing, demand forecasting, production scheduling, and distribution management. Pharmaceutical companies are quite knowledgeable in production record keeping, quality assurance, and batch traceability.

Although many companies are mistakenly paranoid about sharing strategic and operating information, many others are not. Most Baldrige winners and applicants and people from many best-in-class companies are just regular people and are proud of what they have accomplished.

■ When Mid-Columbia Medical Center of The Dalles, Oregon got serious about TQM and benchmarking, they formed the "MCMC University." The director, dubbed "Professor," decided to benchmark the training function and spent five days taking notes at Disney University, and then went on to attend Ritz-Carlton's training session for a week. "They were flattered," the "Professor" said. "We were the only people who had ever asked them if we could attend." Training videos were supplied by Northwest Tool & Die Company, Disney, Harley-Davidson, and Johnson Sausage.

Table 8-2 contains a selected list of companies noted for their best practices in the functions shown.

MEASURE YOUR OWN PERFORMANCE

At this step in the process, your own performance should have been pre-measured; otherwise, there is nothing to compare against the benchmarking data. Moreover, data analysis of best-in-class may proceed aimlessly unless the benchmarker understands what information is being sought.

Having determined with some degree of accuracy the performance of the target firm and the extent of your own performance, it follows that an analysis of the *gap* between the two is necessary. The trickiest part of the process is to compare internal and external data on an equivalent basis. This does not mean that both sets of data must be comparable in the same exact form.

Performing a "gap analysis" of the variation with the benchmarked process involves the problem-solving process treated in Chapter 6. This analysis will reveal:

■ The extent, the size, and the frequency of the gap

■ Causes of the gap; why it exists

■ Available methods for closing the gap and reaching the performance level of the benchmarked process

ACTIONS TO CLOSE THE GAP

Once the *cause(s)* of the gap is determined through problem analysis, alternative courses of action to close the gap become evident. Selecting the right

Table 8-2   Selected Best-Practice Companies

Company	Function
American Airlines	Information systems (long line)
American Express (Travel Services)	Billing
AMP	Supplier management
Benetton	Advertising
Disney World	Optimum customer experience
Domino's Pizza	Cycle time (order and delivery)
Dow Chemical	Safety
Emerson Electric	Asset management
Federal Express	Delivery time
General Electric	Management processes
GTE	Fleet management
Herman Miller	Compensation and benefits
Hewlett-Packard	Order fulfillment
Honda	New product development
IBP	Productivity
L. L. Bean	Distribution
3M	Technology transfer
Marion Merrell Dow	Sales management
Marriott	Admissions
MBNA America	Customer retention
Merck	Employee training
Milliken	Cross-functional processes
Motorola	Flexible manufacturing
NEXT	Manufacturing excellence
Ritz-Carlton	Training
Travelers	Health care management
US Sprint	Customer relations
Wal-Mart	Information systems
Xerox	Benchmarking

alternative course of action is a matter of rational decision making. Among the criteria for weighing the courses of action are time, cost, technical specifications, and, of course, quality. It should be added here that the best source of information on closing the gap may be the best-in-class, because that company has already experienced what the benchmarking organization is going through.

The action plan lists each action step, the time of completion, the person responsible, and the cost, if appropriate. The results expected from each action step should also be listed in order to provide a measure of whether the objective or output of each step is achieved.

The action plan itself represents a process and lends itself to the basics of process control. Hence monitoring, feedback, and recalibration are required.

PITFALLS OF BENCHMARKING

Curt W. Reimann, who heads the Baldrige Award program at the National Institute of Standards and Technology, finds that a lot of people think benchmarking is "instant pudding." It will not improve performance if the proper infrastructure of a total quality program is not in place. Indeed, there is significant evidence that it can be harmful. Unless a corporate culture of quality and the basic components of TQM (such as information systems, process control, and human resource programs) are in place, trying to imitate the best-in-class may very well disrupt operations.

Other potential pitfalls include the failure to:

■ Involve the employees who will ultimately use the information and improve the process. Participation can lead to enthusiasm.

■ Relate process improvement to strategy and competitive positioning. Design to factors that affect the customer's purchasing decision.

■ Define your own process before gathering data or you will be overwhelmed and will not have the data to compare your own process.

■ Perceive benchmarking as an ongoing process. It is not a one-time project with a finite start and complete date.

■ Expand the scope of the companies studied. Confining the benchmarking firms to your own area, industry, or to competitors is probably too narrow an approach in identifying excellent performers that are appropriate for your processes.

■ Perceive benchmarking as a means to process improvement, rather than an end in itself.

■ Set goals for closing the gap between what is (existing performance) and what can be (benchmark).

■ Empower employees to achieve improvements that they identify and for which they solve problems and develop action plans.

■ Maintain momentum by avoiding the temptation to put study results and action plans on the back burner. Credibility is achieved by quick and enthusiastic action.

QUESTIONS FOR DISCUSSION

8-1 What benefits can be gained from benchmarking?

8-2 Identify two or three functions or activities, other than product characteristics, that could be benchmarked by

■ A manufacturer

■ A service company

8-3 How can benchmarking become an intervention technique for organizational change?

8-4 Summarize some actions taken by Xerox, Ford, and Motorola while implementing their benchmarking programs.

8-5 What are the pros and cons of benchmarking based on financial performance?

8-6 Select an industry and list three or four key success factors (e.g., advertising, distribution, engineering, sales) for that industry. Which firm(s), in your opinion, would be appropriate to benchmark?

ENDNOTES

1. Rick Whiting, "Benchmarking: Lessons from the Best-in-Class," *Electronic Business,* Oct. 7, 1991, pp. 128–134. This article provides a good justification for benchmarking and the principles behind it.
2. Bob Gift and Doug Mosel, "Benchmarking: Tales From the Front," *Healthcare Forum,* Jan./Feb. 1993, pp. 37–51.
3. A. Steven Walleck, "Manager's Journal: A Backstage View of World-Class Performers," *Wall Street Journal,* Aug. 26, 1991, Section A, p. 10. This article contains good examples of benchmarking applications in several companies.
4. See "Quality," a special report in *Business Week,* Nov. 30, 1992, p. 66. This report suggests various benchmarking measures for three types of firms: the novice, the journeyman, and the master.
5. Adrienne Linsenmeyer, "Fad or Fundamental?" *Financial World,* Sep. 17, 1991, p. 34.
6. The address of the group is 10 Independence Blvd., Warren, NJ 07059. Florida Power & Light Company, the only U.S. winner of the Japanese Deming Prize, formed Qualtec, a consulting group offering services in quality management.
7. *Wall Street Journal,* May 26, 1992, Section C, p. 15.
8. Perhaps the largest *strategic* database is the PIMS (Profit Impact of Marketing Strategy) collection maintained at the Strategic Planning Institute in Cambridge, Massachusetts.

The database contains the strategic and financial results of over 3000 strategic business units. A member firm can search for strategic "look-alike" firms and benchmark the determinants of good or not so good performance. See Robert D. Buzzell and Bradley T. Gale, *The PIMS Principles,* New York: The Free Press, 1987. See also Bradley T. Gale and Robert D. Buzzell, "Market Perceived Quality: Key Strategic Concept," *Planning Review,* March/April 1989, pp. 6–48.

9. For example, Kaiser Associates, Inc. has a seven-step process which is outlined in a company publication, *Beating the Competition: A Practical Guide to Benchmarking,* Vienna, Va.: Kaiser Associates, 1988.

10. For example, Alcoa's steps include (1) deciding what to benchmark, (2) planning the benchmarking project, (3) understanding your own performance, (4) studying others, (5) learning from the data, and (6) using the findings. See Alexandra Biesada, "Benchmarking," *Financial World,* Sep. 17, 1991, p. 31.

11. Bob Gift and Doug Mosel, "Benchmarking: Tales from the Front," *Healthcare Forum,* Jan./Feb. 1993, p. 38.

12. David Altany, "Benchmarkers Unite," *Industry Week,* Feb. 3, 1992, p. 25.

13. Taken from a company brochure entitled *A Summary of AT&T Transmission Systems: Malcolm Baldrige National Quality Award Application.* AT&T's database contains data from over 100 companies and over 250 benchmarking activities for key processes such as hardware and software development, manufacturing, financial planning and budgeting, international billing, and service delivery. Over 20,000 entries describe benchmarking trips or visits with internal and external customers. Sources of competitive benchmarking information include customers, visits to other companies, trade shows and journals, professional societies, standards committees, product brochures, outside consultants, and installation data.

READING

The following article reports on an extensive study by the Conference Board of Canada on how top Canadian companies and companies around the world designed their TQM management systems. The purpose of the study was to benchmark how some of the best firms in the world are implementing TQM. The major finding is that success depends on how well companies define and meet customer expectations through management systems and organization.

CUSTOMER SATISFACTION THROUGH QUALITY

Catharine G. Johnston and Mark J. Daniel

Through our research and involvement with some of the most successful companies in the world, we have concluded that competitive success can only be achieved by organizations able to create a management system that focuses all resources on delighting customers.

In 1990, the Conference Board of Canada, in co-operation with Industry, Science and Technology Canada, studied how six Canadian organizations redesigned their management systems in an attempt to better understand and ultimately satisfy customers' requirements. All six were recognized for their efforts in total quality by the Canada Awards for Business Excellence. However, it is no longer enough to be at the forefront of your industry in Canada. Globalization of commerce has fostered more and better competitors, hungry for both our export and our domestic markets. To prosper in the future, Canadian organizations will be required to meet world-class standards.

Recognizing the need to benchmark on a global scale, Industry, Science and Technology Canada and the Conference Board widened the field of study and

Reprinted with permission from *Canadian Business Review,* Vol. 18 No. 4, Winter 1991, pp. 12–15, The Conference Board of Canada.

sponsored an investigation of some of the best TQM companies in the world. A group of senior business executives invested extensive resources, not the least of which was their valuable time, to examine how some of the best companies in the world are implementing total quality.

This study was not about gathering facts about numbers of companies that had formal quality initiatives, nor was it about comparing total quality from country to country. It was designed to examine some of the best quality initiatives around the world *from a Canadian business perspective*, and to bring back the lessons they learned during the experience so that activities could be implemented in other Canadian organizations to assist them in meeting the competitive challenge.

The participants were senior executives from a diverse group of Canadian companies representing a variety of industries across the country. Small entrepreneurial companies such as IAF Bio Chem and Nexus Engineering and large multinationals such as Northern Telecom and Xerox participated in this pivotal benchmarking experience. The diverse backgrounds and unique knowledge of these individuals added immensely to the group's learning and resulted in many lively discussions. In total, this team of executives dedicated approximately one month to studying how the best companies in the world derive their competitive advantage through a comprehensive Total Quality Management initiative.

The tour spanned seven months and four countries—the United States, Germany, England and Japan. Our 14 host companies in these countries were selected because of their outstanding achievements in Total Quality Management which had frequently been recognized with a quality award. The diversity of culture, industry and company size provided tremendous insights into how total quality can and must be implemented differently in each individual circumstance.

Each company visit lasted from one half to one and a half days and was tailored to the specific requirements of the Canadian group. Extensive briefings both before leaving Canada and at the beginning of each leg of the tour enabled the group to determine the objectives and specific agenda for each company visit and set the stage for a thorough investigation of the management systems of each of these organizations.

The president and/or other senior executives of each host company walked the Canadian group through each organization's evolution (or revolution!) toward total quality. Each company focused on a different aspect of its quality initiative. The information systems department at 3M, which includes over 900 people, shared its experiences in determining the requirements of and satisfying internal customers; Milliken, one of the leading companies in this area, discussed what it had learned about empowering employees; and the Deming Award winning companies explained how teamwork serves as the foundation of their TQM initiatives.

During the tour, participants, in small teams, focused their attention on a particular aspect of TQM, such as strategic planning or employee empowerment. At the end of each phase, the groups met for half a day to share their assessments on each issue and to discuss the general lessons derived from that part of the tour.

What became immediately obvious was that there is no one answer, no set of instructions for this management system makeover. TQM is a state of mind that finds its ultimate success in the whole organization's willingness to change, in some cases to cast out old ways of managing and working, and to view satisfying customers' needs as the determinant of good decision making. Despite the many differences in implementation strategies, five basic themes emerged.

The Goal

Organizations exist to address human concerns. Their continued existence—and success—depends upon how well they meet customer expectations. Long-term survival and profits depend upon being better than the competition at understanding and satisfying customer concerns.

This concept is deceptively simple but has taken on a new significance for the tour participants. The first realization is that quality must be defined by the customer, not by the supplier. Although this appears to be an obvious truth, many companies admit having chased after targets and measures determined internally, only to have to do an about-face when they finally consulted their customers.

Organizations are therefore developing sophisticated systems to determine their customers' real requirements. Methods range from extensive written and telephone surveys to innovative personal contacts. Matsushita, for example, has built replicas of a typical Japanese home in one of its plants. Homemakers are hired on a one-year contract to test both its products and those of its competitors in order to "see ourselves as we are seen by the customer." Engineers, ergonomists and other company experts observe the use of the various appliances and study the assessments of these homemakers.

Companies are also acknowledging the necessity of looking beyond current needs. Some are even going so far as to determine the *unarticulated* needs of their customers and to investigate what requirements might be spawned by the emerging environment.

Moreover, just "satisfying customers' requirements" may not be good enough to keep customers in the future. "Customer delight," going beyond merely meeting the stated requirements in order to build and maintain fierce customer loyalty, is becoming the target for many leaders.

The Challenge

Once the goal of satisfying or delighting customers is set, the management challenge is to determine the customer's needs, bring these needs into the organization and then satisfy them. The objective is to create a management system that can focus the organization's resources on satisfying customers. All employees, individually and collectively, must continuously improve the processes that deliver products and services to the customer.

Leadership

Designing the integrated management system, ensuring that the customer's requirements are the driving force for the organization and aligning the company's resources to those needs are the responsibility of the organization's senior management. In the companies visited, senior management recognized the need for change, built organizational consensus on the direction of change, and remain actively involved in ensuring that resources are focused on producing satisfied customers.

Over and above this, however, it is senior management's role to make the new and ever-changing management system come alive for all employees. The senior executives in the host companies are the biggest boosters of TQM and, by their actions, signal the way for other employees. At Fuji Xerox, the President spends 25 days per year promoting quality within the organization—giving speeches, handing out awards and listening to the concerns of his employees. Some of the goals these leaders are trying to achieve are described below.

Maximizing Employee Contribution

One axiom of Total Quality is that organizations must eliminate waste. The greatest example of waste in many companies is that of employee contributions, contributions that are lost because of the organization's failure to tap the potential of its employees. With mobile technology and capital, employees are the major source of competitive advantage; enhancing their abilities and their willingness to use those abilities is a key management imperative.

If their potential is to be maximized, employees must be involved in a meaningful way in their work, from the planning through the implementation and evaluation stages. Companies note that the single most important motivator for employees is seeing their ideas fully implemented. It is no coincidence that those companies that respond quickly to employee suggestions and look for ways to implement their ideas are the ones that reap the benefits of a high participation rate.

Continuous Improvement

Global competition for increasingly demanding customers makes "best" and "getting better" the only acceptable standards. Continuous improvement driven by customer requirements is necessary, achievable and above all everyone's responsibility. To foster continuous improvement, it is important for senior management not only to accept improvement ideas, but also to actively encourage everyone to identify and to act on opportunities for improvement.

At the heart of this principle is a powerful philosophy that every part of the process leading up to the customer must undergo continuous improvement and that only those people involved in the process can make the improvements. Continuous improvement of processes must be sought on an individual basis, within functions and across functional and company boundaries.

Employees need access to a new set of resources, many of which are the traditional domain of management. Resources such as process improvement tools, information and time are the enablers that employees need in order to satisfy customers.

Integration of Efforts

Customers are the recipients of many individual efforts; however, it is only through the integrated efforts of all employees and departments that the goal of satisfied customers will be realized. The aim is organizational excellence, not functional or departmental excellence; all of the key players need to work together to achieve a common purpose. In the most successful organizations, these are organized into natural work-group teams and cross-functional teams. Major cross-functional processes and improvements are ensured by formally assigning their safekeeping to senior executives. Reward systems are being changed, authority shared, and people trained to work more effectively together.

The Future Challenge

Success in the competitive environment of the 1990s cannot be achieved on one's own. Leading companies are forming alliances with vendors and distributors to ensure the joint continuous improvement of what they offer to customers. The challenge of being *the best in the world* at satisfying your customers requires an even wider network of co-operation.

With mobile technology and capital, where corporations choose to locate their facilities will depend upon the abilities of the current and potential workforce in the various locations under consideration and the infrastructure available within which to operate. Further and substantial co-operation between businesses and among business, government, labour and educational institutions will be required in the 1990s if Canada is to remain competitive in the world market.

CASE

Benchmarking is useful, perhaps even a prerequisite to TQM, in service indus-tries and for services within business processes in all firms, whether in the manufacturing or service sector. Here are four examples of how benchmarking has been used in such situations. Note the Columbus-Cabrini Medical Center case where benchmarking has been integrated with the budgetary process.

BENCHMARKING:
TALES FROM THE FRONT

Oregon State University

Oregon State University at Corvallis pioneered benchmarking in the academic world. The university picked a half dozen peer institutions—land-grant colleges such as Kansas State, Cornell, and Washington State—and determined which one within that particular universe was best in class by a host of measures, from financial aid and admissions to the scheduling of rooms and cost per athlete. OSU focused on clearly measurable processes, deliberately avoiding such controver-sial, hard-to-measure areas as effectiveness of teaching and research, and used the data to screen for those processes that needed improvement at Corvallis.

"We then turn those processes over to TQM teams," says OSU's former vice president for administration, Dr. L. Edwin Coate. "They do what is necessary, including benchmarking, to work out the problem. It has saved us significant amounts of money."

For instance, the school's workers' compensation premium had surpassed $2 million per year. A TQM team analyzed the problem, identified the areas in which the greatest number of cases were generated (physical plant operations and agriculture), and adopted a few measures that were standard elsewhere. An early back-to-work program encouraged rapid rehabilitation; morning exercises for physical laborers prevented many back injuries. Subsequently, the premium dropped by half, for a savings of $1 million.

OSU's success soon became the talk of the National Association of College and University Business Officers (NACUBO), which launched a nationwide effort of its own. In 1991, consultant Barbara Shafer surveyed 320 data points in 40 schools for NACUBO. The 1992 effort is covering an estimated 60 to 100 institutions; the 1993 effort will expand to include more than 200.

Not only is NACUBO increasing the number of institutions it covers but it is edging into teaching and research, and collecting data on such measurements as the ratio of faculty hours paid to student credits awarded. NACUBO's goal is the creation of a database that its members can use, as OSU used its small sample, to assess their own efforts.

St. Joseph's Medical Center

In January 1992, St. Joseph's Medical Center in Stockton, California, working with the American Productivity & Quality Center's International Benchmarking Clearinghouse (IBC) and 28 other hospitals in the Healthcare Forum's Quality Improvement Networks, set out to benchmark its admissions process. The networks had picked admissions because it is complex and important to customers, and because it has a lot in common with admission, registration, and other information-gathering, people-processing procedures in many other industries. St. Joseph's team decided to do the benchmarking in two phases: During Phase 1, it would compare itself with the best in healthcare; in Phase 2, it would look outside the industry for ideas.

The team made some revealing discoveries during the first phase. St. Joseph's patients, for instance, had to sign an average of 12 forms to be admitted. Some of the best hospitals managed to keep that number to two; a few kept their average below even that. St. Joseph's patients had six to eight interactions with the staff (representing a problem the study team called "everyone asking the patient the same questions"); the best practices needed only three interactions, sometimes only one.

Some new practices at St. Joseph's that have come out of this first benchmarking phase include:

- Verifying patients' insurance before the date of admission
- Training the admitting and finance staff to work out payment plans together
- Cutting the number of inspections given a new chart from four, five, or more per day to one or two
- Naming a quality team to work on reducing the number of forms and questions.

The business and admitting offices are considering the following practices:

- Creating 24-hour financial hotline, or even offering business services 24 hours a day
- Linking surgery scheduling and pre-admission scheduling by computer
- Gathering insurance information by linking doctors' offices with both the admitting and the billing offices of St. Joseph's.

The team hopes to implement improvements throughout all of St. Joseph's eight businesses next.

In September 1992, the Healthcare Forum released the results of Phase 1 of the *Best Practices in Inpatient Hospital Admitting* study. In October The Healthcare Forum/IBC group met to begin Phase 2: looking outside healthcare and comparing its practices to those of American Airlines, Marriott Hotels, Ritz-Carlton Hotels, Avis Rent-a-Car, Prudential Insurance, and other companies. Among some early ideas: Marriott preregisters many customers, escorting them from the curb directly to their rooms, and a few best-practice hospitals have already found that the "direct-admit" process is possible. The complete details of Phase 2 were released in December.

Motorola

Motorola was an early pioneer in benchmarking. Among its other successes, it managed to slash the time taken to close the company's books at year-end from 14 to two days.

In the early 1980s, the company set an ambitious goal: It would improve a set of basic quality parameters tenfold in five years. The goal was reached, based only on internal comparisons, in three years. There were congratulations all around, handshakes, merit badges for all. Then Motorola looked outside. It sent teams to visit the plants of its Japanese competitors. To their chagrin, the teams found that Motorola would have to improve its tenfold-improvement level of quality measures another two to three times just to match the competition.

Kenneth J. Obrzut, director of group sector strategic programs in Motorola's MIS department, offers the moral of the story: "Benchmarking helps determine what your accomplishments really are, and gives you a chance to match or exceed the best in the business."

For one factory in Florida, Motorola has since borrowed an order-entry process from Wal-Mart, adopted Benetton's idea of asking its stores to relay customer preferences on store items directly to headquarters through computer linkup, and even scavenged techniques from Domino's Pizza. Ten years after Motorola began benchmarking, the company routinely fields benchmarking requests from those same Japanese companies it toured the first time around.

Columbus-Cabrini Medical Center

A number of hospitals have used the MECON-PEER database and analysis software to look into their operations and compare them with similar operations nationwide. The ways they have used the information vary, from classic benchmarking to informed analysis to simply putting muscle into a budget squeeze.

For instance, Chicago's Columbus-Cabrini Medical Center first worked in-house, comparing each department's costs, case load, and FTEs to the previous five years. Unless the department could give a reason why the old numbers no longer fit (in one case, the OR's case load had shifted rather dramatically to more labor-intensive operations), the budgetmakers used the most efficient of the previous five years as the basis for the new year's budget. This practice was implemented about five years ago. Every year since, each department's budget has either remained at that same level or at the most recent year's level, whichever is best (again, unless specific reasons for the exception could be documented).

In a second phase, the administration used MECON-PEER to compare each department with similar departments in other central-city general acute hospitals across the country. The rule for the new budget year was: no department, no matter its historical numbers, could have a budget that came in above the 50th percentile in FTEs per unit of service unless it could document a difference that would make a difference. Everyone had to be at least average in productivity. It was not classic benchmarking, and it "was not real popular," as one official put it, but the provable, comparable data helped the administration keep costs in line.

Questions for Discussion

1   Oregon State University was able to improve costs and productivity through the benchmarking process. Did this process improve *customer-perceived* quality? Why or why not? Who are the customers of a university?

2   Respond to Question 1 for St. Joseph's Medical Center.

3   Motorola moved from *internal* to *external* benchmarking. What justified this move? Do you agree?

4   What are the advantages and shortcomings of using benchmarks for budgeting?

5   Assume that the *first* function to benchmark is the critical function involved in customer satisfaction. What function would you nominate for a university, a hospital, and a manufacturer?

BENCHMARKING AT VARIFILM

Compare each of the following TQM criteria to Varifilm and indicate whether the practice in the company is a *strength (S)* or *needs improvement (I)*. Justify your answer.

2.2 Competitive Comparisons and Benchmarking   (S)   (I)

- A systematic approach is used for evaluating and improv-   —   —
  ing the process for selecting competitive comparisons and
  benchmarking information.

- Competitive and benchmarking information and data are   —   —
  used to establish "stretch" improvement objectives.

- Benchmarking information and data are integrated into the   —   —
  improvement of existing processes and/or the development
  of new processes.

- There exists a defined approach for determining specific   —   —
  benchmarking needs and priorities.

- A global competitive intelligence database is collected and   —   —
  used to estimate a variety of competitive indices, including
  sales, capacity, and cost.

- Competitive data are used to create strategies for market,   —   —
  product, manufacturing, technical, environmental, and resource developments.

- An overall rating is needed for suppliers, but specific bench-   —   —
  marks are used to compare against other companies.

Additional Areas for Improvement

_____

_____

_____

ORGANIZING FOR TOTAL QUALITY MANAGEMENT: STRUCTURE AND TEAMS

If you still believe in hierarchy, job descriptions and functional boundaries, and are not experimenting with new approaches to boundaryless/networked/virtual organizations engaged in ever-changing partners, you are already in deep yogurt.

Tom Peters
Forbes

Synthesizing quality values and policies into every person's job and every operation is a complex task that must be supported by an appropriate organizational infrastructure. Management texts universally define organizing as a variation of a statement such as "the process of creating a structure for the organization that will enable its people to work together effectively toward its objectives."[1] Thus, the process recognizes a structural as well as a behavioral or "people" dimension.

This chapter is concerned with the macro dimension of organization: the overall approach the company might take to establish a quality infrastructure. The micro dimension (organizing the "quality department" or the duties of the "top quality manager") is technical in nature and beyond the scope of this book. Both Deming[2] and Crosby[3] treat this in some detail.

Historically, organizations have tended to focus on the classical principles of specialization of labor, delegation of authority, span of control (a limited number of subordinates), and unity of command (no one works for two bosses). The result in many cases was the traditional pyramidal organization chart, cast in stone and accompanied by budgets, rules, procedures, and the chain of command hierarchy. Task specialization was extreme in some cases. The classic bureaucracy thus emerged.

Prior to the current emergence of total quality management (TQM) in the early 1980s, responsibility for quality was vague and confusing. Executive management grew detached from the idea of managing to achieve quality. The general work force had no stake in increasing the quality of its products and services. Quality had become the business of specialists—product specification engineers and process control statisticians who determined acceptable levels of product variability and performed quality control inspection on the factory floor.

Today, it is generally recognized that there are two prerequisites for a TQM organization. The first is a quality attitude that pervades the entire organization. Quality is not just a special activity supervised by a high-ranking quality director.[4] This attitude (culture, vision) was examined in Chapter 2 and is largely a challenge for top management. The second prerequisite is an organizational infrastructure to support the pervasive attitude. Companies must have the means and the structure to set goals, assign them to appropriate people, and convert them to action plans. People must be aware of the importance of quality and trained to accomplish the necessary tasks.

ORGANIZING FOR TQM: THE SYSTEMS APPROACH

A system can be defined as an entity composed of interdependent components that are integrated for achievement of an objective. The organization is a social system comprised of a number of components such as marketing, production, finance, research, and so on. These organizational components are activities that may or may not be integrated, and they do not necessarily have objectives or operate toward achievement of an objective. Thus, synergism, a necessary attribute of a well-organized system, may be lacking as each activity takes a parochial view or operates independently of the others. This lack of synergism cannot continue under the TQM approach to strategic management because interdependency across functions and departments is a necessary precondition.

The concept of an organizational system is shown in Figure 9-1. Inputs to the system are converted by organization activities into an output. Indeed, the sole

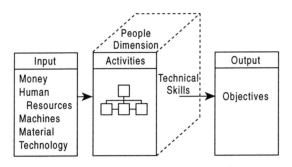

Figure 9-1   The Organization System

reason for the existence of the organization and each activity within it is to add value to inputs and produce an output with greater value. A measure of this conversion of inputs into outputs is known as productivity, and the ratio of output to input must be a positive number if the system is to survive in the long run.

The activities of the organization are subsystems of the whole, but are also individual systems with inputs and outputs that provide input to other systems such as customers and other internal activities. This *chain* of input/output operations is depicted in Figure 9-2.

Despite the simplicity of the concept, it most often fails in practice. Activity supervisors and individuals within activities do not understand the objective or results of their "subsystem," nor can they define their output in measurable terms. When asked to define the output of their jobs, they will answer: "I am responsible for maintenance," or "I work in finance," or "my job is to ship the product." In each case these are statements of activity and not output, objective, or results expected. *Quality* output is stated in such vague terms as "do a good job" or "keep the customer happy." People can describe what they do (activity) but not what they are supposed to get done (objective or result). They may be very efficient at doing things right but ineffective in doing the right things. This failure is critical to organization output as well as structure.

Michael Porter, in his excellent book *Competitive Advantage,*[5] has taken the systems theory a major practical step forward with his concept of *the value chain.* He suggests that "competitive advantage (in this case quality) cannot be understood by looking at a firm as a whole. It stems from the many discrete activities a firm performs in designing, producing, marketing, delivering, and supporting its product." While Porter's concept is expanded to include any of the many sources of competitive advantage, the value chain concept will be used here to focus on the organizational structure for TQM.

The discrete activities of an organization can be represented using the generic

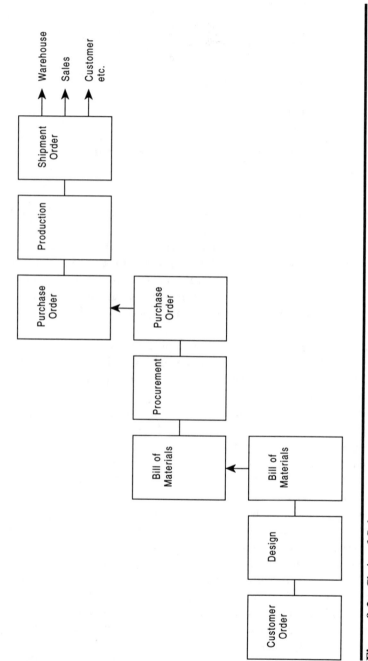

Figure 9-2   Chain of Subsystems

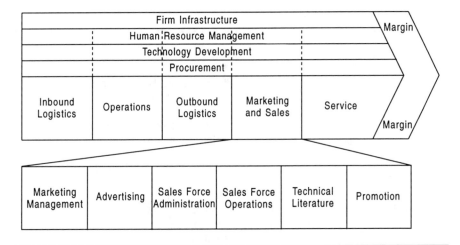

Figure 9-3   Subdividing a Generic Value Chain

value chain shown in Figure 9-3. Note that the activities or organizational functions are comprised of primary and support activities, which may or may not be changed from those listed in Figure 9-3 depending on the firm's industry and its particular strategy. Selected examples of chain activities from Porter's book are summarized in Table 9-1.

Customers, channels, and suppliers also have value chains, and the firm's output of product or service becomes an input to the customer's value chain. The firm's differentiation and its competitive advantage depend on how the activities in its value chain relate to the needs of the customer, channel, or supplier. If quality has been chosen as a competitive advantage, it now remains to determine the customer's value chain and how the product or service can add value to the customer's system. Following this determination, the value chain should be organized into the required discrete activities, each one of which can improve the quality of the output for the purpose of meeting the customer's expectations. Before asking what you can do for the customer, ask what the customer expects to accomplish. The answer forms the basis for a quality organization. In this regard, it should be kept in mind that there are linkages between a firm's value chain and those of its customers, as well as downstream linkages with channels and suppliers. An excellent example of this is Wal-Mart, where a key competitive advantage was achieved through the value chain activity of technology development; in Wal-Mart's case, it was the sophisticated computer-based information system that improved the output of many other activities such as distribution, purchasing, and warehousing.

Table 9-1 Chain Activities

Primary activities	Support activities
Inbound logistics	**Procurement**
Materials handling	Dispersion of the procurement function
Warehousing	throughout the firm
Inventory control	
Vehicle scheduling	**Technology development**
Returns to suppliers	Efforts to improve products and processes
Operations	**Human resource management**
Machining	Recruiting
Management	Hiring
Packaging	Training
Assembly	Development
Maintenance	Compensation
Testing	
Outbound logistics	**Firm infrastructure**
Material handling	Supports entire chain
Order processing	General management
Scheduling	Planning
Finished goods warehouse	Finance, accounting
Marketing and sales	Quality management
Advertising	
Promotion	
Sales force	
Pricing	
Service	
Installation	
Repair	
Training	
Parts supply	

■ A spokesperson for Winnebago Industries, manufacturer of motor homes, concludes, "You must pick the right distribution network. In our case, it is our dealers. We believe we are only as strong as our dealer network. They are our first, last, primary, and most critical link to our end customers."[6]

■ Globe Metallurgical of Cleveland, the first small company to win the Baldrige Award, realized the importance of suppliers in their own value chain. Globe's management determined that the most effective method of assuring compliance with statistical process control and quality approaches in the suppliers' facilities would be to visit each supplier location with a quality improvement team and to train the hourly employees at each location. The program is a vital aspect of Globe's quality system.[7]

■   BSQ Group, an architectural firm in Tulsa, Oklahoma, designs and constructs stores for Wal-Mart. Although the firm's immediate customer is Wal-Mart, they organize their value chain to go downstream with linkages to Wal-Mart's customer: "Many people believe that quality is generally in the eyes of the beholder. Well, in the case of Wal-Mart, that beholder is the store's customer. They are the ones that are helping us define the quality standards that we currently strive to present and it's with them in mind that we begin our study."[8]

ORGANIZING FOR QUALITY IMPLEMENTATION

The traditional approach to organization sees the process as a mechanical assemblage of functions and activities without a great deal of attention to strategy and desired results. The process takes the product as given and groups the necessary skills and activities into homogeneous functions and departments. This approach to building an organization structure has been criticized by Peter Drucker: "What we need to know are not all the activities that might conceivably have to be housed in the organization structure. What we need to know are the load-bearing parts of the structure, the *key activities.*"[9]

Key activities will differ depending on the nature of the organization, its products, and its strategy. What is a key activity in one may not be in another. Advertising may be a key activity in the value chain of Coca-Cola, but not in Boeing Aircraft, where design is the key activity. Back office activity may be a key activity in Merrill Lynch, but not in McDonald's. Firms frequently fail to prioritize or identify key activities in the value chain because of a tendency to organize around the chart of accounts. Some firms focus on those activities where cost, rather than quality or other source of differentiation, is the major consideration.

The value chain concept provides a systematic way to identify the key activities necessary for quality differentiation and a way to group them into homogeneous departments and functions. Indeed, an organization structure that corresponds to the value chain is the most economic and effective way to deliver quality and therefore achieve a competitive advantage.

It should be noted that the Quality Assurance Department is generally not the load-bearing key activity when organizing for TQM. Quality assurance activities can be found in nearly every function of the company if these functions are viewed as links in the value chain. Any activity or function is a potential source of quality differentiation. The ill-defined or elusive word "quality" may be too narrow if it focuses on product or service alone. Moreover, such limited focus may exclude the many other activities that impact the customer's value chain. Not only those functions normally classified as "line" but a variety of "staff" functions as well can be the source of quality in the organization structure. Consider the following sample activities:

Activity	Value to customer
Purchasing	Improved cost and quality of product
Engineering and design characteristics	Unique product
Manufacturing	Product reliability
Order processing	Response time
Service	Customer installation
Scheduling	Response time
Inspection	Defect-free product
Spare parts	Maintenance
Human resources	Customer training

By listing the activities of the organization and comparing them to a value chain such as Figure 9-3, one can see the many potential ways that quality differentiation can be achieved. It should also be noted that these activities can lower customer costs as well.

Production of quality does not stop when the product leaves the factory. Distribution and service are part of the production process. Careful identification of customer value will reveal a number of other opportunities for quality differentiation. For example, buyers and potential customers frequently perceive value in ways they do not understand or because of incomplete knowledge. Scanning a daily newspaper or magazine quickly reveals the many way that both manufacturers and service firms signal subjective, qualitative measures of quality. Do you buy Pepsi Cola for taste or brand image? Do you contemplate the purchase of a Volvo for performance or long life and safety? Consulting and accounting firms signal quality by the appearance and presumed professionalism of employees. Banks are known to build impressive facilities to indicate quality. Charles Revson, formerly of Revlon, once said, "I'm not selling cosmetics, I'm selling hope." The several criteria that the buyer may use to make a buying decision means that there may be an equal number of activities that become *key* activities in the creation of customer value. Porter provides several illustrative signaling criteria,[10] to which firm examples and organization activities that become key in delivery of the criteria have been added here:

Criteria	Firm example	Activity involved
Reputation	Appliances	Advertising
Appearance	Apparel	Design
Label	Athletic shoes	Graphics
Facilities	Bank	Maintenance
Time in business	Whiskey	Distribution
Customer list	Magazine publisher	Marketing
Visibility of top management	Consumer products	Hot line

Of course, having signaled a particular criterion to buyers and potential buyers, it is necessary to deliver as promised, measure the effectiveness of the criterion, and keep customer feedback communication lines open to ensure satisfaction.

Delivery of quality products or services depends on how well the many activities of the company are organized and integrated. The measurement of effectiveness is fundamental to the TQM process (see Chapter 7). It now remains to organize for customer feedback, another *key activity* that impacts other functions and activities throughout the organization.

Measuring customer satisfaction, or dissatisfaction, is an essential but often overlooked activity. What happens when a customer chooses a bank's trust department based on the criterion of experienced personnel, only to be shunted off to a recent college graduate or ignored by a "customer representative"? Research indicates that customers who are satisfied with a bank's quality will tell, on the average, three other people, while those who are dissatisfied will tell eight or nine others about poor quality.[11] How does a customer feel when returning an item under warranty only to be patronized by a retail clerk. One survey found that for every problem incident reported to corporate headquarters, there are at least 19 other similar incidents which simply were not reported or which were handled by the retailer or the front line without being recorded. Most companies spend 95 percent of their resources handling complaints and less than 5 percent analyzing them.

There is a strong correlation between consumer satisfaction with response to problems or questions and the likelihood of purchasing another product from the same company.[12] Yet few customers bother to complain, and of those who do, only a small fraction reach top management. What is needed is the institutionalization of customer service throughout the organization as a key activity to be performed by everyone. Despite this evident need, many companies have neither the activities nor the supporting policies. For many who do, there is a conflict between organization and policies that may have an opposite effect. Covertly measuring quality by using mystery shoppers, holding motivational meetings which employees perceive as paternalistic and patronizing, and paying for sales rather than service are among those policies that may conflict with the need to provide quality products and service.[13] It may be difficult for employees to be quality conscious in the face of policies that discourage this attitude.

THE PEOPLE DIMENSION: MAKING THE TRANSITION FROM A TRADITIONAL TO A TQM ORGANIZATION

The typical company (Figure 9-4a) operates with a vertical, functional organizational structure based on reporting relationships, budgeting procedures, and specific and detailed job classifications.[14] Departmentation is by function, and communication, rewards, and loyalties are functionally oriented. Processes are forced to flow vertically from the top down, creating costly barriers to process flow.

The systems approach to organizing suggests three significant changes, one conceptual and two requiring organizational realignment:

- The concept of the inverted organizational chart
- A system of intra-company internal quality
- Horizontal and vertical integration of functions and activities

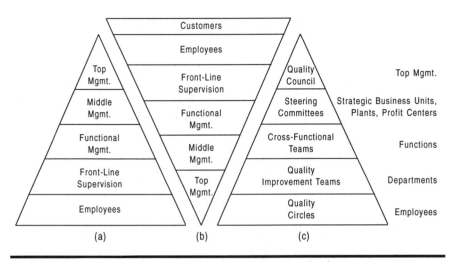

Figure 9-4   Transition from Traditional to TQM Organization

The Inverted Organizational Chart

If you've seen one organizational chart, you've seen them all: the symmetrical pyramid with the chairman at the top and the cascading of authority to successive levels (fourteen at General Motors) until the functions are shown near the bottom of the chart. Front-line supervisors are rarely shown and non-supervisory personnel almost never appear.

Where are the front-line supervisor and the employees? These are the people who deliver quality to the customer. In the eyes of the customer, they *are* the company. The sports fan cares not for the owner or the manager. The players deliver the quality. And so it is with the flight attendant, the bank teller, the auto mechanic, the sales person explaining a product, the person answering the telephone...even the college professor.

Perhaps it is time to put first things first. To make the transition from traditional to TQM management, it may be desirable to *conceptualize* a new organizational chart. Invert the existing one (Figure 9-4b) and put the customer at the top, followed by the employees and front-line supervisors. These are the deliverers of quality. This concept does not change the hierarchy and flow of authority, but the boss is no longer the boss in the old-fashioned sense. He or she is now a facilitator, a coach, and an integrator, whose job is to remove barriers that prevent subordinates from doing their jobs. The same role now falls on middle and top management. Quality is now the responsibility of everyone and not just the quality assurance department.

Internal Quality

The Juran Institute of Wilton, Connecticut delivers a program called "Managing Business Process Quality," which is a technique for executing cross-functional quality improvement among intra-company functions and activities.[15] A key factor in this approach is an organization-wide focus on the customer, including both *internal* and *external* customers. An enlarged definition of quality should be used to embrace all business processes, rather than just manufacturing.

The systems approach, by definition, requires the integration of organizational activities for achievement of a common goal. This goal, under the TQM form of organization, remains the satisfaction of customer requirements, but customers are now considered to be both outside as well as within the organization.[16] The process applies whether relating to a final customer or an internal customer; it is a participative process involving supplier and customer in an active dialogue. Examples include:

■ Metropolitan Life Insurance Company has made a major commitment to improve quality by implementing a *horizontal manage-*

ment approach that is built on management commitment, employee involvement, and knowledge of internal suppliers.[17]

■ Campbell USA has aimed its latest quality emphasis, its "Quality Proud" program, at the administrative and marketing activities of the company. Job descriptions, promotions, pay, and bonuses for all employees are linked to the results of the new program.[18]

As a major step in its transformation to a total quality organization, DEC asked each of its 125,000 employees to answer in writing the following questions:

1. What business process are you involved in?
2. Who are your customers (that is, the next step in the processes you are involved in)?
3. Who are your suppliers (that is, the preceding step in the processes you are involved in)?
4. Are you meeting the expectations of your customers?
5. Are your suppliers meeting your expectations?
6. How can the processes be simplified and waste eliminated?[19]

■ DEC reported that this simple survey had a massive impact. In the short run, countless redundant activities were discovered and eliminated. In the long run, DEC employees now think in terms of meeting both internal and external customer expectations. (This concept is also illustrated in Figure 9-2.)

Aside from the obvious benefits of improvements in quality, productivity, and cost, a system of internal customer quality is important for a number of other reasons:

■ External customer satisfaction cannot increase unless internal customer satisfaction does.

■ No quality improvement effort can succeed without employee buy-in and proactive participation.

■ Focus on internal quality promotes a quality and entrepreneurial culture.

■ An understanding of internal quality policy is an aid in communication and decision making.

■ It is a significant criterion in the Malcolm Baldrige National Quality Award (Section 5.6).

ROLES IN ORGANIZATIONAL TRANSITION TO TQM

Members of a successful organization need a sound understanding of their roles during the transition to a TQM program. People at all levels require orientation as to how they will be impacted under the new philosophy of employee involvement. The improvement process involves a group of complementary activities that provide an environment conducive to improvement of performance for both employees and managers. Each level has a role to play.

The role of **top management** is critical. Many of the most successful companies launched their programs by creating a quality council or steering committee (Figure 4-4c) whose members comprise the top management team. Some multi-division companies encourage a council in each division or strategic business unit (SBU). The council provides a good vehicle for management to demonstrate its leadership in the quality initiative. At Motorola the CEO, who is also the Chief Quality Officer of the corporation, chairs the Operating and Policy Committee in all-day meetings twice each quarter.[20]

Opinions differ as to who should lead or coordinate the TQM effort. One source suggests a new role similar to that of a financial controller, a role that is justified on the basis that quality is now a strategic business planning and management function.[21] Others disagree and suggest that the company should avoid setting up a quality bureaucracy headed by a high-profile quality director. There is general agreement that it should not be headed by a staff department such as personnel or quality assurance. The process should be line led and given back to the business managers who implement it on a daily basis. To reiterate, quality should not be led by a non-line manager.

The major changes are strategic and organizational and have been outlined in this and previous chapters. It now remains for top management to manage the transition.[22]

The role of **middle managers** has traditionally been an integrative one. They are the drivers of quality and the information funnel for change both vertically and horizontally—the go-between for top management and front-line employees. They implement the strategy devised by top management by linking unit goals to strategic objectives. They develop personnel, make continuous improvement possible, and accept responsibility for performance deficiencies.[23]

Front-line supervision has been called the missing link in TQM.[24] At Federal Express, a Baldrige winner, the communication effort is focused on the front-line supervisors because most employees report directly to them. The company realizes that the real purveyors of quality are the employees, and a basic quality concept is candid, open, two-way communication.

Supervisors can make or break a quality improvement effort. They are called upon to provide support to employee involvement teams and create a climate that builds high levels of commitment in groups and individuals.

Quality assurance and the quality professional are faced with good news and bad news as TQM emerges as the load-bearing concern of company strategy. On the one hand, the accelerating emphasis on quality has given them more visibility, and in some cases the reporting relationships have moved to higher levels in the organization. On the other hand, they may now be perceived as a staff support function as quality becomes more widespread and led by line managers.

Philip Crosby indicates that the quality professional must become more knowledgeable about the process of management.[25] The limited tools of inspection techniques and statistical process control have become less important as the more sophisticated approaches of TQM begin to pervade all functions and activities, rather than just manufacturing.

SMALL GROUPS AND EMPLOYEE INVOLVEMENT

In a *Harvard Business Review* article, David Gumpert described a small "microbrewery" where the head of the company attributed their success to a loyal, small, and involved work force. He found that keeping the operation small strengthened employee cohesiveness and gave them a feeling of responsibility and pride.[26]

This anecdote tells a lot about small groups (hereafter called teams) and how they can impact motivation, productivity, and quality. If quality is the objective, employee involvement in small groups and teams will greatly facilitate the result because of two reasons: motivation and productivity.

The theory of motivation, but not necessarily its practice, is fairly mature, and there is substantial proof that it can work. By oversimplifying a complex theory, it can be shown why team membership is an effective motivational device that can lead to improved quality.[27]

Teams improve productivity as a result of greater motivation (Table 9-2) and reduced overlap and lack of communication in a functionally based classical structure characterized by territorial battles and parochial outlooks. There is always the danger that functional specialists, if left to their own devices, may pursue their own interests with little regard for the overall company mission. Team membership, particularly a cross-functional team, reduces many of these barriers and encourages an integrative systems approach to achievement of common objectives, those that are common to both the company and the team. There are many success stories. To cite a few:

Table 9-2   Team Membership and Motivation

Motivating factors	Team membership
Job development (the work)	
Vertical loading	Provides responsibility
Job closure	Team members see results
Feedback	Self-established goals
Achievement	Targets set by teams
Growth/self-development	Training, more responsibility
Recognition	By peers and supervisors
Communication	Team is vehicle for communication (see Chapter 3)

■   Globe Metallurgical, Inc., the first small company to win the Baldrige Award, had a 380 percent increase in productivity which was attributed primarily to self-managed work teams.[28]

■   The partnering concept requires a new corporate culture of participative management and teamwork throughout the entire organization. Ford increased productivity 28 percent by using the team concept with the same workers and equipment.[29]

■   Harleysville Insurance Company's Discovery program provides synergism resulting from the team approach. The program produced a cost saving of $3.5 million, along with enthusiasm and involvement among employees.[30]

■   At Decision Data Computer Corporation middle management is trained to support "Pride Team."[31]

■   Martin Marietta Electronics and Missiles Group has achieved success with performance measurement teams (PMTs).[32]

■   Publishers Press has achieved significant productivity improvements and attitude change from the company's process improvement teams (PITs).[33]

■   Florida Power & Light Company, the utility that was the first recipient of the Deming Prize, has long had quality improvement teams as a fundamental component of their quality improvement program.[34]

TEAMS FOR TQM

The several subsystems or components of a TQM approach were examined in previous chapters. The most critical of these components is employee involvement, and it is the one around which the management system of TQM should be based. It is the most important of the components of TQM and also the most complex. Consider the analogy of an iceberg. Approximately 10 percent of an iceberg is visible, while 90 percent is hidden from view. Imagine that the organizational chart is an iceberg. The visible 10 percent is top management and functional management. The 90 percent, where the true potential for quality exists, is comprised of front-line supervision and non-management employees. Does it not make good sense to tap into the 90 percent which represents a reservoir of ideas for quality and productivity improvements? The vehicle for doing this is some form of *team*.

A 1989 General Accounting Office study found that over 80 percent of all companies had implemented some form of employee involvement.[35] However, the statistic is misleading because responding companies considered a suggestion system as an employee involvement program, which is hardly a systems approach or a linking vehicle. Moreover, the methods most likely to have enduring effects are those that covered the least percentage of employees.

Quality Circles

The most widespread form of an employee involvement team is the quality circle, defined as "a small group of employees doing similar or related work who meet regularly to identify, analyze, and solve product-quality and production problems and to improve general operations."[36] Although the concept has had some success in white-collar operations, the major impact has been among "direct labor" employees in manufacturing, where concerns are primarily with quality, cost, specifications, productivity, and schedules. By their very nature, quality circles were limited to concerns of the small group of members and few cross-functional problems were considered.

The major growth of the circles occurred in the late 1970s and early 1980s, as thousands of companies adopted the concept. Like so many previous movements (e.g., management by objectives, value analysis, zero-based budgeting), however, the concept never met expectations and widespread abandonment resulted. As many as 50 percent of Fortune 500 companies disbanded their circles in the 1980s.[37] The major reason for failure was a general lack of commitment to the concept of participation and the lack of interest and participation by management.[38] From a TQM perspective, quality circles lack the prerequisites of integration with strategy, company goals, and management systems. Organizations can go beyond using circles by creating task forces, work teams, and cross-functional teams.[39]

Task teams are a modification of the quality circle. The major differences are that task teams can exist at any level and the goal or topic for discussion is given, whereas in quality circles members are generally free to choose the problems they will solve. Task teams with the best chance for success are those that represent an extension of a pre-existing, successful quality circle program.[40]

Self-managing work teams are an extension of quality circles but differ in one major respect: members are empowered to exercise control over their jobs and optimize the efficiency and effectiveness of the total process rather than the individual steps within it. Team members perform all the necessary tasks to complete an entire job, setting up work schedules and making assignments to individual team members. Peer evaluation is another characteristic.[41]

A number of common elements are characteristic of self-managed teams:

- **Job design and structure.** The team redesigns the work before implementation and controls the entire job.

- **Supervision.** Traditional supervisors could be absent altogether. Leadership may be assigned according to talent and preference.

- **Quality.** In addition to quality, the teams may become involved in the entire job, including planning, cost, scheduling, and even sales and distribution.

- **Decisions.** Decisions are not confined to quality but may involve all areas that affect the teams. Some may become involved in appraisal, pay, and selection.

- **Customers.** Internal customers are perceived as partners for the purpose of meeting needs of external customers. The primary focus is the external customer.

- **Authority.** If given complete responsibility for the actions of their areas, the teams may have authority and responsibility for growth and profitability.

Cross-Functional Teams

- Computer manufacturer DEC has integrated a range of proven TQM techniques into its program, including cross-functional process improvement teams. One element is strictly home-grown. DELTA (DEC Employees Leveraged Team Activities) is a sophisticated, closed-loop suggestion system designed to discover and address problems. Under DELTA, only an employee who makes a suggestion can dispose of it. He or she also has the responsibility of working with other employees to implement or reshape the suggestion in order to determine whether it is feasible. Thus, DELTA empowers employees and promotes team building, two essential elements of quality management.[42]

The centuries-old hierarchical form of organization with a vertical chain of command was the norm until recently, when organizational complexity demanded horizontal as well as vertical coordination in order to plan and control processes that flowed laterally. If no lateral coordination is achieved, the organization becomes a collection of islands of specialization without integration, a requirement of the systems approach. Linking business process improvement (billing, procurement, recruiting, record keeping, design, sales, etc.) to the key business objectives of the organization is necessary if quality is to become real and relevant. There is widespread agreement that cross-functional teams provide the best vehicle for linking these activities and processes. The concept of linkages is shown in Figure 9-5. Note that a cross-functional approach achieves the objectives of:

- Customers
- Functions
- Processes
- The organization

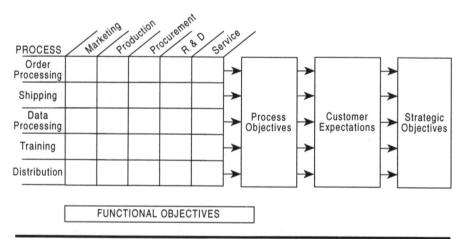

Figure 9-5   Cross-Functional Linkages

Team expert Michael Donovan summarizes a number of trends that will shape the structure and process of employee involvement efforts in the future:[43]

From	To
Perception of employee involvement as a program	Perception as an ongoing process
Voluntary participation	Participation by all members as a natural work team
Quality circles	Several types of teams at many levels
Project focus	Goal focus
Limited management involvement	Active management involvement
Functional management skills	Building participative leadership and facilitation skills into management roles
Employee participation in operating problems	Employee participation in broader issues

QUESTIONS FOR DISCUSSION

9-1   How does an organizational structure that is focused on classical principles (specialization of labor, unity of command, span of management, delegation of authority) tend to inhibit the implementation of TQM?

9-2   Define the concept of *synergism*. How does organizing around the principles of TQM tend to integrate the organization and achieve synergism?

9-3   What is the concept of the *value chain*? How can it be useful in building an organizational structure?

9-4   In organizing for customer satisfaction, what would be a key activity for
■   A brokerage firm
■   An aircraft manufacturer
■   A retail store

9-5   Explain the concept of the inverted organizational chart.

9-6   Explain how membership in a small group might lead to improved motivation and hence improved quality.

ENDNOTES

1. For example, Michael H. Mescon, Michael Albert, and Franklin Khedouri, *Management,* New York: Harper & Row, 1988, p. 323.

2. W. Edwards Deming, *Out of the Crisis,* Cambridge, Mass.: Massachusetts Institute of Technology, Center for Advanced Engineering Study, 1982, pp. 465–474.

3. Philip B. Crosby, *Quality Is Free,* New York: McGraw-Hill, 1979, pp. 69–70.

4. The Conference Board, *Global Perspectives on Total Quality,* New York: The Conference Board, 1991, p. 9.

5. Michael Porter, *Competitive Advantage: Creating and Sustaining Superior Performance,* New York: The Free Press, 1985.

6. Presentation at the Total Quality Service Management Conference, Dallas, May 21–23, 1990.

7. Kenneth Leach, Vice-President, Administration of Globe Metallurgical, Inc. at the Third Annual Quality Conference, June 22, 1990.

8. Presentation at the Total Quality Service Management Conference, Dallas, May 21–23, 1990.

9. Peter Drucker, *Management: Tasks, Responsibilities, Practices,* New York: Harper & Row, 1974, p. 530.

10. Michael Porter, *Competitive Advantage: Creating and Sustaining Superior Performance,* New York: The Free Press, 1985, p. 144. Signals of value are those factors that buyers use to infer the values a firm creates.

11. Keith Brinksman, "Banking and the Baldrige Award," *Bank Marketing,* April 1991, pp. 30–32.

12. American Society for Quality Control, *'88 Gallup Survey of Consumers' Perceptions Concerning the Quality of American Products and Services,* Milwaukee: ASQC, 1988.

13. Mark Graham Brown, "How to Guarantee Poor Quality Service," *Journal for Quality and Participation,* Dec. 1990, pp. 6–11.

14. In 1981, Cleveland Twist Drill, a Cleveland-based manufacturer of cutting tools with $400 million in sales, had over 500 job classifications in a direct labor force that numbered fewer than indirect labor. Joseph L. Bower et al., *Business Policy,* Homewood, Ill.: Irwin, 1991, p. 588.

15. "How to Profit from Managing Business Process Quality," presentation at the Total Quality Service Management Conference, Dallas, May 21–23, 1990.

16. David Mercer, "Key Quality Issues," in *Global Perspectives on Total Quality,* New York: The Conference Board, 1991, p. 11. Mercer is the project director of the European Council on Quality of The Conference Board Europe.

17. Keith D. Denton, "Horizontal Management," *SAM Advanced Management Journal,* Winter 1991, pp. 35–41.

18. Herbert M. Baum, "White-Collar Quality Comes of Age," *Journal of Business Strategy,* March/April 1990, pp. 34–37.

19. U.S. General Accounting Office, *Quality Management Scoping Study,* Washington, D.C.: General Accounting Office, 1991, p. 23.

20. A company handout entitled "The Motorola Story," written by Bill Smith, Senior Quality Assurance Manager, Communications Sector. The committee's meetings are described: "The Chief Quality Officer of the corporation opens the meetings with an

update on key initiatives of the Quality Program. This includes results of management visits to customers, results of Quality System Reviews (QSR's) of major parts of the company, cost of poor quality reports, supplier–Motorola activity, and a review of quality breakthroughs and shortfalls. This is followed by a report by a major business manager on the current status of his/her particular quality initiative. This covers progress against plans, successes, failures, and what he projects to do to close the gap on deficient results, all pointed at achieving Six Sigma capability by 1992." Discussion follows among the leaders concerning all of these agenda items.

21. Al P. Staneas, "The Metamorphosis of the Quality Function," *Quality Progress,* Nov. 1987, pp. 30–33.

22. There are a number of good sources that provide suggestions for managing change. See, for example, Tom Peters, "Making It Happen," *Journal for Quality and Participation,* March 1989, pp. 6–11; Nina Fishman, "Playing the Transition Game Successfully," *Journal for Quality and Participation,* June 1990, pp. 52–56; John Herzog, "People: The Critical Factor in Managing Change," *Journal of Systems Management,* March 1991, pp. 6–11; Ronald Elliott, "The Challenge of Managing Change," *Personnel Journal,* March 1990, pp. 40–49; Edmund Metz, "Managing Change: Implementing Productivity and Quality Improvements," *National Productivity Review,* Summer 1984, pp. 303–314; and Richard Sparks and James Dorris, "Organizational Transformation," *Advanced Management Journal,* Summer 1990, pp. 13–18.

23. G. Harlan Carothers, Jr., "Future Organizations of Change," *Survey of Business,* Spring 1986, pp. 16–17.

24. Nina Fishman and Lee Kavanaugh, "Searching for Your Missing Quality Link," *Journal for Quality and Participation,* Dec. 1989, pp. 28–32.

25. Nancy Karabatsos, "Quality in Transition: Part One," *Quality Progress,* Dec. 1989, pp. 22–26.

26. David E. Gumpert, "The Joys of Keeping the Company Small," *Harvard Business Review,* July/Aug. 1986, pp. 6–14.

27. With apologies to Maslow and Herzberg, who have provided what is probably the most practical approach to motivation. See Abraham Maslow, "A Theory of Human Motivation," *Psychological Review,* No. 50, 1943, pp. 370–396 and Frederick Herzberg, "One More Time: How Do You Motivate Employees?" *Harvard Business Review,* Jan./Feb. 1968, pp. 56–57. A complete review and summary of the writings of both of these theorists can be found in almost any principles of management textbook. For example, see Michael Mescon, Michael Albert, and Franklin Khedouri, *Management,* New York: Harper & Row, 1988.

28. James H. Harrington, "Worklife in the Year 2000," *Journal for Quality and Participation,* March 1990, pp. 56–57.

29. John Simmons, "Partnering Pulls Everything Together," *Journal for Quality and Participation,* June 1989, pp. 12–16.

30. Rick L. Lansing, "The Power of Teams," *Supervisory Management,* Feb. 1989, pp. 39–43.

31. Larry Gerhard and Walter T. Sparrow, "Pride Teams, A Quality Circle that Works," *Journal for Quality and Participation,* June 1988, pp. 32–36.

32. Vladimir J. Mandl, "Team Up for Performance," *Manufacturing Systems,* June 1990, pp. 34–41.

33. Gary Ferguson, "Printer Incorporates Deming—Reduces Errors, Increases Productivity," *Industrial Engineering,* Aug. 1990, pp. 32–34.

34. In company presentation at the Miami headquarters.

35. As reported in Brian Usilaner and John Leitch, "Miles to Go…Or Unity at Last," *Journal for Quality and Participation,* June 1989, pp. 60–67.

36. Joel E. Ross and William C. Ross, *Japanese Quality Circles and Productivity,* Reston, Va.: Reston Publishing, 1982, p. 6. For those contemplating the establishment of quality circles or other quality improvement teams, this book provides an action plan for the process.

37. James H. Harrington and Wayne S. Rieker, "The End of Slavery: Quality Control Circles," *Journal for Quality and Participation,* March 1988, pp. 16–20. For an example of how the Avco division of Textron revitalized their quality circles with management support, see Peggy S. Tollison, "Managers Are People Too: A Case Study on Developing Middle Management Support," *Quality Circles Journal,* March 1987, pp. 12–15.

38. Rick Lansing, "The Power of Teams," *Supervisory Management,* Feb. 1989, pp. 39–43.

39. Edward E. Lawler and Susan A. Mohrman, "Quality Circles: After the Honeymoon," *Organizational Dynamics,* Spring 1987, pp. 42–54.

40. Carol Gabor, "Special Project Task Teams: An Extension of a Successful Quality Circle Program," *Quality Circles Journal,* Sep. 1986, pp. 40–43.

41. Michael J. Donovan, "Self-Managing Work Teams—Extending the Quality Circle Concept," *Quality Circles Journal,* Sep. 1986, pp. 15–20.

42. U.S. General Accounting Office, *Quality Management Scoping Study,* Washington, D.C.: General Accounting Office, 1991, p. 22.

43. Michael Donovan, "The Future of Excellence and Quality," *Journal for Quality and Participation,* March 1988, pp. 22–24

Numerous in-depth surveys have found that TQM efforts have returned expected results in terms of sales, profit, or market share in only a fraction of companies. Successful firms that have achieved these results have redrawn organizational boundaries and redefined communication channels. They have supplanted some functions and organized around redesigned processes. They have empowered teams of employees to achieve clearly defined goals and have recognized achievements.

LESSONS FROM
THE VETERANS OF TQM

Céline Bak

For the past two months, Canada's business community has been abuzz with the success stories hailed at the Canada Awards for Business Excellence. These were successes worth underlining and celebrating.

But what about the untold stories: the failed attempts, the false starts, the stalled change initiatives? In a 1991 *Electronic Business* survey, only 13 percent of CEOs surveyed said that their quality efforts paid off in higher operating income or higher profits. A study of British industry by *TQM Magazine* and A. T. Kearney concluded that while 80 percent of companies had total quality processes in place or were planning their implementation, only one-third of those companies with processes in place had tangible results such as improved market share, lower production cost, documented improvement in customer satisfaction or higher profitability to show for their efforts. Surprisingly, despite the paucity of tangible results, more than two-thirds of these same companies considered their TQM program to be successful!

Reprinted with permission from *The Canadian Business Review,* Vol. 19 No. 4, Winter 1992, pp. 17–19. ©1992 The Conference Board of Canada.

That three-quarters of Canadian companies should be either nurturing or planning quality initiatives is not surprising. The fact that they do so when so few current efforts produce any tangible benefits leads one to wonder why. Have they simply not found the right mix for their business or are they incurable optimists attempting an impossible task?

And what about those companies that have succeeded in sustaining quality initiatives over many years? What can companies whose quality efforts are wavering learn from them?

A year ago, A. T. Kearney set out to document the answer to this question. In the Canadian study described above, two elements distinguished those few companies that could show bottom-line results for their efforts. The first was their focus on business processes and the second, the longevity of their TQ initiatives (defined as three or more years).

We decided to use longevity, the most objective quality of the two, to identify companies whose efforts we would examine in more detail. The generous participation of AMP, Cargill, Pratt and Whitney and Steelcase made this study possible.

At each company, we interviewed a wide cross-section of people, both in

Study Participants

■ **AMP of Canada Ltd**. is a manufacturer and distributor of electric and electronic connecting products for original equipment manufacturers of computers and telecommunications equipment. Its quality efforts began in 1982 and were formalized in 1984.

■ **Cargill Limited** is a diversified agricultural company with operations from coast to coast covering grain, fertilizer and farm chemicals, livestock, feed and seed. Cargill's High River facility had quality built right into the plant. It started its quality processes before the plant opened in 1989.

■ **Pratt and Whitney Canada Ltd.,** the market leader in small gas turbines for corporate and commuter aircraft, helicopters and auxiliary power units for military jets, began its TQM effort in 1988 under the banner "Q+".

■ **Steelcase Canada Limited** is a manufacturer and distributor of office furniture and equipment. Its customer-focused quality efforts were initiated in 1989.

focus groups and individually, about their quality successes. We asked them about what had worked and how they would do things differently next time. The people we met with were candid and forthright. They told us that the road to effective and sustainable quality processes lies in redefining traditional boundaries and the communication channels that make up an organization.

These companies have redrawn boundaries and redefined communication channels by supplanting some functions in favour of redesigned processes, by empowering teams of employees to achieve clearly defined goals and by recognizing achievements.

Organizing by Process

Each participant in our study is in a different stage in its evolution toward organizing around business practices rather than age-old functions. However, each has identified its business processes as sets of linked activities or operations that drive key outputs: customer satisfaction, cycle times and product quality.

These companies are paying attention to key processes such as order fulfillment, procurement and production, in contrast with internally focused functions such as sales, inventory and operations. This might not appear on paper to be a big difference, but for these companies' customers, the difference is fundamental. As key processes begin to prevail over functions, organizational structures and internal boundaries are being redrawn, and the results are improved service quality and shorter cycle times.

However, organizing around processes is not for the fainthearted—the change is painful. In fact, it is so unnerving that participants in this study began consciously redrawing boundaries only after they saw empowered teams frustrated and stalled by functional barriers in their efforts to change whatever was necessary in order to deliver "better, cheaper, faster."

At Pratt and Whitney, new product development has gone from a series of over-the-departmental-wall transactions to an integrated effort with representatives from marketing, engineering, manufacturing, procurement, customer support, and finance working together and halving the product development cycle (from five to two and a half years). A remarkable accomplishment, especially given the fact that the success of this project depended on the integrated efforts of some 5,000 people, including those working at four different stages of engineering: advanced concept design, structural and performance design, product definition and manufacturing engineering. But they're not finished yet. As one Pratt and Whitney manager acknowledged: "A good start but there is work to do still."

AMP has created an environment biased toward organizing around processes rather than functions by not always filling vacancies. Functional fiefdoms break apart as people don more than one hat and organize their activities around what matters most to customers. People are stretched, but they readily acknowledge that if AMP is to survive in the '90s, it has to work smarter.

One of AMP's longest standing cross-functional teams is the "on-time delivery" team. This team, composed of representatives from quality, inside sales, warehouse and inventory control, has steadily improved the order fulfillment process over the last two years. Having achieved seven consecutive months of 98–99 percent delivery "as promised," the team now aims for the same high standards for delivery "as required."

Steelcase's "Focus Factories" have cut cycle times of 8 to 10 weeks to 4 weeks and decreased inventory by 50 percent in two manufacturing areas. Focus Factories bring together all functions in production, inventory ordering, procurement and production scheduling. These cross-functional teams have had a direct effect on customer service through a "Quick Ship" program that ensures delivery of Steelcase's fast-moving items in 12 days or less.

At Cargill, the traditional wall between sales and meat fabrication in the plant is coming down. In the past, when sales submitted a daily request for specific quantities and cuts of beef, the people who filled the order had no way of tracking real-time production against sales' requirements. Sales identified this as an opportunity for improvement and a cross-functional team was struck and charged with improving fabrication accuracy.

The team concluded that fabrication needed information to improve accuracy. It linked a computer to the finished goods scanning system to tell the line when requirements for any given cut have been filled. The result was a 15 to 20 percent improvement in "production accuracy" eight weeks after implementation. What used to be the cause for daily aggravation between sales and fabrication is now an opportunity for continuous improvement.

Empowering Teams with Goals in Mind

Where these companies have been successful, teams have been instrumental in determining how boundaries are redrawn within the organization itself and beyond. In order to be confident about how and where the boundaries should lie and when they should be changed, these teams refer to clearly expressed goals. These goals are woven throughout the organization from overall corporate objectives to targets for specific teams.

Steelcase teams look to a set of clear aggressive targets for the corporation as a whole under the banner "Five-Year Goals of World Class Performance." These goals are understood throughout the organization and enable all teams to set priorities and measure progress in areas such as waste, cycle times, safety and product quality.

At Cargill's High River Boxed Meat Plant, members of the maintenance program set a preventive maintenance program for the areas of the plant with the most costly history of downtime. They know weekly what their efforts are yielding and where resources would be better deployed.

AMP's progress toward team objectives is aggregated and posted in a company-wide "Excellence Index." Every team determines how it contributes to (external) customer delight and determines how to measure that contribution. Each team posts performance data regularly and revisits its measures to recheck their predictive nature.

Pratt and Whitney is now in the process of developing an integrated company plan intended to provide all employees with a clear picture of company goals and objectives. This approach will clarify responsibilities and timing.

Timely Communications and Recognition

Realigning communication channels and recognizing the hard work that goes into these changes are fundamental to redesigning the way the organization and its people work. The study participants have each designed ways to recognize the risk taking that is part of any change.

At Cargill, a team of employees has developed a comprehensive process to recognize both individual and team efforts at four well-defined levels. Cargill also recognizes team safety records publicly and tangibly and recently invited all employees and their families to celebrate the plant's second "Zero Defect Day."

At Steelcase, good teamwork is recognized in a number of ways. Some teams are invited to participate in outside events such as conferences where they present their successes to delegates and company brass alike. All teams are empowered to design their own celebration when they reach their objectives.

AMP celebrates all team accomplishments at its annual showcase. All teams that have implemented process improvement show their success story to their co-workers in a setting similar to that of a trade fair.

Pratt and Whitney is redirecting its recognition efforts away from rewarding individuals with a portion of savings resulted from individual business improvement. Its new recognition process is team-based, and is set to be implemented before year end.

Lessons Learned

So what lessons do these veterans have to pass on to companies whose quality initiatives are not yielding expected results or whose efforts have stalled after an initial flurry of activity?

Organizing around processes begins by recognizing that *processes*, not functions or departments, produce the goods and services that delight your customers and satisfy your business requirements. Teams empowered to improve processes will succeed in their task if customer-driven corporate goals are clearly communicated and understood by all. Making the changes to improve key business processes while keeping on top of the challenges of day-to-day business demands extraordinary effort and steadfast resolve. But recognizing early wins and celebrating successes will help all employees to focus on just how important it is to make these changes.

CASE

The need to modernize sparked this company's move to Total Quality Management. The result? Final test yield percentages in the high 90s and a significant reduction in warranty returns.

ALLEN-BRADLEY COMPANY

One of the marks of a truly quality-minded company is that it strives for constant improvement. Even if things are already going well, there's no reason why an organization can't challenge itself to do even better when it comes to quality.

Many companies implement quality management systems because they need to improve quality. Unlike these companies, however, Allen-Bradley Co. (Milwaukee, WI) found itself in the enviable spot of launching its quality system to position itself for even greater competitiveness in the future.

This manufacturer of industrial automation and quality management components and systems, formed in 1903, has always had a tradition of high quality because of its Old World German and Swiss culture. "The company had the Old World mentality of the value of quality," explains Roger Hartel, vice president of Quality Assurance for the company's Industrial Computer and Communications Group (Highland Heights, OH). "As a result, it always had an enviable market position with all of its products."

Cause for Change

In the mid-1970s, however, three important things occurred that forced the company to reevaluate the way it managed quality:

1. **Management decided to move the company into the "electronic age."** Until that point, all the company's products were electromechanical. Man-

Reprinted with permission of *Profiles in Quality* and the Bureau of Business Practice, 24 Rope Ferry Road, Waterford, CT 06386.

agement realized that the future of the industry would be electronic. As such, the company's quality system would need to be refocused.

At the time, quality was based on a lot of inspection, testing, and rework. This worked well, because the majority of defects in the electromechanical devices were very visual (parts out of shape, out of dimension, cracked, or broken). "Quality problems in electronic components, however, are more subtle, hidden in the software or electronic circuitry," points out Hartel.

Such problems can occur as a result of temperature changes, interactions between and among different products, and so on. "A problem might be there one minute and gone the next," he adds.

Because of this, the company needed a quality system based on prevention, rather than appraisal, simply because appraisal would be difficult; and it would certainly not be cost-effective.

2. **Allen-Bradley was also in the process of acquiring a number of new companies** as part of its strategy to move into electronic manufacturing. But these new companies did not have the strict quality culture of the original Milwaukee facility. And when management attempted to transfer this culture to them, it met with great difficulty.

3. **Part of the company's strategy in moving into electronics involved moving into the world marketplace.** That meant that it had to become world-class in its operations, and, of course, this required quality based on prevention, not appraisal.

Early Problems

To address these challenges, Allen-Bradley implemented a Total Quality Management System (TQMS), one that emphasizes continuous improvement in quality, productivity, and customer satisfaction. It is based on the belief that everything can be improved and that improvement must be continuous.

Early efforts involved implementing many of the standard quality control systems, such as statistical tools and training, problem-solving techniques, manufacturing controls, and supplier management. While the efforts themselves were not difficult to implement, management met with resistance in many locations for two reasons:

- Those locations that were part of the "Milwaukee quality culture" didn't see the need for a new system, since their quality was already so impressive.

- Those locations that were recently acquired by the company often reported that they were too busy solving quality problems to find the time to adopt a new system.

Pressure from management to adopt the new system was one component of success, but another event spurred adoption even more: "Many of the divisions realized the need to move into a just-in-time (stockless) production system," reports Hartel. "In so doing, they quickly realized that they would never be able to manage such a system without a prevention-based quality system."

In other words, there was no way to be able to predict how many individual units would have to be fed into a process in order to produce the right number of final products in a short-run system. "You simply cannot do JIT when you have low yields or when you handle quality by inspection and rework," emphasizes Hartel.

Teamwork: A Crucial Element

Teamwork plays a vital role in TQM. Prior to the introduction of the system, people at Allen-Bradley performed their work to high standards, but did not necessarily do so in a spirit of information exchange and cooperation. "They lacked the awareness of what their internal customers needed," he says. Each department, in other words, set its own standards and procedures without consulting other departments.

An important part of TQM involves turning this mentality around to one of teamwork and cooperation. "The idea is to define how the organization as a whole wants to do business," says Hartel. The next step is to break down these goals into individual steps and elements as they affect quality and service. This requires the visible and permanent involvement of all functions. Hartel refers to the process, which addresses how each function serves and is served by all other functions, as "defining and managing interfunctional deliverables and receivables."

Today, the concept is often referred to as parallel engineering. Unlike other companies that have just begun to adopt this strategy, however, Allen-Bradley launched its teamwork concept a decade ago.

■ **The Process in Action.** From the time a marketing person has the glimmer of a product idea or receives a suggestion from a customer for a new product, until the time the product is actually manufactured and shipped, most companies allow the functions involved to operate somewhat independently of one another. Allen-Bradley insists that all the critical functions work together as a team to design, develop, and manufacture the product. Each function becomes both a customer and a supplier of the other functions. In every instance, each function considers the ramifications of its actions on all the other functions.

Certifiable Quality

Another critical element of TQM success is departmental certification. Each department in the company is required to determine what systems must exist in its department in order to satisfy its part in reaching the company's overall goals. Management then audits these systems to verify that they are in place, that they are working, and that they are achieving the quality improvement results that are expected. When a department achieves these three goals, it is formally certified.

Each year, the department must also be recertified. Recertification audits ensure not only that the systems are in place, working, and achieving quality goals, but that they are improving.

"Each certifiable department must enhance its system by adding new elements to its quality activities," emphasizes Hartel. "Status quo causes atrophy, and there is no place for atrophy. We must continue to grow and improve in our quality efforts."

Therefore, the department must establish its quality improvement goals and state how it plans to achieve them. An additional component of recertification involves surveys of internal and external customers that assess departmental performance.

The Benefits It Brings

As a result of its TQM system, Allen-Bradley has seen dramatic decreases in its internal and external failure costs. For example:

- Final test yield percentages for most products are in the very high 90s. Also, many *first* test yield percentages are in the very high 90s.

- One division that quadrupled its size over the past 10 years has seen an absolute reduction in warranty returns over the same period (representing over a 75 percent reduction in warranty returns).

- Between 1982 and 1988, the company saved in excess of $100 million as a result of reduced quality costs. "We have a payback in excess of 13 to 1 on everything we have invested in quality improvement," Hartel says.

- Allen-Bradley has experienced a dramatic increase in market share, "and we feel that a major portion of this is attributable to improved quality and reduced cost," concludes Hartel.

Questions for Discussion

1 The company needed a quality system based on prevention rather than appraisal. What is the difference? What are the organizational implications?

2 Early efforts involved implementing many of the standard quality control systems, such as statistical tools and training, problem-solving techniques, manufacturing controls, and supplier management. These efforts resulted in resistance. Why? How would you have avoided or overcome this resistance?

3 Why would teams have been more appropriate if the company were organized by process rather than by function? What would be the role of teams in a process organization?

4 Among the benefits achieved by the new TQM system is final test yield percentages in the very high 90s. How would the new system improve this percentage? Would you accept a target of "very high 90s?" If not, how would you go about improving it?

EMPLOYEE INVOLVEMENT
MAKES TQM WORK

**Mark L. Lengnick-Hall, George Heinrich,
and Earl Middleton**

Although many organizations have embraced the philosophy of TQM, not all have been successful in achieving their goals. A study conducted by New York City-based Ernst & Young, in conjunction with the Milwaukee-based American Quality Foundation, found that many companies are floundering in their attempts to implement TQM practices. A key finding from this study is that many TQM programs fail, and others don't reach their potential because employees aren't involved. Without employee involvement, even the best quality program is bound to fail.

Associated Company Inc., a Wichita, Kansas-based supplier of machine parts to aviation companies, knows the importance of employee involvement first-hand. In November 1987, the company implemented *Work Smarter,* a quality program aimed at reducing the company's expensive quality costs caused by high scrap and rework rates and high external failure costs (failures that customers experience).

The first step that Associated took toward quality improvement involved setting the product-failure rate at 0.5%. Top management chose this rate over a zero-defect rate for two reasons:

1. The perfect rate would be unattainable and probably would be demotivating.

2. The cost of achieving zero defects might be greater than the benefits.

In addition to making the quality goal attainable, Associated crafted a plan that would be understandable and meaningful to all of its employees. The plan, which followed the teachings of quality gurus W. Edwards Deming and J. M.

Juran, encouraged employees to be innovative and to take risks. Most importantly, employees knew that they had the opportunity to fail.

Group meetings help Associated communicate TQM to employees.   To facilitate implementation and more-specific goal setting, the company divided its approximately 100 employees into eight groups. In the initial implementation, the quality manager met with each of the eight groups. The quality manager described the magnitude of the quality program, indicated the improvements that were necessary and achievable and explained the actions required. He tried to sell the program to the employees and their first-level managers.

The initial approach failed. The employees were skeptical. They had seen programs come and go, and were not convinced of the need or the possible benefits. The first-level managers didn't oppose the program, but they didn't actively support it.

To focus attention on the waste in manufacturing, the quality manager started placing orange tags on defective parts and broken equipment. One such message stated, "This casting costs $1,378. Can you afford to throw it away?" Another orange ticket read, "This machine costs $6,000 to repair. Can you afford to break it?" the orange tickets helped make the cost of quality meaningful to each employee.

The quality manager then started another cycle of meetings. Now, workers paid much more attention to the cost of quality. Small projects that had high probabilities for success were selected and implemented successfully. Goals were set, and as the groups met these goals, they were rewarded. ACI stressed group rewards to encourage teamwork. Some of the rewards included dinners at local restaurants, movie tickets and $50 savings bonds.

With the iteration of meetings and the successful completion of several small projects, the momentum built quickly. Top management continued to expand the rewards program to include a wider variety of rewards for goals that employees attained. As a result, employees gradually accepted more authority and responsibility for quality, and became more involved in all aspects of the business.

TQM improves scrap and rework rates and decreases turnover.   As a result of Work Smarter, Associated's scrap and rework rates declined quickly and bottomed out at a 0.25% rate. In addition, the company's annual turnover decreased from a high of 200% to 25% after the introduction of the program. A more stable work force that was involved in decision making and quality improvements, along with simple but powerful HR management practices, produced major gains for the company. These practices allowed the company to:

- Redirect its employees to become more quality-conscious
- Set goals that were specific and challenging, yet attainable, which led to increased motivation

■ Link rewards to accomplished goals, which reinforced desired behaviors and made it more likely that employees would sustain their efforts.

In addition, continuous feedback about the groups' progress in relation to their goals made it possible for mid-course corrections and ensured that groups stayed on course toward long-term goals. Finally, by encouraging employee involvement through suggestions and specific work changes, Associated treated its people as human resources to be valued instead of mere labor costs to be minimized.

Questions for Discussion

1   Evaluate the company's two reasons for choosing a product failure rate of 0.5 percent rather than Philip Crosby's suggestion that the target should be zero defects.

2   A number of alternatives for team organizations are described in Chapter 9. Which would be appropriate for this company?

PRODUCTIVITY, QUALITY, AND REENGINEERING

In Japan, we are keeping very strong interest to improve quality by use of methods which you started. When we improve quality we also improve productivity.

Dr. Yoshikasu Tsuda
University of Tokyo

During the mid-1980s, the President's Council for Management Improvement wrestled with the productivity process mandated by Ronald Reagan. However, corporate chief executives encouraged the president to get away from processes that stressed productivity and instead to focus on quality. These events led to the creation of the Malcolm Baldrige Award and the subsequent popularity of total quality management (TQM) in U.S. industry.

The relationship among quality, market share, and profitability was examined in Chapter 1, and it was shown that higher quality leads to both increased profits and greater market share. The following questions now arise: Are productivity and quality related? Are they two sides of the same coin? Can you have both? The answer, of course, is *yes*.

Despite a growing body of evidence that indicates a positive correlation, the misconception exists that productivity and cost must be sacrificed if quality is to be improved. In an annual survey of its members in 1990, the Institute of

Industrial Engineers (IIE) found the general opinion to be that only when productivity and quality are considered together can competitiveness be enhanced.[1]

There may be some justification for the belief that increased quality means decreased productivity, but it seems to be the view of those who rank production ahead of quality as the top priority. It is argued that a program to improve quality causes disruptions and delays that result in reduced output. While this may be the case in the short run, it generally is not true over a longer time period. As will be discussed in Chapter 11 (The Cost of Quality), such an argument usually fails when the costs associated with poor quality are considered.

The argument for a positive relationship was made by Deming, who based it on the reduced productivity that is caused by quality defects, rework, and scrap. He concluded, "Improvement of quality transfers waste of man-hours and of machine-time into the manufacture of good products and better service."[2] Feigenbaum maintains that a certain "hidden" and non-productive plant exists to rework and repair defects and returns, and if quality is improved, this hidden plant would be available for increased productivity.[3] These arguments are straightforward; any quality improvement that reduces defects is, by definition, an improvement in productivity. The same can be said, of course, for services and for those firms in service businesses. The cost of quality improvement rarely exceeds the savings from increased productivity.

To build a case for or against quality improvement based on output or defect reduction alone is to oversimplify. A more convincing case can be built around the proven benefits of TQM. When the broader picture is considered, it can be shown that increasing quality also increases productivity, and the two are mutually reinforcing.[4] Productivity has come to mean more output for the same or less cost. TQM embraces a broader concept and can be perceived as *including* the benefits of productivity when properly implemented. Productivity has become a tactical short-term approach associated with cost reduction, greater efficiency, better use of resources, and organizational restructuring. TQM is longer term and more comprehensive and as such is concerned with cultural change and creating visions, mission, and values.

Examples of productivity improvements resulting from TQM abound:

- Under Joseph Juran's guidance, the Internal Revenue Service's processing center in Ogden, Utah adopted quality as a core value, but also achieved productivity increases of $11.3 million from team and management initiatives.

- NASA's Productivity Improvement and Quality Enhancement (PIQE) program has evolved into a multi-program approach incorporating TQM in the agency and in the contractor work force, which comprises about 60 percent of NASA's total.[5]

■   The introduction of computer-integrated manufacturing (CIM), combined with TQM and self-directed work teams, resulted in a 50 percent increase in productivity at Monsanto Chemical's Fibers Division.[6]

THE LEVERAGE OF PRODUCTIVITY AND QUALITY

If quality has a leverage effect on market share and profitability (as pointed out here and in Chapter 1), what are the bottom line consequences of productivity improvement?

Confining the illustration to the question of profitability leverage, three hypothetical income statements will demonstrate how small (10 percent) increases in productivity will yield much greater results than a similar increase in sales:

	I Before	II Sales up 10 percent	III Productivity improved 10 percent
Sales	$100	$110	$100
Variable costs	70	77	63
Fixed costs	20	20	20
Profit	$10	$13 (+30%)	$17 (+70%)

In situation I, sales are $100, variable costs $70, and fixed costs $20, yielding a profit of $10. In situation II, a sales increase of 10 percent yields a 30 percent profit increase, while situation III shows a 70 percent profit increase with *no increase in sales*. The leverage is even more dramatic if a smaller and more realistic return on sales is used. There are also potential additional companion benefits that can be achieved in quality. Again, the answer lies in TQM and the continuous improvement of all processes.

MANAGEMENT SYSTEMS VS. TECHNOLOGY

Since the time of Adam Smith's historic 18th century book *The Wealth of Nations,* we have been taught to believe that labor specialization accompanied by mechanization was the answer to economic growth and productivity. The Industrial Revolution proved this to be so. Even today, the conventional wisdom of economists tells us that the rate of productivity growth is largely a function of changes in real capital relative to labor.

There is a continuing debate in Washington regarding the "reindustrialization of U.S. industry" or "supply-side economics" as it is came to be known in the Reagan and Bush administrations. The primary domestic objective of these administrations was the improvement of the productivity of American industry by encouraging greater savings and thus investment in capital stock. Competitiveness, it was said, required an overhaul of U.S. technology. It is generally believed that Japan's quality and productivity advantage comes from advanced technology.

It would be a mistake to attribute Japan's success to technology alone and a bigger mistake to consider technology to be the only answer to improved U.S. quality and productivity. It is not labor replacement that is needed but rather improved processes. Why, for example, would a company invest in advanced computer equipment to improve an information system that is flawed or a manufacturing process that is antiquated? In the first case, the technology will provide bad information more quickly so that poor decisions can be made faster. In the second case, process labor may be replaced only to find an increase in lead time, inventory turn, or cost of quality.

Many people think of technology as automation and mechanization, machines and computers, and semiconductors and new inventions, but the term has a much broader meaning. It is a means of transforming inputs into outputs. Thus, technology includes methods, procedures, and techniques which enable this transformation. It includes both machines and methods. This is worth repeating: technology includes methods that improve processes to improve the output/input ratio. Company after company has achieved remarkable increases in both quality and productivity with little or no investment in the hardware side of technology.

No one can argue convincingly against the use of the hardware side of technology to improve both quality and productivity. The problem is that automation and machines require time and money, both of which are in short supply. Management systems take little of either and may be equally or more effective. The solution is to improve the system—the process—before introducing technology. General Motors has spent more on automation than the gross national product of many countries, yet the excessive cycle time from market research to manufacture resulted in the production of cars that were not competitive. While GM was taking eight years to produce a Saturn, Honda took half as long to market a more competitive car. Honda accomplished this by controlling cycle time and processes.

The general tendency is to focus on technology to reduce labor cost and to overlook the improved quality that can be achieved through improvement of related processes and tapping the potential of the work force. Good companies buy technology to improve processes, reduce lead times, boost quality, and increase flexibility.

Capital spending in service industries has exploded, but there has been very little increase in productivity or quality. Jonathan M. Tisch, president and CEO of Loews Hotels, remarked: "Productivity in manufacturing is advancing five times as fast as in the service sector. In the late 1950s we needed roughly one employee for every four occupied rooms and that was the average across the industry. Today's average, nationwide, is one employee for every two rooms. In other words, productivity is half what it used to be. Despite the advent of the computer and the introduction of many so called labor-saving devices."[7] The focus in both manufacturing and service industries has been on labor productivity, but for most businesses capital intensity does not improve labor productivity enough to keep return-on-investment above the cost of capital. For those businesses that become more capital intensive relative to sales, a decline in return on investment is the result, even if a normal increase in productivity is achieved.[8]

PRODUCTIVITY IN THE UNITED STATES

The productivity record in the United States is not good. Our capital-intensive industries—home of industrial engineering and the assembly line, production planning, and the computer—have been beaten by Japan and the leading nations of Western Europe as American labor productivity continues to compare unfavorably with the rest of the industrialized world.[9] It is a critical issue for the nation and for individual firms.

Reasons for Slow Growth[10]

When it comes to identifying causes for what has been called the "productivity crisis," every economist, industrialist, and government official seems to have a favorite culprit. Among the most popular explanations are the following issues.

Management inattention. U.S. Secretary of Commerce Malcolm Baldrige (who died in 1987 and for whom the Baldrige Award is named) stated: "Between our own complacency and the rise of management expertise around the world, we now too often do a second-rate job of management, compared to our foreign competitors." One survey by A. T. Kearney, Inc. (management consultants) concluded that the key to productivity is better management and not continued efforts to produce more pounds of automobile per worker. The decade of the 1980s is noted for top management's diversion from productivity, quality, and growth to leveraged buyouts, restructuring, downsizing, and in many case executive perks and golden parachutes.[11]

Short-term gain. The trend has been to focus on short-term financial ratios while failing to take action to ensure long-term growth and productivity.[12] While no one would recommend overlooking financial data, this type of information suffers from the shortcomings of all accounting data. Moreover, financial figures tend to favor the productivity of capital while overlooking the other inputs of labor, material, and energy.

Direct labor. Focus on direct labor has historically been the one variable cost around which financial control systems are designed. Today, the direct labor share of total production costs is down to 8 to 12 percent on average.[13] Some firms fold these costs into overhead or general and administrative expenses, categories that are frequently overlooked when searching for ideas to improve productivity and quality.

Capital. Capital stock formation is largely dependent on savings. Yet Americans appear to be spending more and saving less, leaving fewer dollars for capital formation.[14] The net savings ratios for the major industrialized nations of the world[15] are as follows:

	Average 1980–89	1990	1991
United States	6.0	4.6	4.3
Japan	16.0	14.3	14.5
Germany	12.5	13.4	12.8
Three other major European countries (France, Italy, UK)	14.1	12.0	12.2

Research and development. Expenditures for research and development in the United States surpass every other nation, yet overseas rivals are outpacing the United States in spending growth. Opinion is mixed as to the impact of R&D on productivity. Some evidence indicates that spending is directed toward product improvement rather than productivity improvement. This is good and is expected. However, as previously suggested, many quality investments also improve productivity. An R&D "peace dividend" may be expected from political events in the former Soviet Union and Eastern Europe as R&D dollars move from defense to programs in industry.

Inflation. Is inflation the cause of productivity decline or is inflation the result of the decline?[16] It is almost certain that lower productivity combined with higher wages does result in inflation. To the extent that inflation results in increased relative cost of plant and equipment as compared to labor and the relative cost of operating capital, there can be little doubt that these are investment *disincentives.*

Government regulation, the shift to a service economy, and the lack of goals and programs are among other reasons that have been advanced for the poor record of U.S. productivity. The cumulative effect, although significant, is difficult to estimate.

MEASURING PRODUCTIVITY

Measuring productivity is somewhat easier than measuring quality because the latter is determined by the customer and may be fragmented and elusive. On the other hand, productivity can also be difficult to measure because it is measured by the output of many functions or activities, many of which are also difficult to define.[17] What is the *measurable* output of design, market research, training, or quality assurance?

Despite these difficulties, measures are needed for each activity and in most cases for each individual front-line supervisor. Standards are needed for comparison against past performance, the experience of competitors, and as a basis for action plans to improve.

Carl G. Thor, president of the American Productivity and Quality Center in Houston, is a pioneer in the productivity measurement process and has worked for many years on the development of a measurement system. His principles of measurement for both productivity and quality include:[18]

- Meet the customer's need—that person who plans to use it. The customer may be external or internal.

- Emphasize feedback directly to the workers in the process that is being measured.

- The main performance measure should measure what is important. This may not be the case with the traditional cost control report.

- Measures should be controllable and understandable by those being measured. This principle may be enhanced by the participation of those being measured.

- Base measures on available data. If not available, apply cost benefit analysis before generating new data. Information is rarely worth more than the cost of obtaining it.

BASIC MEASURES OF PRODUCTIVITY: RATIO OF OUTPUT TO INPUT

Total factor is the broadest measure of output to input and can be expressed as:

$$\frac{\text{Total output}}{\text{Labor + Materials + Energy + Capital}}$$

This measure is not only concerned with how many units are produced or how many letters are typed, but also considers all aspects of producing goods and services. Hence, this measure is concerned with the efficiency of the entire plant or company.

Partial factor measures are established by developing ratios of total output (e.g., number of automobiles, patients, depositors, students, widgets, etc.) to one or more input categories and are expressed as follows for the partial factor of labor:

$$\frac{\text{Total output}}{\text{Labor input}}$$

The same applies to material, capital, and energy. All measures are ratios of quantities. Although some ratios can be expressed in quantitative terms such as units produced per man-hour, others must combine unlike quantities of inputs, such as tons and gallons of products, employee-hours, pounds, kilowatt hours, etc. To solve this problem, a set of weights representative of the relative importance of the various items can be used to combine unlike quantities. Base period prices are the recommended weights to be used for calculating total productivity, although other weighting systems such as "man-hour equivalents" can be used.

Functional and departmental measures are more likely to benefit the company than an effort to apply comprehensive, company-wide coverage. Most firms rely largely on budgetary dollar accounting data to analyze their operations, even though these data include the effects of inflation, taxes, depreciation, and the arbitrary accounting cost allocations previously mentioned. Because these accounting figures are frequently not significantly related to the activity or process under study, it is desirable to develop measures that reflect output and input in more realistic terms. Where financial measures are used, it is appropriate to deflate them to a base benchmark.

It is important to establish function and activity measures because these organizational entities are where productivity and quality are delivered and where processes are improved. It is here where process design and control happens. A sampling of illustrative measures is provided in Table 10-1.

Individual measures provide the individual supervisor and worker with the basic target for improvement of both quality and productivity through individual action planning. Improvement can only occur if measured against some benchmark (target, yardstick, standard, objective, or result expected).

The simplest and most effective way to set a standard is to list the responsibility of the job on a piece of paper and then list the measures (results expected) that would indicate that the job is being performed satisfactorily. This provides a benchmark from which improvement can proceed. For example:

Responsibility	Measure
Maintenance	Maintain an uptime machine rate of 95 percent
Assembly	Assemble 32 units per man-hour of direct labor
Accounts receivable	Maintain an accounts receivable level of 42 days

Having established these measures, or standards, the individual can then write a *productivity or quality improvement objective* (results expected). Taking the examples above, these improvement objectives could be written:

My productivity (or quality) improvement objective is

Action verb	Results expected	Time	Cost
Improve	Machine uptime from 94 percent to 97 percent	By June 30	At no increase in man-hours or preventive maintenance costs
Increase	Actual production from 90 percent of schedule to 95 percent	Commencing this quarter	At the same cost of manufacture

Industry and competitive measures are important for benchmarking against the competition, best-in-class, and others in the industry. These are examined in Chapter 8 on benchmarking.

Many companies set measures of total factor productivity such as output per labor-hour, material usage rates, ratio of direct to indirect labor, etc., but such macro measures provide little in the way of functional or departmental measures from which an improvement plan can be developed. Unlike return on investment

Table 10-1   Function and Activity Measures

Function/activity	Measure
Customer support	Cost per field technician, cost per warranty callback
Data processing	Operations employees per systems design employees
Quality assurance	Units returned for warranty repair as percentage of units shipped
Order processing	Orders processed per employee, sales per order processing employee
Production control	Order cycle time, inventory turn, machine utilization, total production to production schedule
Shipping	Orders shipped on time, packing expense to total shipping expense
Testing	Man-hours per run-hour, test expense to rework expense

(a measure of capital productivity), which can be broken down into each of its determinants, broad macro measures mean little to those lower in the hierarchy who need specific objectives in order to develop an action plan.

WHITE-COLLAR PRODUCTIVITY

Productivity of white-collar workers is no less important than that of direct labor or manufacturing employees. Indeed, in terms of numbers and expense, staff and non-production employees outnumber production employees by a wide margin. Yet the problem of measurement of output is more elusive. Measuring the units assembled per man-hour is not too difficult, but how many reports should an accountant prepare, not to mention the most difficult of all measures— managerial productivity. Peter Drucker tells us that it is "usually the least known, least analyzed, least managed of all factors of productivity."[19] Research has shown that white-collar employees are productive only about 50 percent of the time. The remainder is non-productive time and can be traced to personal delays (15 percent) and improper management (35 percent). Causes of wasted time include:

Poor scheduling	Poor staffing
Slack start and quit times	Inadequate communication of assignments
Lack of communication between functions	Unproductive meetings and telephone conversations
Information overload	

Measuring the Service Activity

Although the manufacturing worker (one who physically alters the product) has been measured for decades by time standards, time studies, and work sampling, it is not as easy to set standards for the non-manufacturing employee or the service activity. It is unlikely that measurement can be achieved in the same way as is done for the manufacturing worker. Nevertheless, a system can be devised to describe the productivity of an *activity* at a point in time and then provide a baseline for judging continuous improvement over time. The system is particularly appropriate for multi-plant or multi-divisional companies with similar products or services and for individual companies within an industry.

The basis for a system of measurement starts with the existing functions and activities of the organization. Each activity is a subset of a particular function. For example, the *activity* of recruiting is a part of the human resource *function,*

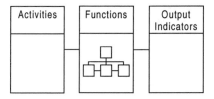

Figure 10-1   Measuring White-Collar (Indirect) Activity

accounts receivable is a part of the accounting function, and so on. The typical organization may identify a hundred or more activities that can be grouped into ten or more functions. This concept is shown in Figure 10-1.

The next step is to identify the *output indicators* that "drive" the activities or cause work in the activities. In other words, if it were not for the work caused by or resulting from the *indicators,* there would be little need for the *activities.* If, for example, there were no personnel employed, there would be no need for employee relations. If there were no purchasing, there would be no need for vendor invoicing. The resources utilized in the activity of vendor invoicing are therefore a dependent variable of the purchasing function. In other words, if activities are the "input" in the productivity ratio of output to input, then the indicators are the "output."

IMPROVING PRODUCTIVITY (AND QUALITY)

Improvement means increasing the ratio of the output of goods and services produced divided by the input used to produce them. Hence, the ratio can be increased by either increasing the output, reducing the input, or both. This concept is illustrated in Figure 10-2, along with a sampling of actions and techniques for improving the productivity ratio. This might be called the productivity wheel.

Historically, productivity improvement has focused on technology and capital equipment to reduce the input of labor cost. Improved output was generally thought to be subject to obtaining more production by applying industrial engineering techniques such as methods analysis, work flow, etc. Both of these approaches are still appropriate, but the current trend is toward better use of the potential available through human resources. Each worker can be his or her own industrial engineer—a mini-manager, so to speak. This potential can be tapped by allowing and encouraging people to innovate in one or more of the five ways described in the next section. Employee ideas can improve productivity, and in most cases this is accompanied by an improvement in quality as well.

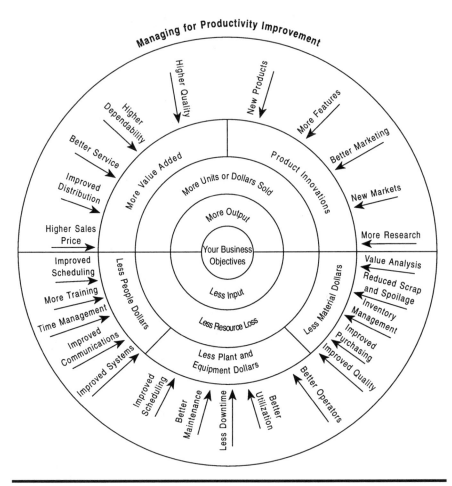

Figure 10-2   Productivity Wheel

Five Ways to Improve Productivity (and Quality) (see Figure 10-3)

Cost reduction is the traditional and most widely used approach to productivity improvement and is an appropriate route to improvement if implemented correctly. However, many companies maintain a somewhat outdated "across-the-board" mentality that directs each department to "cut costs by 10 percent." Staff services are slashed and training reduced, and the result is an inefficient sales force, reduced advertising, and diminished R&D. Maintenance is delayed and machine downtime is increased. The results may be a non-competitive product and loss of market share.

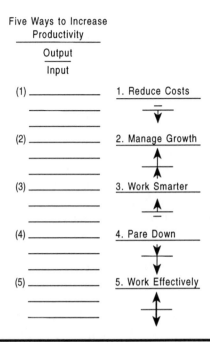

Figure 10-3 Productivity Improvement

Under this "management by drive" approach, people are perceived as a direct expense, and the immediate route to cost reduction is seen as cutting this expense as much as possible. This policy usually leads to employee resentment and is frequently counterproductive. It may result in trading today's headache for tomorrow's upset stomach.

Managing growth is a more positive approach, but growth without productivity improvement is *fat.* The improvement may suggest an investment or cost addition, but the investment must return more than the cost, thus increasing the ratio. Capital and technological improvements, systems design, training, organization design, and development are among the many ways to manage growth while improving productivity and quality. The approach does not necessarily mean additional investment in capital improvement. It can also mean reducing the amount of input per unit of output during the growth period. This may be termed *cost avoidance.*

Working smarter means more output from the same input, thus allowing increases in sales or production with the same gross input and lower unit cost. Many companies think that working smarter means putting a "freeze" on budgets while expecting a higher level of output. Although this may be necessary as a stopgap measure, it is hardly a rational course of action to improve productivity over the longer term. Better ways of improving this ratio might be getting more output by reducing manufacturing cost through product design, improving processes, or getting more production from the same level of raw materials by increasing inventory turnover.

Paring down is similar to cost reduction, except that as sales or production is off, input should be reduced by a proportionately larger amount, thus increasing the ratio. This productivity improvement can frequently be achieved through "sloughing off." In many organizations, there are many more opportunities than are generally realized to reduce marginal or unproductive facilities, employees, customers, products, or activities. Peter Drucker puts it this way: "Most plans concern themselves only with the new and additional things that have to be done—new products, new processes, new markets, and so on. But the key to doing something different tomorrow is getting rid of the no-longer-productive, the obsolescent, the obsolete." This "sloughing off" could apply to customers as well. Remember the 80/20 rule.

Working effectively is the best route to productivity and quality improvement; simply stated, you can get more for less. Some ways in which this can be accomplished are suggested in Figure 10-2.

Examples of Increasing Productivity While Improving Quality

Experience has shown that front-line supervisors and employees have a wealth of innovative ideas for productivity and quality improvement. They have only to be asked. In workshops and seminars conducted for hundreds of participants, there has been a high degree of enthusiasm for setting improvement objectives, defining problems, and organizing action plans for improvement. A few that were converted to action plans and resulted in substantial cost reduction as well as improved productivity and quality are presented here as illustrative examples. Each improvement objective will improve the output/input ratio in one or more of the five ways outlined earlier.

- Improve assembly output by 30 percent by reducing the excessive number and types of fasteners
- Reduce repetitive machine downtime by problem solving
- Set material standards and reduce rework by 10 percent
- Decrease work in process from 45 to 30 days by improved scheduling and shop floor layout
- Improve clerical costs by 30 percent by avoiding duplication with adequate work procedures
- Set standards for setup and improve setup time by 10 percent

- Improve tool revision cost by 50 percent by decreasing lead time from design
- Improve process flow and get 30 percent increased output of presses
- Improve flow of finished goods by improving warehouse layout
- Reduce labor cost by training technicians to replace engineers
- Get more output with less input by cross training and reduction of specialization
- Get more output with same input by better production planning
- Improve bill of materials by reducing custom parts
- Reduce assembly hours by using modular assembly
- Improve reliability by simplified design and design for customer maintainability

CAPITAL EQUIPMENT VS. MANAGEMENT SYSTEMS

Improvements in both productivity and quality have been slowed by two traditional management systems. The first has been the tendency to look to capital equipment as a solution to the problem of labor productivity. In the age of "high-tech," additions to capital have been viewed as the answer to boosting output. There is nothing wrong with this approach. Indeed, as pointed out previously, remarkable gains have been made in mechanization and automation since the Industrial Revolution. However, there are a number of arguments against depending on technology alone. It costs money and takes time, neither of which is an abundant resource.[20] Moreover, direct labor, the focus of capital equipment, is in the range of 8 to 12 percent of total cost of manufacturing. Technology has yet to make significant inroads in the productivity of indirect labor and service industries. Finally, high-tech must be accompanied by low tech—the way workers, supervisors, and managers interact in adapting to new systems.

A basic principle of Economics 101 is illustrated in Figure 10-4. As additional increments of capital are used, productivity increases up to the point where benefits and cost are equal. This is classical economics at its best and reflects Washington thinking about U.S. industrial policy. Figure 10-4 also demonstrates how the productivity curve can be shifted upward by means of improved management systems. This approach costs little and is available immediately. As discussed in earlier chapters, process control and related methods can improve both quality and productivity.

Another shortcoming of the capital investment argument as the primary or sole source of productivity and quality improvement relates to the historical

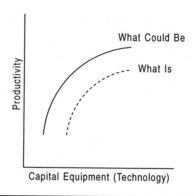

Figure 10-4   Productivity Curve

focus on cost reduction. As discussed in Chapter 11, the traditional cost accounting methods of the past provide inadequate information for decision making in the 1990s. Today, decisions on capital expenditures must be based on overall productivity, improving quality, cutting cycle time, reducing inventory, and adding flexibility. Activity analysis is a first step and it is fundamental to improving *management systems.*

ACTIVITY ANALYSIS

Measurement of an activity output is not sufficient. Questions still remain: (1) Is the output/input ratio a positive number? (2) Can this ratio be improved? Most importantly, (3) does the *value added* by the activity contribute to the goal of the organization and the external or internal customer? The overwhelming majority of people in an organization cannot answer either of these questions, except in general and non-measurable terms. They define their activities in terms of what they are doing, not what they want to get done or whether the output is worth more than the input.

People characterized as *input* supervisors or employees are recognized by their dedication to collecting voluminous data for variance reports or closely examining the details of an expense account. The emphasis is on paperwork and the maintenance of records. They are the guardians of company rules and procedures, but are unconcerned about the value of their service to external or internal customers. The means becomes the end. Emphasis is on form and administration (doing things right) rather than process and results (doing the right things). They confuse *efficiency* with *effectiveness.* The design department is efficient at making repeated modifications to the product without regard for the impact on production. The sales force is efficient at calling on the wrong customers with the wrong product. Staff departments are efficient at providing services to internal customers who place no value on the service because they do not have to pay for it. The focus is on the budget rather than results.

Activity-focused supervisors and employees are intent on what they are doing, as opposed to what should be done. The accountant focuses on preparing the cost report rather than reducing overhead costs. The engineer is concerned only with the technical specifications of design without regard to cost, value analysis, or competitive considerations. When asked to define the results of their jobs, these people will reply with such platitudes as "improve the operations," "keep maintenance costs down," or "stay within the budget." It can be said of bureaucracy that focus on activity rather than results seems perfectly logical to those who are trapped within it. The activity may seem logical to the individual performing it, but to an outsider or a customer it is obviously wasteful.

The historical attention that is paid to budgets and cost control has encouraged a focus on activity rather than non-financial measures that plan and monitor sources of competitive value and *strategic* cost information. For most white-collar and service activities, the purpose of the output is to provide input to another downstream activity that can be viewed as the *internal* customer. A good starting point, therefore, is to determine whether the internal customer's expectation is met by the value provided by the upstream activity. The analysis of these activities begins by charting the flow throughout the organization and identifying sources of customer value in each. The central questions to be asked are what is the value added by the activity and what is the output worth to the supplier and receiver.

The major steps in conducting an activity analysis program include:

- Each unit, function, or activity develops a baseline budget that includes a breakdown of one year's costs.
- Set a cost, productivity, or quality target.
- Develop a mission statement for each unit that answers the question: "Why does it exist?"
- Identify each activity that supports the mission and the end products or services that result from that activity.
- Allocate end-product cost that equals the baseline budget.
- Identify receivers (customers) of the end product or service.
- Develop and implement ideas for improvement.[21]

REENGINEERING

It has been suggested that in order to reinvent their companies, U.S. managers need to abandon the organizational and operational principles and procedures they are now using and create entirely new ones. These new ones can be combined into an emerging idea called **business reengineering**. Michael Hammer and James Champy, authors of *Reengineering the Corporation: A Manifesto for Business Revolution,*[22] call it the next revolution of business and compare its impact with that of Adam Smith's concept of labor specialization.

This managerial idea fits right in with the twin concepts of quality and productivity. Indeed, reengineering, also called process redesign, holds promise for improving quality and productivity: doing more for less—less investment, less time, and fewer people—and also doing it with better quality.

In Chapter 9 (Organizing for Total Quality Management), the classical principles of organization, which focused on structure and activity rather than outcome, were described. It is true that many, if not most, organizations remain committed to the classical principles of labor specialization and bureaucratic structure. The work is specialized and fragmented. Work is passed from one person or process to another. Workers never complete a job, nor do they understand their contribution to the whole; they just perform piecemeal tasks. Traditional process evaluation has focused on *fixing* the process. Business reengineering means starting all over—starting from scratch. **Reorganizing is out: reengineering is in.**

Reengineering a process is confusing and frustrating to some managers. They can identify a process but perceive it as one among "islands of processes" which, when combined, make up the organization. The connection between and integration among processes is elusive. More importantly, they focus on tasks, on jobs, on people, and on structure rather than on outcomes. Order processing is viewed as a series of individual tasks in a process—receiving an order form, picking up goods from the warehouse, and so forth—losing sight of the larger objective, which is to get the goods into the hands of the customer who ordered them. The tasks that make up the process are important, but the customers could care less about them. The customer only wants to know if the process works.

Consider the following scenario at IBM Credit's operations. When a salesperson sold a computer and called to get credit approval, it was important to get the approval rapidly, not only because lending money is a profitable business but also because a delay in approval gave the customer a chance to change his or her mind or get credit elsewhere. The salesperson's call was received by one of fourteen clerical operators who entered the request on a piece of paper. This was the first of *five* steps involving five departments that bounced the request around for periods ranging from six days to two weeks. Ninety percent of that time involved work sitting in someone's in or out basket. When the salesperson would call to learn the status of the customer's financial deal, the information could not be furnished because the request was lost somewhere in the five-step chain.

When one manager took a financing request and walked it through all five steps, it was learned that the actual work took a total of only *90 minutes.* The remaining six days or so was consumed as the request languished in a queue on a desk awaiting movement to the next desk in the process. After reengineering the process, instead of moving the request from office to office, from desk to desk, from pile to pile, one person (called a deal structurer) now processes the entire application from start to finish. There are no handoffs. The result is that the number of requests handled has increased *100 times.*

Reengineering is not reorganizing. It is not new wine in old bottles. It is a rejection of the classical concept of labor specialization and the engineering of tasks. It is the reinvention of the organization through process redesign.

Principles of Reengineering

Creating new rules tailored to the modern environment ultimately requires a new conceptualization of the business process. However, according to Hammer,[23] reengineering need not be haphazard. Some of the principles that companies have already discovered while reengineering their business processes can help jump start the effort for others.

Organize around outcomes, not tasks. This principle calls for the use of one person to perform all the steps in a process. Design that person's job around an objective or outcome instead of a single task. The following is an example of an electronics company which had separate organizations performing each of the five steps between selling and installing equipment.

■ One group determined customer requirements, another translated those requirements into internal product codes, a third conveyed that information to various plants and warehouses, a fourth received and assembled the components, and a fifth delivered and installed the equipment. The customer order moved systematically from step to step, but this sequential processing caused problems. The people getting the information from the customer in step 1 had to get all the data needed throughout the process, even if it was not needed until step 5. In addition, the many handoffs were responsible for many errors. Finally, any complaints from customers were referred all the way back to step 1, which caused inordinate delays in customer service. When the company ultimately reengineered, the assembly line approach was eliminated. Responsibility for the various steps was compressed and assigned to one person, the customer service representative. This person would oversee the entire process. The customer service representative expedites and coordinates the process, much like a general contractor.

Have those who use the output of the process perform the process. In an effort to capitalize on the benefits of specialization and scale, many organizations established specialized departments to handle specialized processes. Computer-based data and expertise are now more readily available, enabling departments, units, and individuals to do more for themselves. Opportunities exist to reengineer processes so that individuals who need the result of the process can perform it themselves. When people closest to the process perform it, there is little need for the overhead associated with managing it. Interfaces and liaisons can be eliminated, as can the mechanisms used to coordinate those who perform the process with those who use it. Moreover, the problem of capacity planning for those who perform the process is greatly reduced.

Subsume information processing work into the real work that produces the information. The previous two principles were used to compress linear processes. This principle suggests moving work from one person or department to another. Most companies establish units which do nothing but collect and process information created by other departments. This arrangement reflects the old rule about specialized labor and the belief that people at lower levels are incapable of acting on information they generate. An accounts payable department collects information from purchasing and receiving and reconciles it with data provided by the vendor. Quality assurance gathers and analyzes information received from production. Redesigning the accounts payable process embodies the new rule, wherein receiving (which produces the information about the goods received) processes this information instead of sending it to accounts payable. The new system can easily compare the delivery with an order and initiate appropriate action.

Treat geographically dispersed resources as though they were centralized. The conflict between centralization and decentralization is that decentralizing a resource gives better service to those who use it, but at the cost of abundance and missed economies of scale. Companies no longer have to make such trade-offs. They can use databases, telecommunication networks, and standard processing systems to realize the benefits of scale and coordination while maintaining the benefits of flexibility of service.

Link parallel activities instead of integrating their results. This principle seeks to forge the links between functions and to coordinate them while their activities are in process rather than after they have been completed. Communication networks, shared databases, and teleconferencing can bring independent groups together so that coordination is ongoing.

Put the decision point where the work is performed, and build control into the process. In most organizations, those who do the work are distinguished from those who monitor the work and make decisions about it. The tacit assumption is that the people actually doing the work have neither the time nor the inclination to monitor and control the work and therefore lack the knowledge and scope to make decisions about it. The entire hierarchical management structure is built on this assumption. Accountants, auditors, and supervisors check, record, and monitor work. Managers handle any exceptions. The new principle suggests that the people who do the work should make decisions and that the process itself can have built-in controls. Pyramidal management layers can therefore be compressed and the organization flattened.

Capture information once and at the source. This last rule is simple. When information was difficult to transmit, it made sense to collect it repeatedly. Each person, department, or unit had its own requirements and forms. Companies simply had to live with the associated delays, entry errors, and costly overhead. However, by integrating and connecting these systems, the company was able to eliminate this redundant data entry, along with the attendant checking functions and the seemingly inevitable errors.

QUESTIONS FOR DISCUSSION

10-1 Give an example of how improving quality can also increase productivity.

10-2 Illustrate how productivity improvement may be more effective than increased sales in improving profitability.

10-3 How can improved management be as effective as technology and capital equipment in improving productivity?

10-4 Why has the rate of productivity increase been low in the United States?

10-5 Choose four or five functions or activities in staff or white-collar jobs and indicate a measure of productivity for each.

10-6 List three of the five ways to improve the productivity rate of input to output, and identify a specific action that could be taken to achieve the improvement.

ENDNOTES

1. Institute of Industrial Engineers, "Productivity and Quality in the USA Today," *Management Services (UK)*, Jan. 1990, pp. 27–31.
2. W. Edwards Deming, *Quality, Productivity, and Competitive Position*, Cambridge, Mass.: Center for Advanced Engineering Study, Massachusetts Institute of Technology, 1982, pp. 1–2.
3. A. V. Feigenbaum, "Quality and Productivity," *Quality Progress*, Nov. 1977, p. 21.
4. This conclusion is suggested by the Profit Impact of Market Strategies (PIMS) database referred to in Chapter 1. The studies suggest that higher conformance and total quality costs are inversely related and better manufacturing-based quality results in higher output without a corresponding increase in costs. See K. E. Maani, "Productivity and Profitability through Quality: Myth and Reality," *International Journal of Quality & Reliability (UK)*, Vol. 6 Issue 3, 1989, pp. 11–23. One empirical study concludes that improvements in quality level may be related to productivity increases. See Daniel G. Hotard, "Quality and Productivity: An Examination of Some Relationships," *Engineering Management International (Netherlands)*, Jan. 1988, pp. 259–266. In one Conference Board research study of 62 firms that attempted to measure the results of quality on profitability, 47 indicated that profits have increased noticeably because of lower costs and/or increased market share. See Francis J. Walsh, Jr., *Current Practices in Measuring Quality*, New York: The Conference Board, 1989, p. 3. See also Colin Scurr, "Total Quality Management and Productivity," *Management Services*, Oct. 1991, pp. 28–30.
5. Joyce R. Jarrett, "Long Term Strategy...A Commitment to Excellence," *Journal for Quality and Participation*, July/Aug. 1990, pp. 28–33.
6. Raymond C. Cole and Lee H. Hales, "How Monsanto Justified Automation," *Management Accounting*, Jan. 1992, pp. 39–43.
7. At the Third National Productivity Conference in Dallas on May 21, 1990.
8. Robert D. Buzzell and Bradley T. Gale, *The PIMS Principles*, New York: The Free Press, 1987, pp. 10–11.
9. Slow productivity growth is not characteristic of all U.S. industries. It has been especially high in the manufacture of computers and TV sets, but negative growth has been the case in petroleum refining and retailing.
10. For a more detailed examination of the reasons for slow productivity growth in the United States, see Joel E. Ross *Productivity, People, & Profits*, Englewood Cliffs, N.J.: Prentice-Hall, 1981 and Joel E. Ross and William C. Ross, *Japanese Quality Circles & Productivity*, Englewood Cliffs, N.J.: Prentice-Hall, 1982.
11. For one popular view of the unwillingness of managers to manage, see Robert H. Hayes and William J. Abernathy, "Managing Our Way to Decline," *Harvard Business Review*, July–Aug. 1989, pp. 67–77.
12. "Productivity and Quality in the 90's," *Management Services (UK)*, June 1990, pp. 28–33. This article reports on a survey of British managers, the majority of whom believe that managers are more interested in short-term financial gain than in long-term productivity. Similar surveys in the United States have had similar results.
13. "The Productivity Paradox," *Business Week*, June 6, 1988, p. 103.
14. National Center for Productivity and Quality of Work Life, *Improving Productivity in*

the Changing World of the 1980s, Washington, D.C.: U.S. Government Printing Office, 1978.

15. OECD, *Economic Outlook,* July 1991, p. 3.

16. Nobel laureate economist Milton Friedman stated that higher wages and the price-wage spiral are an *effect* of inflation, not a *cause.* Milton Friedman and Rose Friedman, *Free to Choose: A Personal Statement,* Harcourt Brace Jovanovich, 1980.

17. Coopers & Lybrand conducted a survey to determine what federal executives know and think about quality management. About half of the respondents said that the lack of dependable ways to measure quality is a major obstacle. The same could be said of productivity measures. David Carr and Ian Littman, "Quality in the Federal Government," *Quality Progress,* Sep. 1990, pp. 49–52.

18. See Carl G. Thor, "How to Measure Organizational Productivity," *CMA Magazine,* March 1991, pp. 17–19. A company-wide system for measuring productivity is quite complex. The American Productivity and Quality Center conducts a three-day seminar on the topic. See also Brain Maskell, "Performance Measurement for World Class Manufacturing," *Management Accounting (UK),* July/Aug. 1989, pp. 48–50. This article identifies seven common characteristics used by world-class manufacturing firms: (1) performance measures are directly related to the manufacturing strategy, (2) primarily non-financial measures are used, (3) the measures vary among locations, (4) the measures change over time as needs change, (5) the measures are simple and easy to use, (6) the measures provide rapid feedback to operators and managers, and (7) the measures are meant to foster improvement instead of only monitoring.

19. Peter Drucker, *Management,* New York: Harper & Row, 1974, p. 70.

20. Carl Thor, president of the American Productivity and Quality Center in Houston, favors management systems. Regarding high-tech additions, he says: "You need a decade's worth of that kind of investment to have an effect." See a special report entitled "The Productivity Paradox," *Business Week,* June 6, 1988, pp. 100–112.

21. For additional ideas on activity analysis, see Thomas H. Johnson, "Activity-Based Information: A Blueprint for World-Class Management Accounting," *Management Accounting,* June 1988, pp. 23–30. See also Philip Janson and Murray E. Bovarnick, "How to Conduct a Diagnostic Activity Analysis: Five Steps to a More Effective Organization," *National Productivity Review,* Spring 1988, pp. 152–160; Paul L. Brown, "Quality Improvement through Activity Analysis," *Journal of Organizational Behavior Management,* Vol. 10 Issue 1, 1989, pp. 169–179. For a more detailed program for implementing an organization-wide productivity improvement program, see Joel E. Ross, *Productivity, People & Profits,* Englewood Cliffs, N.J.: Prentice-Hall, 1981.

22. Harper Collins Publishers, Inc., May 1993.

23. M. Hammer, "Reengineering Work: Don't Automate, Obliterate," *Harvard Business Review,* July–Aug. 1990, pp. 104–112.

CASE

Following a turnaround effort which initially focused on cost reduction, the company profiled in the following article moved into a program of productivity enhancements and then into a quality improvement program. An interesting aside is the way in which the company moved control of operations away from the accountants and into the hands of operating personnel.

WORLD CLASS PRODUCTIVITY AT STANDARD AERO

Paul Sharman

Standard Aero, located in Winnipeg, Canada, is in the business of repairing and overhauling aircraft engines. The company has become one of the largest suppliers in the world for turbine engine and accessory overhaul and repair. The company summarizes its success in two words: "World's Best." It was not always this productive. Among the objectives set by President Bob Hamaberg is to cut the time it takes to overhaul an engine from two months to fifteen days.

In 1989 the company was acquired by Hawker Siddley, a U.K. conglomerate. In the same month as the acquisition, Hamaberg attended a management meeting in the U.K. Dr. Alan K. Watkins, the recently appointed managing director and chief executive of Hawker Siddeley, previously of Lucas industries, led a two-day series of presentations focused on TQM and in particular how Lucas industries had significantly improved productivity and financial results.

Lucas industries had established Lucas Engineering & Systems Ltd. (LE&S) to provide best-practice skills to the process of managing change. LE&S applies modern systems engineering methodologies to the redesign of the business, its

Abridged from *CMA Magazine*, April 1991, pp. 10–12, by permission of the Society of Management Accountants of Canada.

manufacturing systems, organization, and key processes. LE&S provides these services to Lucas businesses throughout the world and also sells similar support services to other businesses, primarily business partners. Watkins' message was essentially: fix the business, not the product.

"When I came back I was convinced we had to re-evaluate the traditional ways of doing things and look at doing things in ways in which we never had before," said Hamaberg. After dwelling on the subject a while, he called his own management meeting and threw down the gauntlet. His message was simple. "I want an order of magnitude improvement in all aspects of our business. Five to ten percent will not do! 75% is the target." He underscored his message by inviting his management team either to sign up or discuss their alternative career plans with him. Initially, management was offended. Gradually, reflecting on Hamaberg's logic, they came on side.

In no time, projects were in flight. The first was a paper reduction program. In three months of examining reports and practices, the company eliminated 20% of its annual paper consumption. Local suppliers were soon visiting the buyers to find out what was going on. The next target was the accounting organization. Hamaberg spent four hours talking with the accountants about TQM and how they might change to provide better service to customers. The outcome of this meeting was both creative and a challenge to the way in which most accounting organizations work.

The six most senior finance managers were reassigned to operations, reporting directly to the business unit managers. Leah Muller, previously controller, used to have a staff of 29 people but now has none. She describes how she initially maintained a safety harness by retaining some of her accounting responsibilities. After a few months, Leah gave up the old activities voluntarily. "I found that I was enjoying myself and making a much greater contribution to the business by being on the front line." Through moving the accounting staff, relations with operating people also improved significantly.

Within a short period of time, accounting record accuracy improved substantially. The business unit accountants were responsible for the accuracy of transactions of all kinds associated with their operation. The emphasis among the now dispersed accounting staff moved from keeping records of other peoples' activities, attempting to capture errors through reconciliations, and clearing accounts and audits, to producing correct entries and documentation at source, hence doing it right the first time. This attitude shift was entirely consistent with the principles of TQM; specifically, build quality in, don't inspect it in. Total accounting staff have been reduced from 40 to 22.

Other organizations quickly followed suit. Engineers were physically moved, and the central sales and marketing organization was completely dismantled and re-assigned to the business unit manager.

Business Redesigned

In December, Hawker Siddeley asked its subsidiaries for competitive proposals to undertake TQM programs. Those selected would receive training and consulting support from Lucas paid for by Hawker Siddeley. Naturally, this was too good an opportunity to be missed. Standard Aero went the extra mile in preparing its proposal, and succeeded. So began what Hamaberg describes as the most exciting part of the redesigning of the entire firm.

The project, which kicked off at the beginning of 1990, was to redesign the complete business. The unit chosen was Standard Aero's biggest: the T56–Allison Engine Overhaul. Where in many companies TQM meant doing what they were already doing better, the Lucas method is to make radical change. T56–Allison Engine Overhaul was to reduce total elapsed time by 75% from the industry norm of 60 days to 15 days. Since the objective was deadly serious, the team assigned full time for nine to ten months was the same group who would stay with the business and run it once the project phase was complete. The team consisted of:

- A director level finance manager
- A senior engineer
- The director of MIS (an engineer who had previously been a business unit manager)
- The business unit director
- A mechanic from production
- An inspector from production

The team was headed up full time by a Lucas consultant who acted as a facilitator. Two training sessions were held. The first, held in the U.K. in May 1990, was attended by two Canadians. The second, a five-day session described as a foundation course, was held in Winnipeg and delivered by three Lucas engineers. Following the foundation course, the project began in earnest. The team worked through five major steps:

1. Identify the business:
   - What is it?
   - Who are the players?
   - What is the market?
   - Analyze the competition.
2. Develop a questionnaire and interview the customers to identify their needs and concerns and to establish a new level of rapport.

3. Evaluate customer complaints and requirements and compare them to competitor information. Develop a strengths and weaknesses analysis.

4. Determine which customers and business they wanted—Lucas calls this scientific marketing.

5. Redesign the business unit relative to the criteria identified in the preceding steps as well as to achieve the 15-day target. This meant evaluating every step of every facet of the business as well as every piece of paper. Eliminating waste activities was achieved by breaking the business into operating cells and then simulating every stage to determine where the bottlenecks were. The design objective for capacity was twice the current level.

In addition, a brand new set of performance measurements was identified using magnetic boards with colored markers showing due dates, the flow of work, and milestone performance. One aspect of this exercise was to implement continuous improvement whereby performance is measured in absolute numbers with the expectation that trends will improve and backsliding is not acceptable. A critical aspect of performance measurement is that the measurements all focus on flow of work in order to meet the customers' needs. This contrasts with the more traditional measurements which tend to focus on efficiency and financial reporting. In some instances, the old measurements were eliminated because they were distracting the organization from doing the right thing. As long as the new stats demonstrate improved performance in absolute terms, then improved profitability may be expected.

Toward Continuous Improvement

After nine months, the first manufacturing cell has been implemented with better than target results. What used to take 30 days now requires only three days. One job which required parts to be moved to another building and three days' elapsed time now stays in the same cell. The whole job takes only a few minutes. The key was to eliminate flow discontinuities and to abbreviate time and distance travelled. Taking advantage of technology to replace old methods has been a critical concern. There are six other cells to be implemented but, together, they should take only six months to design and implement. Walls have already been pulled down and areas prepared.

For T56–Allison Engine Overhaul, the challenge has passed to the marketing people to develop the business, new products and, working with suppliers, the opportunities. Sales people are now required to act more as a technical interface between the product and the customer. Project team members will soon leave their paper-strewn meeting room, decorated with project charts of all kinds, to move to offices co-located with production. There they will run their newly designed and much improved business—a business they have personally examined in excruciating detail and for which they now feel a considerable sense of ownership.

For the company, seven more projects will be undertaken so that every aspect of the entire business will have been evaluated. Meanwhile, reaching 15 days' turnaround is only the first hurdle for the T56 group. With continuous improvement, 15 days will be old news before too long. Company results have already registered the benefit of productivity and TQM steps over the past few years. Earnings were up 45% in the last year on sales increases for the same period of 4.5%. Cash flow exceeded profits by 50%.

Bob Hamaberg clearly believes it is the team effort of a focused group which has delivered the results to date. He described the many communications programs Standard Aero has in place and, also, how the company spends up to 1.75% of revenues on training. No doubt leadership and the application of disciplined techniques have also played critical roles.

Questons for Discussion

1   Justify the way in which the company dismantled the controller's department by assigning the accounting staff to operating units.

2   Was reduction of paperwork the place to start with a productivity improvement program? Explain.

3   Suggest the ways in which productivity and quality would be improved by reducing total elapsed time for overhaul of an engine from 60 days to 15 days.

4   Explain the process of "redesigning" the business. Why does it start with customer requirements?

5   Why is reduction in cycle time so important?

CASE

REENGINEERING AT
AT&T UNIVERSAL CARD SERVICES

In 1992 the Universal Card Services division of AT&T, just 31 months in existence, won the Malcolm Baldrige Quality Award. The division's strong suit was customer satisfaction, although the much improved *customer delight* was chosen as the basis for the company values.

Despite the award, the company found itself with an embarrassment of riches—or more precisely an embarrassment of customers. The success of the company's combination credit card/long-distance phone card was astounding. Charter members would receive a reduced rate credit card that charged several points below market interest rates and had a lifetime membership without an annual fee. In addition, the card gave a 10 percent discount on long-distance calls. The card was launched on the Academy Awards Show. In the first 24 hours, 250,000 inquiries were received, and at the end of one year 5.3 million people had become charter members.

The response overwhelmed the company's ability to accommodate customer inquiries. A major roadblock was information technology. Phone reps were given underperforming "dumb" terminals manufactured by AT&T, the parent company. The reps were unable to integrate information from multiple mainframes and had to bounce from screen to screen while keeping up a conversation with the caller. These computer hardware problems were subsequently solved by the installation of advanced systems, which are under continuing review and reengineering in search of faster response times and greater flexibility. Currently the phone reps field about 1.2 million inquiries per month and answer 95 percent before 20 seconds has elapsed.

Information technology can improve both productivity and quality in a number of ways. For example, the company is testing a voice recognition unit that can reduce costs by more than a factor of 10. A voice response call costs 20 cents as compared to $2.50 for a representative to service the same customer.

Information technology is also valuable for research and data analysis. By analyzing the call-management database, workload forecasts can be made each day or shift to allow for optimum use of personnel between departments.

The company has not overlooked the "soft" side of information technology. The value system of "customer delight" demands rapid, accurate, and courteous responses to customer calls. One-third of the work force which operates in self-directed teams focuses on behavior training, including ways to influence people, how to negotiate, and how to resolve conflicts. These teams have allowed the company to flatten the organization and increase the ratio of associates to supervisors from the current 20 to 1.

Questions for Discussion

1   What is the role of information technology in productivity improvement? What is its role in reengineering? Give examples.

2   Choose a process (e.g., order processing, university registration) and trace the steps in the process to demonstrate how many separate operations are involved. How could the process be reengineered?

PRODUCTIVITY AT VARIFILM

Compare the following TQM criteria to Varifilm and indicate whether the practice in the company is a *strength (S)* or *needs improvement (I)*. The criteria relate to improvement in quality, operations, business processes and support, and supplier quality. It should be noted that improvement in these areas is usually followed by an improvement in productivity (see chapter text).

	(S)	(I)
6.1 Product and Service Quality Results		
■ Key measures of film quality show overall improvement trends. Varifilm is performing better than its best competitor.	—	—
■ Two key measures of on-time delivery (shipment reliability index and delivery satisfaction index) show overall improvement. Varifilm is performing better than key competitors.	—	—
■ There is an overall improvement trend in the order entry error rate.	—	—
6.2 Operational Results		
■ First-pass yield has shown an improvement trend.	—	—
■ Improvement trends are shown for non-conforming product shipped, manufacturing cycle time, and order entry cycle time.	—	—
■ Improvement trends are shown for air emissions and process waste as well as return on equity, profitability, and sales per co-worker.	—	—

Describe how improvement in each of the preceding items should result in reduced cost as well as an increase in productivity of human resources, material, and capital.

6.3 Business Process and Support Service Results (S) (I)

- An overall improvement trend has been shown for accounts — —
  receivable errors and information systems operations. Both
  are approaching or have exceeded the industry standard.

- Improvement trends have been shown for EDI orders and — —
  cost of purchase orders.

- An overall improvement trend has been shown for new — —
  product cycle time and has exceeded the best competitor.

- Benchmarks and industry standards against which Varifilm — —
  compares itself have been flat or have shown no change.
  These should be investigated to ensure that they reflect
  future competitive trends.

- Comparisons for key competitors and best-in-class are pro- — —
  vided for only one measure.

6.4 Supplier Quality Results

- Varifilm has shown overall improvement trends for certi- — —
  fied suppliers, supplier quality rating, and supplier quality
  incidents measures.

- Comparisons of key supplier quality measures to best-in- — —
  class benchmarks are provided for only one measure.

Describe how improvement in each of the preceding items should result in reduced cost as well as an increase in productivity of human resources, material, and capital.

THE COST OF QUALITY

Quality is measured by the cost of quality which is the expense of non conformance—the cost of doing things wrong

Philip Crosby
Quality Is Free

What will it cost to improve quality? What will it cost to not improve quality? These are basic questions that managers need to ask as they focus on the bottom line and company strategic decisions. These questions about the cost of quality have served to draw attention to the quality movement. No one will deny the importance of quality, but it is the confusion surrounding the payoff and the trade-off between cost and quality that is unclear to many decision makers.

It is becoming increasingly clear that whereas the answer to the cost of poor quality may be difficult to obtain, the potential payoff from improvement is extraordinary. Hewlett-Packard estimated that the cost of not doing things right the first time was 25 to 30 percent of revenues. Travelers Insurance Company found that the figure was $1 million per hour. On a positive note, Motorola has reduced the cost of poor quality by about 5 percent of total sales, or about $480 million per year.

COST OF QUALITY DEFINED

The cost of quality has been defined in a number of ways, some of which include:

■   At 3M quality cost equals actual cost minus no failure cost. That is, the cost of quality is the difference between the actual cost of making and selling products and services and the cost if there were no failures during manufacture or use and no possibility of failure.[1]

■   Quality costs usually are defined as costs incurred because poor quality may or does exist.[2]

■   The cost of not meeting the customer's requirements—the cost of doing things wrong.[3]

■   All activities that are carried out that are not needed directly to support departmental [quality] objectives are considered the cost of quality.[4]

These definitions leave unanswered the question: "How much quality is enough?" In theory, the answer is analogous to a principle of economics: basic marginal cost equals marginal revenue (MC = MR). That is, spend on quality improvement until the added profit equals the cost of achieving it. This is not so easy in practice. In economics, the MC and MR curves are difficult to define and more difficult to compute. The same is true of the cost/benefit curves of quality costs. What are the costs of added quality and the "hidden" costs of non-quality? What are the bottom line benefits? Neither of these questions is easy to answer, particularly in view of the long-run strategic implications. The answer lies at the very essence of what the company is about.

THE COST OF QUALITY

The cost of quality or, more specifically, "non-quality" is a major concern to both national policymakers as well as individual firms. Because much of our national concern with competitiveness seems to be focused on Japan, it is interesting to note that some estimates of quality costs in U.S. firms indicate 25 percent of revenues, while in Japan the figure is less than 5 percent.[5] Estimates of potential savings are as high as $300 billion by nationwide application of total quality management (TQM).[6] Feigenbaum puts the estimate at 7 percent of the gross national product and suggests that this figure can be one of the tools used by policymakers in considering the quality potential of the U.S. economy in relation to the country's major competitors.[7]

The cost of poor quality in individual firms and the potential for improvement can be staggering. In *Thriving on Chaos,* Tom Peters reports that experts agree that poor quality can cost about 25 percent of the personnel and assets in a manufacturing firm and up to 40 percent in a service firm. There appears to be general agreement that the costs range between 20 and 30 percent of sales.[8]

The potential for profit improvement is very substantial. One has only to visualize a profit-and-loss statement with a net profit of 6 percent before tax and then compute what the profit would be if 20 to 30 percent of the operating budget were reduced. Add to this the additional strategic benefits and the potential is great indeed.

THREE VIEWS OF QUALITY COSTS

Historically, business managers have assumed that increased quality is accompanied by increased cost; higher quality meant higher cost. This view was questioned by the quality pioneers. Juran examined the economics of quality and concluded that benefits outweighed costs.[9] Feigenbaum introduced "total quality control" and developed the principle that quality is everyone's job, thus expanding the notion of quality cost beyond the manufacturing function.[10] In 1979 Crosby introduced the now popular concept that "quality is free."[11] Today, the view among practitioners seems to fall into one of three categories:[12]

1. **Higher quality means higher cost.**   Quality attributes such as performance and features cost more in terms of labor, material, design, and other costly resources. The additional benefits from improved quality do not compensate for the additional expense.

2. **The cost of improving quality is less than the resulting savings.**   This view was originally promoted by Deming and is widely held among Japanese manufacturers. The savings result from less rework, scrap, and other *direct* expenses related to defects. This is said to account for the focus on continuous improvement of processes in Japanese firms.

3. **Quality costs are those incurred in excess of those that would have been incurred if the product were built or the service performed exactly right the first time.**   This view is held by adherents of the TQM philosophy. Costs include not only those that are direct, but also those resulting from lost customers, lost market share, and the many hidden costs and foregone opportunities not identified by modern cost accounting systems.

The attention now being given to the more comprehensive view of the cost of poor quality is a fairly recent development. Even today, many companies tend to ignore or downplay this opportunity because of a continuing focus on production volume or frustration with the problem of computing the trade-off between volume and quality. This computational difficulty is compounded by accounting systems that do not recognize the expenses as manageable. More on this will be provided later in this chapter.

One survey of 94 corporate controllers found that only 31 percent of the firms regularly measured costs of quality, and even among those firms productivity was ranked higher than quality as a factor contributing to profit. Not surprisingly, the major reason for failure to measure these costs was lack of top management commitment.[13]

Philip Crosby, of "quality is free" fame, is of the firm opinion that zero defects is the absolute performance standard and the cost of quality is the price of non-conformance against that standard. His concept is catching on as more companies set goals such as parts per million, six sigma, and even zero defects. On the other hand, a goal of zero defects may be more costly than the payoff that might accrue. As one approaches zero defects, costs may begin to increase geometrically.

Another of Crosby's principles, which he calls "absolutes," is *measurement of quality:*

> The measurement of quality is the Price of Nonconformance, not indexes....Measuring quality by calculating the price of waste—wasted time, effort, material—produces a monetary figure that can be used to direct efforts to improve and measure the improvement.[14]

This monetary figure, according to Crosby, is a percentage of sales, and he suggests that the standard should be reduced to about *2 to 3 percent.* This measure has been generally accepted, and many firms use it as a target and measure of progress.

QUALITY COSTS

The costs of quality are generally classified into four categories: (1) prevention, (2) appraisal, (3) internal failure, and (4) external failure.[15] *Prevention* costs include those activities which remove and prevent defects from occurring in the production process. Included are such activities as quality planning, production reviews, training, and engineering analysis, which are incurred to ensure that poor quality is not produced. *Appraisal* costs are those costs incurred to identify poor quality products after they occur but before shipment to customers. Inspection activity is an example.

Failure costs are those incurred either during the production process (*internal*) or after the product is shipped (*external*). Internal failure costs include such items as machine downtime, poor quality materials, scrap, and rework. External failure costs include returns and allowances, warranty costs, and the hidden costs of customer dissatisfaction and lost market share. Recognition of the relative importance of external failure costs has caused many companies to broaden their

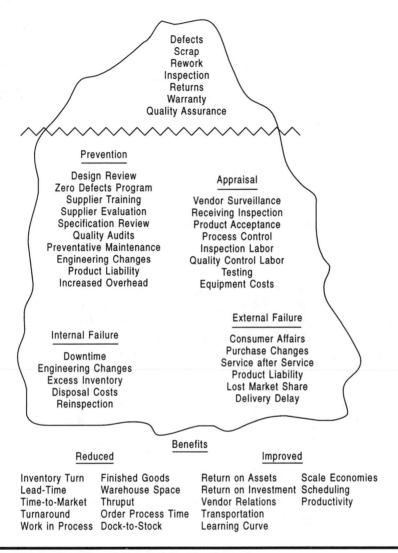

Defects
Scrap
Rework
Inspection
Returns
Warranty
Quality Assurance

Prevention

Design Review
Zero Defects Program
Supplier Training
Supplier Evaluation
Specification Review
Quality Audits
Preventative Maintenance
Engineering Changes
Product Liability
Increased Overhead

Appraisal

Vendor Surveillance
Receiving Inspection
Product Acceptance
Process Control
Inspection Labor
Quality Control Labor
Testing
Equipment Costs

External Failure

Internal Failure

Downtime
Engineering Changes
Excess Inventory
Disposal Costs
Reinspection

Consumer Affairs
Purchase Changes
Service after Service
Product Liability
Lost Market Share
Delivery Delay

Benefits

Reduced		Improved	
Inventory Turn	Finished Goods	Return on Assets	Scale Economies
Lead-Time	Warehouse Space	Return on Investment	Scheduling
Time-to-Market	Thruput	Vendor Relations	Productivity
Turnaround	Order Process Time	Transportation	
Work in Process	Dock-to-Stock	Learning Curve	

Figure 11-1   Benefits of Costs of Quality Control

perspective from product quality to total consumer satisfaction as the key quality measure.

In Figure 11-1, the many costs of non-quality are classified into the four categories outlined earlier: (1) prevention, (2) appraisal, (3) internal failure, and (4) external failure. The figure is an attempt to convey the idea of an iceberg, where only 10 percent is visible and 90 percent is hidden from view. The analogy is a good one because the *visible* 10 percent is comprised of such items as scrap,

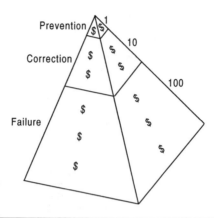

Figure 11-2 1-10-100 Rule

rework, inspection, returns under warranty, and quality assurance costs; for many companies these comprise what they believe to be the total costs. When the *hidden* costs of quality are computed, controlled, and reduced, a firm can acheive the benefits shown at the bottom of Figure 11-1.

Of these types of costs, prevention costs should probably take priority because it is much less costly to prevent a defect than to correct one. The principle is not unlike the traditional medical axiom: "An ounce of prevention is worth a pound of cure." The relationship between these costs is reflected in the 1-10-100 rule depicted in Figure 11-2. One dollar spent on prevention will save $10 on appraisal and $100 on failure costs. As one moves along the stream of events from design to delivery or "dock-to-stock," the cost of errors escalates as failure costs become higher and the payoff from an investment in prevention becomes greater. Computer systems analysts are aware of this and understand that an hour spent on better programming or design can save up to ten hours of system retrofit and redesign. One general manager of Hewlett-Packard's computer systems division observed:

> The earlier you detect and prevent a defect the more you can save. If you catch a two cent resistor before you use it and throw it away, you lose two cents. If you don't find it until it has been soldered into a computer component, it may cost $10 to repair the part. If you don't catch the component until it is in the computer user's hands, the repair will cost hundreds of dollars. Indeed, if a $5000 computer has to be repaired in the field, the expense may exceed the manufacturing cost.[16]

When total customer satisfaction becomes the definition of a quality product or service, it creates a need to develop measures which integrate the customer perspective into a measurement system. This need moves beyond the shop floor and into the many non-product features such as delivery time, responsiveness, billing accuracy, etc. This need also leads to a search for quality, and hence quality costs, in activities not usually recognized as incurring these costs. This will change as more companies realize that all activities can contribute to total customer satisfaction. Thus, quality costs include those factors which lie behind the obvious production processes. Moreover, it becomes necessary to identify the hidden quality costs associated with foregone opportunities.

What is frequently overlooked is the unrealized potential for improved productivity and quality to be achieved by identifying and measuring the difference between no failure (parts per million, six sigma, zero defects, etc.) cost and actual cost. What, for example, would be the payoff from just-in-time, better process control, improved inventory turn, and reduced cycle time in the many cross-functional processes and cost interrelationships in the stream of activities during the life cycle of the product or a service? Each of these actions would improve quality, use fewer resources, and improve return on investment (ROI). How these same actions could also increase market share and profitability was previously examined in Chapter 1. To quote Feigenbaum: "Quality and cost are a sum, not a difference—complementary, not conflicting objectives."[17]

MEASURING QUALITY COSTS

In a 1989 Conference Board survey of 149 large U.S. companies (96 manufacturing), it was found that 111 had a quality process or program. Of the 111 that had a program, 83 attempted to measure quality. The majority of the companies that attempted to measure quality costs compiled the information outside of the accounting system. The breakdown of cost categories reflected a major focus on the direct labor costs of scrap, rework, returns, and costs related to inventory including past-due receivables. There was little evidence to indicate that these costs, once collected, were used to manage processes leading to customer satisfaction quality. Rather, the systems appeared to resemble the traditional cost reduction syndrome discussed in Chapter 10.

An effective cost of quality planning and control systems should be directed toward the basic reason for quality improvement; that is, support of a differentiation strategy. Of course, if a company has not developed a strategy, it becomes difficult to identify those costs of quality that support differentiation of satisfaction in the minds of the customers. For a multi-division or multi-product firm, this strategy may be different for each market segment or strategic business unit. There is little advantage to investing in equipment, overhead, or process improvements which do not add customer value. What is good for Neiman Marcus may not be good for K-Mart.

The cost of differentiation reflects the *cost drivers* of the value activities on which uniqueness is based.[18] Differentiation can also result from the coordination of linked value activities that may not add much cost, but nevertheless provide a cost savings and a competitive edge when integrated.

The measurement and reporting of quality costs to facilitate these strategic demands needs to be provided to users of the information in a form that aids in decision making. Thus, the measurement and reporting of costs of quality should meet the three-part need to: (1) report quality costs, (2) identify activities where involvement is suggested, and (3) indicate interlinking activities.

Activities and functions are not independent. They form a system of interdependencies that are connected by linkages and relationships. For example, purchasing from a low-quality supplier may lead to redesign, rework, scrap, increased field service, and direct labor variance. These linkages are difficult to recognize and are often overlooked. Nor is the conventional accounting system equipped to separate the cost of quality in these linked activities. Virtually all accounting classifications group activities along functional lines and force the reporting of quality costs into several general expense categories such as salaries, depreciation, training, etc. Analyzing the accounts can produce limited estimates of quality costs, but unless the costs are designed into the system, they will be elusive for decisions and action planning.

As one of the steps in the design of a planning and control system, it is useful to identify those activities and linkages between activities where costs occur. Some form of linear or matrix organizational chart or table is useful for this purpose. Departments or activities are listed across the top and costs of quality down the left-hand side. A number (e.g., 1 for primary responsibility or 2 for coordinating responsibility) can be entered at the intersection of the cost of quality category and the activity or function involved. The chart will show overlap among activities and will therefore indicate the need for cooperation, inter-functional teams, and the like. A similar chart can be devised to present cost of quality by activity. Thus, quality costs can be presented based on both cost and activity responsibility, and this form of presentation is more likely to get the attention of top management.

A similar chart can be constructed for reporting the dollar costs of quality. The same format could be used for both budgeting and reporting. Costs can be tabulated by organization unit, by time, by cost of quality categories, or by product. Quality costs can also be normalized for volume by using one or more of the following measures: per direct labor hour, per direct labor cost, per dollar of standard manufacturing cost, per dollar of sales, or per equivalent unit of product.[19]

The most elusive category for reporting is the cost of lost opportunities, which is an external failure cost. These represent the impact of profit from lost revenues resulting from purchase of competitive products and services or from order cancellations due to customer requirements not being met. An additional problem is assigning these *estimated* costs to a quality project or action plan that may prevent recurrence. It is also elusive and difficult to compile the relationships among two or more costs that affect quality costs, i.e., prevention plus appraisal.[20]

The constant theme throughout a cost of quality system is that *costs are not incurred or allocated, but rather are caused.* Cost information does not solve quality problems, nor does it suggest specific solutions. Problems are solved by tracing the *cause* of a quality deficiency.

THE USE OF QUALITY COST INFORMATION[21]

Quality cost information can be used in a number of ways:

- To identify profit opportunities (every dollar saved goes to the bottom line)
- To make capital budgeting and other investment decisions (quality, as opposed to payback, is the driver of decisions to purchase new equipment or dispose of unneeded ones; equipment for rework is not needed if the rework is eliminated or reduced)
- To improve purchasing and supplier-related costs
- To identify waste in overhead caused by activities not required by the customer
- To identify redundant systems
- To determine whether quality costs are properly distributed
- To establish goals for budgets and profit planning
- To identify quality problems
- As a management tool for comparative measures of input-output relationships (e.g., the cost of a reliability effort versus warranty costs)
- As a tool of Pareto analysis (Chapter 6) to distinguish between the "vital few" and the "trivial many"
- As a strategic management tool to allocate resources for strategy formulation and implementation
- As an objective performance appraisal measure

General Electric's cost of quality system is increasingly emphasizing non-product features such as inquiry responsiveness, delivery times, and billing accuracy. The emphasis is on root cause analysis and process improvement: simplifying procedures and reducing cycle time and driving down quality costs while improving customer satisfaction. Internal and external systems measure performance versus customer expectations; these systems also track opportunities that have been lost by non-conformance to customer expectations.[22]

ACCOUNTING SYSTEMS AND QUALITY MANAGEMENT[23]

The shortcomings of accounting information systems were outlined in a previous chapter, and opinions of experts who indicate that accounting information provides little help for reducing costs and improving quality and productivity were reported. The tendency is to *allocate* rather than manage costs. Moreover, the allocation is normally a function of direct labor, an item that has shrunk to 15 percent or less of manufacturing costs. Overhead, at about 55 percent, is spread across all products using the same formula. Accounting also cannot identify or account for the many non-dollar hidden costs of quality and productivity.

Critics claim that management accounting systems should be designed to support the operations and strategy of the company, two dimensions in which quality plays a dominant role. This is increasingly evident in the "new" manufacturing environment, sometimes known as advanced manufacturing technology (AMT), which is characterized by a number of emerging trends. These trends and their implications for quality management were summarized in Chapter 6. Some of the decision-making needs and how traditional accounting practices may fall short in meeting them are listed here:

Decision needs	Traditional accounting
Activity management	Financial accounting
Investment management	Payback or ROI
Non-dollar measures	Dollar accounting
Process control	Cost allocation
Just-in-time	Inventory turn
Feedforward control	Historical control

ACTIVITY-BASED COSTING

The majority of companies that attempt to measure quality costs compile the information and statistics outside of the accounting system. These data are aggregated and do not reflect the true cost of quality or the activity in the process that is causing it. It is worth repeating that costs are not incurred or allocated, *they are caused.* The mere collection of data is of little use unless the data can help identify the drivers of quality costs so that problem identification leads to problem solution.

Activity-based costing (ABC), called "A Bean-Counter's Best Friend" by *Business Week,*[24] can be the system that promises to fill this gap.[25] ABC is a collection of financial and operation performance information that traces the significant activities of a firm to process, product, and quality costs. It is well suited to TQM because it encourages management to analyze activities and determine their value to the customer.

Imagine the case of a firm with excessive warranty costs. The following questions might arise: (1) What is the cost of the returns? (2) What is the cause of the returns and can the cause be traced to a specific activity? Is it the supplier, design, or one of the many activities in production? (3) How can the process(es) be improved to reduce the cost of returns? (4) What is the trade-off between cost of process revision and reduction of warranty costs? (5) What are the strategic implications? The concepts of ABC may lead to some answers.

The concepts of process control and activity analysis were described in Chapter 6 (Management of Process Quality) and Chapter 10 (Productivity and Quality). ABC brings these interlinking concepts together through cross-functional analysis:

- **Process control** documents the process flow, identifies requirements of internal and external customers, defines outputs of each process step, and determines process input requirements.
- **Activity analysis** defines each activity within each process and identifies activities as value added or non-value added based on customer requirements.

Activity analysis applies to internal as well as external customers. When Rear Admiral John Kirkpatrick assumed command of the six U.S. Naval Aviation Depots, he inaugurated the use of TQM. One element of the system was that wherever possible, the internal customer was allowed to demand only those internal products or services desired.[26] Could this be a logical extension of customer satisfaction? If it can be applied to external customers, why not internal customers as well?

The third step is to develop cause-and-effect relationships by identifying *drivers* of cost or quality. In the case of cost, the drivers are the conditions that create or "drive" the need for an activity and hence the resources consumed. If the cost driver relates to a non-value activity, it can be eliminated or reduced. It is estimated that 50 percent or more of the activities in most businesses are cost added rather than value added.[27]

ABC recognizes that activities, not products, consume resources, and process value analysis is needed to assign costs to the activities that use them. The system recognizes that costs are driven by factors other than volume or direct labor. In the case of product costing, the costs are assigned based on their consumption of activities such as order preparation, storage time, wait time, internal product movement, field maintenance, and design. The focus on the process, not the product, suggests a transition to breaking down the floor into smaller cost centers and identifying the cost drivers of each.

Cost drivers are agents that cause activity to happen. Consider an engineering change order (ECO) which causes many activities to occur, such as documentation, production schedule changes, purchase of a new machine, or change in a process. If the ECO is issued to correct excessive field maintenance costs, manufacturing will absorb additional charges, marketing's distribution costs will increase, and customer satisfaction may erode because of delays and field repairs. By using the ABC concept, the true cost of the affected product can be determined as well as its cross-functional impact on budgets and performance.

This ECO example illustrates the impact of engineering and design on product life cycle costs. Roughly 80 to 85 percent of a product's lifetime costs, including maintenance and repair expenses, are locked in at this stage. ABC might provide guidelines to help engineers design a product that meets customer expectations and can be produced and supported at a competitive cost.

The Multi-Product Problem

■ At Rockwell International Corporation, a capital budgeting request for an $80,000 laser was denied because at $4,000 per year in labor savings the payback would take 20 years. Further analysis showed that the process would be reduced from 2 weeks to 10 minutes, moving shipments out faster and saving $200,000 a year in inventory holding costs.[28]

■ Tektronix, Inc. adopted ABC in a printed circuit board plant and found that one high-volume product drew on so many resources that it generated a negative margin of 46 percent and sapped profits from other products. These examples illustrate how "across the board" accounting *allocation* of costs, rather than *management* of costs, distorts the information required for good decision making.

There is great potential for inaccurate costing and control of multi-product lines in a firm with a single overhead center, and inaccuracies in costing increase dramatically when allocation is achieved by direct labor, machine time, processing time, or some other "assignment" method. A major soft drink producer found that the costs of its array of brands varied as much as 400 percent from what traditional cost accounting methods reported.

In summary, ABC decomposes activities, identifies the drivers of the activities, and provides measures so that costs can be traced to the activities that cause the cost.

Strategic Planning and Activity-Based Costing

■ At a meeting of IBM's board of directors in November 1991, various restructuring proposals were considered. One option was to unburden the lines of business from general overhead expenses. For example, the company may remove from its personal computer business the burden of helping pay for research on mainframe computers. (This action was subsequently taken in 1992.)

There is a cost dimension to most strategic decisions. Product lines, channels, locations, brands, segmentation, and differentiation need to be identified, and each decision establishes a linkage between demands and spending on resources. If costs are forecast on the arbitrary basis of some unit directly related to production, the real cost of a product or capital project may be made arbitrarily.[29] ABC can help reveal data for strategic decisions about which product lines to develop or abandon and which prices to increase or decrease. Tracing overhead to activities and then to products may also identify costs that do not contribute to quality and hence to differentiation.

ABC has leapfrogged traditional cost accounting, but it is a new and complicated system. For these reasons, the great majority of companies have not achieved a significant level of sophistication in its use. The basic concept of ABC is that costs of products and quality can be traced to the drivers of activities that consume the resources which *cause* these costs. Research reveals that there is widespread failure to compile the many prevention, appraisal, internal failure, and external failure costs that are "hidden" until identified by a cost of quality management system. If the costs are not identified, there is little chance of tracing them to the process or activity that is causing them. Only the "visible" rework, scrap, and repair/service costs are compiled by more than half of the respondents.

Summary

Is a cost of quality program essential to a quality improvement effort? The answer may be no, but a firm cannot spend unlimited resources without regard for both strategic issues and the cost/benefit equation. Moreover, a cost of quality effort is but one of a system of interlinking efforts that comprise a management philosophy of TQM.

QUESTIONS FOR DISCUSSION

11-1   Select a firm (restaurant, hotel, airline, manufacturer) and list several costs related to quality failure. Estimate these costs.

11-2   What is the estimated cost of poor quality in U.S. industry?

11-3   What is the justification for Philip Crosby's claim that "Quality Is Free"?

11-4   Illustrate each of the four types of costs of quality.

11-5   Why should prevention costs take precedence over the other three classifications?

11-6   What are the benefits of a cost of quality measuring system?

ENDNOTES

1. Doug Anderson, "How to Use Cost of Quality Data," in *Global Perspectives on Total Quality,* New York: The Conference Board, 1991, p. 37.
2. John F. Towey, "Information Please: What Are Quality Costs?" *Management Accounting,* March 1988, p. 40. Apparently this is a quasi-official definition adopted by the National Association of Accountants (NAA).
3. Roger G. Schroeder, *Operations Management,* New York: McGraw-Hill, 1989, p. 586.
4. J. M. Asher, "Cost of Quality in Service Industries," *International Journal of Quality & Reliability Management (UK),* Vol. 5 Issue 5, 1988, pp. 38–46.
5. William Band, "Marketers Need to Understand the High Cost of Poor Quality," *Sales & Marketing Management in Canada,* Nov. 1989, pp. 56–59.
6. Ned Hamson, "TQM Can Save Nearly $300 Billion for Nation," *Journal for Quality and Participation,* Dec. 1990, pp. 54–56. This potential is reflected in the quality improvement potential (QIP) index.
7. Armand V. Feigenbaum, "The Criticality of Quality and the Need to Measure It," *Financier,* Oct. 1990, pp. 33–36. This estimate reflects a national (QIP) index for the gross national product. Feigenbaum is president and chief executive officer of General Systems Company, Inc., which installs company-wide quality systems in manufacturing and service organizations.
8. Financial managers estimate the cost at 25 to 30 percent of sales. See Garrett DeYoung, "Does Quality Pay?" *CFO: The Magazine for Chief Financial Officers,* Sep. 1990, pp. 24–34. See also Lester Ravitz, "The Cost of Quality: A Different Approach to Noninterest Expenses," *Financial Manager's Statement,* March/April 1991, pp. 8–13. A 1990 study of quality in North American banks found that non-quality cost related to unnecessary rework and related factors represented 20 to 25 percent of a bank's operating budget. In Britain, the United Kingdom Institute of Management Services estimates that the cost of

quality non-conformance amounts to 25 to 30 percent of sales. See John Heap and Lord Chilver, "Total Quality Management," *Management Services (UK),* June 1990, pp. 6–10.

9.   J. M. Juran, Ed., *Quality Control Handbook,* New York: McGraw-Hill, 1951.
10. Armand V. Feigenbaum, *Total Quality Control,* New York: McGraw-Hill, 1961.
11. Philip Crosby, *Quality Is Free,* New York: McGraw-Hill, 1979.
12. An excellent discussion of these categories is contained in David A. Garvin, *Managing Quality,* New York: The Free Press, 1988, pp. 78–80.
13. Thomas N. Tyson, "Quality & Profitability: Have Controllers Made the Connection?" *Management Accounting,* Nov. 1987, pp. 38–42.
14. Taken from a promotional brochure by Philip Crosby Associates, Inc. of Winter Park, Florida.
15. The British Science and Engineering Research Council funded a study on quality-related costs as part of a two-year study. A literature review showed the domination of the prevention-appraisal-failure classification, a preoccupation with in-house costs, and little regard for supplier and customer-related costs. See J. J. Plunkett and B. G. Dale, "A Review of the Literature on Quality-Related Costs," *International Journal of Quality & Reliability Management (UK),* Vol. 4 Issue 1, 1987, pp. 40–52. This classification can also apply to non-manufacturing areas. Xerox is one firm that has implemented a well-defined quality program aimed at achieving quality in non-manufacturing services. A model was developed to illustrate the costs of quality based on the prevention-appraisal-failure classification. See Michael Desjardins, "Managing for Quality," *Business Quarterly (Canada),* Autumn 1989, pp. 103–107.
16. As quoted in David A. Garvin, *Managing Quality,* New York: The Free Press, 1988, p. 79.
17. Armand V. Feigenbaum, "Linking Quality Processes to International Leadership," in *Making Total Quality Happen,* New York: The Conference Board, 1990, p. 6.
18. Michael E. Porter, *Competitive Advantage,* New York: The Free Press, 1985, pp. 127–130. Although Porter does not address the specifics of cost of quality, his discussion of differentiation costs provides an excellent dimension to the topic.
19. For more detailed information on methods of compiling quality cost information, see Wayne J. Morse, Harold P. Roth, and Kay M. Poston, *Measuring, Planning, and Controlling Quality Costs,* Montvale, N.J.: National Association of Accountants, 1987. This NAA research study provides a number of actual reporting formats used by responding companies in the survey. For the collection and reporting formats used by ITT and Xerox, see Francis J. Walsh, Jr., *Current Practices in Measuring Quality,* New York: The Conference Board, 1989 (Conference Board Research Bulletin).
20. James T. Godfrey and William R. Pasewark, "Controlling Quality Costs," *Management Accounting,* March 1988, pp. 48–51.
21. For sources of information regarding the use of cost of quality information, see the following: John F. Towey, "Why Quality Costs Are Important," *Management Accounting,* March 1988, p. 40. See also James M. Reeve, "TQM and Cost Management: New Definitions for Cost Accounting," *Survey of Business,* Summer 1989, pp. 26–30; J. J. Plunkett and B. G. Dale, "A Review of the Literature on Quality-Related Costs," *International Journal of Quality & Reliability Management (UK),* Vol. 4 Issue 1, 1987, pp. 40–52; John J. Heldt, "Quality Pays," *Quality,* Nov. 1988, pp. 26–28.
22. Elyse Allan, "Measuring Quality Costs: A Shifting Perspective," in *Global Perspectives*

on Total Quality, New York: The Conference Board, 1991, p. 35 (Conference Board Report Number 958).

23. H. Thomas Johnson and Robert Kaplan, *Relevance Lost: The Rise and Fall of Management Accounting,* Boston: Harvard Business School Press, 1991. Peat Marwick, one of the Big Six accounting firms, scored a major coup by signing Kaplan to an exclusive contract in the field of activity-based cost accounting. See "A Bean-Counter's Best Friend," *Business Week/Quality 1991* (special bonus issue dated October 25, 1991 entitled "The Quality Imperative: What It Takes to Win in the Global Economy").

24. "A Bean-Counter's Best Friend," *Business Week,* October 25, 1991, pp. 42–43 (special bonus issue entitled "The Quality Imperative: What It Takes to Win in the Global Economy").

25. Because ABC is relatively new, there is no widespread treatment of it in the literature. Perhaps the best source of information, at least from the accountant's point of view, is *Management Accounting.* See, for example, Thomas E. Steimer, "Activity-Based Accounting for Total Quality, *Management Accounting,* Oct. 1990, pp. 39–42. See also Michael R. Ostrenga, "Activities: The Focal Point of Total Cost Management," *Management Accounting,* Feb. 1990, pp. 42–49 and Norm Raffish, "How Much Does that Product Really Cost?" *Management Accounting,* March 1991, pp. 36–39. For a managerial perspective, it is suggested that a literature search be conducted for recent writings of Robert Kaplan.

26. Michael D. Woods, "How We Changed Our Accounting," *Management Accounting,* Feb. 1989, pp. 42–45.

27. Michael J. Stickler, "Going for the Globe. Part II: Eliminating Waste," *Production & Inventory Management Review and APICS News,* Nov. 1989, pp. 32–34.

28. "The Productivity Paradox," *Business Week,* June 6, 1988, p. 104.

29. Bernard C. Reimann, "Robert S. Kaplan: The ABCs of Accounting for Value Creation," *Planning Review,* July/Aug. 1990, pp. 33–34. The author reports Kaplan's contention that the "essence of strategy" is to regard all overhead expenses as variable and driven by something other than the number of units. Also, financial reporting is fine for reporting bottom line financial performance but inadequate for strategic decisions.

CASE

The following case study demonstrates how the costs of quality can be traced and reported through an activity-based approach. The purposes of the study were to make management aware of the magnitude of these costs and to provide a baseline from which continuous improvement could be measured.

COST-OF-QUALITY REPORTING: HOW WE SEE IT

Richard K. Youde

Since its founding in 1979, Sola Optical, a manufacturer of ophthalmic spectacle lenses in Petaluma, Calif., has enjoyed rapid and continued growth. While management always had focused on maintaining high levels of product quality and customer service, it had no real understanding of the costs of achieving these goals nor of the opportunities for improvement. Instead, management relied on and gave credibility to traditional financial reporting and cost accounting systems because sales and profits continued to grow.

Three years ago, Sola Optical was given responsibility for the spectacle lens division of a newly acquired business. The integration of additional product lines and three geographically diverse manufacturing plants, along with the doubling of sales volume and the number of employees, added new complexity to the running of the business. Management's attention was focused on the integration process and the bottom line pressures brought with it.

Through this period, management and employees began to think about the application of world-class manufacturing (WCM) concepts such as total quality management (TQM), just-in-time (JIT) manufacturing, quality function deployment, and activity-based costing. While the company had little direct experience

Reprinted with permission from *Management Accounting,* January 1992, pp. 34–38. Copyright 1992 by Institute of Management Accountants, Montvale, N.J.

with the WCM concepts, many employees had been exposed to them through trade journals and seminars.

The company had no previous exposure to cost of (poor) quality reporting, but through the process of implementing WCM it developed a powerful new approach to cost-of-quality reporting that had a positive impact.

TQM/JIT Implementation

Management's interest in world-class manufacturing concepts led to the hiring of a consultant to help establish an approach for its implementation. The work included development of a TQM/JIT execution plan and the calculation of cost of quality (COQ) for the divisional headquarters site, which included the division's largest factory and all marketing, administrative, and engineering support. Sola Optical's financial results, shown in Figure 1, are typical of U.S. manufacturing companies before implementing TQM, showing 20% of sales dollars being consumed by poor quality.

Management accepted the consultant's proposal for implementing Total Quality Management and Just-in-Time techniques including:

- Establishment of a TQM steering committee to oversee the implementation,
- Creation of a dedicated cross-functional TQM resource staff as a new organizational entity,
- Formation of four pilot TQM teams, and
- Contracting for the consultant's services to get the project started.

The total quality management effort initially was focused on operational effectiveness. The steering committee included the divisional president, his

Cost of Quality 20%

Profits 20%

Expenses 60%

Figure 1   Distribution of Revenue

reporting staff, senior manufacturing managers, and TQM resource staff members who were drawn from manufacturing, marketing, quality control, research and development, and finance. The resource staff was given a charter to facilitate the implementation of TQM/JIT within Sola.

Four pilot projects with the greatest opportunity for savings were selected from the manufacturing area, and each one involved improving process yields and product quality. In a dual-track implementation role, the consulting personnel concurrently facilitated quality improvement teams, beginning with the four pilot teams, and provided training to Sola employees in TQM/JIT techniques. Special emphasis was placed on coaching the TQM resource staff who quickly assumed the responsibility of quality improvement teams.

To begin the process of cultural change, management decided to provide TQM and JIT overview training to a large number of employees. Overview/introduction classes totalling 20 hours were given to nearly every employee over a period of six months.

The pilot teams and TQM resource staff were successful, and more teams were formed in manufacturing, distribution, and administrative areas. The new teams were assisted by the consultant and TQM resource staff associates. Members often worked in areas of interest to the individual team members, however, and were not focused in the areas known to offer the most opportunity for savings. In retrospect, it was clear that many teams needed better direction, which could have been provided by better cost-of-quality information.

Classic Cost of Quality

The initial COQ study prepared by the consultants used the classic approach and identified, through interviews with operating and financial managers and employees, costs of (poor) quality and classified them into four categories: prevention, appraisal, internal failure, and external failure.* The purpose of the COQ report was to make management aware of the magnitude of the cost and to provide a baseline against which the impact of future continuous improvement activities could be gauged.

The report demonstrated that relatively few dollars were spent on defect prevention, that appraisal costs were high (because our quality control department used final inspection to assure only good products were transferred to inventory), and that internal failure costs were extremely high. External failure costs were shown to be quite low, attributed to the high level of quality inspections performed and the corresponding high appraisal costs.

---

* Wayne Morse, Harold Roth, and Kay Poston, *Measuring, Planning, and Controlling Quality Costs,* Institute of Management Accountants, Montvale, N.J., 1987.

TQM teaches that dollars spent in preventive activities such as designing product for manufacturability, training, and development of procedures will be recovered manyfold through reduced appraisal and failure costs. By measuring over time the relative costs of prevention, appraisal, internal and external failure, management can observe whether continuous improvement activities are paying off.

Cost-of-Quality Study

The COQ study was successful in alerting management to the magnitude of the costs and was a reasonable baseline against which to measure future performance for the site as a whole. It did not suggest specific actions that individual managers and employees could take to make improvements. Therefore, quality improvement teams did not have the information necessary to focus on the most important problems.

The lack of focus by some quality improvement teams contributed to loss of interest in the process by some employees and frustration of both management and quality improvement team members at the slow progress toward achieving real quality improvements.

Activity-Based Approach

A method had to be devised to ensure that operating managers and quality improvement teams were focusing their activities appropriately in order to assure the success of the TQM/JIT implementation effort. Gaining management's attention and commitment is a basic requirement of world-class manufacturing concepts. Management initially supported the implementation of TQM/JIT and accepted the original cost-of-quality figures. A way was needed, however, to get its buy-in and support of specific quality improvement activities.

One of the limitations of traditional COQ reporting is its failure to associate costs with activities. Activity-based costing has shown that costs cannot be controlled. Rather, one must control activities that in turn cause costs. Relating quality costs to activities greatly enhances the usefulness of the cost-of-quality report.

The solution, in terms of cost-of-quality reporting, lies in applying techniques from world-class manufacturing, such as activity-based costing, JIT and TQM, to the development of quality costs. TQM provides simple statistical tools, such as run sheets and Pareto charts, identifying the most important problems. An activity-based cost-of-quality report works like a Pareto analysis, showing the relative costs of the most important quality-related problems along with the respective cost drivers. JIT is a philosophy promoting the elimination of waste.

Quality failures and all the activities surrounding them fall within the definition of waste.

The Ripple Effect and Ripple Costs

At Sola Optical, we focus on "failures" in COQ reporting because we want to improve the activities that lead to failures, the major contributor to cost of quality. Besides the direct cost of failures, such as the cost of rejected product, we wanted to show the complexity the failure itself added to our processes. Thus, we coined the term "ripple effect," defined as the activities resulting from a real or potential failure. For example, the resources consumed reworking a defective product constitute the ripple effect, as do the activities associated with inspecting a product even when no defect actually exists. We also include in the cost of quality the "ripple cost" (costs of the ripple effect). Results of interviews with managers, supervisors, leads, and workers identified ripple effects of returned goods (see Figure 2).

An analysis of the chart shows that credit memos issued for customer returns result in lost gross profit on the sale. Shown next are the steps in returned goods processing (RGA processing), beginning with the receiving department, followed by the returned goods department and warehouse, and ending with the activities associated with issuing a credit memo. When large returns occur, the very complex production and inventory planning cycle is disrupted because of unplanned inventory. Finally, the chart reminds readers that there is a cost to the customer as well.

Inclusion of the ripple effect charts in the COQ report provides readers with a better understanding of their operations. The use of these charts is a powerful tool, drawing attention to opportunities for improvement. Incorporating the ripple costs, along with the direct cost of failures, in the COQ provides the same effect.

Developing an Activity-Based COQ Report

We identified eight steps (see Table 1) in developing an activity-based COQ report.

1. **Identify cost and service problem areas:** The first step in developing an activity-based COQ report is to identify the most important cost- or service-related problems. At Sola Optical, the division president and representatives from marketing, manufacturing, materials, accounting, management information systems, and customer service were asked to identify the five most important problems/opportunities in terms of costs or customer satisfaction. Then a review of the initial COQ report, prepared by

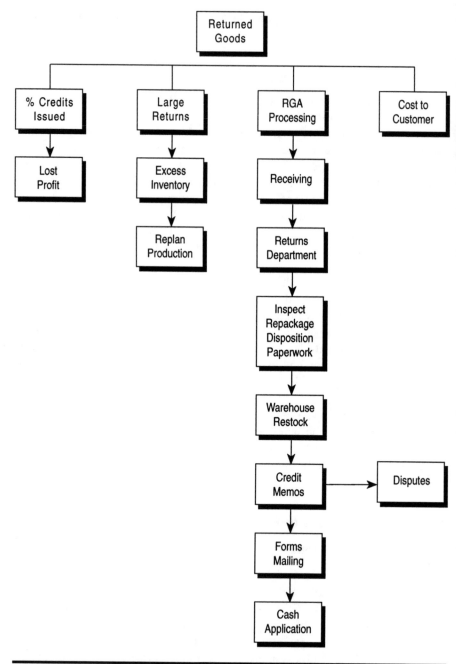

Figure 2   Ripple Effect of Returned Goods

Table 1   Steps in Developing an Activity-Based Cost of Quality Report

■ Identify cost and service problem areas.

■ Summarize problems to a manageable list.

■ Identify ripple effects.

■ Calculate ripple costs.

■ Condense the list again.

■ Summarize information for presentation.

■ Review with managers and steering committee.

■ Publish and present to employees.

the consultants, was conducted to assure no important costs included in it were omitted from the list.

The list was edited to eliminate any ideas that were not related to COQ. For example, one interviewee had identified the need for employee development. But this was considered inappropriate for this purpose.

2. **Condense problems to manageable list:**   The list was summarized and ranked according to the number of responses for each idea. Then a condensed list of ideas was developed based on the number of responses and knowledge of costs and cost of quality. The ideas that remained on the list after this step were those for which data could be collected and for which the cost of quality would be high enough to warrant further consideration.

Some ideas were judged too impractical to include. For example, the cost associated with inaccurate finished goods' inventory records was dropped because of the difficulty in quantifying the costs.

Next, ripple charts were prepared and reviewed with the original interviewees to ensure their accuracy. Changes were incorporated into a final copy of the ripple chart.

3. **Calculate ripple costs:**   Several principles guided the development of costs, especially ripple costs. First, it is important to recognize that the intent of COQ reporting is to provide reasonably accurate information for use in allocating resources, not to develop a complex cost accounting system. The purpose of measurement is to tell the organization whether it is heading in the right direction.

Second, the information needs to be absolutely credible. At Sola, we wanted to avoid challenges to the whole process based on disagreements over minor elements of cost. The approach taken was to include only costs that were easily supportable. Not all ripple activities shown on the ripple charts are included in the cost. The reported cost of quality, therefore, is the minimum, and is in fact understated. But employees can recognize that the ripple chart includes other activities that contribute to cost and system complexity.

Finally, we wanted to make monthly reporting very simple. Costs that are readily available, such as the direct cost of rejected product, would be included as calculated. Costs that are not readily available, particularly those combining cross-functional activities, would be estimated on a per occurrence basis. When monthly COQ reports are prepared only the actual number of occurrences need to be collected. Calculations then are based on the per occurrence cost.

The development of yield-loss costs serves as a good example of this process. Yield loss represents the costs associated with product rejected. The direct cost of product rejected was taken from the cost accounting system and broken down by the major production processes. The cost of one major ripple effect, the quality control department (i.e., inspection), also was available from the accounting system.

The remaining ripple costs, which included disposing of product reject, record keeping, and production costs caused by a higher level of starts, were estimated on a per reject basis. The estimated costs of these activities over a six-month period were divided by the number of reject lenses produced for the same period. Ripple costs for the six areas were calculated by the same methodology.

4. **Condense the list again:**   It may be necessary to condense the list again if the total costs of any of the potential areas are not significant enough to be included in the report. At Sola Optical, it was our original intent to identify 10 of the most significant COQ areas (more would tend to defocus management attention). At this point, our list was condensed to six: yield loss (defective product), mold (tooling) loss, employee turnover, injuries, finished goods stockouts, and customer returns. Two other cost areas, excess finished goods' inventory and machine downtime, looked like strong candidates for inclusion but required more research.

5. **Summarize information for presentation:**   The goal of COQ reporting is to present concise, usable information. Presenting too much detail is a sure way to lose the interest of the audience. It is the responsibility of quality improvement teams to develop and present their own detailed information.

The sequence of presentation should be adapted to the business culture. At Sola Optical, we chose to present overall costs first—shown in total, then annualized as percent of sales and as a cost per employee—followed by the individual COQ areas. Figure 3 shows an example of the total costs chart.

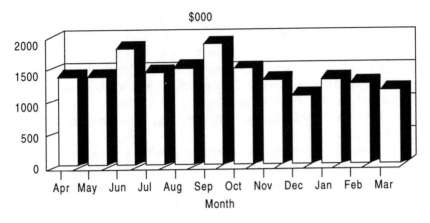

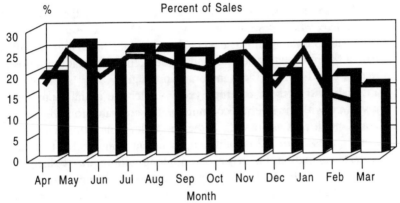

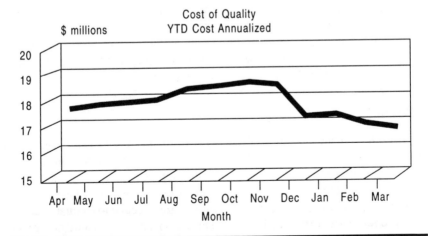

Figure 3   Total Cost of Quality

Individual COQ area costs then are shown together on similarly scaled graphs so that relative value of the costs is obvious. Then charts for each of the COQ areas along with their respective ripple charts are presented. For each area, the total cost per month, annualized cost, percent of the appropriate overall level of activity such as sales or production value, and the activity cost driver are shown.

For each of the COQ areas, costs are broken into direct and ripple costs on the chart.

6. **Review with managers and steering committee:**   The first presentation was reviewed with key managers whose acceptance was critical to the success of the whole reporting process. If at this late date any information was to be challenged, it was better to resolve the problem individually than have the validity of the data undercut in a formal presentation.

    The next step was to present the COQ report to the TQM steering committee, whose key members already had been exposed to the information. This presentation was designed to generate discussion regarding the use of the information so that management, through quality improvement teams, could address these important problems.

7. **Publish and present to employees:**   After the initial report has been reviewed with the steering committee, it is advisable to review it with as many employees as possible so they understand its purpose and contents. Formal presentations to quality improvement teams and to the individual departments within the organization, along with regularly distributed reports, were methods used to improve employee understanding.

8. **Continuously improve the report:**   The COQ report is an ever-changing and improving report based on the needs of the company. As quality improvement teams achieve cost reductions, the specific cost areas being measured will change. There is a continuing need to ensure resources are being applied to the most important problems. The entire process described here should be completed each year to ensure the best information is being provided.

A Powerful Tool

At Sola Optical, the activity-based cost-of-quality report is a powerful tool for managing quality improvement activities. Quality improvement teams are focused in the most important areas with the ripple effect concept being key to this method. Combining cross-functional costs caused by a quality failure into a single metric provides management the information needed to evaluate each type of failure relative to others and focus resources on the most important problems. The activity-based cost-of-quality approach can be applied easily in any business environment.

Questions for Discussion

1   The article states that by relating quality costs to activities, the usefulness of the cost-of-quality report is improved. Explain why this is true and why it might improve the frustration resulting from the original cost-of-quality study.

2   Figure 2 demonstrates the "ripple effect" of returned goods. Explain why returned goods would result in costs related to disputes, excess inventory, production planning, and cash application. What additional costs not shown (e.g., redesign) might be involved.

3   Identify some cost-of-quality data that may be available from accounting records and some that are not. What is the danger of using accounting data? What role should the accounting department play in reducing cost-of-quality?

4   Choose a company or organization with which you are familiar. Refer to Figure 11-1 in the text and identify those costs that result from defects and returns. What is your estimate of the cost as a percentage of sales?

12

ISO 9000: UNIVERSAL STANDARDS OF QUALITY

Companies can comply with Europe's standards—or stay home

Business Week

"Simply put, ISO 9000 has come to be the price of admission for doing business in Europe," says Robert Caine, president of the American Society for Quality Control (ASQC). "Ask any business person who has given up trying to gain entry into the European market what stopped him, and he's likely to answer in code: ISO 9000," concludes Kymberly Hockman of Du Pont's Quality Management and Technology Center. These are among the many experts who are urging U.S. firms to take the ISO Series standards seriously.

Even if a firm does not do business in Europe or does not plan to do so, it should not ignore this accelerating movement to international standards. As will be discussed, the movement is expanding into other areas of the world and into many areas of the U.S. public and private sectors as well.

ISO 9000 is a set of five worldwide standards that establish requirements for the management of quality. Unlike *product* standards, these standards are for *quality management systems*. They are being used by the twelve-nation European Economic Community to provide a universal framework for quality assurance—primarily through a system of internal and external audits. The purpose is to ensure that a certified company has a quality system in place that will enable it to meet its published quality standards. The ISO standards are generic in that they apply to all functions and all industries, from banking to chemical manufacturing. They have been described as the "one size fits all" standards.

ISO AROUND THE WORLD

The European Community (EC) consists of twelve member nations: Belgium, Denmark, France, Germany, Greece, Ireland, Italy, Luxembourg, the Netherlands, Portugal, Spain, and the United Kingdom. The goal of the EC is to create a single internal market, free of all barriers to trade. For products and services to be traded freely, there must be assurance that those product meet certain standards, whether they are produced in one of the EC nations or in a non-EC nation, such as the United States.[1] The EC is using the standards to provide a universal framework for quality assurance and to ensure the quality of goods and services across borders.

The International Organization for Standardization (ISO) is the specialized international agency for standardization and at present comprises the national standards bodies of 91 countries. The American National Standards Institute (ANSI) is the member body representing the United States. ISO is made up of approximately 180 technical committees. Each technical committee is responsible for one of many areas of specialization, ranging from asbestos to zinc. The purpose of ISO is to promote the development of standardization and related world activities in order to facilitate the international exchange of goods and services and to develop cooperation in intellectual, scientific, technological, and economic activities. The results of ISO technical work are published as international standards and the ISO 9000 Series is a result of this process.

In 1987 (the same year the ISO 9000 Series was published), the United States adopted the ISO 9000 Series verbatim as the ANSI/ASQC Q-90 Series. Thus, the use of either of these series is equivalent to the use of the other.[2] The ISO standards are being adopted by a varying number of companies in over 50 countries around the world that have endorsed them. Many people believe that within five years registration will be necessary to stay in business.[3]

By 1992 more than 20,000 facilities in Britain had adopted the standards and became certified.[4] Over 20,000 companies from other EC countries have registered, compared to about 620 in the U.S. The Japanese not only have adopted the standards, but also have mounted a major national effort to get their companies registered.[5]

The EC adopted ISO 9000 in 1989 to integrate the various technical norms and specifications of its member states. By 1991, ISO compliance became part of hundreds of product safety laws all over Europe, regulating everything from medical devices to telecommunications gear. Such products accounted for only about 15 percent of EC trade at that time, but the list of products is growing. Entire industries are encouraging the adoption of the standards.

One example of the impact is reflected in the requirements of Siemens, the huge German electronics firm. The company requires ISO compliance in 50 percent of its contracts and is pressing all other suppliers to conform. A major justification for this action is that it eliminates the need to test parts, which saves time and money and establishes common requirements for all markets.

Even for companies whose products are unregulated, ISO standards are becoming a de facto market requirement for doing business with other EC companies. If two suppliers are competing for a contract or an order, the one that has registered its quality systems under ISO 9000 has a clear edge.

The impact of these standards is reflected by the widespread distribution of the ISO 9000 Series, which has become the best-seller in the history of the ISO, under whose auspices they were developed. ISO 9000 even outsold the universal and long-standing international weights and measurement standards. However, it is worth repeating that ISO 9000 is not standards for products, but standards for operation of a *quality management system.*

ISO 9000 IN THE UNITED STATES

U.S. companies have been slow to adopt these international standards despite the fact that 30 percent of the country's exports go to Europe. Moreover, to the extent that the standards are adopted elsewhere in the world, additional exports will be affected as well. Additional markets both within and outside the United States may be closed to those firms that ignore the requirement or fail to be certified. Du Pont, now a leader in adopting the standards, only began its ISO drive in 1989 after losing a large European order for polyester film to an ISO-certified British firm.

Some people perceive ISO 9000 as a barrier to competition and even a plot to keep U.S. firms out of Europe. This view, of course, is not the case, but a barrier can exist unless the standards are clearly understood.

Additional evidence of growing acceptance lies in the fact that the standards are being integrated into the requirements for manufacturers that make products under contract for several U.S. government agencies, including NASA, the Department of Defense, the Federal Aviation Administration, and the Food and Drug Administration.[6] To date, ISO 9000 registration is required of suppliers to the governments of Canada, Australia, and the U.K.

Du Pont, Eastman Kodak, and other U.S. pioneers adopted ISO 9000 in the late 1980s to ensure that they were not locked out of European markets. They then found that the standards also helped to improve their quality. Now, Baldrige winners such as Motorola, Xerox, IBM, and others are making suppliers adopt ISO. As the movement catches on and as suppliers to suppliers are required to come on board, there may be a geometric leverage effect in the number of companies adopting the standards. This effect may give additional meaning to the often-repeated description of the market as *global* in dimension.

Despite the weight of the evidence that suggests the need to adopt ISO 9000, it appears that many U.S. firms have not done so, nor do they plan to do so. One survey of 254 mid-sized manufacturing firms conducted by the Chicago accounting firm of Grant Thornton found that only 8 percent planned to become certified by the end of 1992 and 48 percent of the senior executives never even heard of the ISO 9000 standards.[7]

The good news is that for those firms planning to become ISO 9000 certified, the process is not all that difficult, especially if the company already has a quality effort underway. Indeed, those companies using total quality management (TQM) are more than half way there. For Baldrige winners, certification would be a relatively simple process.

What is the impact of ISO 9000 for service industries and for those manufacturing firms whose products fall outside the *regulated* product areas? The answer is provided by ASQC:[8]

> Outside of regulated product areas, the importance of ISO 9000 registration as a competitive market tool varies from sector to sector. For instance, in some sectors, European companies may require suppliers to attest that they have an approved quality system in place as a condition for purchase. This could be specified in any business contract. ISO 9000 registration may also serve as a means of differentiating "classes" of suppliers, particularly in high-tech areas, where high product reliability is crucial. In other words, if two suppliers are competing for the same contract, the one with ISO 9000 registration may have a competitive edge with some buyers. Sector and product areas where purchasers are more likely to generate pressure for ISO 9000 registration include aerospace, autos, electronic components, measuring and testing instruments, and so on. ISO 9000 registration may also be a competitive factor in product areas where safety or liability are concerns.

Some American manufacturers have criticized the EC's adoption of ISO 9000, suggesting that the standards are inferior to those used in the United States. Moreover, it is suggested that requiring U.S. companies to conform to the standards will force them to incur larger production costs.[9]

The counter arguments are that the standards will eliminate the hodgepodge of standards that now exist around the world, and production costs will be more than offset by other savings and the increase in productivity and quality.

Criticisms and ignorance of ISO 9000 notwithstanding, there is evidence of a growing acceptance of the standards among U.S. firms. One source reports an increase in registration of 500 percent between 1992 and 1993. Of course, this increase is computed on a somewhat smaller 1992 base.[10] It is interesting to note that the Japanese experience is similar to that in the United States. Initial resistance was largely overcome by pressure to conform to the requirements of the international marketplace.[11]

Involvement of professional and trade associations appears to be growing as firms within a particular industry band together to research how best to meet ISO requirements. The chemical industry has been a leader in this movement. Professional engineers, public utilities, software vendors, and manufacturers of information technology are among the groups with organized efforts.[12] Some have formed a network of support groups.[13]

THE ISO 9000 ANSI/ASQC Q-90 SERIES STANDARDS[14]

Unlike the Baldrige, the ISO 9000 Series and its clone, the ANSI/ASQC Q-90 Series, are not awards programs. They do not require the use of any state-of-the-art system, nor do they require any prescribed method of process control. They are generic and apply to all industries.[15] As a set of requirements for quality systems, these series provide a common measuring stick for gauging quality systems. Leaving the determination of quality levels to the customer–supplier interaction, the series fill the need for a customer's guarantee that a supplier will, within defined limits, be able to deliver products and services as promised.[16] This flexibility and lack of constraining requirements mean that there is no one right way to do ISO 9000. Industries are free to find their own way and perceive this as an opportunity rather than an additional constraint. This freedom can serve as a source of both frustration as well as liberation.

The ISO 9000 Series is so named because it consists of *five* sets of standards, numbered sequentially from 9000. A brief summary of each standards is provided in Table 12-1.

ISO 9001 ensures conformance to requirements during design, development, production, installation, and service. The quality systems requirements[17] are

Management responsibility	Inspection, measuring, and test equipment
Quality system	Inspection and test status
Contract review	Control of non-conforming product
Design control	Corrective action

Table 12-1 Summary of ISO 9000 Standards

Standard	Content	Application
ISO 9000	Provides definitions and concepts. Explains how to select other standards for a given business	All industries including software development
ISO 9001	Quality assurance in design, development, production, installation, and servicing	Engineering and construction firms, manufacturers that design, develop, install, and service products
ISO 9002	Quality assurance in production and installation	Companies in the chemical process industries that are not involved in product design or after-sales service
ISO 9003	Quality assurance in test and inspection	Small shops, divisions within a firm, equipment distributors that inspect and test supplied products
ISO 9004	Quality management and quality system elements	All industries

Document control	Handling, storage, packaging, and delivery
Purchasing	Quality records
Purchaser-supplied product	Internal quality audits
Product identification traceability	Training
Process control	Servicing
Inspection and testing	Statistical techniques

Documentation

Many firms hesitate to comply with the standards due to the onerous task of *documentation.* The advice given to some firms is to "document what you do and do what you document." Nevertheless, documentation actions to comply with the standards are necessary. There are three major tasks:

1. Write the quality manual according to ISO guidelines
2. Document all relevant procedures
3. Write all relevant work instructions

An excerpt from a standard on documentation is as follows.

4.5 Document Control

4.5.1 Document Approval and Issue

The supplier shall establish and maintain procedures to control all documents and data that relate to the requirements of this Standard. These documents shall be reviewed and approved for adequacy by authorized personnel prior to issue. This control shall ensure that: a) the pertinent issues of appropriate documents are available at all locations where operations essential to the effective functioning of the quality system are performed; b) obsolete documents are promptly removed from all points of issue or use.

4.5.2 Document Changes/Modifications

Changes to documents shall be reviewed and approved by the same functions/organizations that performed the original review and approval unless specifically designated otherwise. The designated organizations shall have access to pertinent background information upon which to base their review and approval.

Where practicable, the nature of the change shall be identified in the document or the appropriate attachments.

A master list of equivalent document control procedures shall be established to identify the current revision of documents in order to preclude the use of non-applicable documents.

Documents shall be re-issued after a practical number of changes have been made.

Management Responsibility

The commitment and involvement of top management are requirements for the success of any significant cultural or operational change. So it is with both the Baldrige and ISO 9000. The concern of ISO with management responsibility is reflected in the following series excerpts:[18]

Quality policy. The supplier's management shall define and document its policy and objectives for, and commitment to, quality. The supplier shall ensure that this policy is understood, implemented, and maintained at all levels in the organization.

Management review. The quality system adopted to satisfy the requirement of the standard shall be reviewed at appropriate intervals by the supplier's management to ensure its continuing suitability and effectiveness. Records of such reviews shall be maintained.

Internal quality audits.   The supplier shall carry out a comprehensive system of planned and documented internal quality audits to verify whether quality activities comply with planned arrangements and to determine the effectiveness of the quality system. Audits shall be scheduled on the basis of the status and importance of the activity. The audits and follow up actions shall be carried out in accordance with documented procedures.

The results of the audits shall be documented and brought to the attention of the personnel having responsibility in the area audited. The management personnel responsible for the area shall take timely corrective action on the deficiencies found by the audit.

Corrective action.   The supplier shall establish, document and maintain procedures for:

- Investigating the cause of nonconforming product and the corrective action needed to prevent recurrence

- Analyzing all processes, work operations, concessions, quality records, service reports, and customer complaints to detect and eliminate potential causes of nonconforming product

- Initiating preventive actions to deal with problems to a level corresponding to the risks encountered

- Applying controls to ensure that corrective actions are taken and that they are effective

- Implementing and recording changes in procedures resulting from corrective action

Functional Standards

ISO 9000 standards also require documentation and follow-up performance for all functions affecting quality. Functional requirements are illustrated by the following examples:[19]

- **Design.**   Sets a planned approach for meeting product or service specifications

- **Process Control.**   Provides concise instructions for manufacturing or service functions

- **Purchasing.**   Details methods for approving suppliers and placing orders

- **Service.**   Detailed instructions for carrying out after-sales service

- **Inspection and testing.**   Compels workers and managers to verify all production steps

- **Training.**   Specifies methods to identify training needs and keeping records

BENEFITS OF ISO 9000 CERTIFICATION

The benefits to the organization gained by improving quality in products and services were outlined in Chapter 1. To repeat:

1. Greater customer loyalty
2. Improvements in market share
3. Higher stock prices
4. Reduced service calls
5. Higher prices
6. Greater productivity and cost reduction

These same benefits would be achieved by ISO 9000 certification to the extent that actions leading to certification result in a quality management system. Moreover, certification provides the additional benefit of acceptance by EC customers and others whose criteria of acceptance include ISO 9000 certification.

Experience tends to confirm that companies do achieve these benefits. Consider the following examples:

■ A British government survey revealed that 89 percent of ISO 9000 registered companies reported greater operational efficiency: 48 percent reported increased profitability, 76 percent reported improvements in marketing, and 26 percent reported increased export sales.[20]

■ The British Standards Institution, a leading British Registrar, estimates that registered firms reduce operating costs by 10 percent on average.[21]

■ Du Pont attributes the following results to the adoption of ISO standards in their plants:

■ On-time delivery at one plant increased to 90 percent from 70 percent

■ Cycle time at one plant went from 15 days to 1 1/2 days

■ First-pass yield at one plant went from 72 percent to 92 percent

■ Test procedures were reduced from 3000 to 1100

■ A number of U.S. firms have reported benefits ranging from increased sales to improved communications.[22]

GETTING CERTIFIED: THE THIRD-PARTY AUDIT

Many managers perceive the thought of an audit of any kind as a necessary bureaucratic action that has a very low priority. This negative perception may increase when it is learned that preparation for ISO 9000 certification may take from six to twelve months and that the failure rate the first time around can be as high as two out of three. Nevertheless, a third-party audit is a prerequisite to certification. Speaking of certification, Deming noted, "You don't have to do this—survival is not compulsory!"

The traditional two-party quality audit system relies on the buyer–seller relationship, where the buyer (customer) "audits" the supplier. This puts a burden on both parties. Imagine a supplier with a hundred or more customers, each with their own specific requirements. From a customer's point of view, it would be beneficial if all suppliers could be judged by a single set of criteria.

The third-party audit places great importance on quality systems, a critical factor in the EC. The independent third-party *registrar* certifies that the quality system meets the requirements of ISO 9000.

What is the rationale for a third-party audit? Financial results are measured by financial statements, while product and service outputs are measured by quality. If the impartial third-party audit is required for financial systems, why not a similar check on quality systems? This is particularly important in helping to guarantee quality across international borders.

DOCUMENTATION

There are three basic steps to the registration process:

1. Appraisal of the organization's quality manual
2. Evaluation of conformance to documented procedures
3. Presentation of findings, with recommendations for corrective action

A great deal of *documentation* is required. The justification is reflected in the management axiom, "if you haven't written it out, you haven't thought it out." Moreover, as people come and go, change jobs, and forget a procedure, documentation ensures that a record is maintained for continuity. The simple rule is that if all personnel involved in a given system or procedure were replaced, the new people could continue making the product at the same quality level.

The amount of documentation depends on the nature and complexity of the business. A hierarchical approach involving three levels is generally acceptable:

■ **Level 1:** An overview type of quality manual consisting of policies that meet the requirements of the ISO standard for which certification is sought.

■ **Level 2:** Functional or departmental operating procedures in terms of "who does what."

■ **Level 3:** Work instructions that explain how each task is to be accomplished.

The criteria for approval are simple: "Can you say what you do and do what you say?" Questions such as the following may be asked: Is the process control system adequate for your needs? Is it understood by those who run the process? Are they properly trained to operate the process? Is the documentation up to date? Do you have an internal audit system that regularly assesses whether the control system is functioning as it should be?

POST-CERTIFICATION

The third-party audit and subsequent certification, if achieved, should be viewed as a means, not and end to be achieved. The importance of preparation for certification lies not so much in the certification itself, but in the quality system that results from the effort leading to it.

The customer is the ultimate beneficiary of the quality system, and any effort to obtain ISO 9000 certification without customer communication can be a waste of time and a compromise of any system that may result.

Certification is a beginning, not an end. Continuous evaluation, feedback, and fine-tuning are suggested. Who will perform this internal and continuing "audit" following certification? The responsibility, of course, is top management's. The role of the internal auditor, if any, is not clear. Should the role include getting ready for certification or maintaining post-certification requirements, or both?[23] The role is not clearly assigned and may represent an opportunity for internal auditors.

CHOOSING AN ACCREDITED REGISTRATION SERVICE

Quality managers who decide to implement an ISO 9000 system are confronted by two related issues: how best to implement the new system and how to ensure that certification will be recognized by customers. This latter issue will normally be settled if certification is recognized by legitimate accreditation bodies.

U.S. firms located in Europe normally utilize one of the many accrediting bodies in those countries. Many are government sanctioned, such as Raad voor de Certificatie (RvC) in the Netherlands and the National Accreditation Council for Certification Bodies (NACCB) in the United Kingdom. IBM's Application Business Systems Division was the first American-based firm to be certified in all of its business lines. Certification was gained after an audit by Bureau Veritas Quality International.[24]

No single firmly established registrar-accredited authority is recognized in the United States, and confusion exists as to which auditors are accredited by whom. Two non-governmental groups—the Registrar Accreditation Board (RAB) (an offshoot of the ASQC) and ANSI—have carried out a joint effort to develop accreditation requirements for ISO 9000 auditing companies operating in the United States.[25] The creation of the ANSI/RAB accreditation program is the nearest source of credible U.S.-based registrars.

A number of criteria should affect the decision on the choice of a registrar, including their knowledge in the specific industry and in the auditing of quality systems, how many similar firms they have registered, their turnaround time for audit results, their re-audit schedule should complement the business cycle of the firm, and, most important, they should be accredited.

As a general rule, it is probably not wise to shop around for the lowest price, because the cost of an audit is small compared to the overall cost of the registration effort.

ISO 9000 AND SERVICES

The standards apply not only to the manufacturing process, but to after-sale service and to service departments such as design within the manufacturing firm as well. Additionally, the standards also translate to the service sector. They specifically address quality systems for service as well as production. Indeed, ISO 9000-2, a separate guideline, was issued to explain ISO criteria in terms of selected service industries.

In the United Kingdom, standards are being used by educational institutions, banks, legal and architectural firms, and even trash collectors. At London's Heathrow Airport, British Airways PLC adopted ISO standards to reduce complaints of lost cargo and damaged goods. In the United States, a growing number of transportation companies will not transport hazardous material unless the shipper is ISO certified.

There is some evidence that the ISO 9000 Series is receiving more interest from service organizations in the United States than in Europe. Service firms in consulting, purchasing, and materials management are expressing interest. It is believed by some that the greater interest by U.S. service firms is based on strategic considerations as ISO 9000 is perceived as a "market differentiator."[26]

THE COST OF CERTIFICATION

A frequently asked question is: "How much does certification cost?" This is a legitimate concern, although the question may be accompanied by another one: "What is the payoff?"

There is no set answer to how much it costs and how long it takes. Each company is different. The answer depends on such factors as company size, product lines, how far along the company's existing systems are on the quality continuum, whether consultants are used, and the implementation strategy adopted. It can cost a small company $2,000 to $25,000 in consulting fees for advice on developing a quality system.[27] Employee time in creating the system is additional and can be the largest cost.

The major determinant is the firm's starting position. If the company has just won a Baldrige Award, registration of a plant or business might take just a few days. However, if the system must be created from the ground up, it can take a year and cost $100,000 or more.[28]

ISO 9000 VS. THE BALDRIGE AWARD

The ASQC reports that one of the most frequently asked questions regarding the ISO Series is: "Aren't the Baldrige Award, the Deming Prize, etc. equivalent or better 'standards' than the ISO Series?" The answer, replies ASQC, is quite simple: "You can't hope to meet the expectations of any of these programs if you aren't already implementing the ISO 9000 (ANSI/ASQC Q-90) standards in your company. These standards provide the foundation on which you can build your quality management and quality assurance systems so you may ultimately achieve a high level of success. Moreover, the ISO 9000 Series is the only system accepted internationally."

The Baldrige is a much more comprehensive program than ISO 9000. It is truly a TQM system, whereas the ISO Series is much more limited in scope. It is a basic standard, a minimal requirement, and can be worth about 200 to 300 points in the Baldrige program. For example, it does not address the human resource dimension, as does the Baldrige. On the other hand, a company implementing the Baldrige criteria is in a much better position to implement the ISO standard.

The Baldrige criteria are much more specific. The guidelines spell out what is expected in detailed language. In contrast, the ISO Series is designed to be inclusive, not exclusive. It does not mandate that one approach be used over another. As long as you can say what you do and do what you say, you can get your system registered. This generic nature of the standards can be a source of frustration as well as liberation.

For those companies whose quality systems are on the low end of a TQM continuum, ISO may be a starting place on the road to eventually achieving a TQM system. Certification also has the advantage of putting the organization on a level playing field with the competition worldwide.

IMPLEMENTING THE SYSTEM

Although the series provides guidance on the required attributes of the quality system, the standards do not spell out the means of implementation. Once a decision is made to adopt the standards and seek certification, the following major steps will facilitate successful change:

- Recognize the need for change and get the commitment of top management.
- Incorporate quality in the strategic plan as the linchpin of differentiation.
- Formulate and adopt a holistic quality policy statement adapted to ISO requirements. Get support and commitment from all managers.
- Determine the scope of the business to be certified. Will it be a particular process, related facilities, a geographical site, or the whole company?
- Determine the status of the current quality system through an internal audit. Define the *gap* between where you are and what it will take to close the gap.
- Estimate the cost in time and money and implement the plan by organizing the necessary action steps.

QUESTIONS FOR DISCUSSION

12-1 Why is it important for U.S. firms to comply with ISO 9000?

12-2 Compare the standards of ISO 9000 with those of the Baldrige Award.

12-3 Does ISO 9000 contain product standards or standards for operation of a quality management system? Explain the difference.

12-4 Answer the criticisms that meeting ISO standards will add to production costs.

12-5 What are the five sets of standards? Summarize each.

12-6 What are the benefits of ISO 9000 certification?

ENDNOTES

1. Gary Spizizen, "The ISO 9000 Standards: Creating a Level Playing Field for International Quality," *National Productivity Review,* Summer 1992, p. 332. This is an excellent summary of the provisions of ISO 9000.

2. The ANSI/ASQC Series is available from ASQC headquarters through the customer service department (Tel. 800-248-1946). The ISO 9000 Series is available from ANSI (Tel. 212-642-4900). Keep in mind that the ANSI/ASQC Q-90 Series is *identical* to the ISO 9000 Series.

3. Suzan L. Jackson, "What You Should Know about ISO 9000," *Training,* May 1992, p. 48. This is a good primer on ISO standards. ISO 9000 was adopted by the EC in 1990 as a global standard of quality. Its stringent requirements ensure that products manufactured along ISO 9000 are world class. See Jack Cella, "ISO 9000 Is the Key to International Business," *Journal of Commerce and Commercial,* Jan. 25, 1993, p. 88. Even China is moving toward adoption of the standards according to Ed Haderer, "Setting Tough Standards," *The China Business Review,* Jan.–Feb., 1993, p. 34. The Shanghai-Foxboro Company Ltd., an affiliate of the U.S.-based Foxboro Company, became the first company in China to attain ISO 9000 certification.

4. "Want EC Business? You Have Two Choices," *Business Week,* Oct. 19, 1992, p. 58. In the U.K., where the standards have become most widely embraced, over 80 percent of large employers with payrolls over 1000 are registered. See Kymberly K. Hockman and David A. Erdman, "Gearing Up for ISO 9000 Registration, *Chemical Engineering,* April 1993, p. 128.

5. Donald W. Marquardt, "ISO 9000: A Universal Standard of Quality," *Management Review,* Jan. 1992, p. 50.

6. "U.S. Firms Lag in Meeting Global Quality Standards," *Marketing News,* Feb. 15, 1993.

7. Jeffrey A. Tannenbaum, "Small Companies Are Finding it Pays to Think Global; Firms Win New Business by Adopting International Quality Standards," *Wall Street Journal,* Nov. 19, 1992, Section B, p. 2. See also *Marketing News,* Feb. 15, 1993, p. 1.

8. American Society for Quality Control, "ISO 9000," a brochure prepared by the Standards Development Department of ASQC, P.O. Box 3005, Milwaukee, WI 53201 (Tel. 414-272-8575).

9. Milton G. Allimadi, "New Quality Standards Draw Fire from US Group," *Journal of Commerce and Commercial,* Jan. 4, 1993, p. 4.

10. Mark Morrow, "International Agreements Increase Clout of ISO 9000," *Chemical Week,*

April 7, 1993, p. 32. This article attributes the success of ISO 9000 to its brevity (20 pages) and its simplicity. Since its inception, over 30,000 companies have registered.

11. Marjorie Coeyman, "ISO 9000 Gaining Ground in Asia/Pacific," *Chemical Week,* April 28, 1993, p. 54. In some parts of the Asia/Pacific region, the ISO 9000 quality standards have almost become domestic standards.

12. In a 1993 conference of the National Society of Professional Engineers, the topic of compliance with the EC's ISO 9000 quality control standards was discussed. See Jane C. Edmunds, "Engineers Want Quality," *ENR,* Feb. 8, 1993, p. 15. For Power Transmission Distributors (The Association), see Beate Halligan, "ISO Standards Prepare You to Compete," *Industrial Distribution,* May 1992, p. 100. The concern of the public utilities industry is reported in Greg Hutchins, "ISO Offers a Global Mark of Excellence," *Public Utilities Fortnightly,* April 15, 1993, p. 35. The computer industry's concern is reflected in Gary H. Anthes, "ISO Standard Attracts U.S. Interest," *Computerworld,* April 26, 1993, p. 109.

13. "Support Group Formed for Companies Seeking ISO 9000," *Industrial Engineering,* March 1993, p. 8. The National ISO 9000 Support Group will provide information, support, advice, and training at low cost to any American company interested in the ISO 9000 process. The goal of the group is to allow the free exchange of information and questions between companies seeking ISO registration.

14. Copies of the standards are available for a small fee from the American Society of Quality Control (Tel. 414-272-8575) and the American National Standards Institute (Tel. 212-642-4900).

15. Donald W. Marquardt, "ISO 9000: A Universal Standard of Quality," *Management Review,* Jan. 1992, p. 51. See also Kymberly K. Hockman, "The Last Barrier to the European Market," *Wall Street Journal,* Oct. 7, 1991, Section A, p. 14.

16. Michael E. Raynor, "ISO Certification," *Quality,* May 1993, pp. 44–45.

17. Adapted from John D. Flister and Joseph J. Jozaitis, "PPG's Journey to ISO 9000," *Management Accounting,* July 1992, p. 34.

18. Adapted from Kymberly K. Hockman and David A. Erdman, "Gearing Up for ISO 9000 Registration," *Chemical Engineering,* April 1993, p. 129.

19. Adapted from *Business Week,* Oct. 19, 1992 and ASQC *ANSI/ASQC Q-90-1987— Quality Management and Quality Assurance Standards.*

20. Gary H. Anthes, "ISO Standard Attracts U.S. Interest," *Computerworld,* April 26, 1993, p. 109.

21. Donald W. Marquardt, "ISO 9000: A Universal Standard of Quality," *Management Review,* Jan. 1992, p. 52.

22. See Elisabeth Kirschner, "Nalco: Registration in Context," *Chemical Week,* April 28, 1993, p. 71. See also Marjorie Coeyman, "FMC: The Benefits of Documentation," *Chemical Week,* April 28, 1993, p. 69.

23. See Giovanni Grossi, "Quality Certifications," *Internal Auditor,* Oct. 1992, p. 33–35 and Gary M. Stern, "Sailing to Europe: Can Auditing Play a Role in the New International Quality Standards?" *Internal Auditor,* Oct. 1992, pp. 29–33. Both of these authors, who are members of the internal auditing profession, argue for an expanded role for internal auditors in the certification and follow-on process.

24. "IBM, Help/Systems Receive ISO Certification," *Systems 3X-400,* Feb. 1993, p. 16. ABS won the Baldrige Quality Award in 1991.

25. Emily S. Plisher, "Seeking Recognition: U.S. Auditors Build Their Base," *Chemical*

Week, Nov. 11, 1992, pp. 30–33. See also a special report entitled "Confusion Persists on Issue of Registrar Accreditation," *Chemical Week,* April 28, 1993, p. 42. As of April 1993, ANSI/RAB had accredited 27 quality system registrars. The "unofficial" list is contained in this endnote citation.

26. Gary Spizizen, "The ISO 9000 Standards: Creating a Level Playing Field for International Quality," *National Productivity Review,* Summer 1992, p. 335.

27. This is the estimate of OTS Registrars of Houston, an ISO 9000 registrar. "Small Companies Are Finding it Pays to Think Global; Firms Win New Business by Adopting International Quality Standards," *Wall Street Journal,* Nov. 19, 1992, Section B, p. 2.

28. Donald W. Marquardt, "ISO 9000: A Universal Standard of Quality," *Management Review,* Jan. 1992, p. 51. See also Ian Hendry, "ISO Standardizes Quality Efforts," *Pulp & Paper,* Jan. 1993, p. S4. Several of these firms report a cost of certification of about $112,000. Also, General Chemical's Green River plant achieved certification at an estimated cost of $150,000. Rick Mullin, "General Registers Green River Site: First ISO 9002 for Natural Soda Ash," *Chemical Week,* April 28, 1993, p. 59.

The author is truly one of the world's best pioneers of the quality movement. Upon the death of Deming in December 1993, he became the last of the major gurus. In this article he predicts that the 21st century will be the century of quality and the label "Made in the USA" will again become a symbol of world-class quality. His prognosis for Europe is gloomy, partly because of its dependence on ISO 9000 as the standard for total quality management.

ASSESSING QUALITY GROWTH IN THE US

J. M. Juran

At the beginning of the 90's, a few major US companies (about 50 of the Fortune 500 companies) had attained world-class quality. Others were in various stages of their quality journey; some had not started, some had started over, some were making progress, and some were well along. We don't know the numbers at each of these stages—the research hasn't been done.

That doesn't sound like much progress, but the situation is better than it seems, because meanwhile we have accumulated useful work in process. The successful companies, though few in number, have proved that world-class quality is attainable in our culture. Companies that have become US role models and their results are benchmarks for the rest of the economy. From successful companies, we learn what works. From unsuccessful companies, we learn what does not work.

This emerging body of know-how is helping CEOs to shed their ignorance of how to manage for quality. Our CEOs have learned much by visiting successful companies, by hearing their presentations at conferences, and by attending meetings.

Reprinted with permission from *Quality*, October 1993, pp. 48–49. A publication of Chilton Publishing, a Capital Cities/ABC, Inc. Company

That emerging body of know-how is changing the strategies adopted by CEOs. During the 80's many quality initiatives focused on exhortation—banners and slogans. Alternatively, they focused on a remedy without knowing what the disease was. Now CEOs increasingly use the managerial sequence: establish the vision, policies, and goals; train the hierarchy in managing the quality process; establish responsibilities; and provide resources. The final step in the sequence is motivating and training people how to use the necessary tools.

I sometimes get flak from the statisticians for assertedly downgrading their field. However, that is not my position. I agree, training in statistical tools is essential. But we should not start with statistics. We should start by agreeing on goals and how to reach them.

What Lies Ahead?

Back in 1966, shortly after one of my visits to Japan, I spoke at a quality conference in Stockholm. I predicted that "The Japanese are headed for world quality leadership, and will attain it in the next two decades, because no one else is moving there at the same pace."

That was in 1966. After that bull's eye, it might be best for me to quit while I'm ahead. Nevertheless, some trends are so clear that I venture another prognosis.

Global Outlook

We are witnessing a rapid expansion of international competition in quality. This expansion is caused by the convergence of forces such as:

- Proliferation of multinational companies.
- Increased global competition.
- Emerging regional markets that spur competition and destroy protectionism.
- Environmental protection.

From this information we can derive a logical prediction: The 20th century has been the century of productivity. The 21st century will be the century of quality.

U.S. Perspective

During the 80's, a few US companies demonstrated that world-class quality is attainable in our culture. Forces now at work are urging more companies to attain world-class quality. The results achieved by successful companies have been widely publicized, stunning, and stimulate other companies to go after similar results.

Furthermore, successful companies are serving notice to suppliers: "You must attain world-class quality if you wish to remain a supplier." This requirement is propelling itself into the entire supplier chain.

The Malcolm Baldrige National Quality Award has generated intense interest in the industrial sector. The award is prestigious, and it serves the winners in the marketplace and in public relations. Beyond the applicants for the award, it has stimulated a great many companies to conduct self-audits against the criteria. It has also stimulated creation of similar awards for states, regions, and even such backward sectors of the economy as government, health, and education.

These forces appear to be irreversible and lead to some additional logical predictions. During the 90's the number of companies that attain world-class quality will rise by an order of magnitude. During the next century the label "Made in the USA" will again become a symbol of world-class quality.

European Outlook

Next, we turn to the outlook for Europe. In a sense, it is hilarious to talk of Europe as though it were a single entity. The commonalities, however, justify a wide-angle look.

The European countries have not been as intensely invaded by Japanese products as has the US. In addition, European countries have retained a higher level of protectionism. All this has created a lag—European countries have been slow to respond to the growing quality crisis. They will pay a price for this lag during the 90's and into the next century.

The Europeans adopted the so-called ISO 9000 series of standards in response to the growing quality crisis. The standards are voluntary—they are not a legal prerequisite to selling products in Europe. But they have been so cleverly marketed that whoever hopes to sell products in Europe must meet registration criteria for ISO 9000. Registration to ISO 9000 has in effect become a license to market in Europe.

The ISO standards have a degree of merit. The criteria define a comprehensive quality system. The registration process might rid companies of the plague of multiple assessments that have burdened them in the past. However, the criteria fail to include some of the essentials needed to attain world-class quality, such as:

- Quality goals in the business plan.
- Quality improvement at a revolutionary rate.
- Training in managing for quality.
- Participation by the work force.

All in all, my prognosis for Europe is gloomy. In my view, many European companies are in for a massive letdown. They will get registered to ISO 9000, but this alone will not enable them to attain world-class quality.

And On to Japan

Paradoxically, one reason for Japanese leadership in quality is that they lost the war. That defeat did not cause them to give up their goal of gaining a place in the sun, although it did cause them to change their grand strategy. Reaching that goal would now have to be done by superiority in trade rather than in armaments.

To achieve superiority in trade required getting rid of Japan's reputation for poor quality. That posed quite a challenge, but the defeat opened their minds and made them willing to adopt new ways, including a revolutionary rate of quality improvements, year after year. Several decades of using those new ways then brought them to world leadership in quality.

Given their achievements to date, and the associated momentum, it is safe to predict that the Japanese will remain among the world quality leaders well into the next century.

We should also note the entry of a subtle influence that is likely to affect share of market despite residual differences in quality. That influence is patriotism. The urge to "buy American" has always been a force in the marketplace. Other things being equal, this force is usually decisive in the decision to buy. If other things are too unequal, the gap can overcome the force of patriotism. Patriotism is willing to forgive a narrow gap, but not a wide one.

During the 80's, the gap between Japanese and US quality was narrowed noticeably by some of our companies. That action enabled those companies to recapture some market share. We can expect the quality gap to continue to narrow in the decades ahead. This will translate into changes in market share as customer perception catches up with the facts. The more our companies narrow the competitive gap in quality, the more the urge to "buy American" takes over in the marketplace. Patriotism steps in even before the gap has been fully closed.

Editor's note: This article has been excerpted from a talk by J. M. Juran given at the Business Roundtable CEO Quality Forum, 1993 by Juran Institute, Inc.

CASE

PPG'S JOURNEY TO ISO 9000

John D. Flister and Joseph J. Jozaitis

Many management accountants have heard about ISO 9000 but don't really know what it is or how it may affect their organizations. One fact is clear—ISO certification is becoming a requirement for companies to remain competitive in the international markets, particularly Europe.

At PPG Industries' Specialty Chemicals Division we started our journey to ISO 9000 in July 1991, and our goal is to be certified before the end of the year. Currently we are preparing for the preliminary audits.

During the past year we learned that achieving ISO 9000 can be summed up in four simple steps:

- Document what you do.
- Do what you said you will do.
- Control nonconformance.
- Control change.

We also discovered that the costs of achieving certification are not small. A typical estimate for auditing and registration fees alone is around $35,000. This figure does not include the enormous amount of time involved by many individuals in the organization. In addition, future costs are involved in maintaining certification.

On the positive side, the payback can be enormous. The resulting reduction in the price of nonconformance will often offset much of the cost.

What Is ISO 9000?

PPG Industries, Inc. was established in 1883 and makes flat glass and fabricated glass products, continuous-strand fiberglass, decorative and protective coatings, and industrial and specialty chemicals. PPG Specialty Chemicals includes domestic and international facilities and is committed to becoming a world-class supplier in the surfactant and specialty chemicals market. Our department managers were introduced to the ISO standards during a presentation by representatives from a PPG Fiberglass plant that had just been registered to the ISO 9002 standard.

ISO 9000 is a series of five international quality standards developed by the International Organization for Standardization (ISO) in Geneva, Switzerland. The ISO 9000 standard provides some basic definitions and is a road map to using the other standards in the series.

The ISO 9001, 9002, and 9003 standards are for external quality assurance purposes for use in contractual situations. ISO 9001 ensures conformance to requirements during design and development, production, installation, and servicing. Therefore, engineering and construction firms and manufacturing companies who design, develop, produce, install, and service their products are covered under this standard. The quality system requirements for ISO 9001 are listed in Table 1.

ISO 9002 specifies a model for quality assurance when only production and installation conformance is required. This standard is particularly relevant to process industries where specific requirements for products are stated in terms of an established design or specification. Chemicals, food, and pharmaceutical companies generally seek certification under ISO 9002.

ISO 9003 requires only conformance in final inspection and testing. This standard concerns small shops, equipment distributors that inspect and test the products they supply, or divisions within an organization such as laboratories.

ISO 9004 contains guidance on technical, administrative, and human factors

Table 1   ISO 9001 Quality Systems

Quality System Requirements	
Management Responsibility	Inspection, Measuring, and Test Equipment
Quality System	Inspection and Test Status
Contract Review	Control of Nonconforming Product
Design Control	Corrective Action
Document Control	Handling, Storage, Packaging, and Delivery
Purchasing	Quality Records
Purchaser Supplied Product	Internal Quality Audits
Product Identification and Traceability	Training
Process Control	Servicing
Inspection and Testing	Statistical Techniques

affecting the quality of products and services. This standard provides guidelines for developing and implementing a quality system.

When we began our journey we discovered that much of the chemical industry was seeking registration to the ISO 9002 requirements. Deciding on the appropriate standard for our business was not easy. Because our company is a specialty chemical manufacturer, the design and development of new products is an important feature of our business. Our general manager believed that ISO certification would differentiate our business from our competitors. It would also, he believed, encourage our two manufacturing plants to work more closely with our research and development facilities.

Getting Started

The first major step was to create the quality project manager position to organize and manage all activities. The co-author of this article, Joseph J. Jozaitis, was named to this position. Because PPG Specialty Chemicals has been using the total quality process for several years, our second step was to assign Quality Action Teams (QATs) to each of the quality system requirements of the ISO 9001 standard listed in Table 1. Twenty teams of more than 100 employees at three different sites were selected by the project manager. These teams are cross functional, include representatives for the appropriate sites and departments, and have the necessary skills. Their purpose is to:

- Understand the requirement of its section of the standard.
- Evaluate what we currently do pertaining to that section.
- Recommend additions or new procedures needed to conform to the standard.
- Implement any new requirements or work with departments to implement the new methods or tasks.

Last July, team chairpersons met with their individual teams and reviewed the ISO standard and the information given to them about the project. It was very important to get each team going in the right direction, and this effort needed more attention and education than we thought originally. Some teams had a clear task ahead of them. Others were confused and uncertain about how to deal with the generic language of the standard because the same requirements can be applied equally to companies making chemicals or to companies designing computer systems and software.

Sources of Information

We decided not to use consultants to help us with the certification. Instead, we built up a network of information sources to answer questions and keep the teams going in the right direction.

An important resource for us is the PPG Fiberglass site because its managers have already achieved certification. They have been helpful in areas such as calibration and laboratory testing. We have been able to apply what they have experienced to our specific situation.

The quality projects manager is the contact person for all ISO matters. He has developed a broad base of knowledge about ISO through his attendance at training sessions on the ISO 9000 standard and quality auditing process with several site quality coordinators and the director of quality for the PPG Specialty Chemicals group. Together they form a network to share information on specific topics. Other groups involved include customers and vendors and the individuals responsible for our actual registration audit.

Progress Is Made

The job of the quality projects manager is to keep the teams focused on the standard. While several teams did not attack the problem aggressively, others charged ahead but went off on a tangent and lost sight of the real issue.

Although each team has worked at a different pace, they all agree that our current quality system shares several common features. First, most of our current system is good and can be used to satisfy the ISO requirements. In those areas that are lacking, additions can be made so that all functions conform to the standard. The teams also came to the realization that we are underdocumented and have a tremendous amount of procedures to write or rewrite.

Finally we identified a need for a cultural change. The total quality process was changing our way of thinking about requirements and work processes. Our goal is to nurture this new culture and avoid shortcuts that may lead to nonconformance. We have found that the ISO standard encourages and often insists on improvement. When any change becomes part of your process, that change must be documented and controlled.

The Quality Manual

The team involved with quality systems is responsible for writing the quality manual. The manual states our business unit's quality policy as well as our policy and commitment to each of the 20 sections in the ISO 9001 standard.

The quality manual details exactly what we do in each specific area to conform to the requirements of the standard. It also notes standard operating procedures (SOP) and other documents to point the reader toward greater detail for a given work process or function.

The manual was created from sections contributed by the teams. The quality projects manager assembled the manual with help from the quality systems team. The manual also documents standard operating procedures, process instructions, specifications, laboratory test methods, and other procedural documents.

The portion of the manual that covers what we do in each specific area to conform to the ISO standard is the central document of our quality system. We decided to completely replace our old manuals and structure our documentation to conform to the sections in the ISO 9001 standard.

Internal Quality Audits

As the QATs were completing their tasks and the individual departments began to take on the workload, the internal quality audit function acted as the driver to bring the tasks to a close. The internal quality audit teams are responsible for highlighting areas of nonconformance within each department.

The internal quality audits are designed to simulate the audits we will be receiving from the ISO registration body. These audits will be run by people familiar with our system. We believe that if we can pass our own internal quality audits we should not encounter problems with an external audit.

Our first system-wide audit was conducted in December 1991. It was called a "survey" and was used to help departments identify what they needed to do to be in compliance with the standard. We created a work list to help each department decide which standard operating procedures needed formalization. This audit was a huge success and got all departments moving in the right direction.

The second system-wide quality audit began in April 1992 and as of this writing is still in progress. For this audit we are concentrating on compliance with the quality manual, on the existence of all documentation required by the quality manual, and on a detailed check of records to see if we do what our procedures say we should do.

Where Do We Stand

Each department is currently busy writing standard operating procedures for their respective areas. This documentation ensures consistency within the departments and throughout the organization.

All relevant procedures must be documented, and all relevant work instructions need to be written. This documentation is referred to in the quality manual but is not a part of it. These documents should say what we do, not what we think we do. The work instructions are written in a "how to" fashion and can be used for training purposes.

Management's Role

The role of management in any project as extensive as ISO 9000 cannot be overemphasized. It is critical that top management supports the project and even participates in it. If you don't have top management support in this project, do not even start the journey.

Providing resources to the project is one of the crucial roles of management. In our particular situation, it was discovered early in the process that our quality control department had a disproportionate amount of the work to accomplish and that a shifting of personnel was required to meet our goals. Removing this roadblock, as well as others encountered along the way, could be accomplished only at our director level. The directors met, and the situation was resolved quickly, reinforcing the priority status of the ISO project.

Actual participation in the QATs was particularly useful. At PPG Specialty Chemicals, the director of operations was on the internal quality audit team and participated in the quality audits. This situation certainly assigned a higher level of importance to be in compliance for the audits and to follow up on any audit corrective actions.

In any business, there are many projects in process at any one given time. The ISO 9000 project calls for an extensive amount of manpower, which has meant that not all projects could be accomplished. If this fact is acknowledged by management, everyone realizes the importance of the ISO project.

The Challenge Ahead

Although we have yet to be certified, the process has been a positive experience. We still have some problems to resolve, but we have realized benefits from our efforts.

The ISO 9000 standards ensure customers that their suppliers have documented proof that basic quality systems are in place. Because of this documentation, customers will not feel the need to audit suppliers. As a result, companies save time and money.

Companies also benefit from the certification process because it forces them to look at their quality system in great detail. This kind of examination results in better procedures, better documentation, and more consistency in their processes.

Questions for Discussion

1   The company assigned Quality Action Teams (QATs) to each of the quality system requirements of the ISO 9000 standard. Is this an appropriate organizational alignment of teams? Why or why not?

2   The ISO standards require a great deal of procedural documentation. Why do you think that the documentation is more rigorous than the Baldrige?

3   If you were assigned the task of writing a quality manual (an ISO requirement), what general topics would you include?

4   Top management support is critical to ISO certification and success. How would top management demonstrate this support?

13

1993 VARIFILM
CASE STUDY

OVERVIEW

Business Description. Varifilm provides $3 billion worth of specialty plastic films and recycled products each year to the food and industrial market segments. Film is used for food packaging, food sacks, product packaging, pallet wrapping, construction barrier film, electrical insulation, and a wide variety of industrial applications. The Varifilm product is not sold directly to consumers. In addition to the basic product research, development, and customer engineering, support is provided through operations and Research, Development and Engineering (RD&E). These activities are coordinated through sales and customer service. Varifilm works actively with industry councils and two leading universities to maintain its leadership role in the food and industrial packaging markets. Varifilm's Recyclables business uses its own and customer scrap to produce pallets, spools, and fence posts.

Key Quality Requirements. Our customers report five key requirements which are tracked to measure customer satisfaction. They are:

This case study is in the public domain. It has been abridged and modified to more nearly meet the instructional needs of the text. The source is the Malcolm Baldrige National Quality Award.

- Product Quality
- On-Time Delivery
- Ease of Access
- Price
- Knowledge of Coworkers

Product quality includes film properties such as stretch percent, gage (thickness), tear, seal strength, and burst strength.

Organization Structure.　The company is organized into three strategic business units, each headed by a vice-president: (1) food packaging, (2) industrial films, and (3) recyclables. Varifilm is a functional organization with a matrix structure to drive major initiatives and the business process. Three cross-functional business teams, led by the marketing/sales leader, include Food Packaging, Industrial Film and Recycling. The three regional organizations (Europe, Latin America and the Far East) adopt and use the business team initiatives as appropriate.

Customer Base.　The customer base includes construction insulation manufacturers, fabricated housing, hundreds of consumer goods manufacturers and food processors who utilize shrink and stretch film, and retail chains for sacks (plastic bags). The construction industry uses Varifilm's products in fence posts for road and farm applications.

Markets.　Varifilm markets its products worldwide. The Recyclables operation currently provides products to North America only. Within the U.S., plants are strategically located so that all major market regions are viable. International plants have been strategically located near suppliers and market centers. In several cases, U.S. suppliers and customers are mirrored internationally. These partnerships have provided cost benefits to all concerned. Varifilm has been selective in the international markets it has chosen to participate in. Trade barrier changes in North America and Europe will be beneficial to Varifilm. Two additional sites in Eastern Europe and Asia are being considered.

Market Share Region	Varifilm	Company A	Company B	JFC	Strongest Region Competitor
USA	47%	30%	28%	0%	30%
Europe	16%	21%	0%	14%	32%
Asia	21%	0%	13%	32%	22%
South America	26%	22%	15%	0%	28%
Japan	0%	0%	14%	48%	30%

Position in Industry.   Varifilm competes directly with two other companies (Ref. Item 7.6) in the North American market. In Europe and Asia, there are regional competitors along with one of the U.S. competitors. The strongest threat competitively is a Japanese firm (JFC) who is currently building a plant in southern California. (Ref. Item 3.2.)

Technology.   Primary resin received by rail car is processed by heating and extrusion. Chemicals are added to develop specific properties, and some products require multiple layers. In-line conversion equipment further processes (i.e., forming sacks) and packages the film. The recycling process is one of formulating and molding. Additives are used to stabilize the product and create proper color. Advanced computer process controls unique to the industry have been codesigned and developed with computer and equipment suppliers. This advanced technology has been responsible for the improved product uniformity and control. All film operations run continuously. The industry is capital intensive.

Suppliers.   Resins, molds, dies, conversion equipment, inks, chemicals, and ideas are all critical elements to Varifilm's success. Supplier partnerships are developed not only with traditional suppliers but with Universities and Industry trade groups. The number of suppliers has been reduced by 33% over the past three years while supplier certification, supplier quality, and supplier satisfaction have all increased. (Ref. Items 5.4, 6.4.) While the products purchased by Varifilm are generally not unique, partnership programs with suppliers have led to special codeveloped formulations and equipment.

Customer Partnerships.   Customer focus and customer partnerships targeted on value to the customer are key to Varifilm's increasing market share. Customer visits, coworker visits, customer product design teams, and product engineering support all have led to understanding and meeting present and future customer requirements. Electronic order entry and computer tracking of Just-In-Time delivery are examples of customer-partnership-directed service improvements.

Regulatory Environment.   Varifilm operates in the world market and, as such, is committed to be a responsible citizen. In addition to normal FDA and OSHA regulations, there are a wide variety of Common Market and Asian regulations.

Future.   There are four major issues facing Varifilm in the next ten years.

1. The nature of the market and the competitive threat from JFC in the United States.

2. Europe and Asia provide major expansion opportunities. Two new plants are under consideration.

3. Recyclables has created a major new product opportunity. Expansion of this business is limited by the availability of recyclable waste plastic. Fence post demand is expected to double in the next five years.

4. The Packaging Research Alliance project of formable plastic, while creating a major new product line, will exceed our ability to provide technical support.

Union/Management Relationships. All production coworkers are represented by the Film Workers United. The union has been a proactive force for quality. It participates in all quality training, has representatives on business leadership teams and site teams, and attends all quality leadership conferences.

CATEGORY 1.0
LEADERSHIP

1.1 Senior Executive Leadership

1.1a Our senior executives are effective at developing and maintaining a customer focus within Varifilm and at creating an environment for quality excellence because they have gone through a genuine and profound personal transformation.

Our senior executives are personally and visibly involved in quality, since it is Varifilm's model of doing business. Leadership has experienced first-hand the consequences of not being customer-focused and not having sufficiently shared quality values. Leadership works to create a shared quality vision and meet the needs of customers, suppliers, and coworkers. The new leadership model has shifted from telling coworkers what to do and "getting things done through people" to "meeting the needs of coworkers as they work to accomplish their jobs and achieve process supremacy and customer satisfaction."

Phase I (1975–1982) Process Management. The first phase of quality at Varifilm consisted of a detailed process management system along with a sophisticated statistical quality control system for continuous manufacturing.

Phase II (1982–1989) Total Quality Management. The year 1982 was an important turning point when John Romig, our President at that time, introduced and committed the company to Total Quality Management (TQM). This extended the quality process beyond manufacturing and introduced the quality principles through broad training and quality actions through team-based activity.

To firmly and consistently establish our commitment to this new approach over time, we hold Quality Leadership Conferences every other year, bringing together up to 150 top managers and selected participants from within their organizations to unite and consolidate Varifilm's leadership behind shared principles.

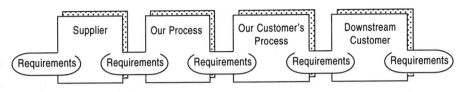

Customer Requirements Chain

At the end of the '80s, Total Quality Leadership began to move into its current and most exciting stage. We realized that we needed to more dynamically involve our people as individuals and team members in feeling personal responsibility for and ownership of the Varifilm quality environment and the values that support it.

As a definition of our quality aspirations, we adopted and implemented the Varifilm Continuous Improvement Criteria (VCIC). To revitalize and improve our quality process, fostering a more personal sense of ownership of the Varifilm quality environment, we implemented Self Managed Teams.

VCIC decides "what" we improve; the Self Managed Teams describe "how" we improve. Key measures are what we track.

Phase III (1989–) Quality Integration.   The third phase of quality at Varifilm builds on the first two phases and adds the strengths of recent teaching in Partnership/High Performance Work Systems (HPWS), Diversity, and Quality Leadership. Union management partnership teams now exist in all facilities, and HPWS teams are the result, with two plants regularly being benchmarked for their organization changes and quality achievement.

If there is a single moment when this third phase really began, it was May 1989, when our senior executives spent an intense week of transformation together at an Outward Climb facility working directly with Outward Climb staff and Mark Hurry, a well-known expert in organizational change, leadership, and empowerment. As a symbol of their shared realization that the pursuit of quality requires bold leadership, our senior executives renamed themselves the "Invincible Team" (I-Team).

With the experience they shared and the intense discussions they exchanged, the I-Team developed a foundation for improved Total Quality Leadership and culture change which included:

- Establishment of a new Purpose and Vision based on achieving success through meeting the needs of key partners in our business: the customer, the coworker, society, and the stockholder. (See Item 1.1b.)

- Adoption of the Baldrige Criteria as the improvement framework, naming it the Varifilm Continuous Improvement Criteria.

- Creation and adoption of the Self Managed Team process to deal with the human side of quality for all Varifilm coworkers.

- Recognition that we need to create an atmosphere characterized by valuing the individual, respect, trust, responsibility, teamwork, support and anticipation if we are to be successful in making the broad changes needed. These are focus areas in the Self Managed Team process.

Each member of the I-Team is committed to spending a minimum of one-third of his/her time on quality-related activities such as customer contacts, establishing values, and supporting coworkers.

1. Responsibilities include customer visits, communication, and participation in new product development. The I-Team also regularly hosts customer visits and opens all quarterly customer quality orientation sessions. Customer satisfaction is also one of the Key Indicators reviewed at each quarterly operations review.

2. Varifilm Quality Values (Goal, Policy, Definition) were established at the beginning of Phase I and reviewed and improved at the beginning of Phase II. These values were included in the original training, and the revised values have been rolled through the company using a large-scale model to gain acceptance and speed implementation.

3. The business planning process has, for the past two years, integrated quality, Key Indicators, customer requirements, satisfaction goals, and projections into the planning process. Unit goal measurement is ongoing. A formal review of Key Indicator (KI) progress is done quarterly with all 200 KIs being reviewed (Each unit has approximately ten KIs.). The I-Team's systematic review of each group allows for unit discussion of its measures and provides the opportunity to recognize improvements. This is an important regular feature of the I-Team meetings.

4. Although recognition is most often done at the unit level, the I-Team actively participates and hosts the biennial Quality Achievement Conference to recognize quality achievements.

5. I-Team members communicate quality values to customer contacts and outside organizations or groups of their choice. Each has also adopted one of the company's major initiatives (Key Indicators). I-Team member responsibility includes supporting teams as they work on their topic, participating in one work team or related educational or benchmarking experience, and being the advocate in I-Team meetings.

1.1b The purpose of Varifilm is to be committed to broad partnerships, and we strive to continuously improve our relationships.

Item	Phase II	Phase III
Values	Quality The individual Total Quality Management Integrity Leadership Customers	Quality The individual, respect Total Quality principles Integrity, trust Teamwork, support Partners, anticipation
Goal	Deliver error free products on time every time	Deliver error free products on time every time
Principles	Meet requirements Error free work Manage by prevention Continuous improvement	Meet requirements Error free work Manage by prevention Continuous improvement Knowledge through benchmarking
Customer Objective	Meet the requirements	Customer delight—be first in customer satisfaction and factors leading to customer satisfaction
Coworkers	Participation	Empowerment
Suppliers	Meet requirements	Partner in value
Stockholders	Provide return	Earn trust, respect needs
Community	Good citizen	Good citizen
Environment	Protect	Improve

Historically, quality values go back to our founders' belief in "value and service for a fair price." This belief was rediscovered in Phase II and stated in the form of our quality Goal, Policy, Principles and Actions. Our "Quality Model" emphasized customer requirements and the importance of continuous improvement. In Phase III this quality foundation was expanded to include broader understanding of partnership, diversity, and quality leadership. The concept of partners included the customer, supplier, coworkers, stockholder/investor, the community and the environment. We are committed to meeting the needs of all partners with the customer being our main focus. All partners, however, must be satisfied.

These values are the basis for many kinds of consistent communication both within and outside the company. They are the foundation of strategic planning (Item 3.1) and our interactions with partners. These values are discussed in formal and informal interactions with members of the I-Team who were personally involved in developing and adopting them.

Our values are regularly reinforced in two ways: (1) annual reviews are included in the *Company News* sent to each coworker; and (2) each coworker team develops its own purpose and vision in support of the company values. In this way, coworkers actively participate in internalizing and putting into practice Varifilm values. This translation of values into the local environment and work group is a unique and highly effective approach that goes beyond normal communication. Most teams display Purpose and Vision statements in their work areas. For example, the following representative declaration is prominently displayed in an Illinois plant:

> *We are committed to meeting ALL customer requirements and supporting each other through teamwork, communication, dedication, ideas, respect, and support. We are committed to continuous improvement and striving to be the best!*

In addition to its annual issue dealing with our quality values, the monthly *Company News* recognizes teams as they "live" their purpose and vision.

1.1c Varifilm's values and customer focus are regularly communicated and reinforced through I-Team personal examples, the supervisor newsletter, and at the semi-annual, two-day leadership meeting of the Management Committee (top 150 managers). This meeting always focuses on quality, with an outside speaker and group discussion. Each leadership team member tracks quality activities such as talks, customer contact, recognition activity, seminars taught and attended, and time involved in Management By Walking Around (MBWA). Members have exceeded their goal of ten activities/month/person for the past three years.

Cliff Bass, *President & CEO.* Systematically visits major customers for improvement ideas and systematically visits each Varifilm site worldwide yearly.

Mike Archer, *Vice-President, Industrial Film.* Regularly participates in plant and RD&E recognition activities, participates on the Quality Council, co-teaches Module 3 (Process Improvement), and led the Order Entry Process Improvement Team.

Carl Baker, *Vice-President, Food Packaging.* Systematically visits one plant per quarter to listen to people, and routinely visits the plants of our three major customers to determine how we can assist them with their continuous improvement efforts.

Leroy Jones, *Vice-President, Recyclables.* In 1991, visited approximately 30 potential customers to understand how our new business venture can best meet long-term environmental issues, as well as meet short-term customer needs. Holds regular "Let's Talk" meetings.

Art Axel, *Vice-President, Quality.*   Gives 15–20 Director's Awards per year to coworkers, suppliers, and/or customers in recognition of outstanding quality accomplishments. Leads efforts to achieve 100% ISO Certification of our facilities and our suppliers' facilities.

Lisa Seavey, *Vice-President, Human Resources.*   Strategic leader of our people development processes. Manages and revises personnel systems and is the champion of the HPWS and Diversity programs. Transferred hiring responsibility to the individual units and teams.

Terry Spade, *Vice-President, Varifilm Far East.*   Leads our culture change in the Far East. Personally leads the Self Managed Team training.

1.1d   Our senior executives systematically and continuously improve their own processes. The I-Team is committed to continuous improvement in leading the quality effort. The I-Team utilizes surveys after talks and at its monthly meeting. Teams, presenters, and participants are surveyed. The I-Team reviews the results of their activities listed in 1.1c to improve.

Individually, our leaders read articles and books, and the team spends one week per year in group training and benchmarking activities. Members have attended the annual Malcolm Baldrige National Quality Award's Quest for Excellence Conference, and leaders of three Baldrige winners have spoken to the leadership team. Every two years a survey of coworkers is conducted. Several questions deal directly with senior leadership and are tracked by the I-Team.

1.2 Management for Quality

1.2a   Each business unit or plant translates Varifilm's values into requirements for all levels of management and coworkers. Several specific processes are used:

VCIC/Partnership Teams and Responsibilities.   During Phase II, each unit had a quality steering committee and teams based on the quality actions. With the use of Baldrige Assessment (VCIC), and since Phase III, each unit has a leadership team responsible for VCIC and a partnership team responsible for HPWS. The use of VCIC ensures continuous improvement and alignment of quality values and customer focus. Unit management is responsible for leading the processes and reporting annually to the I-Team.

Strategic Planning.   The strategic planning process, which uses customer satisfaction data, customer requirements, and Key Indicators, defines responsibilities and promotes customer focus and quality values. (See Category 3.0.)

Customer Requirements Model.   The Customer Requirements Model of Phase II established the internal and external supplier/customer model with requirements. This process is still used to develop inter-unit requirements.

Cross-Functional Teams. Varifilm's teams and partnerships (HPWS) define responsibilities and foster cooperation between units. Cross-functional teams run the various businesses.

Management Committee Meetings. These meetings are used to communicate values and responsibilities.

1.2b Our real objective is to create customer value and satisfaction, improve quality, and reduce costs by understanding and meeting customer requirements and living our values.

Varifilm's customer focus and quality values are communicated in a variety of ways. In addition to Purpose and Vision (see Area 1.1b), Key Indicators which align with customer requirements and are a part of the gain-sharing program are used to directly align coworkers with customer requirements. Basic benchmarking of manufacturing processes has been expanded to all organizations to determine how to accomplish each task more effectively with fewer people. The objective is to improve quality, reduce cost, and eliminate non-value-added work. We use a variety of analysis tools, including process flowcharting, and the seven old and new tools for identifying potential improvements. Visits to and from customers also solidify customer focus.

1.2c Each organizational unit regularly reviews the progress of its improvement efforts, key processes, and key indicators as an outcome of the VCIC.

The Leadership Team reviews Key Indicators quarterly, and each month one unit's Key Indicators are reviewed in detail. Key Indicators are displayed prominently as part of the HPWS and gain-sharing displays. To assist units not performing according to plans and goals, our objective is to ensure accountability, without encouraging improper actions, to meet a numerical goal. We, therefore, focus strongly on solving problems versus assigning blame. Frequent Leadership Team contact provides support as needed rather than waiting for reviews.

1.2d Three tools are used regularly to evaluate and develop improvement plans for awareness and integration of quality values.

1. The Baldrige Assessment, conducted every two years, provides unit assessment of the area along with action plans.

2. The Coworker Climate Survey (CCS), also done every other year, provides detailed information and comparisons between units and with leading companies through the Wheaton Group summaries.

3. Customer satisfaction surveys include questions related to this area. (See Category 7.0.) In addition to the formal survey process, interviews have

been used with all partners to better understand adopted values and to gain perspective on where improvements need to be made.

CATEGORY 2.0
INFORMATION AND ANALYSIS

2.1 Scope and Management of Quality and Performance Data and Information

2.1a   The scope and types of data and information we use are extensive. Figure 2.1 displays our key types of data and information and the computer systems on which they reside. How each supports quality improvement is evident from the data descriptions and from details given in other parts of this application.

Our quality and performance data meet the following criteria: related to customer satisfaction, required for performance analysis, consistent, quantifiable, objective and verifiable, meet industry standards, enable comparisons, meet government requirements, and can be transferred electronically between systems.

Each unit develops its own Key Indicators, which are measures of customer satisfaction, factors leading to customer satisfaction, and process measures. These indicators, along with financial measures, are reviewed by the I-Team quarterly and monthly, or more frequently by each unit.

2.1b   We ensure reliability, consistency, standardization, and rapid access to data and information through the use of computer systems and networks.

Our use of computer technology is one of our strengths. We are supported by a Corporate Information Systems Team of 100 people located in Norco, Whiting, and the plant sites. These resources keep abreast of changing technology, acquire and test appropriate software and hardware improvements, and maintain our systems. They employ systematic structured approaches to ensure software quality. Software development and modification are verified by user testing in a pilot-level environment before being put into full-scale use. The listing of systems in Figure 2.1 is an indication of the utility of our computer network.

Approaches used to ensure rapid and accurate data transfer include automated laboratory data entry at all manufacturing sites and Electronic Data Interchange (EDI) with customers and suppliers.

Update and review of quality and performance data are organized via our Process Management System (deals with information documentation; see Area 5.2a) and by site and business progress review approaches.

Computerized information transfer via electronic mail is highly used/de-

Data	Information Systems
Customer-Related	
Order Entry	Electronic Data Interchange
Customer Complaints, Returns	Problem Report System
Customer Satisfaction Survey	Market Research Survey
Product Performance	Customer Data Interchange, Product Management System
On-Time Delivery	Distribution Management System
Internal Operations	
Product Properties	Product Management System
Process Specifications	PMS and Plant Manufacturing Systems
Process Control	PMS
Yields	Plant Manufacturing Systems
Inventory Effectiveness	Finished Product Maintenance System
Preventive Maintenance	Preventive Maintenance Achievement System
ISO Certification	
Company Performance—Employee Related	
Employment History	Coworker Information System
Personal Data	CIS
Coworker Views	Coworker Climate System
Career Development Plans	Coworker Promotion System
Community Participation	PC databases
Key Indicator Performance	PMS and Financial Information Analysis System
Training Activity	CIS
Suggestion Activity	CIS
Company Performance—Safety, Health and Environment	
Safety Incidents	Plant Databases, Varifilm Safety Reporting System
Waste	Waste Information System
Materials Safety	Materials Safety Data Sheet
Environmental Incidents	Plant Databases, Corporate Prevent Incidents Systems
Company Performance—Quality Performance	
Complaints	PRS
Competitive Comparisons	Competitive Databases
Market Share	MRS, Personal Computer Databases
Benchmarks	QUality Information System
Gain Share	Unit Records
Quality Survey Trends	QUIS, Plant Database
Supplier Performance	
Material Specifications	PMS
Supplier Total Quality Trends	Supplier Database
Cost & Financial	
Annual Budgets	Financial Information Analysis System
Customer Sales	DMS, FIAS
Sales & Earnings	FIAS
Capital Expenditures	Investment Management System

Figure 2.1 Example of Varifilm Data

ployed for communication within Varifilm. Every salaried coworker around the world has an account, and most hourly people have access to electronic mail. All cafeterias have E-mail desks for use by any coworker, and many customers and suppliers also have accounts. Messages can be easily sent to any account around the world. We also make extensive use of voice mail systems.

2.1c Continuous improvement of the scope and management of data is essential in this information age. Continuous improvement processes used throughout Varifilm are also used to improve the scope and management of our data. The assessment process, customer input, and the Process Management System (PMS) are used to map, measure and improve our processes. The use of EDI, electronic mail and common databases has dramatically reduced cycle time. Voice mail wait time is monitored and managed at 15 seconds or less between 8 a.m. and 9 a.m., the busiest time of day. (Ref. Item 6.3.)

Methods to improve the scope and quality of data and information include:

Process	Improvements
Benchmarking	Helped us see the power of cycle time as a measure
Customer Input	Measurements of our performance in meeting delivery time requests
	Measurement of response to request for information
Computer Technology	Improvements in data entry capability
Key Indicators	Improvements in reporting and identification processes
User "Steering Teams"	Expanded functionality of the Product Management System

An indicator of data/information adequacy is audit results of our quality system.

2.2 Competitive Comparisons and Benchmarking

2.2a Benchmarking and competitive comparisons are used extensively in Varifilm to address a business or function's critical success factors and priorities—importance for customer satisfaction, impact on success in the marketplace, operational performance, impact on strategic/industry needs, and competitive activities.

We select benchmarking partners from within the company and the industry and search for best practices wherever they can be found. We have had much success linking like functions and operations from different geographical locations.

Selection criteria include:

- International business
- Strong financial performance
- Capital intensive, manufacturing-based company
- A Baldrige winner or finalist
- Recognized leader in the industry
- Strong reputation in the function being studied
- Performance metrics

2.2b   We have steadily increased the number and scope of our benchmark studies and competitive comparisons.

In 1989, Varifilm hired the T. A. Barns consulting firm to prepare functional excellence benchmarking studies of "Best of the Best" practices such as service, productivity and yield comparisons. Since then, Varifilm has developed its Benchmarking Team led by three internal experts. Ad hoc committees, marketing surveys, and customer and supplier contacts provide data for strategic planning and analysis of competitive practices. The three experts also act as coaches for business teams and HPWS teams who are interested in benchmarking.

Our benchmark studies have increased from 4 in 1989 to 20 in 1992. Figure 2.2 lists some of the studies conducted since 1990 and shows the scope and sources of competitive and benchmark data.

The Varifilm Finance and Planning Department collects and uses vendor comparative data as part of its supplier partnership program.

Competitive comparisons have always been a strong focus of our business teams. We use data from our global competitive intelligence databases to estimate indices of competition (sales, capacity, cost, etc.). Based on trends assessment, we use "competitive intelligence" to develop strategies for market, product, manufacturing, technical, environment, and resource developments which we document in the annual Business Plan (see Item 3.1). One innovative way to collect competitive intelligence is our trade show debrief process which is led by our benchmarking experts.

2.2c   The Varifilm Benchmarking Process (Figure 2.3), resourced by our experts, helps us build synergy from numerous studies of best practices. Comparisons between our processes and best-in-class processes point out opportunities for improvement. This information is used by our business and/or functional teams to develop solutions to attain improved performance. Where possible, non-industry comparisons are also used. Much has been learned from the service and support sectors.

Study Focus	Number of Participants	Study Application
Product & Service Quality		
Customer Service	4 companies 3 Baldrige winners	• One-Call-Quote System • Cellular phone for each sales representative
Customer Focused	4 companies	Introduced innovative design process and cycle time management (Omega/CTE process)
Customer Satisfaction		
Recyclable Competitive Study	6 companies	Decision to start up Recyclables business
Domestic Film Competitive Study	7 companies	Reorganization of the Electrical business
Customer Satisfaction Survey	25 top customers	Defined key success indicators for customers of Industrial Wrap; incorporated into business plans
Internal Operations, Business Processes, Support Services, Coworkers		
Computer Systems	5 companies, 1 supplier	Designed and implemented our global on-line interactive order entry system
High Performance Work System	5 companies	Developed our HPWS
Child Care	3 companies	Pilot program developed
Film Distribution	1 educational institution 3 service companies	• Revised organization structure • Decentralized decision-making
Plant Safety	3 leading companies in safety	Developed safety training program
Maintenance	2 airlines 3 industrial companies	Developed plans to improve craftsmen effectiveness and scheduling
Suppliers		
Supplier Partnerships	5 leading companies	• Revised certification process • Improved recognition program

Figure 2.2   Representative 1990s Benchmark Studies

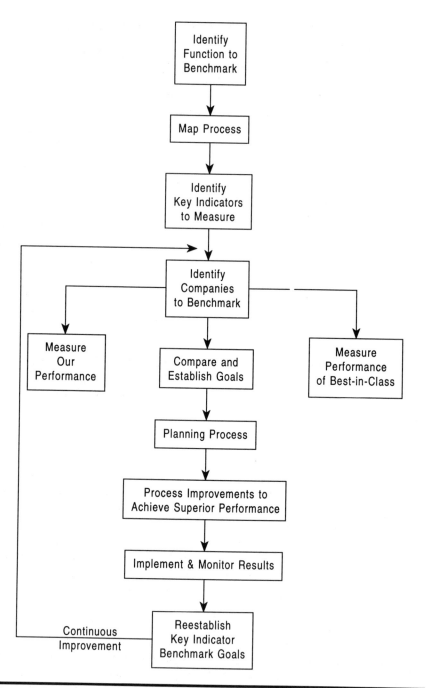

Figure 2.3   Varifilm Benchmark Process

2.2d   Varifilm has a Benchmarking Resource Center, comprised of a manager and three experts.

We actively participate in a network of professional benchmarkers and in professional associations such as the American Benchmarking Center and the Strategic Benchmarking Institute to evaluate new approaches for identifying best-in-class companies. We search computerized databases to identify companies recognized as leaders in specific areas. We also employ consultants to gather business information and metrics to identify companies that are "excellent" in specific functions.

2.3 Analysis and Uses of Company-Level Data

2.3a   We use a variety of approaches to collect customer data, which are routed to the specific groups for aggregation/analysis. For example, customer purchase information is directed to Marketing; complaint information goes to Technical Marketing and Manufacturing; new technology information goes to the Technical organization; and strategic information goes to business leadership. Most of the time, our customers communicate information directly to the appropriate group.

Problem information requiring immediate or near-term action is distributed, as quickly as possible, to people responsible for resolution (electronic mail is usually used). Customer-identified problems are automatically given top priority. Our Technical Marketing and Manufacturing people give these problems top priority until they are resolved. If a problem is not easily resolved or demands additional resources, business leadership gets involved to shift resources to ensure resolution.

Performance in each of our five key customer satisfaction requirements is tracked vs. customer satisfaction. This analysis has confirmed that what customers tell us is in fact a determinant of customer action as measured by market share. Representative summary charts are shown in Figure 2.4.

For service quality performance, our customer satisfaction survey points us to direct measures, such as percent of product meeting delivery time commitment. A corporate study has uncovered a correlation between non-management visits to customers and overall customer satisfaction. Customer satisfaction has led to long-term contracts and has improved market share, especially in a period of economic uncertainty such as 1992.

Each of our businesses is led by a leadership team comprised of the overall business leader, leaders for each major function (e.g., human resources, partnership team representative, manufacturing, marketing, technical) and others as appropriate. For purposes of overall planning and review, customer data are systematically organized and brought into team meetings. Marketing and Tech-

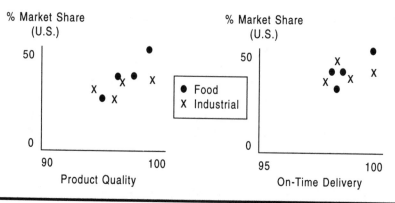

Figure 2.4 Varifilm Key Customers

nical Marketing are the key organizations for data analysis/aggregation and presentation. For the business planning process, described in Category 3.0, customer data brought into the process include satisfaction data, product and service performance data, new product information, strategic partnership factors, and competitive information.

2.3b Manufacturing and Technical groups are responsible for performance data in manufacturing; however, every support function deals with its performance data (e.g., the Information Systems organization analyzes computer performance). Generic operational measures, commonly tracked at every level, are cycle time of key processes and defects important to internal or external customers.

Operational performance is systematically reviewed within each sub-unit of the business (e.g., plant site, Technical group, Information Systems group). When a problem is found, that sub-unit is responsible for correcting it. When resources and priorities are an issue, the I-Team or Business Team is involved. More often, operational data are used for continuous improvement. Teams analyze performance data using problem-solving skills to capitalize on performance that exceeded expectations as well as correcting poor performance.

The analysis and priority setting process includes:

1. Identify issues.

2. Determine revenue at risk.

3. Prioritize issues.

4.   Identify performance measures.

5.   Determine targets.

Each functional organization brings its operational analyses as input to the business plan development process. Key Indicators include First Pass Yield, inventory measures, environmental measures, safety measures, and functional performance measures.

2.3c   Each business has financial analysts and market strategists who analyze and summarize financial and market trends.

We have corporate standards for the analysis of financial information [e.g., calculation of Return on Asset (ROA), After Tax Operating Income (ATOI), cash flow, profit margin, and fixed cost productivity]. Market trend analyses vary depending on the competitive environment. Data are reviewed regularly and summarized for use in the planning process.

2.3d   Specific analysis cycle time is one key indicator (e.g., financial closing cycle). The basic key indicator is achievement of bottom line results (e.g., Do we have the "right" data at the right time to focus our efforts to achieve cost reduction and increases in revenue, market share, and profit?).

Past correlation studies have highlighted some issues important to both profitability and customer satisfaction. It is expected that further study in 1993 of VCIC item scores will uncover additional insight.

Customer surveys are leading indicators of purchase intent, lagging indicators of performance. In 1989, the top ten process issues were identified. Pre- and post- "Fix" purchase intent surveys were conducted. We have been able to track improved sales and now rank key product/process attributes.

Benchmarking gives us new ideas on analysis methods and key indicators. Cycle time reduction techniques include flowcharting and identification of "non-value-adding work." We used both of these methods in reducing the financial closing cycle by 70%. We benchmarked a leading Korean company's "Management By Planning" process to learn about integrating data for business planning. Approaches which help us integrate all analyses for effective decision-making include:

■   Multifunctional business leadership team. Owners of each type of data are represented on the team.

■   Our partnership focus ensures that all key bases are touched in the planning process.

CATEGORY 3.0
STRATEGIC QUALITY PLANNING

3.1 Strategic Quality and Company Performance Planning Process

3.1a   We have an integrated, systematic, and rigorous business planning process. In the late 1980s, we began integrating our quality and business plans. Today, all businesses have totally integrated their quality and business plans—*all* key quality factors impacting external customers and *all* key quality requirements impacting internal operations are included in the business plan. The Strategic Quality Planning Process (SQPP) model was developed in 1990 to ensure this integration. (See Figure 3.1.) The I-Team adopted SQPP for Varifilm strategic quality planning.

SQPP includes:

1. Analysis of the critical factors including VCIC assessment;

2. Planning: Strategic Business Intent; Alignment with Varifilm's Mission, Policy, Values; Business Operating Plans;

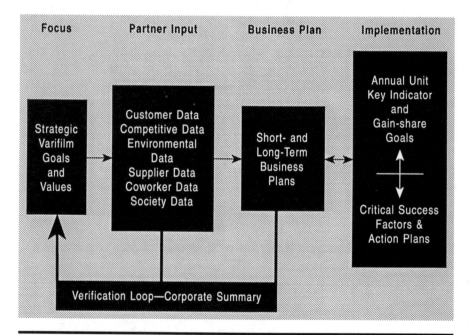

Figure 3.1   Strategic Quality Planning Process

3. Implementation: Deployment to the work units;

4. Input from coworkers across levels, sites, functions, suppliers, and customers;

5. Focus on our partners.

Business plans address customer requirements; competitive pressures; financial, market, and societal risks; our process and service capabilities; and our supplier capabilities. We use a variety of information sources from inside and outside Varifilm. (See Category 2.0, Figure 2.1.)

Customer Requirements	Customer surveys, Product Specification Reviews, customer teams, focus groups, Fitness Reviews, and I-Team and coworker visits
Competitive Environment	Customer/supplier feedback, benchmark studies, trade assessments, reports of competitive intent, production capability, quality of products and services
Risk Analysis	Market team assessments, government requirements, societal concerns, corporate financial/market reports, global financial/market assessments, capital expenditure needs assessment, environmental cycles
Our Capability	Controlled Operating System (COS) updates, technology assessments, supplier technology developments, technical/ engineering reports, Cpk
Supplier Capabilities	Supplier partnership, Cpk, Joint Specifications Development, certification audits, Material Specification Reviews, ISO 9000
Future Business Factors	Customer surveys, Vision, and Mission

Our businesses analyze their data to (1) assess where they are versus their quality goals, profit objectives, competitors, and industry trends; and (2) identify improvement opportunities.

To ensure that quality factors are included in the business plan, most businesses get feedback on customer-related and internal performance-related requirements from coworkers, customers, and suppliers via the Total Quality Fitness Review. VCIC is an integral part of the Total Quality Management (TQM) process.

All businesses develop a portfolio which includes an assessment of their financial performance and strategies, Key Indicators, and their total VCIC assessment score and goal. The I-Team reviews this information to (1) verify alignment with Varifilm's Vision, Mission, and continuous improvement strategies; and (2) authorize resource plans.

The calendar of planning processes is rigorously followed:

March–April   Business Customer Satisfaction Surveys completed.

May–June   Quality assessment complete (VCIC every two years).

June–August   Business strategy reviews are completed.

September   Costs and profit objectives are established.

November   Corporate alignment is achieved. Budget (one year) and Plan (five year) finalized. Key Indicators finalized.

December   Critical Operating Tasks for the coming year are established. Unit, team, and individual objectives set, aligned with goals.

Each business uses the aligned business plan to develop critical operating tasks, which are shared with all coworkers to enable them to stay focused on continuous improvement.

3.1b   Varifilm's strategic direction is guided by the Board of Directors and the I-Team. Business selection and emphasis follow the direction set during the annual planning process. Direction is discussed and reviewed with the board annually.

Realignment of the work processes has started with the introduction of process management concepts and the Phase III Partnership/HPWS work redesign. The partnership effort encourages process and analysis and process redesign.

The five-step partnership process is:

1. **Change event:**   Unit meets to hear from customers, suppliers, and leadership. Requirements, competitors, and vision are presented.

2. **Design team:**   A cross-functional design team is formed to develop and present a new structure which will meet the requirements of customers and coworkers. (Presentation and acceptance follow.)

3. **Work teams established:**   Work teams are established and develop their own process flow.

4. **Training:**   Cross-training occurs on redesigned process and job responsibilities.

5. **Implementation and continuous improvement.**

The same process analysis and improvement in Step 3 are now part of a course for HPWS teams. The teams use the process to improve and measure their own processes. Unit Key Indicators are aligned and improvement measured. Once the process is mapped, the ongoing team annually reviews its process for improvement. Several plants have hired JIT Associates to implement similar process improvement team training. Since 1990, six plants have implemented the process. (See Item 4.1.)

Unit and team activities, aligned with the strategic plan (see Item 3.1), are reviewed quarterly by the Invincible Team Key Indicator review and the annual unit review (see Item 1.2). Operational performance, energy and material utilization, waste reduction, productivity, product quality, and labor are all included.

3.1c   Each work unit develops implementation action plans and schedules.

Business leaders communicate the critical operating tasks throughout their organizations. Presentations are made at each site, and they are available on videotape and electronic bulletin board systems at each site so everyone can become familiar with them. After the initial presentation, a cascading approach is used.

1. Supervision discusses strategies and plans applicable to their work units. Suppliers are also engaged in this process as appropriate.

2. Resources are committed to achieve the desired results outlined in the critical operating tasks and are based on scope and priority.

3. Business leaders "close the loop" by modifying the plan, as required, based on coworker and supplier input.

Our coworkers are empowered to update their systems and processes as part of their continuous improvement efforts. Graphs and charts of business measures (Key Indicators) are prominently displayed so everyone can track progress toward meeting strategic intent and gain-sharing goals.

Gain-sharing was negotiated in 1991. Each plant or unit has a gain-share committee, consisting of leadership, coworkers, and union representatives. The committee selects 3–5 customer-related goals that must include a customer service, product quality, and cost goal. These goals are submitted to and approved by the I-Team to assure fairness. Payout is targeted at 5% of annual salary if goals are achieved. The potential range is 0–10%. Gain-share aligns key indicators to each individual coworker. This is one tool used to align Varifilm's goals.

3.1d   Our multifunctional teams coordinate business plans and facilitate alignment with Varifilm plans. (Ref. Area 2.3a.) Members of the planning group attend courses and seminars given by leading business schools to stay abreast of leading edge technologies. Based on their learnings, they identify improvement opportunities in our planning process and implement changes as needed.

3.2 Quality and Performance Plans

3.2a   Our businesses use customer requirements, competitive intelligence, and assessment of internal capabilities to define key quality factors and company performance requirements.

Key quality factors are based on customers' perceptions obtained from our customer partnership meetings and verified through our satisfaction surveys. Factors vary from business to business. However, those common to our main businesses include product quality; on-time delivery; commitment to the customer's industry; partnership; responsiveness to and understanding of customer requirements; and new product development. In addition to customer satisfaction and related directions, we also set goals for coworker and public responsibility.

Key company performance requirements are derived from the needs of our defined partners and are defined through the planning process. Major items are VCIC score, First Pass Yield, cost and revenue, profits, waste, EPA-related emission levels, safety, public perception (most admired), and coworker satisfaction.

3.2b   Varifilm's short-term quality and performance directions and goals focus on opportunities critical to our partners and utilize Key Indicators. (See Figures 3.2 and 3.3.)

Each business develops its short-term quality goals and objectives consistent with the five-year business plan. The goals focus on actionable results which address key customers' requirements and are aligned with Varifilm's goals and directions. These goals are documented in each business plan as well as in each business' critical operating tasks for the year. Short-term goals are most visible in the Key Indicator reporting and in each unit's gain-sharing objectives. As an example, Figure 3.3 shows some quality goals for three of our businesses.

3.2c   Varifilm long-term goals ensure our future! To achieve long-range goals, our businesses identify their global capital equipment, facilities, education and training, and personnel requirements for their plans and strategies.

Specific long-term goals include being the low cost producer of industrial and food packaging film and having the number one market share in those markets in which we compete.

Key Indicators are projected for five years. Generally, Varifilm's goal is to double or halve (as appropriate) the Key Indicator in four years. This goal creates a stretch approach, which has supported continuous improvement but also created a paradigm change mentality.

		Partners		
Coworkers	Society	Stockholders	Customers	Suppliers

Short-Term Goals 1993

Complete 20-hour SMT training Part time Work Option Coworker Satisfaction Gain-share Diversity training	Day Care Pilot 10x EPA requirements	ROA top quartile Make Most Admired Company List	Goals specific to business (see Figure 3.3) Customer	Reduce supplier base by 30%

Long-Term Goals 1996

>95% work force in High Performance Work System Teams by 1993	20x EPA requirements	ROA top quartile Growth 12%/year Market share leader	Goals specific to businesses (See Figure 3.3)	100% certified suppliers

Figure 3.2   Varifilm Short- and Long-Term Goals

Business	Goal	1991 (Actual)	1992	1993	1998
Food	Product Change Cycle Time	12 hrs.	8 hrs.	4 hrs.	2 hrs.
Packaging	Product Introduction Cycle Time	10 mos.	6 mos.	4 mos.	2 mos.
	% Earnings from New Products	14%	23%	25%	25%
	On-Time Delivery	90%	99%	99.9%	6 Sigma
Industrial Film	On-Time Delivery (Request)	85%	95%	99%	100%
	First Pass Yield	80%	85%	90%	95%
	Customer Satisfaction Index	80	85	90	95
Recyclables	Customer Satisfaction Index	85	90	95	97
	Employee Satisfaction	55%	60%	68%	72%
	Broken Promises (On-Time Delivery)	0.8%	0.2%	0%	0%
	VCIC Score	450	550	650	750

Figure 3.3   Examples of Business Quality Goals

3.2d All Varifilm businesses are keenly aware of market trends and competitive directions and develop their improvement plans so they can continue to perform well in the foreseeable future.

A clear example of this approach is illustrated by our Food Packaging business. This business is primarily domestic in focus and has tough domestic competitors. At this point in time, a leading Japanese film company (JFC) is building a state-of-the-art plant in southern California. We can project the selling price and product quality. In a dramatic display of commitment to the business, Varifilm committed $500 million to upgrade our equipment and laid out a plan to improve quality and hold or reduce cost in order to counter this strong competitive threat. We project our quality and price levels to be very competitive. Specifically, in Food Packaging's "Critical Operating Tasks," goals are identified for 1993 through 1998, and projected benchmarks are given for each.

CATEGORY 4.0
HUMAN RESOURCE DEVELOPMENT AND MANAGEMENT

4.1 Human Resource Planning and Management

4.1a Human Resource management has closely aligned itself with the businesses and goals of Varifilm. Since the implementation of Phase II and Phase III, Human Resources (HR) has been actively involved as a functional member of each business. As part of the business planning process, training and involvement requirements are defined. The focus has changed from phase to phase. During Phase I, HR focused on supervisor development, job descriptions, grievance procedures, process specification development, and negotiations. Phase II brought TQM training, statistics training, team training, participation, recognition, affirmative action, and coworker feedback systems. Phase III moved to coworker involvement, HPWS, coach training, diversity training and implementation, and coworker-developed skill training.

Our human resource management approach is a vital part of achieving coworker partnership. Our HR goals reflect a commitment to people development, from the constant goal of improving safety to the short- and long-term goals cited in Area 3.2c (Self Managed Teams, HPWS training, gain-sharing, diversity). We address these various goals through our efforts in education and training, recruitment, involvement, empowerment, and recognition. Long-term goals focus on the work team of the future, including the technical training that will be required.

Human Resources has its own set of Key Indicators which align and support business indicators. We envision an environment that truly and totally VALUES

PEOPLE. That means being caring enough, and conscientious enough, to place the needs of our people at the heart of everything we do, at the center of all our aspirations. It means HR management that translates our concern for people into the total fabric of all that we are.

1. **Education and Training.**   Varifilm's "People Value"—"Value and Respect for the Individual"—We realize that only by achieving the growth and development of our people can we attain our quality and performance objectives. Education and training are important for developing Varifilm people, and we apply these methods to promote health and safety, co-worker development, involvement, skill development, diversity, and greater customer focus. We respond to changing business and customer needs with our quality education programs.

    Phase II: With intensifying competition, we needed greater involvement with our customers. We implemented TQM training, customer requirement training, and quality skills training. These initiatives greatly increased customer contact for heightened coworker sensitivity to customer needs and continuous improvement.

    Phase III: SMT/HPWS process management, understanding the business, and creating work teams in a variety of learning experiences. This phase moves to a system of performing work in which all coworkers join together to drive the quality of the business results, and performance is valued over rank.

    Empowerment: Hundreds of ad hoc teams sprang up in the '80s for specific tasks and still function today. Currently, there are many self-directed (empowered) teams which operate and maintain the business processes.

2. **Mobility, Flexibility and Changes.**   HPWS, emphasizing performance over rank, will further empower coworkers, and our gain-sharing for all coworkers is reducing artificial distinctions. We are proud of our progress and are determined that it continue.

3. **Recognition.**   We enthusiastically recognize and reward individual and team contributions. That conscientiousness makes a difference. We recognized 23% of our work force in 1991 with monetary awards and have met our goal of 25% in 1992. (See Area 4.4b.) Highly effective, non-monetary coworker awards include plaques, mementos, tickets, merchandise, dinners, celebrations, donuts and coffee, and letters of recognition. Many of these are given by coworkers. HPWS, when fully deployed, will reward skills and performance, not seniority.

4. **Recruitment.**   We are convinced that, to remain competitive, our work force must reflect an increasingly diverse society. That is why our proactive

hiring goal requires that new hires at the management/professional level reflect the diversity of our country which we need as a company to succeed. This recruitment requirement also stands for our non-U.S. units. We also have an upward mobility goal that stipulates parity by 1998 at all levels, including the executive payroll and Board of Directors.

4.1b   Our goal is a well-trained, diversified, empowered work force.

Hiring Diversity.   Since 1979, our goal for hiring women and people of color for management/professional positions is 45–50%. We have exceeded that goal in each of the last five years.

Upward Mobility.   Our goal is to achieve parity at every level of the professional and managerial group with the representation of women and people of color within the Varifilm work force. Thus, if 24% of professional and managerial coworkers are women (as is currently true at Varifilm), then women should be 24% of every level all the way up to the Board of Directors and CEO.

Currently, we have 24% women and 13% people of color at parity up to the manager level. Above that, the percentages fall off significantly. We have proactive programs to increase manager and above representation.

Retention.   Our goal is to retain all coworkers we hire.

Diversity.   Our goal is to value diversity and utilize the unique skills, abilities, and interests of each individual. We recognize that to be successful Varifilm coworkers must work in a quality way and that the skills and abilities of all coworkers are required. We offer seminars and workshops on racial and gender diversity. We have changed our perspective from expecting the individual to fit the organization to helping the organization accept and manage diverse and unique individuals.

Affirmative Action.   Our diversity training and approach has replaced

Item	1988	1989	1990	1991	1992
Minorities in Management as % of Total Hires	35%	39%	58%	60%	55%
Salaried Females as % of Total Hires	15%	15%	18%	23%	25%
Wage Roll Females as % of Total Hires	45%	45%	46%	47%	49%
Salaried Blacks as % of Total Hires	10%	10%	11%	12%	13%
Wage Roll Blacks as % of Total Hires	15%	15%	15%	15%	15%
% Turnover Per Year	8%	6%	5%	6%	4%
% Minority Turnover Per Year	12%	8%	7%	6%	5%

Figure 4.1   Hiring Diversity

past affirmative action programs. While we are committed to affirmative action and measure and report as required by the government, our goals and objectives are much more aggressive. We offer affirmative action support for those seeking assistance in correcting any situation or in filing a complaint. The program has resulted in special training for several individuals. We support outstanding local minority students with scholarships and summer job programs.

One Salary Roll by Year-End, 1995. We are committed to an environment that genuinely values people. As an expression of that idea, we will achieve one salary roll by the end of 1995. Administratively, all coworkers will be on salary and will receive the same treatment regarding development and pay, while meeting legal requirements, without regard to type of position.

Interviewing Process Improvements to Better Reflect Needs. To ensure that we hire operating people with value for teamwork, risk-taking, and diversity, we have changed our hiring process to include three interview levels, job orientation including one three-hour team-building session, peer evaluation, and exercises to demonstrate problem-solving abilities, basic skills, and special technical skills. HPWS teams are now doing their own hiring using this documented process.

4.1c We use data from coworker surveys to improve the development and effectiveness of our work force and support processes. In the mid '80s we instituted the Coworker Climate Survey to measure coworker attitudes, understand the issues affecting coworkers, measure our progress and assess our future course. The survey monitors 11 Key Indicators among all coworkers such as well-being, satisfaction, and involvement.

Management compares survey results among sites, against the Corporate Leadership Survey (initiated in May 1991 and used throughout the Company at all levels) and against the Wheaton data (compares Varifilm to 13 other major companies). The Coworker Climate Survey (see Area 1.2d) and VCIC process are also used to measure changes and identify areas for proactive or corrective action.

Our turnover of all rolls is so low that it has ceased to be a reported measurement. We still track for diversity purposes. Historical data are only used for hiring and researching projections. We attribute this to pay and benefits, treatment of people, recognized opportunities for advancement, high ethical standards, and concern for doing the right thing.

What is more, when turnover is decreased and people are involved in continually improving their results together, it only makes sense that mutual loyalty and teamwork build. That is what seems to be happening more often at Varifilm.

4.2 Employee Involvement

4.2a   Our Self Managed Team (HPWS) process and opportunities for improvement suggestion systems actively seek and utilize coworker contributions.

The Team Training Process is a tremendous investment in our people. Its initial phase is a four-day seminar, "Encouraging Empowered Teams" (EET), for team leaders or a two-day seminar, "Self Managed Teams," for all coworkers.

In training, when a person learns that he/she can safely take more of a risk than he/she had believed, whether climbing a pole or jumping off a ledge—especially with the total and active support of the team cheering him/her on, that same coworker becomes more willing in the work place to handle the risk of a new idea, to offer feedback for improvement, or to push him/herself to make a change enhancing personal performance.

A series of four continuous development modules (one day each for team members and three days each for skill development, with one point person per team) are led by coworkers and follow the introductory piece. These modules integrate involvement and empowerment with a specific quality improvement project. (See Figure 4.2 for an overview of each module.)

We also share this training with our direct and downstream customers and suppliers. At our Whiting plant, for example, a cross-functional team of marketing and plant people participated in the two-day session with people from one of our largest customers. They shared their business concerns and needs. As a result of successful interchanges like these, we plan to share our process with more direct and downstream customers.

The training modules emphasize the success of synergy and enable teams to develop and empower themselves. Each natural work group team completes a meaningful quality project that improves some part of its actual work performance. Every coworker is a member of a team with which he/she interacts for an ongoing series of developmental experiential learning activities.

Most coworkers participate on or with several teams. We have natural self-directed work teams, task teams, design teams, customer partnership teams, supplier partnership teams, safety teams, quality teams, etc. Typically, these

1. **Team Organization Concepts**	Values, Vision, organization structure, recognition, participation
2. **Work Redesign**	Concepts of work redesign, how to get started
3. **Process Improvement**	How to map, measure, and improve a process
4. **Problem-Solving Skills**	Varifilm's problem-solving approach and process

Figure 4.2   Self Managed Team Modules

	Open Line				Suggestions	
	Wage Roll		Salaried			
Year	Actual	Goal	Actual	Goal	Actual	Goal
1988	100	—	10	20	550	500
1989	180	100	15	20	800	750
1990	111	100	20	20	1000	1000
1991	89	100	25	20	2000	1500
1992	37	50	19	20	3500	2500
1993	—	25	—	20	—	4000

Figure 4.3   Coworker Involvement in Open Line and Suggestion Systems

teams are cross-functional, spanning coworker levels to get the skills, knowledge, and abilities required to achieve the improvement objective.

Suggestion Systems traditionally offer opportunities for coworkers to contribute their ideas to improve safety, quality of product or service, the workplace, or other aspects of the business. Empowered learning teams have now taken over administration of the suggestion systems and brought about significant improvements in cycle time and quality of suggestion and time to implementation. Participants receive initial feedback within 3 days concerning the status of their suggestions and periodically thereafter regarding progress toward implementation. Monetary awards are given based on tangible savings or intangible value.

To promote a free flow of coworker communication, we have an open door policy and open line written process. Any coworker can discuss any suggestion, problem, concern or idea with any member of management and receive an immediate response. This is consistent with our move from a hierarchical management system to a teamwork/involvement culture, encouraged by OE and our SMT process. With the Open Line Process, a written question or suggestion receives the normal three-day written feedback. As teams have become a way of life, open line volume has significantly decreased.

4.2b   Our Self Managed Team process is synonymous with increased coworker empowerment, responsibility, and innovation.

SMT increases coworker responsibility in many self-directed work teams, cross-functional teams, and tasks teams—empowering all coworkers at all levels. Our training initiatives enable coworkers to interact successfully with customers and suppliers on scheduled customer plant trips, quality task teams, and problem-solving teams.

Wage roll coworkers now lead visits to customer plants and orientations of customers visiting our facilities. These visits by coworker teams to customer sites not only improve performance, they also enhance satisfaction. They help our people now realize that they are seen as more than just "bodies" to perform a task; they are thinking, creative members of the team who can achieve more if they have a chance to know and experience more. In addition, through these contacts, coworkers often generate a personal sense of loyalty to their customers—"Mary needs it this way. I know because I was there and she is counting on us!" The enthusiasm and perspective these customer contacts build are, frankly, nothing short of wonderful, and a critical part of understanding and meeting our customer requirements.

All categories of coworkers are linked to empowerment through the business objectives and key indicators. With clear goals, training, and encouragement to act, everyone is involved in continuous improvement activities. Management or leadership's role is to support teams as they do their job. Unit leadership is also empowered to redesign team activities and, when combined with HPWS activities, major improvements have occurred.

4.2c SMT participation, CCS data, participation in our suggestion systems, and use of tools are used to evaluate the extent and effectiveness of coworker involvement.

Coworker involvement, empowerment, and innovation are measured through the Coworker Climate Survey, tracking/assessing coworker suggestions and their results, and team participation. Our suggestion goal is for every coworker to make at least three suggestions per year. We ensure that all rolls participate.

Self Managed Teams. Participation was 96% for team leaders. Eighty-one percent of other team members, spanning all categories of coworkers, attended either the two-day or four-day training process.

Suggestions come from a broad cross-section of coworkers, with most submitted by wage roll coworkers. Salaried coworkers generally discuss their suggestions with their team, who can decide to adopt and implement them. (Ref. Area 4.2a.)

Operational Linkage. Key Indicators are reviewed by the I-Team once a quarter and each unit once a year. Coworker involvement data are not only reviewed but analyzed in context with all other unit data. (Ref. Item 3.1.)

Coworker Climate Survey Results. Figure 4.4 shows the percentage of favorable coworker responses by category, many of which measure some aspect of perceptions around involvement. Most categories have shown improvement during a time of change with HPWS, significant training and cultural redirection activities, and a national recession. We attribute this to our focus on the individual, team training, self managed teams, customer focus, and strong leadership involvement.

	Percent Favorable		
Survey Index	1988	1990	1992
Capacity to Act	30	42	61
Coworker Satisfaction	48	55	65
Coworker Involvement	25	42	58
Quality Leadership	52	49	67
Customer Focus	32	43	62
Commitment to Values	65	68	72
Communications	68	68	68
Training	40	43	45
Recognition	47	51	67
Valuing Diversity	32	70	75
Continuous Improvement	35	68	76

Figure 4.4   Wage Roll Coworker Involvement

	Percent Favorable			Benchmark Top Quartile
Survey Index	1988	1990	1992	
Capacity to Act	40	45	50	48
Coworker Satisfaction	68	71	75	64
Coworker Involvement	45	48	59	51
Quality Leadership	71	74	75	62
Customer Focus	51	53	67	58
Commitment to Values	67	72	77	67
Communications	65	66	70	65
Training	55	45	49	57
Recognition	45	48	67	66
Valuing Diversity	32	40	55	60
Continuous Improvement	39	70	80	55

Figure 4.5   Salaried Coworker Involvement

4.3 Employee Education and Training

4.3a   Everything we do in Varifilm flows from our concepts of vision, our partners, and the business direction established by senior management.

1. It was in that context that the I-Team focused on Total Quality Leadership and training in areas of Organizational Effectiveness, Focus on the Customer, and Self Managed Teams.

   Most of our businesses decided to become global players and, therefore, need ISO 9002 certification. A natural result was the training given to coworkers who will be responsible for achieving ISO certification.

   At the site level, training programs are in place for all categories of coworkers. Programs include new coworker orientation (two days quality and two days values, unit goals, introduction to products), extensive general and job-specific safety training, step-by-step standard practices, equipment training, and Controlled Operating Procedure training.

   All coworkers learn basic quality skills of problem-solving and self-managed teams. At the job skills level, training needs are performance based. Qualification is determined by test results—for technicians, lab operators, environmental system operators—or by peer or supervisor follow-up.

   At the individual level, job training is jointly determined by task and personal developmental objectives. For example, as individuals and teams move toward greater self-management, they need the tools/skills to perform their present tasks or prepare for the next ones (e.g., Statistical Process Control, Pareto analysis, cycle time reduction, specific job skills and leadership).

   Courses on quality and continuous improvement are developed and presented by corporate resources in Logistics and Operations and Human Resources. They offer courses in Total Quality Management (Phase II), Statistical Process Control, Design of Experiments, Problem Solving, Data Collection and Display, Statistics, Leadership of Continuous Improvement, Principles of Coaching, Fundamentals of Continuous Improvement, etc. Corporate course catalogs are continually upgraded and made available to coworkers on-line.

2. The introduction of SMT training was delivered by an outside consulting group at the five special centers established for the purpose. Consultants then trained "trainers" on the four SMT modules. The trainers, in turn, trained all teams on these modules and the team point-people on the more detailed material.

   Additional methods of dissemination are:

   - Off-site training facilities and outside consultants/equipment vendors
   - Internally developed workshops and seminars
   - Experiential learning

- Cascaded training (values)
- Individual and team training
- On-the-job training
- Self-training through access to training sections at sites which contain lending libraries and equipment that coworkers can check out for practice. The Corporation also offers an electronic catalog of course offerings and educational resources.
- Self-paced computer-aided training
- Traditional classroom approach

4.3b   Quality and related training has increased significantly.

A new plant coworker is trained for about 160 hours initially. About 25% (40 hours) is devoted to quality training. Training areas include: Quality orientation of policy, principles, values, SMT training, safety rules and procedures, equipment operation, dealing with hazardous materials, Process Management System, job procedures, Controlled Operating Procedures, quality checks, communicating quality issues, coordinating quality with internal suppliers and customers, terminology, Statistical Process Control, Product Quality Management, product specifications, product identification, and setting up equipment. When operators transfer from one area to another, they are trained on the equipment and standard practices for their new area of responsibility.

Average participation in SMT training in 1992 was 20.6 hours for every coworker in Varifilm. Our goal is to complete the processing with all coworkers by the end of 1993, which translates into another 28 hours/coworker.

Other job-related quality training available to our coworkers includes: Basic Statistics, Problem Solving, Statistical Process Control, Statistical Design of Experiments, Product Quality Management, Analysis of Variance, Strategy of Experimentation, Total Productive Maintenance, ISO 9000, Self Assessment– Malcolm Baldrige, Continuous Flow Manufacturing, Total Quality Management, Quality Circles, and Quality Function Deployment.

4.3c   Skill testing and participant feedback are used to evaluate and improve our training effectiveness. "Hard" skills (e.g., technician, laboratories, operator testing) are done in the classroom and laboratory to verify understanding of theory and practical application. Follow-up is done through job cycle checks. (See Area 4.3a.) "Soft" skills like empowerment and leadership are critiqued at the end of training so each participant can feedback learning and verify that training is adequate. Feedback forms are provided to instructors to enable them to improve their presentations. Coworker certification (first try) is tracked as a measure of course effectiveness.

4.3d Our coworker education and training trends show outstanding gains.

During the past four years, average hours of quality and related training per coworker per year for salaried people went from 15.0 to 111.0 ('88 to '92) and from 8.7 to 117.0 for wage roll. The forecast for '93 is 120 and 120, respectively.

4.4 Employee Performance and Recognition

4.4a Our recognition, promotion, compensation, reward, and feedback processes support quality and performance objectives.

In 1982, Varifilm tied its formal recognition policy to Quality Leadership as part of our quality principles to "Create an environment in which we value and recognize quality and innovation, increase individual involvement and teamwork, and seek full use of our talents to ensure that worldwide quality leadership is achieved and continually improved." In short, we intend that recognition should become the norm, rather than the exception.

Our processes recognize both business success and personal growth. Each unit has its own instant recognition program consisting of a thank-you card and small gift (less than $5 movie ticket, car wash, etc.). These can be used by any coworker and have averaged 2–3 per person per year over the past five years. Each unit also has a more formal unit quality award where individuals or teams submit a one-page write-up, and one (or more) is chosen for recognition each quarter. Both are considered non-monetary recognition vs. reward.

Recognition of personal growth for salaried coworkers is primarily driven by the Annual Progress Review process of annual discussion of contribution and development. This becomes the basis for promotion, salary, bonus, and other principal monetary rewards.

Wage coworkers discuss their contributions and needed improvements with team members and unit leaders as part of their training selection and gain-sharing reviews. Quality is an integral element in these discussions.

To support the recognition of personal growth and achievement, there are a number of specific awards that celebrate demonstrated success in Marketing (Customer Focus Award), Technology (Scientific Medal), Quality Leadership (Invincible Award), and Problem Solving (Root Cause Award). These Varifilm awards are augmented by business center awards recognizing functional and business excellence in creativity or a trait highly valued by the business center. At each site, newsletters, bulletin boards, flashing display boards, and video news recognize both team and individual success, allowing all to celebrate the success of their colleagues. Self Managed Teams encourage self-recognition among coworkers in work groups. Coworkers decide who should be recognized, and peer recognition is encouraged. As an example, in several areas at the Camden plant, the Suggestion System was revised by wage roll coworkers who now evaluate the suggestions.

We make a conscious effort to recognize teams as well as individuals. In some instances, we reward an entire business. One plant celebrated its business success by taking everyone on a one-day boat trip. This trip provided reward and recognition while reinforcing value for team building and encouraging even higher commitment to business excellence.

4.4b   Our Coworker Climate Survey provides feedback on how well coworkers rate our recognition programs.

Our key method for evaluating recognition effectiveness is the CCS. Specific questions are included that focus on recognition. Improvement teams are established to take action on those items identified for improvement. We also use the Baldrige Assessment process to measure each business' effectiveness in recognizing coworkers and to recommend changes for further improvement.

4.4c   Our coworker recognition and rewards have increased across all categories.

Before the end of 1982, fewer than 1% of coworkers received monetary awards. The Instant Recognition program provides thousands of instant recognition events each year. In addition all coworkers benefit from the gain-sharing program whose goals are tied to quality Key Indicator improvement and Varifilm performance. Gain-sharing has provided an annual payout to unit coworkers ranging from 1.4% to 9.7% of their annual salaries each year since 1991.

4.5 Employee Well-Being and Satisfaction

4.5a   Safety and health are top priorities.

All of our quality improvement programs are conducted with this mind-set. We benchmark our safety performance and procedures against leading companies in safety. Varifilm believes that all safety and health incidents, injuries, and job-related illnesses are preventable. As such, each job-related incident, injury, or illness is thoroughly investigated for cause and remedy by a team of coworkers. Investigations are publicized at the site (and elsewhere, if appropriate) so that each coworker can benefit from the learning.

We also have Safety, Health, and Ergonomic Teams at each site. These teams are made up of coworkers from all job levels. They implement programs to increase awareness, improve the work environment, and reduce injuries or illness. The CCS shows a top quartile (77–80%) for favorable comments on safety and health.

Coworkers also can train for fire brigade, emergency squad, or career/education enhancement programs. A cross-functional team at our Norco plant conducted a work and family survey in 1991 to learn more about total coworker needs and how the company might better support them. This ongoing study was initiated by coworkers and received full management support.

4.5b Developmental and job training are used extensively to support coworker development and/or accommodate change.

Developmental and job training are managed through our Tuition Credit Program, Job Training Programs, and Reassignment Programs. Our coworkers are encouraged to attend developmental and technical courses and seminars. Through our Promoting The Individual system, they are given opportunities to grow with their needs and interests. We also have a policy of promotion from within. Mentor programs are becoming increasingly prevalent as a way to improve communication and share career possibility ideas among coworkers.

Support for coworkers includes a variety of programs (complete health care programs):

- Holistic Health—our workplace health program
- Personal and family counseling programs
- Health club/YMCA membership support
- Alcohol & Chemical Dependence Rehabilitation
- Classes (family safety, boating safety, defensive driving, firearm safety, rape prevention, substance abuse awareness)

plus many other benefits (Coworker Assistance Program, site recreational areas, pre-tax savings plans, Child Care Locator, Flex Time, Parental Leave, Tuition Refund).

4.5c Coworker satisfaction is determined by Coworker Climate Survey results and one-on-one meetings with coworkers and their supervision.

4.5d On- and off-the-job safety and coworker satisfaction are indicators of coworker well-being and morale. Varifilm teaches and practices safety excellence, both on and off the job. Our safety performance is comparable to the best in the world. Our coworkers enjoy working conditions that are two times safer than the plastics industry average and ten times safer than all industry. Our sites compete for world safety records.

Our concerns for coworkers' on- and off-the-job safety inspired the development of the Individual Safety Program (ISP). ISP rape prevention and personal protection classes have received many awards and have been shared with our customers. Our coworker satisfaction is high. Our 1991 CCS data indicate 69% favorable response to the Business Success/Job Security category and 71% favorable response to the Like My Role category. The rate of coworker turnover is low, about 1% for salaried and 1.75% for wage roll (excluding retirements). These figures continue to be tracked for continuous improvement.

While about 80% of our wage roll coworkers are unionized, most belong to local, independent unions. Positive labor-management relations are most significantly demonstrated by the occurrence of no strikes in 18 years. Sensitivity to coworker needs has resulted in the fact that the union was asked to participate in the organization of all three U.S. Varifilm plants built since 1976.

We believe that we have been creating an environment within Varifilm—and our human resources are an important reason why—in which the continuous improvement approach becomes the limitless supply of fuel to keep the "pilot lights" burning when we ignite them in ourselves and our people. They will burn even more brightly in the years ahead, with even more satisfied and trained coworkers who even more fully help us meet the needs of the other partnerships to which we are so strongly committed. (Ref. Area 4.2d.)

CATEGORY 5.0
MANAGEMENT OF PROCESS QUALITY

5.1 Design and Introduction of Quality Products and Services

5.1a   We have a long, successful history of product and service innovations. We began the Varifilm business based on our successful research into film-based products. Since then, we have developed thousands of variants to respond to changing market demands and specific customer needs.

Traditionally, most Varifilm products were designed by first envisioning a product concept, developing market test samples to assess customer receptivity, and scaling directly from a semi-works scale to full production. Varifilm's **Controlled Operating Procedures (COP)** detail the six stages of product design and introduction.

More recently, Varifilm has developed marketing structures which provide more direct intelligence on market trends, customer needs, and processing capabilities. Varifilm's Technical Marketing resources identify new product/process ideas through interactive discussions with direct and downstream customers. Customers' needs and processing changes are translated into engineering and product specifications.

Still, we needed to increase the success rate of our product development and accelerate our "time-to-market" to remain competitive. In 1989, Varifilm conducted a benchmark study, "Customer-Focused Product/Process Development" against "best-in-class" companies. The study showed us that we needed to make improvements in product design leadership, methodology, and supplier partnerships. The "Omega" and Cycle Time Excellence (CTE) approaches address these needs.

"Omega" Process, developed in 1990 by a Varifilm Self Managed Team, enhances the methodology, organization, and customer/supplier involvement of Varifilm's COP approach. (See Figure 5.1.) The Food Packaging, Electrical, and Construction businesses (about 80% of sales) have implemented "Omega."

Cycle Time Excellence (see Figure 5.1), a product management methodology licensed by Timeclock Associates for new product design, mandates leadership involvement in the process. CTE components include:

- A Program Approval Committee of a business' top leaders to authorize and direct the product development;

- A cross-functional Product Development Core Team to conduct development;

- Phase reviews to ensure organizational alignment to proceed, stop, or repeat; and

- Documented methodology in product development guidance.

	COP	Omega Process	CTE
Customer requirements translated into design	Interactions with customer teams define define customer requirements. Requirements translated into design in Stage 1.	Customer partnership developed using QFD	Application of QFD using cross-functional teams assures translation into design
Quality requirements early in process	Product and process controls are established and tested to assure quality in Stage 3	Cross-functional teams address quality requirements in Stage 2; product and process controls are tested	Quality requirements are addressed in Stage 2. Team monitors process until completion.
Designs integrated to include all phases of production and delivery	Supporting systems verified in Stage 5	Supporting systems identified in Stage 4	Supporting systems tested in Stage 5
Process control plan	COP documentation in Stage 5	COP documentation in Stage 5	Documented Control Plan in Stage 4

Figure 5.1 Product Design Approaches

Recyclables adopted CTE in early 1991 and expanded to nine product development projects by year-end. Industrial plans to adopt it in 1993.

Customer requirement translation, addressing of quality requirements, production/delivery integration, and development of a process control plan are described in Figure 5.1.

5.1b   We identify product and service performance specifications during Stage 2, "Planning and Design" or "Feasibility," and we review them at the end of each test run and modify if necessary. Process specifications, developed during Stage 2, address process capability requirements.

5.1c   We conduct benchmark studies to identify improvement opportunities.

Our businesses pilot new practices they deem will add the greatest value and, based on their experience, expand and deploy to other sites and businesses. For example, as a result of our 1990 Customer Focused Product/Process Development benchmark study, we examined and tested the "Omega" and CTE processes. Our people are learning the QFD and robust design concepts imbedded in these processes. By year-end 1991, we completed our "Film Quality" benchmark study to identify further opportunities to improve our design processes.

5.2 Process Management: Product and Service Production and Delivery Processses

5.2a   Our overall system for manufacturing quality control is our Process Management System (PMS). PMS was developed in the mid-1970s by Food Packaging with our corporate statistical consulting group and deployed throughout Varifilm in the early 1980s. PMS is based on the concept of a "controlled process." We explicitly define a Controlled Process for each of our products through documentation and standard systems to ensure consistency each time we manufacture a given product. PMS includes the following components:

- A "Controlled Operating System" (COS), which documents equipment specifications, material specifications (for supply), production orders, Controlled Operations, Controlled Processing Procedures, Control Practices, measurement test methods and assessments, and plant tests and results for all production and measurement processes required for each product
- Routine variability analysis using process and measurement data
- Process control
- Measurement control
- Product release
- Management of change (modified processes, transfer of production between sites, etc.)

■ Product handling, packaging, and distribution

■ Supplier quality

■ Annual audits

We define our PMS in a set of Varifilm *Controlled Operating Procedures.* Over 15 (down from 30) full-time people administer PMS and keep COP up-to-date. Because of this fully deployed and refined approach, we have been able to achieve ISO 9002 registration in 90% of our units, generally in less than one year after starting. PMS is now a team responsibility.

Within PMS, we measure product properties which predict successful customer end-use requirements. A representative list of our product properties for Food Wrap is shown in Figure 5.2.

For all important properties, we use statistical methods to detect drifts from aim. We have used Statistical Process Control (SPC) since the mid-1970s. We have refined this method so that it calculates how far off-aim the process has drifted, highlights ineffective and control responses to signals, and provides automatic adjustments to minimal drifts as well as notifying the operator of the drift and adjustment.

As a final quality test, we release the product from our manufacturing operation based on a statistical sampling of a defined "lot" of product. This procedure ensures that all products routinely released for shipment meet all COS, On-Aim, and product property requirements, and conform to Product Release and Product Segregation System limits.

5.2b We quickly move to understand and eliminate the root causes for any processes which are out of control. We have a rigorous system to handle out-

---

FDA Approved Materials for Direct Food Contact Surfaces

Gage (Film thickness)

Tear (Both machine and cross direction)

Sealing Temperature

Tack Temperature

Maximum Seal Strength (Both machine and cross direction)

Odor

Taste

Print Quality

Product Resistance

Figure 5.2 Representative Food Wrap Product Properties

of-control occurrences. Where the process is not automated, a manual adjustment is required, and a documented corrective action procedure is followed. This procedure is designed to identify and correct the root cause, and test for closure.

The Problem Solving Skills Module (Module 4) provides a structured approach for teams and individuals to determine and verify root cause. The problem analysis portion includes explaining the deviation, defining it, developing possible reasons, and testing and verifying reasons. As reported in Area 4.3b, 70% of all coworkers have been trained in this module.

If the measurement process is out of control, we suspend routine testing on the affected instrument and initiate diagnostic and corrective procedures immediately.

5.2c   We aggressively pursue a variety of "world-class manufacturing technologies" to improve our manufacturing and delivery.

1. **Process Simplification.**   All businesses use our PMS to reduce the variability of the manufacturing process. Electrical is using an expanded improvement process (Module 3) to optimize material and information flow from suppliers to customers and Continuous Flow Manufacturing to streamline the manufacturing process. Construction is piloting Advanced Process Control techniques to develop a process model which analyzes the ability of manufacturing technology to make products. Application of Continuous Flow Manufacturing at our Gary Construction Film Plant increased First Pass Yield by 8% and reduced work in progress and cycle time by 40%.

2. **Benchmark Information.**   Benchmark studies have identified opportunities for improvement (see Item 2.2), and we continue to develop plans which address the areas in which we do not match or exceed "best of the best."

3. **Process Research and Testing.**   Statistically designed experiments are widely used to optimize product and process quality. Statistical analysis of process data identifies sources of variation. Manufacturing technology committees representing each plant identify best practices, equipment, and approaches to be adopted.

4. **Information from Customers of the Processes.**   Customer information is consistently evaluated with respect to how we can improve product quality, cycle time, and overall performance. Our Product Development Core Team (PDCT) reviews customer input monthly.

5. **Challenge Goals.**   Challenge goals are set after extensive benchmarking of companies who have addressed the area under consideration and deemed

to be "best in class." Varifilm has found that business teams and HPWS work teams establish challenge goals using this methodology. Not only has credibility been given to the goal, but methods of achieving it are also learned.

5.3 Process Management: Business Processes and Support Services

5.3a The day-to-day management of support services and business processes is guided by our quality philosophy that taking immediate corrective action to determine and eliminate root causes of internal and external customer concerns and problems prevents defects.

We use one-on-one interactions, team meetings, and networks to assess procedures required to meet internal customer needs. The Self Managed Teams distribute How Are We Doing (HOW) questionnaires to their internal customers to identify opportunities for improving service. About 300 HOWs have been generated since mid-1990. This report solicits information on internal customer needs and expectations as well as assessment of the service performance. Interaction with the appropriate marketing and customer service organizations and coworkers is used to identify external customer requirements.

1. All businesses have adopted Varifilm quality tools to reduce business activity cycle times. A business group, working with its quality functional leader, defines (1) core activities, (2) cycle time for each activity, and (3) associated costs. A cost/time profile is created which shows costs per function and potential savings by reducing time required to perform activities within the function (Module 3, Figure 4.2).

2. The concept of "Key Indicators" has been adopted by manufacturing and support groups. Through defined Key Indicators, groups use process performance data to focus and measure improvement. All support groups use this approach.

3. Monthly and quarterly audits conducted by the functional leadership team measure compliance with key quality measures. Annual audits of Process Management Systems and Controlled Operating Procedures are conducted by another site's resources. ISO Registration forms a key assessment of on-site support functions and contract processing. Cycle time and defect reductions are part of the Total Quality Fitness Reviews.

5.3b Root cause elimination and process management in our business process are essential to meeting our customers' demands and expectations. People directly responsible for a given business process evaluate problems to identify and

Function	Key Indicator	1993–4 Goals	Frequency of Review
Info Systems	Up-time	99.95%	Monthly
Procurement	Cost–Order processing	<$10	Yearly
	% Orders EDI	80%	Monthly
	Number of suppliers	–5%	Monthly
Warehousing	No. Quality/ Service Incidents	0	Monthly
Transportation	Variations/100 Loads	0.5%	Monthly
	Carrier Quality	99.5%	Monthly
Maintenance	Cost/Replacement Investment	3.0%	Quarterly

Figure 5.3   Support Service Key Indicators and Goals

eliminate the root cause. If a prompt solution is not possible, a team is assigned to solve the problem. (Ref. Area 5.2b.)

5.3c   All support organizations and teams are active in improving the effectiveness of their functions. Our Quality Leadership improvement focus is a strong driving force to make this happen.

The improvement processes described for manufacturing are used to improve support processes.

On a broad scale, the Self Managed Team process led groups through a structured process of improvement based on customer needs. This training is available throughout Varifilm. (See Area 4.2a.)

1. **Process Analysis/Simplification.** Process analysis/simplification and/or redefinition are pursued. We use flowcharting and benchmarking to help achieve more effective operations.

2. **Benchmark Information.** Benchmarking studies have identified opportunities for improvement (see Item 2.2), and we continue to develop plans which address the areas in which we do not match or exceed "best of the best."

3. **Process Research and Testing.** Statistically designed experiments are widely used to optimize business process quality. Statistical analysis of process data identifies sources of variation. Committees representing each business process identify best practices, equipment, and approaches to be adopted.

4. **Alternative Technologies.** We are accelerating the application of such leading edge technologies as cycle time reduction and SPC to our business processes.

5. **Information from Customers of the Processes.** Networks and cross-functional teams (including internal customers) are key for quality support activities across Varifilm. For example, Information Systems and Customer Service network in a Communications Excellence Team. Teams and networks are empowered to set requirements and improvement projects, but each is accountable for accomplishments.

5.4 Supplier Quality

5.4a We use the following key indicators to monitor and rate our supplier quality:

We formed the "Ingredients Quality Systems Committee" in January 1987 to "partner" with our suppliers to improve our raw materials. This self-directed, multi-site, cross-functional team developed, implemented, and manages systems to update material specifications, assess ingredient quality, rate supplier performance (see Item 6.3), eliminate problems, maintain an informational database, reward and recognize excellence, certify suppliers, and assist suppliers with their systems.

5.4b We certify suppliers for materials which meet a performance level judged to be in "full compliance with Varifilm's requirements" (see table).

5.4c We are constantly reviewing our procurement activities to ensure that we not only work with "state of the art" incoming materials, but also are viewed by our suppliers as a "preferred customer."

We annually review the performance of our Purchasing Department in selecting and describing to suppliers who are capable of supplying materials which consistently meet our standards and specifications. To this end, we have reduced the number of suppliers over the past three years by 33% while improving the view of Varifilm as a supplier by 53% of our customers.

5.4d We are encouraging ISO registration for our suppliers, and we are formally recognizing excellent performance. We benchmark Best-in-Class companies to improve our Supplier Quality Program processes and strategies. (See Area 6.4b.)

We recognize a supplier's successful attainment of our highest confidence in total quality partnering by Varifilm Certification and increased business where possible. Basic requirements for Varifilm Certification are:

- Proactively upgrade material specifications and ISO Certification
- Only conforming product was shipped within the last year
- Quality assurance as verified by ISO Certification or Varifilm on-site audits
- Evidence of continuous improvement
- Supplier Total Quality Rating (Scale 1–5)
- Use of statistical techniques

We also have a three-tiered, formal recognition system to acknowledge supplier successes:

- *Quality Leadership Award* for excellent ratings over time
- *Quality Progress Award* for a significant single event, or for significant improvement in overall rating
- *Partners Award* for good partnering, as determined by Varifilm sites working with the supplier.

Various levels of Varifilm management are involved in supplier recognition, appropriate to the level of recognition being given. There is a requirement to present the award to the supplier's *employee* at his/her location. To strengthen its responsiveness with suppliers, Varifilm has an annual "Supplier Day" as part of National Quality Month. Art Axel, Vice-President of Quality, gives awards to 10–15 suppliers whose quality contribution during the past year deserved recognition.

Supplier Requirements	
Product	Conform to Material Specifications
Quality	Statistical Process Control Quality Management System Quality Plans and Improvement Goals
Value-Added	Total Pricing (including Varifilm process savings) Inventory Management Support Provided
Service	Order Handling and Invoicing On-Time Delivery Safety Environmental Responsibility
Capability & Technology	Technical Service RD&E Resources and Application

Method	What Is Assessed	Who Assesses	Frequency
Internal PMS Audit	Adherence to PMS by manufacturing sites	Corporate Quality Assurance	Every 6 months
ISO 9000 Audits	Quality Systems adherence	Wrights Register Quality	Every 6 months
Total Quality Fitness Reviews	Business performance vs. Baldrige criteria	Corporate Quality Resources	Every 24 months
Safety & Housekeeping Audits	Conditions, equipment, and practices comply with safety regulations	Site Environmental, Health & Safety	Monthly
Customer Surveys	Satisfaction with products & services	Varifilm Marketing 3rd Parties	Annually
Supplier Audits	Supplier quality mgmt. system capability	Division Quality Assurance coordinators	Every 12–24 months
Product Specification Review	Variability in product consistency & suitability	Cross-functional Product Teams	Annually
Mgf. Process Checks	Adherence of process to PMS specifications	Control Operators	Every 1–8 hours
Process Hazard Audits	Adequacy of process hazards safeguards	Site Environmental, Health & Safety	Every 2 years
Accounting Audits	Adherence to accounting procedure requirements	Independent Internal & 3rd-Party Auditors	Random, but at least annually

Figure 5.4   Varifilm Assessment Strategies

5.5 Quality Assessment

5.5a   Across Varifilm's businesses and product lines, many approaches are used to assess systems, processes, practices, products, and services. (See Figure 5.4.)

The unique product assessment approach we use was briefly described in Area 5.2. Each quarter we input product and measurement variances, customer specifications, release limits, and the sampling plan. As output, we obtain the percent of product that complies with our customers' specifications. If this assessment tool indicates a degradation in compliance, we often make changes before customers detect the problem.

Our document system specifies what must be documented, when, and by whom; documentation standards; who can access the document; responsibility for maintenance and update; and security procedures (see listing of "Controlled Operating Process" documents in Area 5.2a). Products/sites which have achieved ISO Certification have demonstrated that their document control systems meet ISO standards.

We follow strict guidelines for review and retention requirements of written and computerized documents. Each organization or support group is responsible for updating its documents to reflect technology, practice, and quality improvements.

5.5b Assessment findings are systematically presented to and reviewed and analyzed by appropriate business and plant teams to implement corrective actions. All audits require follow-up action to correct any deviations detected. Immediately following an audit, responsibility is assigned to achieve/restore conformance. Subsequent audits include examination of actions taken in response to previous audits. We train auditors to be competent in the subject they audit (e.g., PMS, process hazards) as well as the audit process.

CATEGORY 6.0
QUALITY AND OPERATIONAL RESULTS

6.1 Product and Service Quality Results

6.1a & b Our key internal measure of product quality is the "Process Capability Index" (Cpk), and our measures of service quality are on-time delivery and order processing error rates.

For a given property, Cpk is the ratio of customer specifications to the range of our performance and directly compares our performance with our customers' needs.

Our immediate goal by year-end 1993 is to achieve a Cpk level of 1.33 (the benchmark level for process industries) for at least 65% of key processes. We have also set a longer range Cpk goal of 2.0 within five years to meet world-class benchmark standards.

In addition, Varifilm has shown improvement in product quality and performance through improvements in film stretchability (elongation), which results in thinness (gage) of films; the number of breaks per roll (film strength); and failures of film formed into bags (film sealing capability). In both measures we have exceeded Best-in-Class targets.

Our principal measures of on-time delivery are the percent of orders meeting committed shipment date (Shipments Reliability Index—SRI) and percent of orders meeting our customer's request date (Delivery Satisfaction Index—DSI).

Overall performance in SRI has improved from 79% in 1989 to 94% in 1992, while the DSI has improved from 77% to 86% over the same time period. Our current goal is 95% for both the SRI and DSI. Customer surveys indicate our direct competitors are not doing as well as Varifilm in either of these areas.

The improvement in on-time delivery, both SRI and DSI, is directly attributable to our ability to measure and improve the performance of the processes contributing to order fulfillment. Through the use of the Varifilm quality improvement process we learned that many orders were not shipped on time due to errors in the orders. As a result, we started to measure the **order processing error rate** and can now see a direct correlation between improvements in reducing the number of errors at order entry and on-time delivery, with an overall goal of reducing the number of errors at order entry to 0.01%.

The **percent of invoice errors** is another internal measure of our ability to deliver outstanding products and services which meet our customer's requirements and expectations. A longer range objective is to be equal to "world-class" companies which have 0.2% invoice errors.

6.2 Company Operational Results

6.2a & b   We monitor performance on operational measures of importance to our partners. Operational productivity, efficiency, and effectiveness of manpower, processes, and other resources impact all partners. Our two key drivers—reduced cycle time and reduced defects—continue to serve as cornerstones for all operational processes and are reflected in the indices used.

Operational Measures Focused on the Customer Partner

First Pass Yield.   Since this performance measure was adopted in 1985, the average has steadily improved, and the range of performance among businesses has been reduced. Our benchmark studies reflect the industry leader's First Pass Yield to be about 94%. Our goal is 95%, with some of our businesses currently performing above that level.

Nonconforming Product Shipped.   Another operational measure we track is the percent of product shipped which did not fully conform to all specifications. We only ship nonconforming product after a full evaluation of potential customer impact, notifying the customer and securing agreement, and properly labeling as nonconforming. We have significantly reduced the nonconforming products we ship. To our knowledge, we are the only company in the film industry which tracks this index.

Varifilm's Total Quality Process also identified **manufacturing cycle time**, the time from order "to make" is received on the manufacturing floor to shipment to the distribution center, as a key driver to improved customer satisfaction. It also helps identify the major areas to manage our raw material, work in process, and finished goods inventory and correlates well with our progress in reducing them. Film manufactured product cycle time improved in 1992 to 2.8 days from 4.6 days in 1989.

Finally, we also measure the time it takes to enter an order. We achieved an improvement in the **order entry cycle time** from 53 hours in 1989 to 2 hours in 1992. Our goal is less than 30 minutes.

Operational Measures Focused on the Society Partner

We have a rigorous program to control **air emissions** from our plants. Our environmental goals are consistent with federal and state environmental standards. Because of the success of this program, the original projection of 64% reduction of Superfund Amendments and Reauthorization Act (S.A.R.A.) Title 313 emissions ("right to know") by 1993 has been revised to 70% reduction.

Our plants are systematically reducing the amount of **process waste**. Varifilm's goal of 64% reduction by 1995 has been upgraded to 75%. In 1993, we expect to generate less than one ton per day (dry weight) of process waste compared to over 30 tons per day in the '87–'88 base period.

Operational Measures Focused on the Stockholder

Our earnings also steadily increased throughout the end of the '80s and into the '90s. This also correlates well with sales per coworker, which shows a steady increase in sales per coworker since 1989.

6.3 Business Process and Support Service Results

6.3a & b   Our support functions have improved their performance versus goals. Our Business Support Services also focus on reduced cycle time and elimination of defects. A key improvement tool is the Varifilm Total Quality Process "Business Cycle Time." Teams of coworkers from all levels within these services identify non-value-adding activities which can be eliminated, thus reducing overall cycle time. Eight sites are deploying this process.

Each function developed continuous improvement goals, consistent with the Varifilm Continuous Improvement Criteria, and tracked its performance opposite these goals. Benchmark goals are used for Information Systems, Transportation, Maintenance, and Business Services. Product development processes have been benchmarked, and our business-specific cycle time goals are "stretch goals" based on past performance.

Accounts Receivable Errors (ARE) are calculated and reported monthly. After an overall increase in AREs in mid-1990, the rate was brought back to the 1989 levels by teams which used such tools as Pareto and cause-effect analyses to identify causes and corrective actions. Currently, business teams are conducting root cause analyses and planning corrective actions which address "pricing discrepancies."

Information Systems are another key business process at Varifilm. Since 1989, the percentage of **time the company's information systems have been operational** has increased from 93% to over 98%, the industry standard. These improvements are estimated to have saved Varifilm over $143 million by reducing hours lost by coworkers using these systems and increasing our ability to promptly interface with our customers at all times. Our current goal is 99.95%.

Information system improvements also enabled Varifilm to convert the number of **customers placing orders electronically through EDI** from 17% in 1989 to 63% in 1992, well above the industry standard.

Use of EDI also led to a reduction in the cost of processing a purchase order of $25 in 1989 to $18.10 in 1992. Our goal for 1993 is $10, or $2 below the industry standard.

We also measure the time it takes to introduce new products to our customers. Known in Varifilm as **New Product Cycle Time**, this measure calculates the time from commitment to a customer to provide a new product until delivery of production quantities. We achieved an improvement from 58 months in 1989 to 36 months in 1992. Our goal is to further reduce this to 30 months in 1993.

6.4 Supplier Quality Results

Our supplier program has progressed since 1987 toward meeting our goal of: "We will only purchase from suppliers who use quality management systems, including statistical techniques, meet all agreed-upon specifications, and continuously improve the quality and value of their products and services."

6.4a & b   Our suppliers are continuously improving the quality of their products and services. In 1989 we benchmarked supplier quality with five site-visited Baldrige companies. We selected these companies because our experience with them indicated they have superior supplier quality programs. The benchmarked companies have an active program to reduce their supplier base in order to leverage their resources and impact total quality of purchased materials. They achieved 20% to 70% reductions over a five-year period. Varifilm began to focus on reducing the number of suppliers in 1989. The goal is a 50% reduction in supplier base by the end of 1992. This study revealed our supplier systems (specifications, Total Quality requirements, auditing, SPC use, etc.) are excellent. However, we were impressed by the approach of these companies and adopted four key program performance metrics.

Certified Suppliers totaled 24 key suppliers by year-end 1992, down from 51 in 1989. These companies supply about 80% of our total raw material volume. Our goal is to certify all strategic materials suppliers using our supplier partnership process by the end of 1993.

Total Quality Ratings of Key Suppliers. We have rated 41 suppliers, accounting for over 90% of our raw materials volume. The current average score is 4.1 (Scale 1–5, 5 = "excellent"), with no supplier rated less than 3.0, "below satisfactory." Moreover, the percent now rated 4.6–5.0 is 26% compared with 2% during our 1989 rating. This represents an average rating increase of 0.5, exceeding the 1993 goal.

% Out-of-Date Product Specifications has decreased significantly. Our goal is to have no out-of-date specifications. We currently have a 5% level of out-of-date specifications compared to 3% average in the companies we benchmarked.

CATEGORY 7.0
CUSTOMER FOCUS AND SATISFACTION

7.1 Customer Expectations: Current and Future

7.1a We continuously review our methods of evaluating and improving our ability to meet the current and near-term customer requirements and make improvements when warranted.

1. Our customers are grouped by market—Food Packaging, Industrial Packaging, and Recyclables. In each grouping we constantly monitor customer requirements and expectations through surveys, partner feedback, complaints, gains and losses of customers, product performance, and trade literature. We review and prioritize these requirements to ensure that we are addressing our customers' most important requirements. Each business team or plant is responsible for prioritizing and tracking action.

2. We collect customer information by the methods described above. This information is directed to the appropriate product management teams who are responsible for managing our customer relationships. The information we collect includes: the product and service features most important to our customers, how Varifilm is doing, and how our competitors are performing. Priorities are based on (1) what is most important to our customers; and (2) differences between Varifilm's performance and our competitors in these areas. Our product management teams continuously receive and evaluate customer information.

Formal third-party telephone surveys are conducted annually of existing and potential customers. These data are formally reviewed by the business teams on a quarterly basis and verified by business team members' personal feedback from customer and market visits.

In addition, Varifilm exhibits at various trade shows including InterPak and the annual convention of the Institute of Food Technologists (IFT). The object of exhibiting is not only to sell products, but also to use a structured approach to gather customer-related information.

3. Once a year, our technical marketing and technical sales groups join our major customers' technical sales group in making their sales calls. This provides opportunities to learn about our indirect customers' problems and opportunities.

7.1b Our continued success depends on our ability to understand and meet our customers' future needs.

1. Each of our businesses focuses on the time horizon which is most critical to its customers' future needs. While some of our Industrial and Food Packaging businesses realize they must focus on the critical time horizon of three–five years, Recyclables is often thinking 20 years ahead. All our businesses, however, are aware of trends that will affect the plastic film business into and beyond the year 2000.

2. We deal with technological, competitive, societal, and demographic factors which may impact customer requirements, expectations, or alternatives in three major ways:

    ■ Varifilm has developed collaborative arrangements with the Total Quality Management, Food Science, Packaging Science, and Polymeric Chemistry Programs at a leading private and a leading state university. These partnerships provide an opportunity for undergraduate students to intern in our plants and laboratories, in support of basic research in food, packaging, and polymeric sciences. In addition, we have developed a mini-sabbatical program which allows for an exchange of university faculty and our scientists and engineers. This program provides us with information needed to determine future technologies.

    ■ Each business tracks its specific global business environment factors. Our economists develop specific economic information relevant to each business, and resources within the business keep abreast of demographic and technical trends and forecasts.

    ■ Our RD&E resources study basic trends affecting technology and consumer patterns. One model is "substitution." Recyclables substitution for metals is only about 10% underway in the U.S., and much less in other areas of the world. Substitution helps us understand consumer use patterns on a macro scale.

3. Through interaction with our customer partners and their customers, we collect information about our competitors' customers and other potential customers. We then interact with these potential customers directly at trade shows, trade association meetings, and indirectly through our interactions with equipment manufacturers to determine how we could best meet their needs.

4. We project the relative importance of our key product and service features into the future:

    ■ Through discussions of future needs between our customers and our Marketing and Technical Marketing Representatives.
        Our I-Team members also hold formal meetings with our major customers' top leadership.

    ■ Through our total customer partnership process we better understand future consumer needs. We frequently conduct focus group meetings with our customers' marketing representatives to identify consumer needs. When needs are clarified, we develop a value chain partnership, fully linking all customers from Varifilm to the retailer. This total partnership works to develop the new offering that will meet consumer needs.

    ■ Recyclables uses the continuous improvement process to understand and meet new customer needs. It is based on the premise that the business exists to enable customers to design increasingly productive solutions to their own waste problems. The "iteration" step is where a Varifilm/customer team jointly identifies better ways to meet customers' needs. Critical to this process are strong partnerships formed with strategic customers.

5. Each business segment within Varifilm quarterly reviews its market segments for changes which might either threaten the market for existing or new products or provide opportunities for new products or services.

7.1c   Since understanding future customer requirements and expectations is so important to us, finding better ways to do it is built into all the approaches given above. Annually, a cross-functional team (Post Mortem Team) reviews the short- and long-term projections over the past five years, rationale for making these projections, and actual current events. Root cause analysis is conducted to determine why specific projects were not on target from either a positive or negative point of view. Strategies are then implemented to increase the accuracy of our projects.

Working with multiple companies throughout the value chain is perhaps the most important method for improving our ability to understand future market-place needs. Vertical alliances are growing factors of our business.

7.2 Customer Relationship Management

Because we sell to over 2,500 customers, we develop relationship strategies to meet the needs of: (1) *Major Customers*—our partners; and (2) *All customers* from the small, independent businesses to Fortune 500 companies. Less than 10% of our total customers account for 80% of our sales volume. However, sales volume alone does not define our partners. Our criteria for customer partnerships include: customers whose market objectives are aligned with our marketing and technology capabilities; technology, product, or market leaders; and those with needs compatible with our knowledge and resources.

7.2a & b Personal contact is the primary way we determine what is important to our customers. We understand the value chain for our products, and we place resources at various parts of the chain so we can better understand customers' needs.

Our primary customer contacts, their roles, their logistics, and/or technology support are shown in Figure 7.1. Standards are set by first researching issues important to the customer, such as knowledge and courtesy of coworkers or clarity of information. Key drivers are then identified, measures defined and then tested for accuracy.

Our End-Use Marketing, Marketing, Technical Marketing, and Customer Service Representatives (CSRs) build and maintain partnerships with strategic customers through regularly scheduled meetings and Total Quality Fitness Reviews. We also survey customers to verify our understanding of their needs and assess our performance in meeting them. In addition, Technical Marketing enhances our relationships with our customers through on-site assistance in solving problems, whatever the cause. This also helps us ensure realistic customer expectations.

7.2c Our goal is easy access to knowledgeable, consistent contacts for all customers and regular follow-up through normal communication channels.

Our CSRs, the focal point of our day-to-day customer assistance and follow-up, are available by phone during normal working hours. We provide emergency access for our customers so they can reach us after hours and on weekends and holidays. If CSRs are unable to answer questions or address problems, they contact appropriate resources. Marketing personnel visit our strategic customers once a week and our smaller customers once a quarter. Technical Marketing representatives travel to our larger customers' plants 2–3 times per week, and

Account Managers, through customer relationships, develop business strategies for major customer accounts. Logistics/technology support: location near customer, electronic and voice mail, and computer access to order and sales data.

Marketing, through customer relationships, develops business strategies to fulfill all customer needs. Logistics/technology support: location near customer, electronic and voice mail, and computer access to sales, market, and product data.

Technical Marketing, working with customers, identifies key product and service features which meet customer needs, provides technical assistance, and seeks ways to improve our products. Logistics/technology support: plant and laboratory investigative support, electronic and voice mail, and computer access to sales, customer, and product data.

End-Use Marketing services the "downstream" customer—captures key information and reflects consumers' likely market behavior relative to products made from our film. Logistics/technology support: location near industry decision makers (e.g., California, Florida and Texas for Food Wrap), electronic and voice mail, and computer access to sales data.

Customer Service Representatives receive, expedite, and track customer orders (key contacts for follow-up on recent transactions). Logistics/technology support: location within the business they support, electronic mail and computer access to sales and warehouse data, order entry and Problem Report System.

Coworker visits to customers define detailed requirements and establish joint commitments. (See Figure 7.2.)

Figure 7.1   Primary Customer Contacts

they visit smaller customers as needed to deal with quality and service concerns and new product implementation strategies.

Communication with our direct customers is not limited to our primary contacts; it occurs across organizational levels. In addition to our personal contact, our businesses maintain widely advertised 800 telephone numbers to offer specific product information. We also use this contact as a source of customer information including needs/requirements.

Each business ensures that customer assistance is available when needed through an 800 telephone number, product hotline, and voice mail systems available 24 hours/day, 7 days/week. Our major customers are also connected to our electronic mail systems. Our Electrical business utilizes a Call All Customers Program in which manufacturing operators at our plant phone small customers who normally would not have contact with a marketing representative.

We also maintain EDI systems which provide customers direct access to our Product Quality Management and order entry systems. (See Item 2.1.) Our customers choose the communication tools which work for them. Some routinely use electronic devices, such as voice mail and/or electronic mail, in their busi-

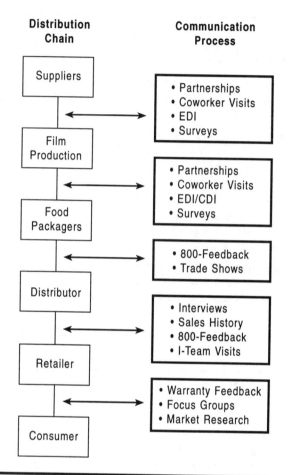

Figure 7.2 Food Packaging Distribution Chain with Communication Networks

nesses and therefore feel comfortable using automated devices in their dealings with us; however, smaller companies who have fewer electronic systems prefer the personalized "human" contact. Our customers make their preferences known through their daily contacts with us and in their survey responses.

For our largest customers, we send an electronic status report every morning to report the day's shipments, and we send additional status reports as needed throughout the day. When this report is received by the customer, it is reviewed. If a problem is spotted, a dialogue is initiated between the CSR and the customer to ensure that the supply will be uninterrupted.

We also use a variety of communication tools and strategies to reach custom-

We will respond to customer inquiries as follows:

Product delivery	90% while on the phone; 100% within 24 hours
Price	95% while on the phone; 100% within 24 hours
Product line	90% while on the phone; 100% within 24 hours
Technical	Response within 24 hours

Figure 7.3   Representative Customer Service Standards

ers at all levels in the distribution chain. The distribution chain and communication networks shown in Figure 7.2 illustrate the use of different strategies to reach our "downstream" customers.

7.2d   Although we have always had service standards, in 1990, we identified the need for more quantitative, fully deployed service standards aligned with the Baldrige criteria. Cross-functional teams within each business were charged with upgrading their standards, reviewing them with customers, documenting them, deploying them throughout the business, measuring performance, and reporting results to the people who influence our ability to meet standards. By the end of 1993, all will have deployed improved service standards.

7.2e   Our businesses select qualified people for customer contact positions, provide training to ensure their success, and provide the support they need.

The primary method we use to ensure a common vision for guiding customer contact coworkers is their SMT experience. We continually reinforce this with our publications, including "Quality Reports."

1. The vast majority of our customer contact personnel are selected from within Varifilm. Each business identifies and selects its customer contact personnel with assistance from our human resource consultants.

2. Our customer contact career progression paths are not linear. A person may move from manufacturing to CSR or Technical Marketing to Marketing. Career options are defined in the booklet, *Your Personal Choices*.

3. Many courses are offered to assist people in improving their relationship management skills—"Business Communications" (which includes learning telephone styles), "Effective Negotiating," "Effective Product Management," and "Face-to-Face Selling." Our "Telephone Courtesy" course provides training in listening and talking to customers on the phone.

4. We increasingly empower our customer contact coworkers. Technical Marketing representatives can authorize up to $10,000 for an individual

claim settlement. The CSR can set up new customers, authorize less-than-truckload shipments, initiate product returns, and authorize payments up to $2000 per incident to reimburse customers for out-of-pocket losses.

5. Coworker morale is assessed informally and formally. Daily interactions with management, customers, and peers provide opportunities to informally assess morale and attitude shifts and provide support. Coworker morale is tracked formally through the Coworker Satisfaction Survey. (See Area 4.2d.)

6. Customer contact coworkers are recognized and rewarded by peers, teams, managers, and corporate management. Every business and function has its own system of peer recognition for outstanding efforts.

7. Customer contact positions are highly valued. Although people are reassigned within the customer contact positions, turnover is low (<1%). The primary reason for leaving is promotion or career broadening.

7.2f All businesses create Problem Reports (PRs) to track complaints, status, and resolutions.

1. When we receive a customer complaint, we strive to (1) satisfy the customer, and (2) resolve the problem.

    In 1990, we computerized PRs in our businesses to store and aggregate complaint information. We do not distinguish between formal and informal complaints. All are logged, and our Product Management representatives immediately begin investigation into the causes of the problems. Held accountable for resolving complaints, they solicit input from other marketing and manufacturing resources, including obtaining and analyzing samples. Solutions are documented in the Problem Report System (PRS). Our businesses track resolution cycle time for each reported trade problem to ensure minimal elapsed time from notification to problem resolution. Each business reviews its unresolved PRs to monitor progress, assign additional resources, if needed, and share learnings.

    Our computerized systems enable us to sort and aggregate complaints by business, customer, product, plant, and type of problem; and trade reports are used to share our learnings with other sites.

2. As part of the problem review described in (1) above, types and frequency of complaints are reviewed to determine the root cause and action necessary to eliminate them. In many cases, there is a direct correlation between complaints and input from customer requirements and expectations and the source of complaints received, which reinforces the priority given projects aimed at meeting customer requirements and expectations.

7.2g Varifilm Continuous Improvement Criteria biennial evaluations, Total Quality Fitness Reviews with customers and our own people, and our annual third-party customer satisfaction surveys are used to evaluate and improve our customer relationship management practices.

1. Methods used to gain customer feedback and confidence include direct contact with customers by our customer contact personnel who, through establishing strong personal relationships, are able to gain a better insight on how to improve their performance as well as Varifilm's overall performance.

2. Customer responses to specific survey questions are the key indicators we use to evaluate our customer relationship management practices.

    In our customer satisfaction survey, we ask our customers to evaluate the effectiveness of our relationship management and customer contact performance. For example, customers are asked, "How good is Varifilm Construction at working with customers as partners to improve their relationship?"

    Each business reviews this information annually to identify improvement opportunities. Goals and strategies are developed and prioritized based on the results. (See Item 3.2.)

7.3 Commitment to Customers

7.3a Our history of commitment to the film industry, our product innovations, the range and quality of products and services, and our responsiveness to new requirements build customer confidence in us; and we back this confidence with a range of implicit and explicit guarantees.

For all our products, we explicitly guarantee conformance to the Product Specifications Record, a formal document of all the product information needed for customer and/or end-use processing requirements. Many customers rely on this guarantee in lieu of their own materials testing. All businesses routinely update Product Specification Records during annual reviews for those product properties that reflect improvement.

Our commitments extend beyond our direct customers to the consumer. We test, certify, and warrant all products carrying the Varifilm certification mark. In Food Packaging, all new food wrap seeking certification is tested in our Olson laboratories. If the sample is not up to standard, our technicians work with the customers' technicians to identify and correct root causes. We document the certification status of our customers' products including all aliases (brand/style names). This information is used by our Consumer Warranty Team to quickly respond to consumer questions.

Although we only provide the film which goes into food wrap, our "Xtra Shelf Life" warranties include (1) Full warranty against flavor loss of foods and beverages wrapped in Xtra Shelf Life; and (2) Varifilm will replace any wrap that does not perform as warranted. Varifilm maintains a "1-800-NEWFILM" telephone number to provide information and resolve warranty issues.

Communication of these commitments is carefully drafted by "third-party" sources with the intent of bringing the customer's perspective into the interpretation of the commitment. These commitments use simple, universally understood words and phrases and are always printed using 12 point type or larger.

Before any commitment is transmitted to customers, the draft is reviewed with at least 3 customers to establish a clear understanding of content and meaning.

7.3b We use the feedback from our customers and consumers to evaluate and improve our commitments.

In 1991, after reviewing the VCIC, Food Packaging decided to make its guarantee more explicit to ensure customer understanding. This guarantee, now found on all rolls of film and every order and invoice the customer receives, states:

> *"We are committed to meeting your requirements. If you are not completely satisfied with our film, we will replace it or credit your account for the cost. Please call us at 1-800-FIXIT4U. "*

This warranty does not change the existing implicit warranty; it avoids a gap between customer expectation and delivery by ensuring that all customers understand it.

7.4 Customer Satisfaction Determination

7.4a We determine customer satisfaction through personal contacts, the third-party customer satisfaction surveys, and our Total Quality Fitness Reviews.

1. Our businesses are defined by product, geographic region (United States, Europe, Far East, Latin America), and market. We organize market segments within each business around end-use applications, which are characterized by similarities in customers, product requirements, and distribution channels. We currently serve over 40 major market segments. Market segments are also defined by customer groups with similar processing capabilities.

    Through personal contacts, our Marketing and Technical people provide information on how customers in each market segment think we are doing. (See Area 7.1a.) Our customer surveys and Total Quality Fitness Reviews provide quantifiable information which help us verify this feedback. Survey results are grouped by product, key market segment, function in the customer's organization (RD&E, Purchasing), and by "sales" or "strategic customers." Key customer satisfaction requirements are:

1. Product Quality
2. On-Time Delivery
3. Ease of Access
4. Price
5. Knowledge of Coworkers

2. Our Customer Satisfaction Surveys assess what our customers value in a supplier; identify product quality, marketing support, customer service, and business effectiveness issues where improvements would increase customer satisfaction; and determine how our customers compare us with our competitors.

We interview key customer decision makers within the various functions (e.g., Research & Development, Purchasing and Business managers) who are knowledgeable about the use of our product in their operation. Because of their positions, their responses correlate directly to anticipated future market behavior.

Our businesses use a survey process developed in collaboration with and conducted by Customer Surveys Inc. (CSI). Respondents are asked early in the 20-minute interview to identify competitive suppliers. After rating the relative importance of a series of quality factors, customers are asked to rate Varifilm and each competitor on a 0–5 scale. (The scale is explained to each respondent, and a word anchor is provided for each number. For example, 5 is excellent, outstanding, the best; 4 is good, better than average.) CSI uses retired business executives, who are at ease talking with our external customers. The customers' narrative comments, including their views of our strengths and weaknesses, are documented for our use.

Use of a third-party firm to conduct the survey, customer anonymity, and the use of business executives as interviewers ensure objectivity. Survey design ensures validity—consultants have incorporated validation questions throughout the survey. After results have been tabulated, answers to these questions are compared to assure validity.

Since we began customer satisfaction surveys in 1989, we have completed 24 surveys, interviewing over 1600 customers, including customers in Korea and Europe. Each business conducts the survey annually. Electrical experimented with quarterly surveys; however, because customers reported this approach was too time-consuming, they now survey annually.

Businesses also use interviews with customers during the Total Quality Fitness Review process. (See Item 3.1.) These reviews are global and include customers outside the United States. Customer input on the Fitness Review and the customer survey showed a strong correlation in 1989 and 1990, so we now rely more on the customer satisfaction survey for customer input.

7.4b We compare customers' satisfaction with our performance versus our competitors.

1. At least twice a year, all businesses conduct an internal Trade Leader Assessment of Product Quality. Technical Marketing representatives ask our customers a series of questions to determine their level of satisfaction on product suitability and consistency. (See results in Item 6.2.)

2. Using customer survey data on in-kind competitors, we compute Indices of Relative Competitive Position for customer satisfaction. One index is the average rating gap between us and the average of all competitors for each quality factor, weighted for relative importance. The second index, used as a benchmark, is the rating gap between us and a "hypothetical" BEST competitor, created by the best score for each factor, weighted for relative importance. Customers also provide a "one-shot" overall satisfaction rating of Varifilm and our competitors using the 0–5 scale.

    Because of the limited number of in-kind competitors, our Recyclables' products businesses use a more generalized comparison in their surveys. Their customers compare us with other suppliers in the areas of product, customer service, market representative, and general business.

7.4c Our businesses use customer feedback and their experience to evaluate the survey process and recommend improvements. Business leaders review recommendations from the survey teams and make improvements before the survey is rerun. We annually upgrade our questions to improve clarity, understandability, and explicitness. We continue to revise our list of survey participants so we get the information we need.

We moved away from a quarterly frequency to an annual cycle based on customer feedback. Electrical upgraded its survey to use "paired comparisons" of importance and satisfaction to provide greater accuracy than the 0–5 scale.

Market teams use a variety of approaches to integrate survey feedback with other customer inputs. Comparisons are cross referenced with information from our direct personal contacts with customers. Food Packaging confirmed the assessment accuracy of its marketing personnel by including several of them as respondents to the customer satisfaction survey. Their responses closely matched the customers in both relative importance and satisfaction levels.

7.5 Customer Satisfaction Results

7.5a   Overall, we have maintained a consistently high level of customer satisfaction in the areas important to our customers.

The target measures (product quality, on-time delivery, ease of access, index-price) have been achieved in 1993 and in all cases have exceeded our best competitors.

Leadership reviewed the 1991 survey results and identified responsiveness and customer relationships as opportunities for improvement. Programs were initiated in 1992 to improve these areas. In 1992, customers reported improvements in customer partnerships, responsiveness, understanding of customer requirements, and sales representatives. These improvements are also reflected in our competitive comparison.

Each of our specialty products businesses asked customers to rate our year-to-year progress in overall performance in the areas of products, service, marketing representative, and general business. Ninety-four percent of the customers who rated us believe we are performing better than or the same as we were last year.

7.5b   Our customer dissatisfaction indicators support findings that our customers are satisfied with our products and services.

The number of complaints (Problem Reports) per million pounds shipped is extremely low (see Figure 7.4).

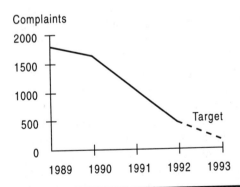

Figure 7.4   Customer Complaints per Year

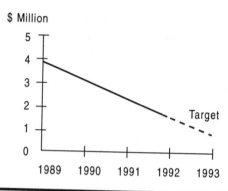

Figure 7.5   Customer Claim Dollars

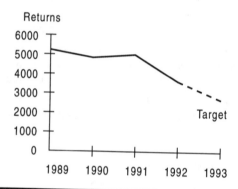

Figure 7.6   Number of Customer Returns

Our claim dollars and our returns (see Figures 7.5 and 7.6) are also small. Varifilm has also received numerous awards from customers and government agencies. The number increased from 11 in 1980 to over 100 in 1992.

7.6 Customer Satisfaction Comparison

7.6a   Varifilm businesses enjoy a competitive advantage in customer satisfaction. Our customers compared us with competing suppliers. They rated us higher than the average of all our competitors and comparable to the best-rated competitor in both 1991 and 1992.

7.6b   We maintain long-term relationships with our strategic customers. Our businesses use sales history data to track sales by customers and by market segments quarterly. Given the nature of our businesses, analysis of trends in losing customers to competitors is not very insightful. For example, our Construction business sells to 95% of the existing plants—the number is decreasing as plants go out of business or companies merge. Strong end-use preference and performance warranties drive the majority of retailers to carry our products, which in turn exerts pressure on the plants.

7.6c   Our businesses are industry leaders, as demonstrated by our large market share. We have increased our market share during the past four years. Using data published by the Film Economic Bureau, an industry-supported association, we track market share for these businesses monthly. However, we do not view market share as the only indicator of customer satisfaction. Our businesses use these data and trends to better understand competitors' tactics, strategies, and intent regarding markets and capacity utilization.

Changes in market share of businesses do not surprise us; they usually reflect protracted negotiations for major programs in the industry or competitive consolidations.

Varifilm has itself developed unique long-term "value" contracts where quality improvements are shared with our customers. These aggressive partnerships assure future market share and growth

Our Recyclables business has few, if any, in-kind competitors. We generally measure their growth in new applications or substitution rates for functional competition. Where we have in-kind competition, Varifilm is the leading supplier, and we enjoy the largest market share.

INDEX